MANAGEMENT CONCEPTS

ORGANISATIONAL BEHAVIOUR

HUMAN RESOURCE MANAGEMENT

MANAGEMENT CONCEPTS

ORGANISATIONAL BEHAVIOUR

HUMAN RESOURCE MANAGEMENT

Dr. Niranjan Pani

KUNAL BOOKS
New Delhi-110002 (India)

KUNAL BOOKS
4596/1A, First Floor,
11, Daryaganj, Delhi-110 002
Ph. 011-30125412
Email: kunalbooks@gmail. com
Email: kunalbooks@yahoo. co. in

Management Concepts, Organisational Behaviour, Human Resource Management

First Published 2009
ISBN 978-81-907129-3-4

PRINTED IN INDIA

Published by Prem Singh Bisht for Kunal Books, New Delhi and
Printed at Deepak Offset Press, New Delhi

To

My father Sri Ananata Charan Pani

And mother Smt. Sashi Pani

Preface

Management of Organisations, its people is very attractive in modern era. Target is performance, work and satisfaction of customers. To this much have been studied and written on Organisation, Organisational Behaviour, Management of Enterprises and techniques and Human Resource Manage-ment. Here an attempt has been made to present the ideas of reputed authors as to the all the three facets of and inside of Organisation briefly. Succinctly it can be declared that though the piece of work is not original writing yet concise, orderly and lucid presentations of facts are made in this book. The purpose of this book is to help the student fraternity.

Part One, is Management concepts. In it Concepts of Management, Approaches to Management, Challenges to Management in 21st Century, Theories of Management, Comparative Management practices of US and Japan, Work Motivation, Leadership, Communication Decision Making, Planning, Management of Change, Managerial Control, Conflict Management, Strategic Management, Total Quality Management, Trade Unionism and Workers Participation in Management have been examined.

To put it again the book is intended for students of Management, Commerce and Public Administration. The whole gamut of study is divided into three parts.

Part two, is Organisational Behavior. In it some selected topics – OB, Foundations of OB, Organisational Culture, Organi-sational Design, Organisational Change and Organisational Development – are discussed. Other topics – Leadership, Decision-Making, Organisational Motivation and Organisational Communication are placed in next part.

Part Three is Human Resource Management. In it Concept of HRM, Personnel management and HRM, Human Resource Planning, Job Analysis, Job Designing, Recruitment, Selection, Training and development, Career Management, Performance management, Compensation, Collective Bargaining, Human Resource Audit, Human Resource Information System and Future of HRM are portrayed in a intelligible manner.

No doubt, this endeavour will benefit students, researchers, teachers and professionals in the field concerned. I will appreciate, if constructive criticism and suggestions could be forwarded to us to enhance the quality and usefulness of this, which we will incorporate in subsequent edition of the book with due acknowledgement.

Dr. Niranjan Pani

Acknowledgements

For this book I am thankful to a number of prolific authors on the above subjects–SP Robbins, Keith Davis, F. Luthans, Udai Pareek, Knootz, Stroner, C. B. Mamoria, K. B. Aswasthappa and many others whose ideas, thinking and writings are reflected in this book. More particularly this book is enriched with the thought provoking and experience cooked thoughts of the experts mentioned in the book.

Again, I am thankful to Sri Santap Sanghari Mishra, M. Phil. and my scholar whose unceasingly effort make this work possible. Further, I am indebted to my partner Puspa Dash who cooperated a lot to give it to a final touch. I am also thankful to Prof BK Patnaik for his loving and forceful inspiration which is mingled in this piece of work. And I am also thankful to my father, mother and other family members for their smiling blessings and wishes for this book. Also I am thankful to Lali, Bobli, Soni, Moni, Kanha, Chani, Bubun and Anni for their silent wishes for this work.

As already stated, to present the authentic information we have drawn upon the works of various men of letters in the field. I owe a deep sense of gratitude to all of them. I am equally grateful to my mentor, seniors and colleagues for their guidance, cooperation, inspiration and assistance while working on this project. Finally, Mr. Prem Singh Bisht of Kunal Books, New Delhi deserves all appreciation for evincing keen interest in this and materialising it superbly in the present shape.

***Saraswatipuja*, 2009** **Dr. Niranjan Pani**

Contents

PART THREE: HUMAN RESOURCE MANAGEMENT

PART I

MANAGEMENT CONCEPTS

Chapter one

MANAGEMENT CONCEPTS

Learning Tips

- Management is a process of planning, organising, staffing, leading and controlling for fulfilling organisational goals. It is an attempt to build future with excellence.
- People responsible for utilising resources, fulfilling goals of organisation and building interpersonal human relationship are called managers.
- Managers are top, middle and front line ones to perform liaison, monitor and negotiator roles in organisation. For this purpose they utilise technical, human, conceptual and design skills.
- Managers of global arena are to face challenges in 21st century. Need for vision is necessary as they have to face globalisation and liberalisation. Concern for ethics is necessary because decision of managers have much impact on in-out of organisation. And new managers have to confront cultural diversity.
- Planning is the core of management. Decision-making is the heart of Management. Organising is building structures for achievement of goal. Staffing is maintaining a creative human resources. Leadership is to persuade followers for organisational goals for tomorrow amidst increasing competition. To inculcate motivation among people is a formidable challenge to managers. Communication is nerve centre of organisation. And controlling is the feedback to decision-point.
- Managers are dealing with customer satisfaction, employees development, and quality product / service.
- At work place managers strategically face conflict, and provide congenial atmosphere for workers' participation.
- Competence building, effectiveness facilitating, and Excellence creating are the motto of New Managers.

MANAGEMENT: DEFINITION, NATURE AND PURPOSE

In general terms management means getting things done by other organisational members. It is connected with handling of resources – human and physical – for accomplishment of selected objectives. And this endeavour involves a process of planning, organising, directing and controlling, staffing and leading. Also Fayol's model of management consists of five functions – to forecast and plan, to organise, to command, to co-ordinate and to control. To put it succinctly, it can be said that Management is the process of designing and maintaining environment in which individuals working together in groups, efficiently to accomplish selected aims. (Koontz & Weihrich: 1994). To get a vivid picture of management and its boundaries, this basic definition covers the following areas:[1]

- As manager, people carry out the managerial functions of planning, organising, staffing, leading and controlling.
- Management applies to any kind of organisation-simple, complex, small, big, profit making and loosing, etc.
- It applies to managers at all organisational levels – lower, middle and top.
- The aim of all managers is same, i.e. to create a surplus.
- Managing is concerned with productivity.
- It implies effectiveness and efficiency.

Further, it in not out of way to point out that managers are people responsible for achieving effectiveness by directing people efficiently in an organisation In this context one question comes to our mind, why we read management? The simple answer is managers are key to build relationship in an work situation to achieve goals. Obviously, the numbers of factors are connected with management – functions of management, skills of manager, and challenges of management in 21st century.

The term 'management' is used in many senses. It should not be confused with a person or a group of people. Management is a process made up of definite functions. Those who perform these tasks, to reiterate, are managers. No standard terminology has yet been evolved in this field as would satisfy everyone. Thus management is sometimes confused with administration and sometimes with organisation. Some writers equate the terms administration and management. Others go further and subordinate administration to management[2]. The widely ubiquitous and prevalent view, however, is of Meyor. Accordingly, management in contrast to administration is a purely internal concept characterising any activity performed in an organisational unit. Also a similar confusion exists as to the relationship between organisation and management. Some exponents regard organisation as merely one of the many functions of management. The fact however is that, organisation is the anatomy or the structure while management is the philosophy or the process. So Seckler Hudson viewed organisation will be regarded as the division and unification of effort towards some goal or policy. Management will be regarded as the collective utilisation of human resources and material in an effort to reach the known goal. In other words, organisation is the framework or apparatus of administration, while management is the running of it. To put it in the words of Millet, public administration is an instrument for the exercise of political power. Administrative organisation is the formalized structure for exercising certain powers of government. On the contrary, management is the group of persons and the process by which organisation is animated to accomplish declared tops. Management, as a result, is a process of achieving a desired goal. However, management is not doing things, but getting them done through managers. Essentially, it is an act to achieve objectives through the efforts of others. According to Terry, [3] management is the accomplishing of predetermined objective through the efforts of other people. If we break the word 'management', it will be 'manage+men + t'. The management is to manage men tactfully for accomplishment of a common objective in an effective way. Further pointer to this is that the goal can only be attained through group action and not individual action and the goal is selected not random. Essentially, managing is an important human activity and is essential for coordination of individual effort. Management like other practices is an art. It is known how. It is doing things in the light of the realities of a situation. Yet managers can work better by using the organised knowledge about management. It is this knowledge that constitutes a science. Thus managing as practice is an art, and the organised knowledge underlying the practice may be referred to as a science.

Nature of Management

To understand the nature of management one has to note a number of accompanying characteristic features of the same. They are:

1. *Universality of Management Process*

It means that the fundamental functions of management are a sort of distinct skill and are performed by the manager regardless of the type of enterprise, the major activities or the level at which the manager works. Management according to this view is a technique which can be studied and training in its application acquired. Such skill can also be transferred from one field to the other. The entire concept of generalist administration is predicted upon this assumption. There is a growing trend towards the transfer of personnel at the managerial level from public sector to private sector and *vice versa*. It is in this sense that management may be called a science. And process of management is omnipresent to all sectors.

2. *Management as Team Work*

Management is multi–manager activity. It is collective endeavour by a team. The process of management is not confined to one particular step or level in an organisation. It is present in the entire organisation at many different hierarchical levels of authority and responsibility. In the words of Fayol, "management is neither an exclusive privilege nor a particular responsibility of the head, or senior members of the business, it is an activity spread like all other activities, between head and members of the body corporate." According to him, the work of each class of employees in an industrial concern requires some managerial ability.

3. *Management as Profession*

A profession has been defined as a calling or vocation in which one profession is supposed to have acquired specialized knowledge which is used either in instructing, guiding or advising others. The present managerial class fulfills these conditions. True, complete professionalisation is a day dream and an impossibility. Of course there is greater feasibility of it in staff positions than in operating ones. Again, management can not be a profession in the sense of accreditation by a third party similar to admission to the bar or license to practice medicine. However professionalism has its advantages. Apart from giving the managers a professional pride in their job, it also helps, in the acceptance of the functions of management.

The purpose of management is very clear, because it is indispensable for any organisation. Managers are charged with the responsibility of taking actions that will make it possible for individuals to make their best contributions to group objectives. Management thus applies to small and large organisations. It is the first-rate management that can put the organisation in the right path of development.

MANAGEMENT: ITS NEED

It is not easy to evolve a universally accepted ordeal of a good management. Standards devised to measure the quality of performance are bound to vary from time to time, place to place and community to community and to say it is related to its environment. Experts are prone to judge the effectiveness of management by the extent of accomplishments of targets. They are interested primarily in results and performances. But it is quite possible that results may be attained by incredible costs in men, money and materials, and by the use of wrong procedures and iniquitous means. Attention must, therefore, be given to means as well. So, H. Simon focused rational behaviour which is primarily a yardstick to realize reasonably a given end. Further, Luther Gullick regards efficiency as a single ultimate value. Similarly, Waldo regards efficiency and economy as twin beacons of good management. But what is efficiency? It is a compendious term and may include varied attributes like swiftness in action, economy in cost, proper procedure, maximum utilisation of resources, etc. Efficiency is said to have three aspects–1) physical efficiency which is the relationship between physical quantities consumed and produced, 2) business efficiency which is the relationship between amount of money spent and income received, and 3) social efficiency which is the relationship between the human costs incurred and human satisfactions produced. In other words, efficiency is the relationship between the input and output in terms of materials, money and men. There is still another aspect of efficiency, namely the state of personal relationship within the organisation. More particularly, effectiveness is the achievement of objectives and efficiency is the achievement of goals with least amount of resources.

Millett adds three services to the needs for management– satisfactory service, responsible performance and good government. Satisfactory services mean:

- Fair and equitable service i.e. equal treatment to all citizens on the part of management,
- Timely service, i.e. service to be effective and must be in time,

- Ample service, that is right quantity at the right place and at the right time,
- Continuous service, i.e. service unobstructed by rain, snow, sky or dark night and and
- Progressive service, i.e. a service which improves in quality and performance.

Responsible performance of the public service means that management provides direction for administrative effort by working with and through those institutional devices which exist to express the will of a democratic society. An arbitrary and irresponsible management can hardly fulfill the aspirations of people in modern times. That is why management today has to be democratic and responsible, and not bureaucratic and irresponsible. Good government or good management has been the goal ever since the times of Plato and Aristotle. But throughout history, the term has been differently interpreted. To Luther Gullick him the true goals of management are to make the conduct of affairs technically sound, politically responsible, publicly acceptable, professionally approved and socially constructive.

Moreover, in this regard, the American Management Association has prescribed the following ten needs for management.

1. Definite and clear-cut responsibilities should be assigned to each manager.
2. Responsibility should always be coupled with corresponding authority.
3. No change should be made in the scope or responsibilities of a position without a definite understanding to that effect on the part of all persons concerned.
4. No employee occupying a single position in the organisation should be subject to definite orders from more than one source.
5. Orders should never be given to subordinates over the head of a responsible manager. Rather than do this the officer in question should be supplanted.
6. Criticism of subordinates should, whenever possible, be made privately and in no case should a subordinate be criticized in the presence of executive or employees of equal lower rank.
7. No dispute or difference between executives or employees as to authority or responsibilities should be considered to trial for prompt and careful adjudication.
8. Promotions, wage changes and disciplinary action should always be approved by the executive immediately superior to the one directly responsible.

9. No executive or employee should ever be required, expected to be same time an assistant to and critic of another.
10. Any executive whose work is subject to regular inspection should whenever practicable be given the assistance and facilities necessary to enable him to maintain an independent check of the quality of his work.

Goals of Manager

Briefly, to restate the goals of all managers are to create surplus, to turn 'burn out' of the enterprise to 'glow ups,' to transfer 'will way' to 'way way' and convert 'wish horse' to 'work horse'. They must establish an environment in which members of enterprise strive to complete goals with minimum cost, time. resource and dissatisfactions. Enterprises are excellent if they are: 1) oriented towards action, 2) concerned with customer satisfaction, 3) appreciated managerial autonomy and 4) driven by organisation's mission (Peters & Waterman: *In Search of Excellence*). Managers are central to attain enterprise's excellence. To add to this, another goal of manager is productive. Besides, in performing the roles managers must be honest, frugal and preferred.

While performing, effective managing is the concern of each manager. All managers carry out managerial functions – planning, organising, staffing, leading and controlling. But the time spent for each function differs with Top, Middle and Lower level managers in organisational hierarchy as given in Figure - 1.1.1.

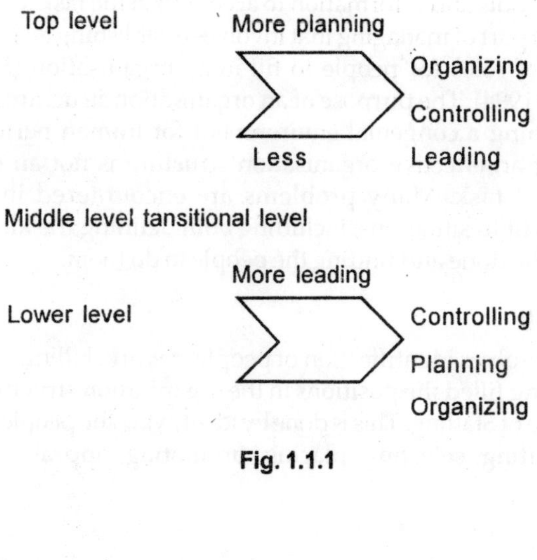

Fig. 1.1.1

FUNCTIONS OF MANAGEMENT

The functions of managers[4] provide a useful framework for organising management knowledge. To this Gullick, explained that the functions of managers are planning, organising, staffing, directing, coordinating, reporting and budgeting, i.e. POSDCRB. According to Fayol, the functions of managers are planning, organising, commanding, controlling and coordinating (PO3Cs). In fact functions of managers are numerous. The chief functions of manager can be discussed under the following heads:

1. Planning

Planning is a rational approach to goal attainment. It involves selection of missions and objectives and the actions to achieve them. It requires decision-making - choosing future courses of action from among the alternatives. No real plan exists until a decision- a commitment of human or material resources or reputation- has been made. Before a decision is made, all that exists is an academic study, an analysis or a proposal.

2. Organising

In organisations people are working together in groups to achieve some goals. Obviously, they must have roles to play, much like the parts actors fill in a drama. The concept of a 'role' implies that what people do has a definite purpose or objective. They know how their job objective fits into group effort and they have the necessary authority, tools and information to accomplish the task. Organising then is that part of managing that involves establishing an intentional structure of roles for people to fill in an organisation (Koontz & Weihrich: 1994). The purpose of an organisation structure is to help in developing a congenial environment for human performance. Designing an effective organisation structure is not an effortless managerial task. Many problems are encountered in making structures fit to situations, including both defining the kind of jobs that must be done and finding the people to do them.

3. Staffing

Staffing involves identification of people at work. Filling workforce and keeping filled the positions in the organisation structures is the other name of Staffing. This is done by identifying the people available and recruiting, selecting, placing, promoting, appraising, career planning, compensating and training or otherwise developing both new entrants and current job holders to accomplish their tasks effectively and efficiently.

4. Leading

Leading is the influencing of people so that they will have a say to organisation and group goals. It has to do predominately with the interpersonal aspect of managing. All managers would agree that their most important problems arise from people, their desires and attitudes, their behaviour as individuals and in groups so the effective managers need to solve them by performing the functions of leading. Leadership implies followership. People tend to follow those who offer them a means of satisfying their own needs, wishes and desires. Evidently, it is understandable that leading involves motivation, leadership styles and communication. Leading, as such, is a crucial factor in managing.

5. Controlling

Controlling is essentially a matching activity. It measures and corrects the activities of subordinates to ensure that events conform to plans. It evaluates performance against goals and plans, explains where negative deviations exist. Further by taking actions to correct deviations, it helps to ensure achievement of plans. Planning precedes controlling, so, plans are not self achieving. Plans guide managers in the better utilisation of resources to accomplish specific goals. Then follow up activities are checked to determine whether they conform to the plans. Control activities generally relate to the measurement of achievement. As methods of controlling, the budget for expense, inspection records and the record of labour hours lost, are generally familiar. Each measure shows whether plans are working out properly or not. If deviations persist, it recommends necessary correction.

The functions of management are given in the following Figure 1.1.2.

6. Coordinating

In addition, it can be said that coordination is the essence of managership. Some authorities consider coordination to be a separate function of the management. It seems more accurate, however, to regard it as the essence of managership, for achieving

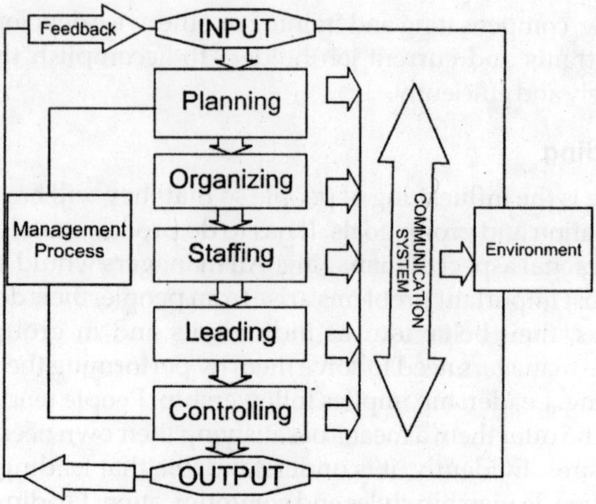

Fig. 1.1.2: Management process

harmony among individual efforts toward the fulfillment of group goals. Each of the managerial functions note above –planning, organising, staffing, leading and controlling - is an exercise contributing to coordination. Moreover the whole function is presented graphically in Figure 1.1.3.

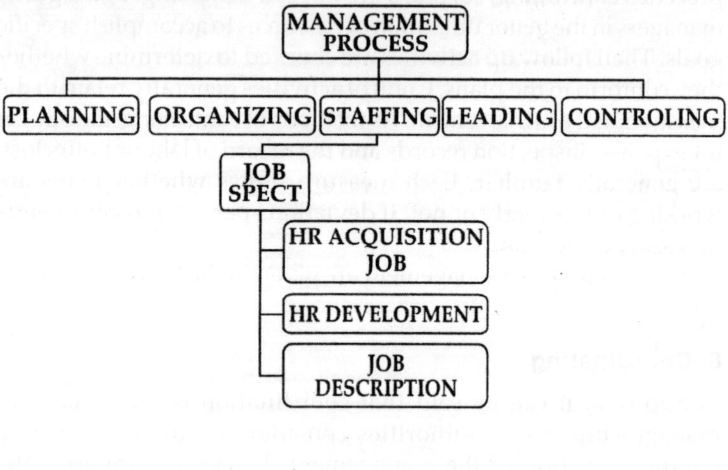

Fig. 1.1.3:

New Role

Nothing is constant except change. Organisations and functions of managers are changing. In coming days a perceptible phenomenon is varied changes at work place and with work cultures.

- Average company will be small and they will employ few people.
- Traditional hierarchy will replace horizontal division of work.
- A network of specialist will dominate work place. Work situation shall be paradise of technicians.
- Service management will gain momentum. Preproduction management will take back seat.
- Need for redefinition of work with constant learning, pay for performance, more thinking, creativeness and competence building will be order of the age.

To meet this changing new work culture managers are required to infuse their functions with vision, ethical analysis, and responsiveness to cultural diversity and new ideas of work and work place. Further modern manager should be imbibed with dog's philosophy – work as watch dog. WATCH stands for Word, Action, Trust and Character. Another feature, competence building, is needed for new manager. This means the capacity to make moon to football and *vice -versa.*

Moreover, manager should inculcate the habit of seeing things not in piecemeal but in totality – 'total perception.' A small story will illustrate the character in question. A man showed a pot filled with big stones. A manager was asked to comment on the filling status. He said it was filled. Then it was filled with small stones in the gap between big stones. Another manager was asked about the status. He also replied in the same manner. Again the man filled the pot with sand between gaps of small stones. Now the person asked if the container is full? A manager with the character reflecting total perception replied no it is not yet full. Only it is full when it is filled with water up to overflow out of the pot.

To add to it, modern enterprising managers are to depend on tuition but on intuition; interdependence instead of independence. Moreover new managers put prominence on policy making, planning, developing system, monitoring performance, coordinating, coaching, modeling, setting standards, building culture, risk taking, team building, empowering and competitiveness and quality.

Managerial Skills

There are three managerial skills as defined by Robert L Katz:

- Technical skill - Technical ability to work in managerial setting. *Managers at* lower level should possess more of this skill than middle and top level managers.
- *Human skill* - Capacity to deal with people in the organisation. Managers at all level should possess this skill.
- *Conceptual skill*- Designing and problem solving skill. Top level managers should possess more of this skill.

APPROACHES TO MANAGEMENT

To reiterate, management is the process of creating and maintaining an organisational setup in which individuals working together in groups, competently to bring about preferred aims. There are many approaches to management analysis such as:

1. *Empirical or case approach:* It analyses experience through cases. It makes out success and failures. Side by side this approach is limited by the fact that situations are all different.
2. *Interpersonal behavioural approach:* It focuses on interpersonal behaviour in three areas - human relations, leadership and motivation. Important fact is Its base rests on individual psychology.
   The negative side of this approach is it ignores few functions of management - planning, organising and controlling.
3. *Group behaviour approach:* This approach gives prominence on behaviour of people in groups. It is based on sociology and social psychology. Also it is identified with Organisational Behaviour. Over and over again this approach is not integrated with management concepts, principles, theory and techniques.
4. *Co-operative social systems approach:* It is a combination of both interpersonal and group behavioural aspects leading to a system of cooperation. Its expanded concept includes any co-operative group with a clear purpose.
   For the study of management, this field is too broad. At the same time it overlooks many managerial concepts, principles and techniques.
5. *Socio-technical approach:* In this approach, technical system has great effect on social system- personal attitudes and group behaviour. Its focal point is on production, office operations,

and other areas with close relationships between the technical system and the people.

This approach highlights on blue collar and lower level office work. And also it ignores much of other managerial knowledge.

6. *Decision theory approach:* Its focus is on the decision-making process, and decision makers–persons or groups making decision. Some theorists use decision-making as heart of all enterprise activities.

   The limitation of this approach is that there other functions of management than making decisions. The hub is at the same time too narrow and too wide.
7. *Systems approach:* Systems concepts have wide applicability. True, systems have boundaries. Simultaneously, they also interact with the external environment. That is to say, organisations are open systems. It identifies the importance of studying interrelations of planning, organising and controlling in a system as well as in many subsystems.

   To put it in other words it analyses 1) the interrelatedness of systems and subsystems, and 2) the interactions of organisations with the external environment. From this angle it can hardly be considered a new system and approach to management.
8. *Mathematical approach* – Model building in Management is replete with mathematical processes, concepts, symbols. In this regard it looks at management as a purely logical process, expressed in mathematical symbols and relationships. Besides, it is true many concepts in management cannot be modeled on mathematics line though mathematics is regarded as a useful tool. And hardly is it considered as an approach to management.
9. *Situational Approach:* Contingency or situation/circumstances play an important role in this approach so far as managerial practices are concerned. Contingency theory recognizes the impact of given resolution of problems on organisational behaviour patterns and management at large. Situation analysis is very complex. So it is very intricate to foresee and find out contingency factors and interrelationship between cause and effect.
10. *Managerial roles approach:* This approach is provided by Henry Mintzberg. The moot point in this approach is – what managers do? From the observations of the activities of five chief

executives, Mintzberg categorized ten managerial activities / roles, under three headings. This classification was because he believed managers were not performing only classical functions but the following ten varieties of other activities.

A. Interpersonal roles

Figure head role	: Legal / Social nature of function
Leader role	: Responsible for motivation and direction of sub-ordinate.
Liaison role	: Linked with outsiders. Provides network of outside contacts.

B. Informational roles

Recipient role	: Monitor role in handling information
Disseminator role	: Passing outside information to insiders
Spokesperson role	: Passing information to outsiders.

C. Decision roles

Entrepreneurial role	: Blends opportunities with environmental forces for change.
Disturbance	: Solves problems of organisations. handler role
Resource allocator	: Approves budgets for work role
	Negotiator role : Represents organisation at negotiations.

This approach is criticized on the ground that the sample of the approach is too small, as noted above only five executives. So the result of this is necessarily, prejudiced conclusion. Fact is that in Minzberg's approach structuring and other strategies of management are neglected. In spite of this his classification of roles are related to modern functions of management. They are given below:

Mintzberg's role	*Modern functions*
• Resource Allocator Role	Planning
• Entrepreneurial Role	Planning
• Interpersonal Role	Leading
• Informational Role	Can be fitted with number of managerial functions.

11. *McKinley's 7-s Framework:* After Managerial Role approach this approach is identified as one of the recent approaches to

management in recent years. This Seven S' approach is developed by McKinsey company and the theme was based on two books – *The Art of Japanese Management* (RT Paseale & Ors) and *In Search of Excellence* (Peters and Waterman). The seven 'S' are:

i. Strategy
ii. Structure
iii. Systems
iv. Style
v. Staff
vi. Shared values
vii. Skills.

This approach's factors are connoted with letter 'S' but the meaning of the word is different. For example, by skill in management, it is meant as technical, human and conceptual. But in 7-S framework it means capabilities of organisation as a whole – its strength and weakness. The plus point in this approach is that it was tested in Harvard and Stanford B Schools and 7-S is supporting modern managerial functions, thereby this approach supplemented and improved organisational effectiveness. A comparative

Mc Kinsey 's 7 S Framework	*Modern management functions*
1. Strategy Systematic action and allocation of resources to achieve organization's aim.	Strategy , Policy and Planning
2. Structure Organizational structure and Authority - Responsibility	Organizing , Organizational Structure, Department/line staff, Authority and Decentralization
3. Systems. Procedures and process such as: Information systems, Manufacturing process, Budgeting and control process.	Controlling- especially the system and process of controlling, control techniques, information technology, productivity and operation management
4. Style Management Behaviour and Organizational Behaviour to achieve organizational goals.	Leading
5. Staff The people in the enterprise	Staffing dealing with recruitment, selection, training,

Contd.

and their socialization into organizational culture.	promotion, performance appraisal and compensation management.
6. Shared Values (Subordinate goals). The value shared by the members of an organization	Leadership and, effective organizational culture
7. Skill Distinctive capabilities of an enterprise	Strategy, policies and planning

Source: R T Pascale & AG Athos, *Art of Japanese Management*

presentation of both 7-S framework and Modern Management Functions is given below for better clarity of understanding.

True 7 –S framework pinpointed the key features of the management process and attempted to analyze the relationship between number of variables there in. As noted above the terminology / nomenclature may not be clear and appropriate. But its contributions to the field of management knowledge cannot be refuted.

1. Operational Approach

Operational approach, otherwise known as Managerial Process approach developed by Koontz, draws together concepts, principles, techniques and knowledge from other fields and above discussed managerial approaches. This identifies the management knowledge; this endeavor is to develop science and theory with practical application. It differentiates between managerial and non-managerial knowledge. It develops classification system built around the managerial functions of planning, organising, staffing, leading and controlling. A better illustration of Operational Approach is given in Figure 1.1.4.

1. *System's theory*
   A. Applied Systems Theory
   B. Socio-technical System
   C. Cooperative Social System
   2. Sociology / Social Psychology
   D. Group Behaviour

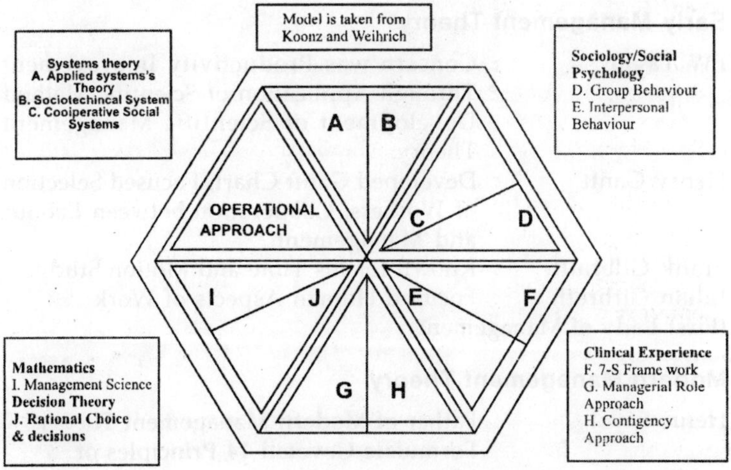

Fig. 1.1.4: Operational Approach/Management Process Approach

E Interpersonal Behaviour

3. *Clinical experience*
   F. 7-S Framework
   G. Managerial Role Approach
   H. Contingency Approach
4. *Mathematics*
   I. Management Science
5. *Decision theory*
   J. Rational and Decisions.

The functions of managers are accentuated in the operational approach/Management Process Approach.

THEORIES OF MANAGEMENT

As to management theory little study was made before 1950s. Essentially, the pattern of management analysis became obscure. So it is terned as 'management theory jungle' (Knootz & Ors, 1994). Particularly, the evolution of Management theory starts with F W Taylor. Since then prolific writers were and are enriching the discipline. To state briefly;

Early Management Theory

FW Taylor : Concern was Productivity Improvement
• Through Application of Scientific Method Development of Scientific Management Theory.

Henry Gantt : Developed Gantt Chart, Focused Selection of Workers, Cooperation between Labour and Management.

Frank Gilbraith : Known for his Time and Motion Study.

Lilian Girbreth : Focused Human Aspects of Work
(First Lady of Management)

Modern Management Theory

Henri Fayol : Father of Modern Management Theory Formulate Coveted 14 Principles of Management

Behavioural Theory

Hugo Munsterberg (1912) : Applied Psychology to Industry and Management

Walter D Scott (1911) : Applied Psychology to Personnel Management

Max Weber (1947) : Developed theory of Bureaucracy

Vilfredo Pareto (1917) : Father of Social System approach

Elton Mayo (1932) : Study of Social Attitudes and Relations of Work Group at Work Place.

Systems Theory

Chester I Barnard: Comprehensive social system to managing.

Modern Management Thoughts

Peter F. Drucker : General Management

W. Edward Deming : Introduced Quality Control

Douglas McGregor Nature of Man / Theory 'X' & 'Y"

Frederic Hertzberg : Two Factor Theory

Robert R Blake : Managerial Grid Theory

Rensis Likert : Leadership Theory

Abraham Maslow	: Needs Theory of Motivation
Laurence Peter (1969)	: Peter Principle –People get promoted to a level where they are Incompetent
William Ouchi (1981)	: Theory 'Z" Adoption of Selected Managerial Principles to US environment] Japanese
Peter and Waterman (1982)	: Identified Characteristics of Excellent Enterprises

Now it is pertinent to analyze the main ideas of few important management thinkers.

CLASSICAL THEORY: Administrative and Managerial

The classical theory of organisation is also known as the structural theory. It has been pronounced notably by Henri Fayol, Luther Gullick, Lyndal Urwick, J. D. Mooney, A. C. Reily, M. P. Follett and Shelton,, etc. These writers argue that administration is administration, regardless of the kind of work being undertaken within which it is performed. Then they proceed to identify the important elements in the processes of administration as well as features common to all administrative structures.

The most important concern of the classical theory is the formulation of certain universal principles of organisation. It deals with primarily formal organisational structure. The theory assumes that there are certain fundamental principles on the basis of which an organisation can be established to achieve a specific objective. The watchwords of this approach are efficiency and economy.

FAYOL: Father of Modern Management Thought

Henri Fayol was a creative writer on technical and scientific matters as well as management. The most outstanding of his writings is his book General and Industrial Management (1916). Henri Fayol observed that management was an undertaking common to all human activities. Fayol's ideas about managerial activity are presented in the context of his writings on industrial undertakings. The totality of activities of an industrial undertaking is divided into the following six groups as depicted in figure 1.1.5.

1. **Technical activities:** Production manufacturer, adaptation.
2. **Commercial activities:** Buying, selling exchange.
3. **Financial activities:** Search for and optimum use of capital.
4. **Security activities:** Protection of property and persons.

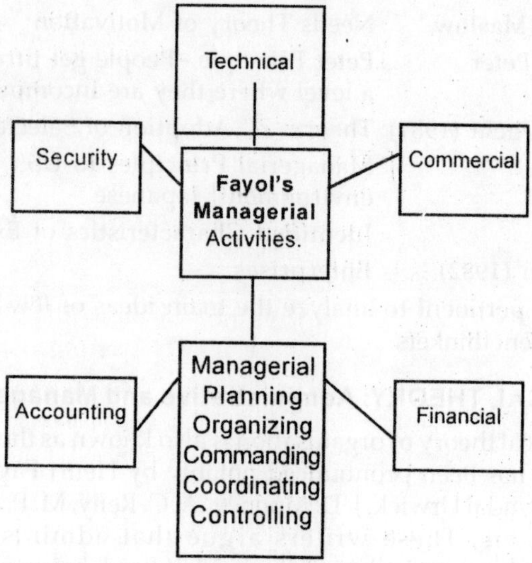

Fig. 1:1.5

5. **Accounting activities:** Stock taking, balance sheets, costs, and statistics.
6. **Managerial activities:** Planning, organising, commanding, coordinating and controlling.

Fayol also suggested that managers should have the following attributes:

1. **Physical:** Health, vigour, appearance.
2. **Mental:** Ability to understand and learn, judgment, mental vigour and adaptability.
3. **Moral:** Firmness and willingness to accept responsibility.
4. **General Education:** General acquaintance with matters.
5. **Special Knowledge:** Be it technical, commercial, financial or managerial.
6. **Experience:** Knowledge arising from the work proper.

Henri Fayol stated that the principles of management are not rigid. On the contrary, they must be capable of adaptation to various enterprises and settings. From his discussion of management theory, "Fayol derived fourteen principles. These are the following:

1. **Division of work:** Specialisation of labour produces more and better work with the same effort.

2. **Authority and responsibility:** Authority should commensurate with responsibility. In other words, the occupant of each position should be given enough authority to carry out all the responsibilities allocated to him.
3. **Discipline:** Obedience should be observed in accordance with the standing agreements between the firm and its employees.
4. **Unity of command:** For any action, an employee should have only one boss.
5. **Unity of direction:** One head and one plan for each activity.
6. **Subordination of individual interest to general interest:** The remuneration paid for services rendered should be fair and afford satisfaction to both personnel and the firm.
7. **Remuneration:** The remuneration paid for services rendered should be fair and afford satisfaction to both personnel and the firm.
8. **Centralisation:** The degree of initiative left to managers varies depending upon top managers, subordinates and business conditions.
9. **Scalar Chain (hierarchy):** The line of authority of superiors ranging from ultimate / top authority to the lowest ranks in the hierarchical ladder.
10. **Order:** Once the basic job structure has been devised and the personnel to fill the various slots have been selected, each employee occupies that job wherein he/she can render the most effective service.
11. **Equity:** For the personnel to be encouraged to fulfill their duties with devotion and loyalty there must be equity based on kindliness and justice in employer-employee relations.
12. **Stability of tenure:** Suitable conditions should be created to minimize turnover of employees.
13. **Initiative:** The ability to think afresh would act as a powerful motivator of human behaviour.
14. **Espirt de corps:** Harmony, union among the personnel of an organisation is a source of great strength in that organisation.

Gullick and Urwick

American and British administrative thinkers had applied their minds to develop the organisational or management theories further. Among such writers the names of Gullick and Urwick merit special mention. The book entitled *Papers on the Science of*

Administration edited by them in 1937 is considered to be an important milestone in the development of since of administration. Deriving inspiration mainly from the works of F. W. Taylor and H. Fayol, the two authors have developed the classical theory of organisation, a landmark or pointer which is also known as the "Administrative Management" theory. They believed it to be possible to develop a science of administration based on these principles.

One remarkable feature in the writings of these authors is the importance they attached to the structure of administration while almost neglecting the role of men in the organisation. Having stressed the substance of the structure as a designing process Gulick and Urwick devoted their attention to the discovery of principles based on which the structure may be designed. Gullick enumerated ten principles of organisation. In working out these principles Gullick was very much influenced by Henri Fayol's fourteen basic elements of administration. Gullick principles are itemized as:

1. Division of work or specialisation.
2. Bases of departmental organisations.
3. Coordination through hierarchy.
4. Deliberate coordination.
5. Coordination through committees.
6. Decentralisation.
7. Unity of command.
8. Line and staff.
9. Delegation, and
10. Span of control.

Among the ten principles of administration listed out, Gullick laid special emphasis on division of work. The other classical administrative theorist also made the division of labour as the central tenet of his approach. Work division implies that the job to be performed be broken into its component functions and again each of the component functions be broken down into simple repetitive activity. At each stage the sub-division of work is followed by the inter-relating of the divided parts. Thus, Gullick said that division of work and integration are the bootstraps by which mankind lifts itself in the processes of civilisation. However, Gullick was cognizant of the limitations beyond which the division of work can not go. Also, Urwick identified eight principles of organisation. They are listed as under:

1. Principle of objectives.

2. Principle of correspondence.
3. Principle of responsibility.
4. The scalar principle.
5. Principle of span of control.
6. Principle of specialisation.
7. Principle of coordination.
8. Principle of definition.

Urwick felt that the administrative organisation is still unexplored field and there are many unknown factors for a fuller understanding and appreciation. He, therefore, suggests that his principles are a framework of thought and an array of ideas which would help others to synthesize out of their own experience. Gullick also recognized the executive functions and coined the new nomenclature "POSDCORB"- a buzz word now - incorporating all functions. Each letter in this word represents one important function of the managers.

The Coveted Seven Functions: POSDCORB

P **Planning:** Planning is concerned with the recognition of the various activities required to reach the goal and arranging them in terms of priorities and sequence so that the objective of the organisation may be reached in a systematic and efficient manner.

O **Organisation:** After planning the activities of administration one should think of the structure of administration, namely organisation through which the activities are put into operation and objectives are achieved.

S **Staffing:** Staffing is concerned with all aspects of personnel administration. Thus recruitment, appointment, promotion, discipline, retirement, etc. are function which must receive due attention of the managers.

D **Directing:** It relates to the orders is-sued by the managers to the subordinates directing the activities of administration.

Co **Coordination:** Coordination relates not only to the evidence of conflict and duplication in organisation but to secure co-operation and team work between the various units and employees.

R **Reporting:** It is the responsibility of the executive to keep himself posted with the progress of activities in the organisation. A good communication system is imperative through which such progress is reported to the executive.

It is thorough reporting that the executive becomes aware of the problems in the organisation for which he may initiate corrective measures by issuing necessary directions.

B **Budgeting:** Budgeting covers the entire field of financial administration. As finance is indispensable for any administration the executive has to pay adequate attention to matters like budgeting, financial procedures, and accounting.

Besides Fayol, Gullick and Urwick, M. P. Follett, Mooney and Reiley also contributed to the classical theory. Accordingly, organisation is a formal structure of plans, amenable to creation in accordance with clearly understood principle. Here it is pertinent to say that the classical theory views organisation as a machine, considering human beings mere cogs. Hence the classical theory is discernible by four features as given below:

- Impersonality
- Specialisation
- Hierarchy
- Efficiency.

Further, it is manifested by six philosophical characteristics:

1. It is atomistic in the sense that it sees the individual in isolation from fellowmen.
2. It is mechanistic as it does not explain the dynamics of organisational behaviour.
3. It is static.
4. It is voluntarism
5. It is rationalistic.
6. It does not take any note of non-economic incentives.

In spite of considered merits Classical theory is criticized on the ground that each principle has been proved to be neither empirically valid in organisational functioning nor universally applicable which has led H. Simon to dub them as proverbs. The classical theory is also criticized for its neglect of human element in work. It treats organisation as a closed system, completely unconnected with or uninfluenced by the external environment. Its obsession with the normative aspect of the functioning of organisations leads to its neglect of the study of actual and informal behaviour patterns in the formal organisational structure.

SCIENTIFIC MANAGEMENT THEORY

F.W. Taylor was pioneer in developing the first systematic organisation theory. An engineer by profession, he is regarded as the father of scientific management. He was the first to advocate the adoption of scientific methods in the field of industrial work processes and management to promote industrial efficiency, harmony and economy.

During the latter half of the 19th century, when the industrial revolution had reached a stage of culmination point the rapid expansion of business and industry added new pebbles of problems to industrial planning and management. The working conditions in the factories were chaotic. The work methods, tools and procedures were neither standardized nor planned for efficiency and effectively. Choice of methods of work was mainly left to the workers themselves resulting in considerable ad hoc planning and incompetence. Rapid industrialisation had given rise to a new managerial class who were being called upon to face new problems not encountered earlier. So to fulfill this need and find ways to lift up industrial productivity Taylor came out with his ideas on "Scientific Management." This term is coined by Lowis D. Brandies first and subsequently used by Taylor in his widely known book, *Principles and Methods of Scientific Management*.

The major goals of scientific management were to raise industrial output by systematic application of scientific methods of work to managerial problems and work procedures in industries establishments. Taylor in his book made certain fundamental assumptions that are explained below:

1. Industrial processes can be made open for scientific observation and experimentation.
2. The standard time prescribed for each operation can be produced at a designated standard of efficiency and economy.
3. The workers can be trained by the management in the best methods for achieving the industrial objectives.

Principles of Scientific Management: Pointer to Management

Taylor accentuated in the interest of society's prosperity, the close collaboration and deliberate cooperation between the workmen and the management while campaigning for the application of scientific methods. To put it succinctly, Taylor's philosophy of management was based on mutual interests and on 4 basic principles.

The Four Principles

1. Development of a True Science of Work

When science is viewed as an "organised knowledge", every act of a workman can be reduced to a science. In the interest of the worker and the management, it is necessary to know, what constitutes a fair day's work. As a result the worker cannot be condemned unnecessarily by the boss and management can also get maximum benefit from the workers. This needs a scientific investigation of a large daily task to be undertaken by qualified and skilled workers. This can be completed by gathering traditional knowledge of the workers. The results of investigation have to be classified, tabulated and reduced into rules and laws to unearth the ideal working method. Essentially, such development of science of work will incur 'Quadruple benefits' – it enables the organisation to produce more, make possible the workers to receive higher wages and a huge profit to the enterprise and thereby lower cost products to customer. This is, therefore, nothing but indication of Total Quality Management.

2. Scientific Selection of the Workmen

To ensure the effective performance of the scientifically developed work, there is also a need to select the worker scientifically focusing physical and intellectual qualities. This needs deliberate study of the aptitude, nature and performance of the worker. Consequently, this will lead to find out what possibilities and limitations one has to encounter, for future development. He insisted that every worker must be systematically and thoroughly trained. It is the responsibility of the management to develop the worker offering him opportunities for advancement to do the job to the fullest realisation of his natural capacities. Employees also should accept the new methods, tools and conditions willingly and enthusiastically. Seemly this is a pointer to Human Resource Development by centering on training for development.

3. Scientific Education and Development of Workmen

To enable the worker to do his job and to ensure that he may not slip back to the earlier methods of doing the work, there must be somebody to inspire the workers. Taylor felt that, this was the sole responsibility of the management. He believed that workers were always willing to cooperate the management, but there is much opposition from the side of the management.

4. Intimate and Friendly Cooperation between the Management and the Workmen

In the traditional management theory, the worker bore the entire responsibility for work. Simultaneously the management had lesser responsibilities. But Taylor's scientific management assumed equal responsibility between management and worker. This attitude of work creates between them an understanding and mutual

KPSM: Keyprinciples of scientific management

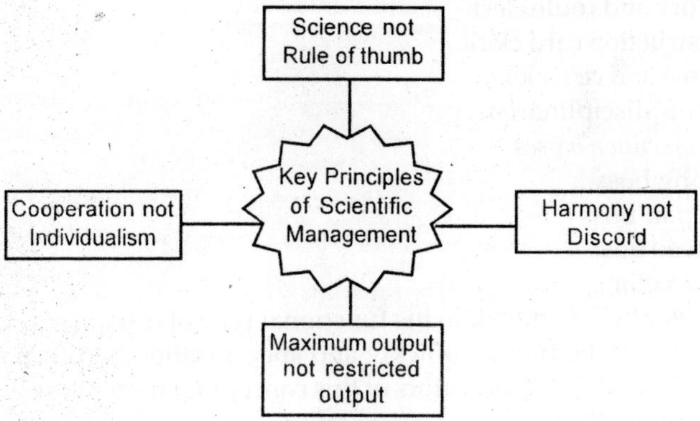

dependence. There will also be constant and intimate cooperation between them. All this will result in elimination of conflicts and innovation of cooperation. So the philosophy of the above principles may be summarized. A graphic picture is given below.

Basics of Scientific Management

1. Science not rule of thumb.
2. Harmony not discord.
3. Cooperation not individualism.
4. Maximum output not restricted output.
5. Development in each greatest efficiency and prosperity.

Creative Mechanisms

Taylor also developed some more mechanisms to serve his principles of scientific management, they are as follows.

1. **Functional Foremanship:** - Taylor doubted the efficacy of the 'linear' system or the military type of organisation in which each worker is subordinate to only one boss. He replaced this BOSS AND I system with what is called functional order from eight narrowly specialized supervisors. Thus he divided the work not only among workers but also among supervisors. Of the eight functional bosses, there are four for planning and four for execution – two cardinal principles of administrative management.

Four *planning bosses*
- Work and route clerk
- Instruction card clerk
- Time and cost clerk
- Shop disciplinarian

Four *execution bosses*
- Gang boss
- Repair boss
- Speed boss
- Inspector

Taylor believed that, in his functional type of organisation, the foreman can be trained quickly and specialisation becomes very easy. Other pointer indicators of this conceptual framework are:
- Time study
- Standardisation of tools.
- Desirability of a planning department.
- Exception principle in management.
- Use of slide rules.
- Payment according to differential rate.
- Routing system.
- Modern cost system, etc.

Taylor observed and admitted that scientific management is not an efficient device. It is not a new scheme of paying men. It is not a new system of figuring costs. It is not a time study or motion study. And it is not innovation of foremanship. Admittedly, scientific management, above all a complete mental evolution on the part of workers and management. It demands the realisation of the fact that their mutual interest is not antagonistic and mutual prosperity is possible only through mutual cooperation. Without this feeling of grand mental revolution on both sides scientific management is not a reality.

A Look: From Critical Angles

1. **Reaction of Trade Unions:** The trade unions were against the modern methods of increasing output by the introduction of the premium bonus system. The labour leaders considered Taylorism is not only destroying the trade unionism but also destroying the principle of collective bargaining. They treated it as a menace to the community at large and main cause for increasing unemployment. Trade Unions felt that, Taylor was more interested in the mechanical aspects of work and not much concerned about the total work situation.
2. **Reaction of managers:** Taylorism was also often attacked by managers. Those who wanted quick promotions to the high managerial positions without any merit based on higher education opposed Taylor's stand.
3. **Reaction of thinkers:** The fertile thinkers who attacked Taylor include Sheldon, M. P. Follett, Sam Lewis John, Elton Mayo and Peter F Drucker, etc. They charged that Taylor's scientific management was impersonal and under emphasized the human factor. This criticism led to a series of experiments in industrial sociology and social psychology later on.
4. **Anatomy of work:** Another criticism of Taylor is that he did not properly understand the anatomy of the work. His emphasis on the minute division of the work and specialisation was severely disparaged. If the work gets depersonalized, the worker becomes a mere cog in the machine and the relations between the workers and the executives become remote as a result of which he lacks the sense of participation in the work. It may even lead to automation of the workers which may have physiological and neurological consequences. Taylor's division of working people into planning and executive ones is not conducive at all.
5. **Negative initiatives**: Behaviouralists charged that Taylor's method of scientific management sacrifices the initiative of the worker, his individual freedom and the use of his intelligence and responsibility. Herbert Simon and March have described the scientific management as the physiological organisation theory.

HUMAN RELATIONS THEORY

Human relations theory develops on the critical edifice of Scientific Management. The essence of human relations theory lies in its primary emphasis on human beings, psychological motivations and informal group behaviour. This theory centers on management as a web of interpersonal relationships. It lays greater stress on the behaviour of role occupants in an organisation than on the formal structure of the organisation. The protagonists of this school argue that since management and administration involves group effort and collective endeavors of people the study of management must be concentrated on the individual as a socio-psychological being. Further this should be more concerned with his motivations.

The greatest single influence of the human relations theory came from the Hawthrone experiments which were carried out in USA by Elton Mayo and his colleagues. The findings were first published in *Management and the Worker* (F. J. Roethlishberger and W. J. Dickson) in 1939. The Hawthrone studies carried out at the western Electric Company at Hawthrone in USA is a historic landmark in organisational theory, since it helped to develop the human relations school of organisation. The immediate objective of the study was to measure the effect of improving lighting on workers output and the socio-psychological problems of the industrial workers.

Elton Mayo concentrated on the study of worker's behaviour and production capacity taking into consideration physiological, physical, economic, social and psychological aspects. He called this approach as "clinical approach." He undertook the first research programme in 1923 in a textile mill near Philadelphia and named "The First Enquiry." Hawthrone studies were conducted in four phases:

Four Phases

1. *Illumination Experiment (1924-27):* To determine the effect of different levels of illumination on worker's productivity.
2. *Relay Assembly Test Room Experiment (1927):* To observe the effects of various changes in working conditions on the worker's output and morale.
3. *Mass Interview Programme (1928-31):* To explore the employee's feelings by talking to them. It is also called ventilation therapy.
4. *Bank Wiring Experiment (1931-32):* To understand how the norms that controlled each member's output, were established by the informal organisation.

After the final phase, it was found that the workers had a clear-cut standard of output which was lower than management target.

The group according to its standard plan did not allow its members to increase or decrease the output. Although they were capable of producing more, the output was held down to maintain uniform rate of output. They were highly integrated with their social structure and informal pressure was used to set right the erring members. The following code of conduct was maintained for their group solidarity.

1. One should not turn out too much work. If one does, he is a "rate buster."
2. One should not turn out too little work. If one does, he is a "chesler."
3. One should not tell a supervisor anything detriment to an associate. If one does he is a "squealer."
4. One should not attempt to maintain social distance.

Howthrone Findings: Mayo and his colleagues concluded that:

i. Not the physical conditions of work, but the social and psychological factors at the workplace determine the employee's morale and output.
ii. Organisation is a social system.
iii. Non-economic rewards significantly affect the worker's behaviour, output and morale.
iv. Workers are not inert isolated but social animals.
v. Division of labour strictly on specialisation is not necessarily the most efficient approach.
vi. The workers have a tendency to form small social groups.
vii. Workers react to management as members of informal work groups rather than as individuals.
viii. Leadership style of supervision, communication and participation play a central role in worker's behaviour, satisfaction, and productivity.

Essentials of the Theory

The writers of this theory have concentrated on three elements:

1. **The Individual:** Human Relations theory emphasizes differences among individuals. For them each worker is unique. Each worker brings to the job situation certain attitudes, beliefs and ways of life, as well as certain skills. Each person has certain hopes and expectations of job situation.
2. **Work Groups:** The second element of this theory is its emphasis upon social aspect of work groups. The informal organisation

that exists within the structure of the formal organisation is emphasized. The theory focuses its attention on the social aspects of man. Mayo, thus, concluded that man's social situation in his work group ranked first and the work was incidental.

3. **Participative Management:** The third element of the Neo-classical theory is Participative management. It means participation of workers in decision-making about their work conditions. The workers discuss with the supervisor and influence the decisions that affect them. It leads to increase in productivity.

Human Relations Theory: Look from Critical Angle

1. The theory ignored several factors of employee's attitude and behaviour, particularly those operating outside the organisational environment like the social background of workers. Its assumption concerning human motivations failed to recognize the complexity and diversity of human needs. Only human relations approach partly satisfied these needs. It ignored the possibility that the conflict of interests between the workers and management might make the whole approach inapplicable.
2. It was criticized on the ground that the theory tried to substitute human relations oriented supervisors for union representation. Mayo was disapproving of for not understanding the role of unions in a free society. Loren Baritz and others condemned Mayo's theory as anti union and pro management.
3. Critics like Carry pointed out that the Hawthorne group selected in their fist experiment "cooperative girls" who were willing to participate in the research programme and this type of research was worthless, since a sample of five or six could not be taken as a reliable sample to make generalisations.
4. Peter F Drucker found fault with human relations theory for their lack of awareness of economic dimension.
5. Mayo was also criticising for his sentimental concentration on the members of organisation to the neglect of its work and purposes and a general softness and lack of direction.
6. Mayo also has been criticized as encouraging a paternalistic domination of the private lives and even the private thoughts of the individuals by their employers.
7. Critics argue that there was no place in Mayo's philosophy for conflict and he sought to achieve organisational harmony

through the subordination of individual and group interests by he administrative elite.

8. Benedics and Fisher have argued that Mayo's failure as a social scientist to a large measure due to his failure to define sharply the ethical pre-suppositions of his scientific work.

Thus to conclude, it can be said that the human relations theory of organisation arose as a reaction to the basic doctrines of classical theory. References to the famous experiments still abound, but so many specialists have since developed their own particular approaches that human relations theory now forms one of the most tangled thickets within the administrative theory jungle.

BEHAVIOURAL THEORY

Since 1887, when this subject as a separate discipline was born, a number of approaches exist to the study of public administration. Modern behaviouralism which developed in the late 30's and 40's of 20th century is mainly concerned with the scientific study of man's behaviour, in diverse social environments. It started as a protest against traditional approaches in the social sciences.

In public administration, behaviouralism as a distinct line of study started in the 1930s with the human relations movement. Later it was developed by Chester Barnard, Herbert Simon,, etc. Simon argued that, administrative behaviour is a part of the behavioural sciences and the study of public administration should involve the study of individual and collective human behaviour in administrative situations. The behavioural approach in administrative studies has the following salient features:

Salient Features

1. Its literature is descriptive rather than prescriptive, with the studies on motivation being an exception.
2. Increased attention is paid to the individual based on more realistic research concerning motivation, decision-making and the nature of authority.
3. Informal relationship and communication among members of an organisation is emphasized.
4. Operational definition of terms and empirical study is also emphasized based on rigorous methods, such as field study, laboratory experiment or use of statistical methods.

5. Though not exclusively, it is chiefly concerned with quantification and formal theory construction.
6. It is interdisciplinary in character.

According to the Behaviouralists, all human actions one motivated by social, economic political or psychological environment from which they come. So they adopt an integrated and interdisciplinary approach. This approach aims at substituting empirical and realistic judgments for the purely value oriented. So, it is value neutral. It also emphasis's a scientific approach to the study of administrative problems and their solution.

The behavioural approach in public administration has given an additional impetus to scientific research and systematic theory constriction. Public administration also dealt with cross-cultural studies of administrative behaviour. As a result, knowledge in comparative public administration was developed. In the field of comparative public administration, Robert Presthus and Michael Crozier have conducted empirical studies of bureaucratic behaviour in different socio and cultural perspectives. In India also; a number of scholars like Pai Panandiker, C.P. Bhambri, etc. have used behavioural techniques in research.

Critical Analysis

Behavioural approach has been carped for being of limited utility in the analysis of all types of administrative phenomena. Study of man as a social animal is really praiseworthy. But it can not be considered a part of the administrative sciences unless the resulting knowledge is particularly applicable to the administrative man. Again the behavioural science is largely valid and applicable to small social groups, where as the study of public administration deals with larger communities. The total exclusion of values from a study of administrative problems and phenomena will make the study of public administration rather sterile and irrelevant to the vital issues of modern age. Contribution of Simon to this theory is discussed in this book under Decision-making later.

4. CHALLENGES TO MANAGEMENT IN 21ST CENTURY NEED OF COMPETENCE

Commonly management is accepted as a specific discipline, having its own basic problems, specific approaches, specific concerns, skills, techniques and fundamentals. Management is a practice rather than a science. Its practice is always based on knowledge. Its boom world over has proved that a professional manager must be more than either a bureaucrat or a technocrat. As Peter F Drucker opined that a manager can not be confined to his discipline, can not be content with manner of his skills, his tools and his techniques. Management is universal which transcends any particular environment and yet management is not culture free for it is a social function. As such, it is socially accountable as well as culturally crashing. No organisation whether economic, political, social or even religious can survive without management. Principle of management is now universally used not only for managing business organisations but also educational social, military and even governmental organisations. Management is the technical process in all forms of organisation, though it may vary in its complexity with the size of organisation. In the words of Claude S. George, "Management is the central core of our national as well as personal activities, and the way we manage ourselves and our institutions reflect with alarming clarity what we and our society will become."

Other Challenges to Management

- Cultural diversity.
- Ethics and social responsibility.
- Total quality management
- Generation gap.
- Decision-making
- Planning and strategic management.

Cultural diversity is the biggest challenge to management. It is very difficult for an organisation to accept the alien culture where it has to operate. Ethics and social responsibility force the management to deviate from its predetermined goal or contribute to the delay in the achievement of goal. Due to heavy competitions among different organisations, there is a continuous demand on quality. Without quality, an organisation will never survive now-a-days. So how to achieve total quality management is the biggest question for every organisation. Generation gap has also its impact on management. Differences are set of values held by different age groups are called generation gaps. As we approach the 21st century a number of commentators has observed a new generation gap between a kind of attitude called baby boomer and a kind of attitude called baby booster. The baby boomers were born during post world war II and baby boosters were born after 1964. The implications for managers are significant, because this gap can present a challenge to the long standing idea that managers must be motivators and the employees need motivating pushes. Busters think, boomers are blocking their way while boomers want busters to "wait your turn." Busters think boomers do too much politicking and too little work, while boomers think busters are naive about work place relationship. Busters think, boomers are stuck in the old hierarchies, while boomers think busters have no respect for authority. Busters think boomers are not current on technology (Stroner & ors). Problems in decision-making also impose challenge to management. Rational decision-making proceeds on the belief that managers can transform a complicated web of facts, assumptions, objectives and well-informed guesses into a clear decision. Decision-making is an effort to exercise control over the organisation's destiny. But this faith has been challenged in recent years. More and more, an adaptive approach to decision-making has emerged as a way to think about what managers can do and can not expect to accomplish. According to adaptive thinking, the results of decision action are jointly produced by what your organisation does and what other organisations are doing at same time. Two versions of the adaptive approach to decision-making are: game theory and chaos theory. Game theory is the study of people making interdependent choices. It highlights the explicit role of human relationships, and interactions in decisions. Chaos theory is the study of dynamic patterns in large social system. It pays close attention to the instability of a system. Another challenge is planning and strategic management. There is a trend in strategic management towards more collaborative efforts between people at different organisations called as collective strategy. The idea is that strategic managers have reason to worry not only about their own enterprise's strategy but also a sense of direction for some collection of enterprises that have common concerns.

MANAGER IS IN NEW ROLE: A FAÇADE OF ORGANISATION

As to role of managers, Henry Mintzberg undertook a study which consisted of observations of five chief executives. To put it again, on the basis of this study, ten managerial roles were identified and grouped into interpersonal informational and decision role.

- International roles.
- Figure head role
- Leader role
- Liaison role
- Informational roles.
- Recipient role
- Disseminator role
- Spokesperson role
- Decision roles.
- Entrepreneurial role
- Disturbance handler role
- Resource allocator role
- Negotiator role.

But in the changing scenario, the managers should travel beyond such defined roles. Many new roles have to be performed by the manager in the 21st century. Obviously, managers' functions are redefined. The manager must be effective and efficient. All over the world there is established definition of management in its changing scenario with Men, Money, Material and Machines - 4 'M's for building up competitive strength of a nation, irrespective of the fact whether it is a developed or developing. Management is the dynamic, life giving and life support system. Without management, resources of production will remain only unproductive or underproductive resources. So manager's role must be tapped, harnessed, and utilised for the quality of life. In this regard managers should be like a helicopter. Helicopter provides the view of a terrain which cannot be had on the ground. Professional managers in their respective disciplines need such a view for optimal performance in their jobs. Only then can they improve their performance, qualitatively as well as quantitatively.

So in 21st century, for a manager a number of new roles are prescribed in addition to the roles prescribed by Mintzberg.

The innovative new roles are:

- Planning
- Directing
- Motivating
- Controlling
- Researching
- Thinking
- Decision-making
- Leaving

- Organising
- Listening
- Strategy making
- Appraising
- Training
- Communicating
- Team building
- Monitoring
- Reviewing
- Evaluating
- Writing
- Goal setting
- Managing Time
- Presentation

With this mangers can fly high for people, for organisation and for customers.

References

1. Koontz and Weihrich, *Essentials of Management*, Tata McGraw Hill Publishers, New Delhi.
2. Meyer, *Management Science*, McGraw Hill Publishers, New York.
3. G. R. Terry, *Principles of Management*, Richard D. Irwin, Homewood, 1970.
4. Koontz and Weichrich, *op. cit.*

Chapter two

GLOBAL AND COMPARATIVE MANAGEMENT[1]

Management theory is universal. But its practice varies from country to country. In fact the practice totally depends upon the socio-politico and legal-economic environment of that country.

In France, government planning on a national scale helps co-ordinate plans of individual industries and companies. The government's aim is to utilise most effectively the country's resources and to avoid expansion in uneconomic areas. Although governmental planning which is also extended to regional areas – is carried out by relatively few, but competent, people, cooperation and assistance are provided by other governmental departments, employer's organisations, unions and consumers. The plan which is generally revised every five years, attempts to obtain economic growth, price stability, a balance in foreign payments and a favourable employment situation. Managers then, are not only constrained by 'Le Plan' but also aided by it, since it produces a great deal of information upon which they can draw for preparing plans for their own enterprise. At times, the plan becomes a global strategy helping specific industries. There is a close relationship between government planning and firms, especially those that are owned and directly aided by the government.

In the past and to a lesser extent today the German cultural environment favoured reliance on authority in directing the workforce, although it was often benevolent authoritarianism. Even today, while managers may show concern for subordinates, they also expect obedience. It is almost a paradox that, on the one hand, the managerial style is characterized by considerable use of authority, while on the other hand, labour by law, is represented by and actively involved in managing large corporations. In 1951, a law was passed that provided for codetermination, which requires labour membership in the supervisory board and the executive committee of certain large corporations. Furthermore, a labour director is elected as a member of the executive committee. This position is a difficult one. Labour directors supposedly must represent the interests of the employees and at the same time, must make managerial decisions that are in the best interest of the enterprise.

Managing in Australia is influenced by that country's moralistic stance and its emphasis on political and social value, achievement and risk taking. Italian managers are operating in an environment of low tolerance for risks. Italians are very competitive, but at the same time they like group decision-making. Management in Austria is characterized by self-realisation and leadership. Independence and competitiveness are valued. The tolerance of risk taking is rather low there. In Britain, security is important and so are resourcefulness, adaptability and logic. Individualism is also highly valued. In case of Russia, important decisions were largely made by central planners. However the need for decentralisation has become evident. The managerial power even extends to the decision of firing an employee. But this authority may be more theoretical than real, because the state guarantees employment. Thus the dismissal may amount to a transfer of the employee to another organisation. Raising the status of the managerial elite is a new phenomenon in Russia but management education lags for behind that in most western nations. Moreover, Japan and United States management are regarded as model for other countries

USA AND JAPAN:[2] THE PRACTICE OF MANAGEMENT

Japan, one of the leading industrial nations in the world, has adopted managerial practices that are quite different from those of other economically advanced countries in the western world. Important features of Japanese management practice are:

- lifelong employment,
- great concern for the individual employee, and
- emphasis on seniority.

Typically, employees spend their working life with a single enterprise, which in turn provides employees with security and a feeling of belonging this practice brings the culturally induced concept of 'Wa' (harmony) to the enterprise, resulting in employee loyalty and close identification with the aims of the company. However it also adds to business costs, because employees are kept on the payroll even though there may be insufficient work. Consequently, firms are beginning to question the practice of life long employment. Indeed, changes appear to be in the making, but they are slow. What is often overlooked, however, is that this permanent employment practice, knows 'nenko' is used only by large firms. It is estimated that the job security system applies to only about one third of the labour force closely related to lifelong employment is the seniority system, which has provided privileges for older employees who have been with the enterprise a long time. But there are indications that the seniority system may be superseded by a more open approach that provides opportunities for advancement for young people.

The managerial practice of decision-making in Japan is also considerably different from that in the USA. It is built on the concept that changes and new ideas should come primarily from below. Thus, lower level employees prepare proposals for higher level personnel. Supervisors, rather than simply accepting or rejecting suggestions, tactfully question proposals, make suggestions and encourage subordinates. If necessary, proposals are sent back to the initiator for more information. Japanese management then uses decision-making by consensus, lower level employees intimate the idea and submit it to the next higher level, until it reaches the desk of the top executive. If the proposal is approved, it is then returned to the initiator for implementation. Although the decision-making process is time consuming, the implementation of the decision because of the general consensus at various levels of management is swift and does not require additional 'selling'. An important characteristic of Japanese decision-making is the large amount of effort that goes into defining the question or problem. There is a great deal of communication before a decision is actually made. American managers are often accused of making decision before defining the problem. In contrast Japanese management makes a decision only after long discussions of the issue.

The Americans increasingly examine Japanese management rightly or wrongly to find answers to this productivity crisis. Besides, life time employment and consensus decision-making, there are other characteristics that distinguish Japanese from American management practices. These are mentioned below:[3]

Japanese Management: In Brief

Planning

- Long term orientation.

- Collective decision-making with consensus.
- Involvement of many people in preparing and making decision.
- Decision flow from bottom to top and back bottom up approach
- Slow decision-making and fast implementation of the decision.

Organising

- Collective responsibility and accountability.
- Ambiguity of decision responsibility.
- Informal organisation structure.
- Well-known common organisation culture and philosophy, competitive spirit toward other enterprises.

Staffing

- Young people hired from B-school, hardly any mobility of people among companies.
- Slow promotion through ranks.
- Loyalty to the company.
- Very in frequent performance appraisal for new employees.
- Appraisal of long-term performance.
- Promotions based on multiple criteria.
- Training and development considered a long-term investment.
- Life time appointment.

Leading

- Leader acting as a social facilitator and group member.
- Paternalistic style.
- Common values facilitating cooperation.
- Avoidance of confrontation, sometimes leading to ambiguities, emphasis on harmony.
- Bottom up communication.

Controlling

- Control by peers.
- Control focus on group performance.
- Saving face.
- Extensive use of quality control circles and TQM concept.

USA Management: A Brief Sketch

Planning

- Primary short term orientation.

- Individual decision-making.
- Involvement of peoples in making and selling the decision to persons with divergent values.
- Decisions initiated at top, flowing down. Top down approach
- Fast decision-making, slow implementation requiring compromise, often resulting in suboptimal decisions.

Organising

- Individual responsibility and accountability.
- Clear and specific decisions responsibility.
- Formal, bureaucratic organisation structure.
- Lack of common organisation culture, identification with profession rather than with company.

Staffing

- People hired out of schools from other companies, frequent company changes.
- Rapid advancement desired and demanded.
- Loyalty to the professions.
- Frequent performance appraisal for new employees.
- Appraisal of short term results.
- Promotions based primarily on individual performance.
- Training and development undertaken with hesitation.
- Job insecurity prevailing.

Leading

1. Leader acting as a decision-maker and head of the group.
2. Directive style.
3. Often divergent values, individualism sometimes hindering cooperation.
4. Face to face confrontations, common emphasis on clarify.
5. Communication primarily for down.

Controlling

- Control by superior.
- Control focus on individual performance.
- Fixing blame.
- Limited use of quality control circles.

Theory 'Z'

In theory 'Z', selected Japanese managerial practices are adapted to the USA environment. One of the characteristics of type 'z' management practice is an accent on the interpersonal skills that are needed for group interaction. Yet, despite the prominence on group decision-making, responsibility remains with the individual (which is quite different from the Japanese practice, which emphases collective responsibility.) There is also an emphasis on informal and democratic relationships based on trust. Yet the hierarchical structure still remains intact. Participative management facilitates the free flow of information needed to reach consensus. Formal planning and objectives are important, but numerical measures are not excessively emphasized. Instead, a corporate philosophy and corporate values guide managerial actions. People are seen as whole human beings not simply as factors in production. However the Japanese practice of very infrequent performance appraisals and promotions is not highlighted by theory 'Z' type companies. In short, these companies selectively use some Japanese managerial practices but make adjustments for the environment prevailing in the USA.

References

1. Koontz and Weihrich, *Essentials of Management*, Tata McGraw Hill Publication.
2. *Ibid.*
3. *Ibid.*

Chapter three

PLANNING

In designing an environment for the effective performance of individuals working together in groups, a manager's most essential task is to see that everyone understands the groups purposes and objectives and its methods of attaining them. If group effort is too effective, people must know what they are expected to accomplish. This is the function of planning. It is the most basic of all the managerial functions. Planning involves selecting missions and objectives and the actions to achieve them. It requires decision-making that is choosing from among alternative for future course of action. Plan, thus, provides a rational approach to pre-selected objectives.

Planning bridges the gap between present point and future point. It makes it possible for things to occur which would not otherwise happen. Planning is an intellectually demanding process. In it, estimates, planning and control are inseparable. Any attempt to control without plans is meaningless.

A plan can encompass any course of future action, which clearly shows that plans are varied. They are classified as:

1. **Purpose:** The purpose identifies the basic function of an enterprise or agency or of any part of it. Every kind of organised operation has, or at least should have if it is to be meaningful, purposes or missions. In every social system, enterprises have a basic function or task which is assigned to them by society. The purpose of the courts is the interpretation of laws and their application. The purpose of a university is teaching and research and so on.
2. **Objectives**: Objectives are the ends toward which activity is aimed at. They represent not only the end point of planning but the end toward which organising, staffing, leading and controlling are aimed.
3. **Strategies**: Managers increasingly use strategies to reflect broad areas of an enterprise operation. Strategies mean.

- General programs of action and deployment of resources to attain comprehensive objectives.
- The program of objectives of an organisation and their changes, resources used to attain these objectives and policies governing the acquisition, use and disposition of these resources.
- Determination of the basic long term objectives of an enterprise and the adoption of courses of action and allocation of resources necessary to achieve these goals.

The purpose of strategies is to determine and communicate, through a system of objectives and policies, a picture of the kind of enterprise that is envisioned. Strategies do not attempt to outline exactly how the enterprise is to accomplish its objectives, since this is the task of countless major and minor supporting programs.

4. **Policies:** Policies are also plans in that they are general statements or understandings which guide or channel thinking in decision-making. Not all policies are statements. Policies define an area within which a decision is to be made and ensure that the decision will be consistent with and contribute to an objective policies help decide issues before they become problems, make it unnecessary to analyze the same situation every time it comes up and unify other plans, thus permitting managers to delegate authority and still maintain control over what their subordinates do policies ordinarily exist on all levels of the organisation, ranging from major company policies, the rough major department policies to minor policies applicable to the smallest segment of the organisation. Policies are guides to decision-making. It is a means of encouraging discretion and initiative.
5. **Procedures:** Procedures are plans that establish a required method of handling future activities. They are guides to action, rather than to thinking and they detail the exact manner in which certain activities must be accomplished. They are chronological sequences of required action.
6. **Rules:** Rules spell out specific required actions or non-actions, allowing no discretion. They are usually the simplest type of plan.
7. **Programmes:** Programmes are a complex of goals, policies, procedures, rules, task assignments, steps to be taken, resources to be employed and other elements necessary to carry out a given course of action. They are ordinarily supported by budgets.

8. **Budget:** A budget is a statement of expected results expressed in numerical terms. It may be referred to as a numberized program.

Steps in planning: The planning process involves a series of steps as mentioned in the diagram below:

Being aware of opportunity
↓
Setting objectives or goals
↓
Considering planning premises
↓
Identification of alternatives
↓
Comparing alternatives in light of goals sought
↓
Choosing an alternative
↓
Formulating supporting plans
↓
Numberising plans by making budgets

Fig. 1.3.1

1. *Being aware of opportunities:* Although it precedes actual planning and is therefore not strictly a part of the planning process, an awareness of opportunities in the external environment as well as within the organisation is the real starting point for planning. It is important to take a preliminary look at possible future opportunities and see them clearly and completely planning requires realistic diagnosis of the opportunity situation.
2. *Establishing objectives:* The second step is to establish objectives for the entire enterprise and then for each subordinate work unit. This is to be done for the long term as well as for the short range. Objectives specify the expected results and indicate the end points of what is to be done, where the primary emphasis is to be paced and what is to be accomplished by the network of strategies, policies, procedures, rules, budgets and programes.
3. *Developing premises:* The third logical step in planning is to establish, circulate and obtain agreement to utilise critical planning premises. Such as forecasts, applicable basic policies and existing plans. They are assumptions about the environment

in which the plan is to be carried out. It is important for all the managers involved in planning to agree on the premises. Forecasting is important in premising.

4. *Determining alternative courses:* The fourth step in planning is to search for and examine alternative courses of action, especially those not immediately apparent. There is seldom a plan for which reasonable alternatives do not exist and quite often an alternative that is not obvious proves to be the best. The more problem is not finding alternatives but reducing the number of alternatives so that the most promising may be analyzed.
5. *Evaluating alternative courses :* After seeking out alternative courses and examining their strong and weak points, the next step is evaluating the alternatives by weighing them in the light of premises and goals.
6. *Selecting a course:* This is the point at which the plan is adopted. Occasionally, an analysis and evaluation of alternative courses will disclose that two or more are advisable and the manager may decide to follow several courses rather than the one best course.
7. *Formulating derivative plans :* When a decision is made, planning is seldom complete. Derivative plans are almost invariably required to support the basic plan.
8. *Numberising plans by budgeting:* After decisions are made and plans are set the final step in giving them meaning is to numberize them by converting them to budgets. The overall budgets of an enterprise represent the sum total of income and expansions, with resultant profit or surplus and budgets of major balance sheet items.

Further Readings

1. George R Terry, *Principles of Management*, Homewood, Richard Irwin, 1988
2. David Hussey, *Corporate Planning: Theory and Practice*, Oxford Pergamer, 1982
3. Peter F Drucker, *Management: Tasks, Responsibilities and Practies*, New York, Harper & Row, 1974
4. Dalton E, McFarland, *Management Principles and Practices*, New York, MacMillan, 1994.

Chapter four

DECISION-MAKING

Decision-making is the heart of management. It is the core of Planning. Seckler Hudson made clear that, decision-making in government is a plural activity. It is an imperative part of a political process. Also decision-making is an indissoluble and indispensable component of the management processes. In fact, whatever a manager does, he does through decision-making only. The end products of managers' works are decisions and actions. The importance of decision-making in management is such that H. A. Simon called management as the 'heart of decision-making'.

Decision-making may be viewed as the process by which individuals select a course of action from among alternatives to produce a desired result. It is a process made up of four inters related phases.

1. *Explorative (searching):* The decision maker must find occasions for making a decision. He must take a realistic appraisal of where the organisation is and what are the current problems? Asking what should be done? And what are the challenges?
2. *Speculative (analysing):* The decision maker should analyze various factors affecting a decision problem so that on appropriate response can be obtained. How to take advantage of the challenging opportunities in the environment? And how to utilise the resources to get maximum benefit?
3. *Evaluative (weighing):* The decision maker is expected to make a cost benefit analysis of various alternatives, asking what are the costs? And what are the potential benefits?
4. *Selective (commitment):* This is accusation of making a choice among alternation.

So in other words, decision-making is the process by which the decision maker tries to jump over the obstacles placed between his current position and the desired future position. The decision-making process can be depicted in the following Figure 1.4.1

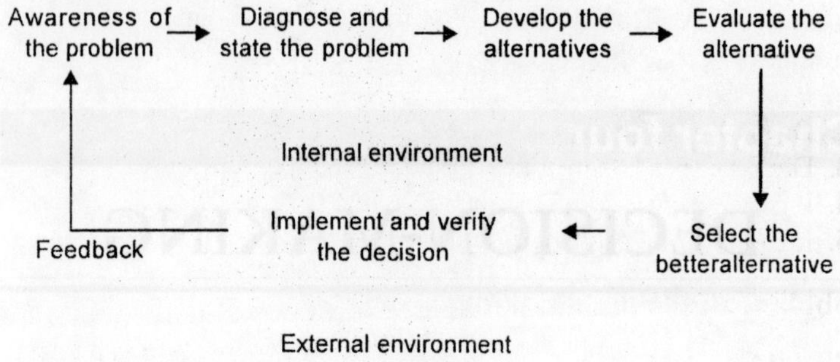

Fig. 1.4.1

Further while selecting an alternative Managers can use three basic approaches as explained in Figure 1.4.2.

- Experience
- Experimentation
- Research and analysis.

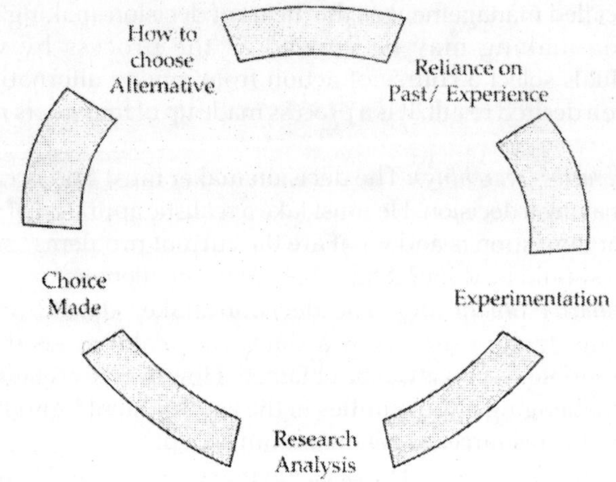

Fig. 1.4.2

Nature: Decision-making should be distinguished from two things, i. e. choice making and problem solving. According to G. P. Huber, choice making is narrow in space and refers to choosing one option from a set of alternative options. Problem solving is abroad term and refers to the broad set of activities necessary to find and implement the course of action. So the decision-making process is different having following features:

1. It is a goal oriented process.
2. Decisions imply alternatives.
3. Decision-making is a analytical intellectual process.
4. It is a dynamic process.
5. It is not the entirely of management.

Problems in Decision-Making

There are a number of problems in decision-making að it is a very complex process. Some problems are:

1. **Involvement in Routine:** It has been found that the executives tend to use a large part of their time in making routine decisions. Prof. March of Carnegie Institute of Technology has conducted a lot of research on business decision-making. He made the subjects perform simple administrative jobs involving three kinds of activities, i.e. routine kind of communication to subordinates, intermediate planning and general planning.
2. **Which Problem to Solve:** The question would not arise if the problems are limited and resources adequate are adequate. But this is a rare pointer. For example, in making a national plan, choices have to be made between building of dams, construction of railway lines, promotion of industries, etc. At a lower level, a Chief Executive may have to decide whether to meet the trade representatives or to attend a conference or to meet the officers of Government. An administrator therefore has to learn to set priorities. The latter ones keep changing according to the importance of the problems at hand.
3. **Propriety of Decisions:** This is the problem of deciding as to what is the right decision. This subject to the conflict between observing the form and carrying out the spirit. Whether the emphasis should be on following strictly the rules and procedures or some other criteria one to be applied. The correct view appears to be that rules and procedures are meant to systematize the work and to improve efficiency and not to be used as criteria for judging the propriety of a decision. The real test is whether the decision promotes general interest.
4. **Bias:** Elimination of bias from decision-making is part of the general problem of rationality in the decision-making. Bias is a vague term difficult to define making. Bias is a vague term difficult to define precisely. It means a swaying influence or undue

learning to one side. Bias, is not a conscious or deliberate phenomenon in the sense that decision maker may not even be aware of it. Bias has nothing to do with unethical conduct like favoritism, nepotism, etc. which are all deliberate acts. Bias in the decisions can be judged by observing whether the decision has derived from norms and whether such deviation, if any can be justified before an independent person on objective rather than subjective grounds.

Factors in Decision-Making

There is no unanimity about the factors that penetrate the decision-making. Some say that the major factors are institution, facts, experience and authority.

Seckler Hudson has listed twelve such factors viz.

1. Legal limitations
2. Financial limitations
3. Mores
4. Facts
5. History
6. Morale
7. Future
8. Superiors
9. Pressure Groups
10. Staff
11. Subordinates
12. Nature of the Program

Different factors may be important at different times and in different situations. In one word factors are situation savvy. A decision is taken depending upon the criteria believed to be important in any particular situation. This is the situational view of the decision-making process.

Theories of Decision-making

As already mentioned, decision-making involves the choice of a particular course of action from among a number of competing alternatives. Theories of decision-making concerned with the question as to how such a choice is made. Generally, there are three theories of decision-making:

1. Rational theory
2. Incremental theory
3. Behavioural theory (H. Simon).

Rational Theory

According to this theory the decision maker first isolates the problem for decision and then identifies various alternative solutions. The costs and benefits of all the alternatives are then worked out and compared with each other. The best alternative is chosen according to the decision criteria decided prior and in advance. On the face of it, this appears a very simple model assuming the decision maker to be a rational person as it assumed in the study of economics. The theory has, however, been subjected to severe criticism on account of the tacit assumption it makes.

The theory assumes that the problems are all known to the decision maker. But it is not a fact. The problems for decision require a greater deal of investigation to isolate. The apparent problem may not be the real problem. Further decisions are for the future. Future is obscure. Evidently, all alternatives are not fully explored before taking decisions.

Another facile assumption of the theory, on the pattern of rationalist economic theory, is that all the alternative solutions of the problem chosen are known to decision maker. It is further implicit that all the consequences of the alternative solutions are also known to the decision maker and that he can instantly compare their costs and benefits. This is not true, away from ground reality. Even if all the alternatives and their costs and benefits are known, it may not be possible for the decision maker to reach a conclusion on account of the conflicting values that may be applicable to the situation. Certain alternatives may not even be available to the decision maker in view of the decisions already taken and executed.

Incremental Theory

The criticisms of the rational theory are to some extent answered by the incremental theory. According to this approach the various processes of decision-making like the selection of the problem and analysis of various alternatives, etc. are not very clearly demarcated. The decision maker considers only a few alternatives for dealing with the problems. These differ only marginally or incrementally from the existing policies. The change takes place slowly. The problem gets redefined and another incremental decision is taken. It is a continuous process in which decision is generally by consensus. For that reason, it is easy to implement.

Obviously, incremental decision-making can not result in big changes. The process is essentially very slow, but has several advantages over the rational decision-making process.

Firstly, the process avoids violent changes which may at times give rise to social and political instability.

Secondly, the incremental decision-making process reduces the risks and costs of decisions which have often to be taken under conditions of uncertainty.

Thirdly, the problem of data collection, analysis of alternatives, etc. remain within manageable limits so that impossible burdens are not placed on the decision makers.

The incremental decision-making process has however, also been criticized by many. It has been said that the process being based on consensus, tends to favour the most powerful and privileged sections of the population. It is incapable of processing bold initiatives favouring the poor and the down trodden. Nor can it make for big and decisive changes.

Behaviour Theory of H. Simon

H. Simon attacked the classical theory of organisation, based mainly on structural approach. He said that the so called principles of organisation were mere proverbs and often lead to contradictory and inconsistent results. He therefore tried to study the question in another way, *viz.* by observing the behaviour of the managers in the organisation.

Simon views an organisation as a structure of decision makers. According to him decisions are made at all levels of the organisation. He divided the decision-making process into three phases:

- Intelligence activity
- Design activity
- Choice activity.

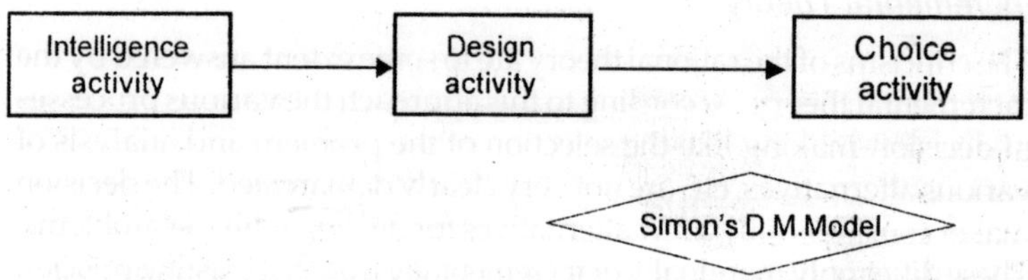

In his famous book antitled*Administrative Behaviour* Simon developed his ideas on the decision-making process. Simon explains that decision-making basically involves choice between alternative plans of action and choice in turn involves facts and valves. A fact is a statement of reality indicating the existing deed, act or state of things. A factual premise can be proved by observable and measurable means, value is an expression of preference. A value premise can only be subjectively asserted to be valid. Simon is aware that most premises have both factual and value elements. To bring out the difference between the fact and value, the means ends distinction is used. Simon concludes that behaviour in an organisation is a complex network of decision process and intently rational in character adjusted to the goals that have been erected. Speaking of the complex network of decision-making process, Simon says that each decision involves the selection of a goal and a behaviour relevant to it. The ambiguous similarity between means ends and fact value is clarified through a definition that in so far as decisions lead to the selection of final goals, they may be treated as 'value judgments', and in so far as decisions implement such goals, they may be treated as 'factual judgments'. Simon does not refer to value decisions and factual decisions.

Simon expounded the necessity of being rational in making a choice. He defined rationality as one concerned with the selection of preferred behaviour alternatives in terms of some system of values where the consequences of behaviour can be evaluated. He explained rationality in terms of means construct. Mean is instrumental purpose and ends in ultimate purpose. If appropriate means are chosen to reach desired end, the decision is rational. It is difficult to separate means from ends because an apparent end may only be a means for some future end.

Simon had difference of opinion as to the concept of 'total rationality'. According to the behavioural theory, optimality is a utopian concept. There is no way to identify optimality and establish a measure for goodness. The decision-making process can not be a scientific process where there are no explicit, clear cut and idealized goals. Real life challenges, item and cost limitations, political pressures from internal and external constituencies force the decision maker to work under conditions of "bounded rationality." It means that he rarely tries to find out the optimum solution to a decision problem. Instead of conducting an exhaustive search, he searchers for a limited number of alternatives and stop when they are able to meet the standards established by them previously to satisfy there goals. This search stops at a point that meets their subjective standards. They select a course of action, whose consequences are good enough. Subjective rationality would be preferable to objective rationality where people have to take decisions under time and cost limitations.

Thus instead of searching for and choosing the best alternatives, administrators accept decisions that are only good enough rather, than ideal. Such decisions are referred to as 'satisfying' decisions the Scottish word meaning satisfying or pleasing.

Information processing abilities	External factors	Time and cost limits
	BOUNDED RATIONALITY	
Organizational objectives	Decisions Maker	Personal Factors
	Satisfying decisions	

Classification of Decisions

Programmed and Non-programmed

Simon also made a classification of decisions. He made a distinction between two types of decisions, i.e. programmed and non-programmed. Decisions are programmed or structured to the extent that they are repetitive and routine in nature. Non-programmed or unstructured decisions are those which are nobel, unstructured and consequential and have to be tackled independently. The techniques to deal with programmed decisions are habit, knowledge, skills and informal channels. Selection and training of executives possessing higher skills, innovative ability, etc. is the techniques to deal with non-programmed decisions. Simon suggests that it is possible to construct mathematical models to make a rational choice. The application of mathematical tools, operation research, electronic data processing, system analysis, and computer can profitably used to make decisions. With the increased use of computers and simulation models, more and more decisions can become programmed, which in turn increases rationality making process. Besides, decisions are made under complete knowledge- Certainty: Increasing Knowledge – Risk and under lack of knowledge – Uncertainty. To Uncertainty modern approaches or techniques are Risk Analysis, Decision Tree and Preference Theory. Further, decisions are facilitated by Decision Support System (DSS) and Management Information System (MIS). Also there is an important role of creativity and innovation in decision-making. And creativity is enhanced by techniques of Brainstorming and Synectics

MODELS OF DECISION-MAKING

Henry Mintzberg's Model

In the following Figure 1.4.3 a view of Simon and modification by Mintzberg is exhibited.

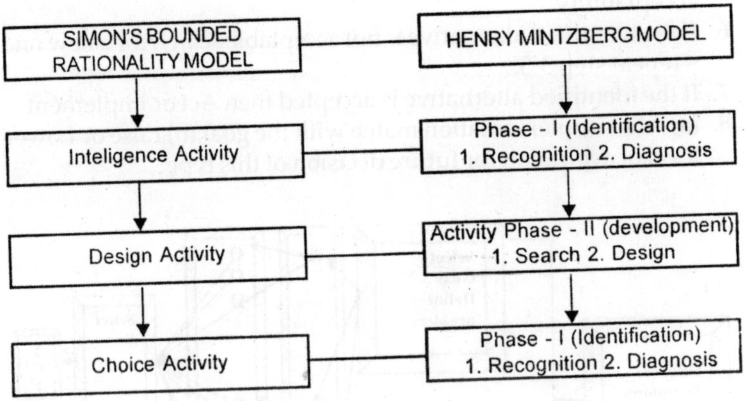

Fig. 1.4.3: Model of decision-making

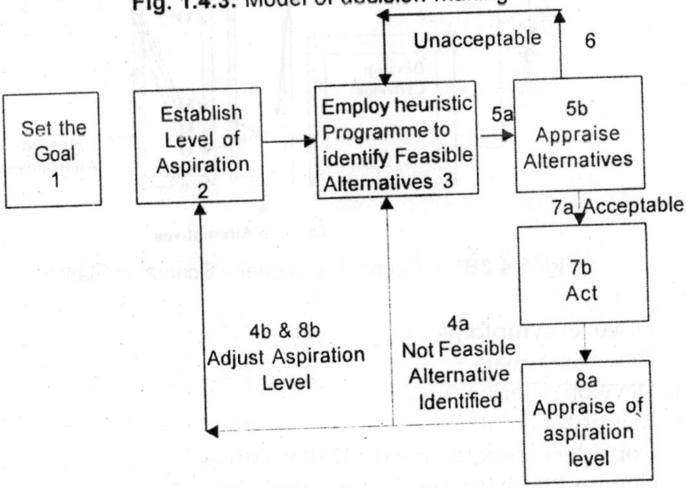

Fig. 1.4.3: A Bounded rationality Model - Administrative Man

Behling and Schriesheim's: DM Models

1. Set the goal or define problem
2. Establish an appropriate level of aspiration or criterion level
3. Employ heuristics (guiding rule for yielding satisfactory solutions) to identify promising alternatives
4. If no feasible alternative is identified (a) Lower the aspiration level (b) begin the search for new alternative by repeating step 2 and 3
5. (a) Feasible Alternative identified (b) Appraise or evaluate for acceptability
6. If the identified alternative is not acceptable search for a new one – repeat step 3-5.
7. If the identified alternative is accepted then Act or implement
8. (a) After implementation match with the goal;(b) raise or Lower level of aspiration for future decision of this type.

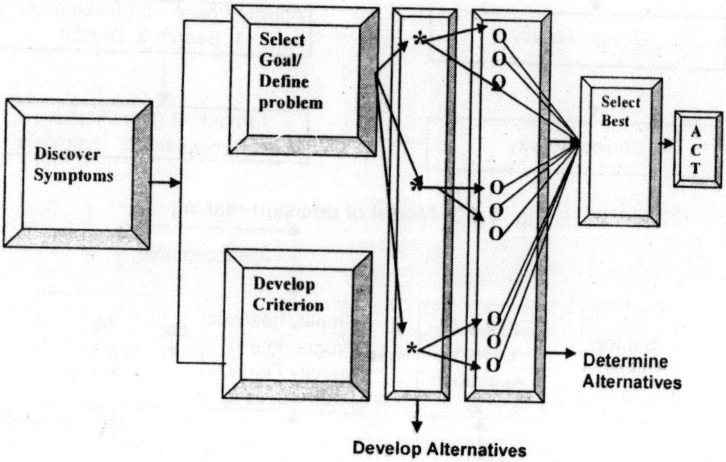

Fig. 1.4.3B: II. Econologic model – Economic Man

1. Discover symptoms
2. Determine goals
3. Develop criterion
4. Identify alternatives
5. Consider consequences of all alternatives
6. Choose Alternative by Comparing Consequences
7. Act or Implement decision

3. Implicit Favourite Model –Games Man Model

(Developed by Soelberg (1967)

Decision rule not justifying implicit Favourite

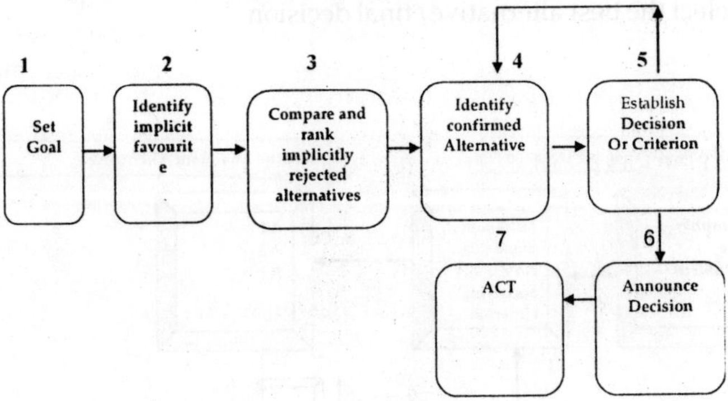

Fig. 1.4.3C

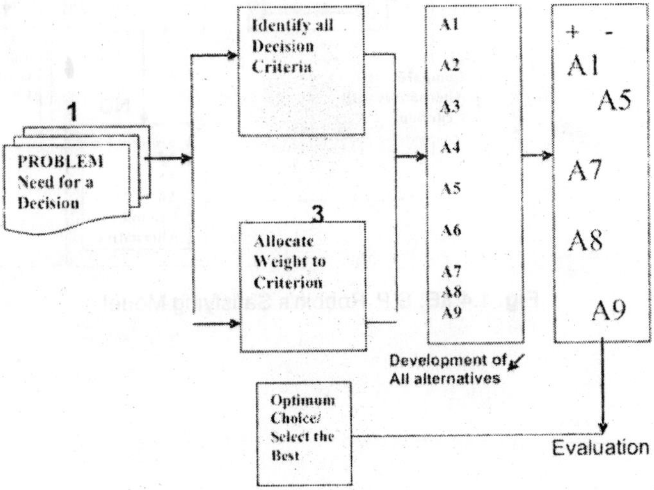

Fig. 1.4.3D: Robbin Three Models: Optimising Model

1. Set Goal/ascertain the need for a decision
2. Identify the decision criteria
3. Allocate weights to the criterion
4. Develop the alternatives
5. Evaluate the alternatives
6. Select the best alternative/final decision

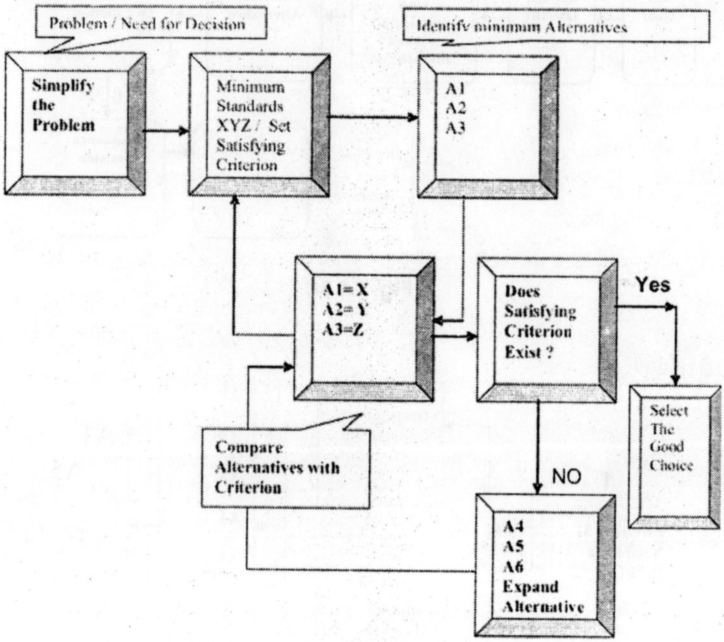

Fig. 1.4.3E: S.P. Robbin's Satisfying Model

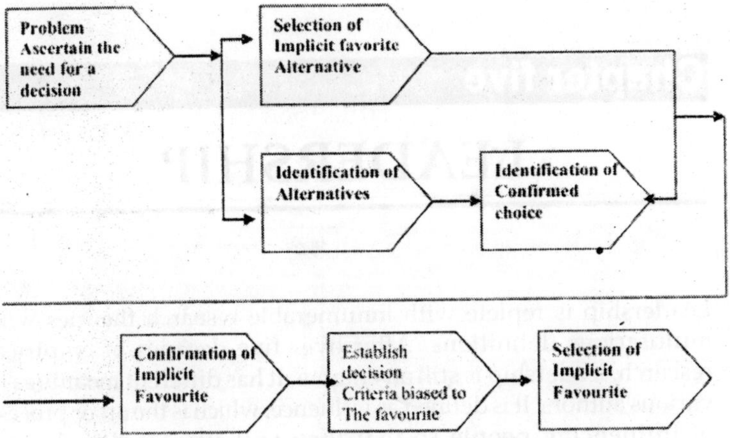

Fig. 1.4.3F: S.P. Robbin's Implicit Favourite Model

Further Readings

1. Fremont A Shull, Andrew L. Delbeeq and Llcummings, *Organisational Decision-Making*, New York, McGraw Hill, 1970.
2. Herbert A Simon, *Administrative Behaviour*, New York, Free Press, 1976.
3. Henry Mintzberg, *Research on Strategy Making*, Proceedings of Academy of Management, 1972.
4. Herbert G. Hicks, *The Management of Organisations*, New York, McGraw Hills, 1972.

Chapter five

LEADERSHIP

Leadership is replete with innumerable research theories with multifarious definitions. After over five decades of empirical research, leadership is still an enigma. It has different meanings to various authors. It is defined as influence, which is the art or process of influencing people so that they will strive willingly and enthusiastically towards the achievement of group goals. Ideally people should be encouraged to develop not only willingness to work but also willingness to work with zeal and confidence. Leadership is a value loaded term. It is defined as the process of influencing group activities towards the achievement of goals in a particular situation.

According to George V. Dixon, "Leadership is in the eye of the follower." Pfiffner has described leadership as "the art of coordinating and monitoring individuals and groups to achieve desired ends." Koontz and Odonell have described leadership as "the activity of persuading people to cooperate in the achievement of a common objective." Terry has defined leadership as "the activity of influencing people to strive willingly for mutual objectives."

The above definitions contain many important points:

1. Leadership is a relationship between two or more people in which influence and power are unevenly distributed.
2. Leadership do not flourish in vacuum. The essential of leadership is followership.
3. Leadership is essentially a continuous process of influencing behaviour.
4. Leadership is essentially a continuous process of influencing behaviour.
5. Leadership is something a person does, not something one has. It is something that emerges, that grows and that is achieved.

Essentials of Leadership

Leaders envision the future. They inspire organisation members and chart the course of the organisation's development. Every group of people that performs near its total capacity has some person as its head who is skilled in the art of leadership. To this four major elements are noticeable.

1. The ability to use power effectively and in a responsible manner.
2. The ability to comprehend those human beings have different motivation forces at different times and in different situations.
3. The ability to inspire.
4. The ability to act in a manner that will develop a climate conducive to responding to and arousing motivations.

Theories of Leadership

The leadership literature is voluminous, and much of it is confusing and contradictory. In order to make our way through this forest, we consider three approaches to explain what makes on effective leader.

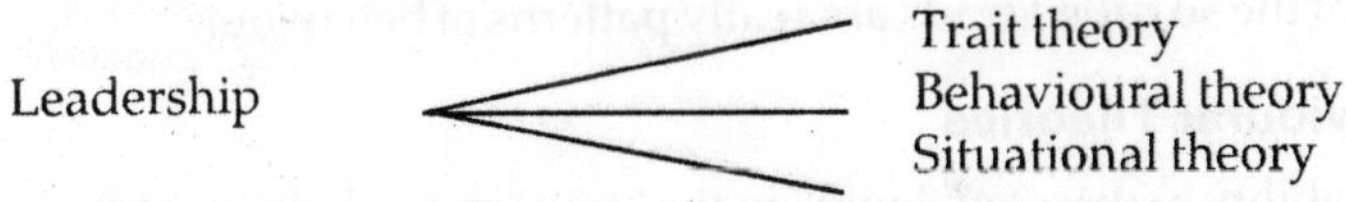

The first sought to find universal personality traits that leaders had to some greater degree than non leaders. The seconded tried to explain leadership in terms of the behaviour a person. Both approaches have been described as "false starts", based on their erroneous and over-simplified conception of leadership. The third used contingency models to explain the inadequacies of previous leadership theories in reconciling and bringing together the results of research findings.

Rather recently, attention has revisited to traits, but from a different perspective. Researchers are now attempting to identify the set of traits that people implicitly refer to when they characterize someone as a leader. This line of thinking proposes that leadership is as much style-projecting the appearance of being a leader as it is substance.

Trait Theories

Prior to 1949, studies of leadership were based largely on an attempt to identify the traits that leaders possess. Starting with the 'Great

Man Theory' that leaders are born and not made. The belief dated back to the ancient Greeks and Romans. The researchers have tried to identify the physical, mental and personality traits of various leaders. The great man theory lost much of its acceptability with the rise of behaviourist school of psychology.

Many studies of traits have been made. Ralph M. Stogdill had identified specific traits related to leadership ability; five physical traits (such as energy, appearance, height, etc.); four intelligence and ability traits, sixteen personality traits (such as adaptability, aggressiveness, enthusiasm, self-confidence, etc.), six task related characteristics (such as achievement drive, persistence, initiative, etc.) and nine social characteristics (cooperativeness, interpersonal skill, etc.).

In general, the study of leader's traits has not been a very fruitful approach to explain leadership. Not all leaders possess all the traits. And many non-leaders may possess most or all of them. Also, the trait approach gives no guidance as to how much of any trait a person should have for leadership. Furthermore, many studies have been made which do not agree as to which traits are leadership traits or what their relationships are to actual instance of leadership. Most of the so called traits are really patterns of behaviour.

Behavioural Theories

The inability to discover "gold" in the "trait" mines led researchers to look at the behaviours that specific leaders exhibited. There are several theories on leadership behaviour and styles. The important of them are:

- Leadership based on the use of authority.
- Likert's four systems.
- Managerial Grid.
- Leadership involving a variety of styles, ranging from a maximum to minimum use of power and influence (leadership continuum).
- Ohio State studies.
- University of Michigan studies.
- Scandinavian studies.

Styles based on the Use of Authority

Leaders were seen as applying three basic styles.

1. Autocratic
2. Democratic or participative
3. Free rein.

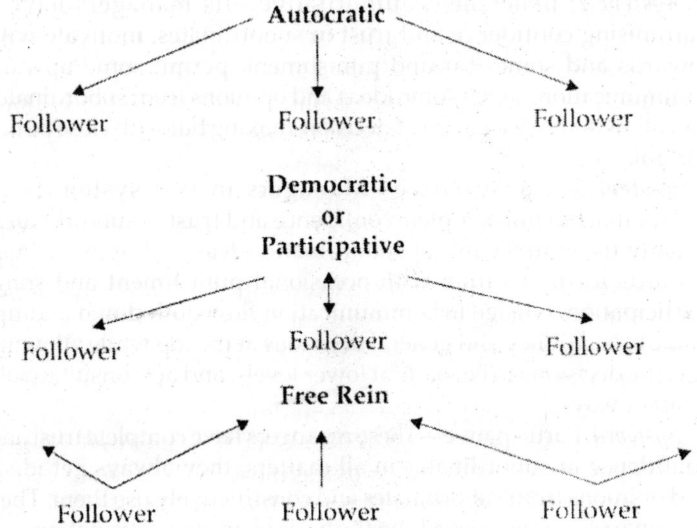

The autocratic leader commands and expects compliance, is dogmatic and positive, and leads by the ability to withhold or give rewards and punishment. The democratic or participative leader consults with subordinates on proposed action and decisions and encourages participation from them. This type of leader ranges from the person who does not take action without subordinate's concurrence to the one who makes decisions but consults with subordinates before doing so. The free rein leader uses his or her power very little, it at all, giving subordinates a high degree of independence in their operations. Such leaders depend largely on subordinates to set their own goals and the means of achieving them, and they see their role as one of aiding the operations of followers by furnishing them with information and acting primarily as a contact with the groups' external environment.

Likert's Four System: Rensis Likert and his associates at the University of Michigan have studied the pattern and styles of leaders and managers for three decades. Likert has suggested four systems of management.

System 1: Exploitive authoritative—Its managers are highly autocratic, have little trust in subordinates, motivate people through fear and punishment and only occasional rewards, engage in downward communication and limit decision-making to the top.

System 2: Benevolent authoritative—Its managers have a patronising confidence and trust in subordinates, motivate with rewards and some fear and punishment, permit some upward communication, solicit some ideas and opinions from subordinates and allow some delegation of decision-making but with close policy control.

System 3: Consultative—Managers in this system have substantial but not complete confidence and trust in subordinates, usually try to make use of subordinates ideas and opinions, use rewards for motivation with occasional punishment and some participation, engage in communication flow both down and up, make broad policy and general decisions at the top while allowing specific decisions to be made at lower levels, and act consultatively in other ways.

System 4: Participative—These managers have complete trust and confidence in subordinates in all matters, they always get ideas and opinions from subordinates and constructively use them. They also give economic rewards on the basis of group participation and involvement in such areas as setting goals and appraising progress toward goals. They engage in much communication down and up and with subordinates, encourage decision-making through out the organisation and operate among themselves and with their subordinates as a group. Likert found that those managers who applied the system four approach to their operations had greatest success as leaders.

Managerial Grid: A well-known approach to defining leadership styles is the managerial grid developed by Robert Blake and Jane Mouton.

The grid has two dimensions: "Concern for People" and "Concern for production". Blake and Mouton have emphasized, the phrase "concern for" is meant to convey "how" managers are concerned about production or "how" they are concerned about people, and not such things as "how much" production they are concerned about getting out of a group.

"Concern for production" includes the attitudes of a supervisor toward a wide variety of things, such as the quality decisions, producers and processes, creativeness of research, quality of staff services, work efficiency and volume of output. "Concern for people" is interpreted in a broad way. It includes such elements as degree of personal commitment toward goal achievement, maintenance of the self-esteem of workers, placement of responsibility on the basis of trust rather than obedience, provision of good working conditions, and maintenance of satisfying interpersonal relations. This leadership pattern is explained in Figure 1.5.1

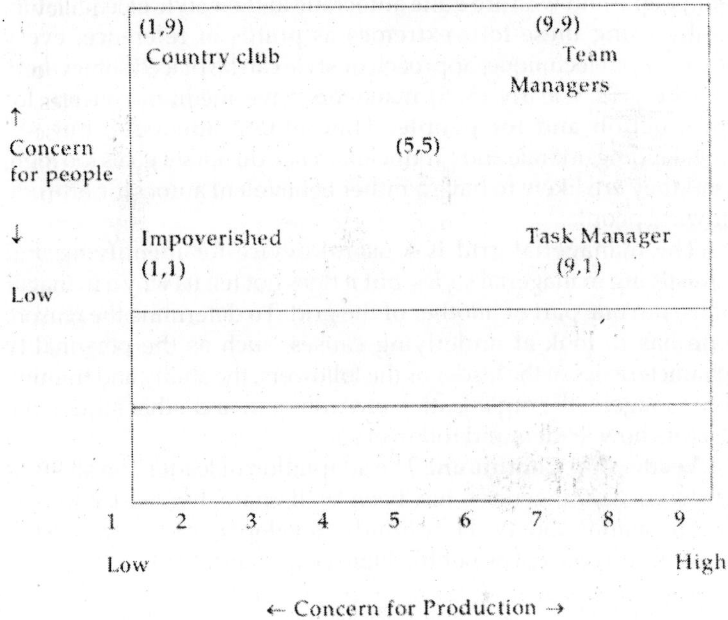

Fig. 1.5.1

Remarkably, Blake and Mouton recognize four extremes of style:

(1, 1) *Style-Impoverished* – Managers concern themselves very little with either people or production and have minimum involvement in their jobs. To all intents and purposes, they have abandoned their jobs and only mark time or act as messengers communicating information from superiors to subordinates.

(9, 9) *Style-Team managers:* These Managers display in their the highest possible dedication both to people and to production. They are the real team managers who are able to mesh the production needs of the organisation with the needs of individual.

(1, 9) *Style-Country club:* These type of managers have little or no concern for production but are concerned only for people. They promote an environment in which everyone is relaxed, friendly and happy and no one is concerned about putting forth coordinated effort to bring about organisation goals.

(9, 1) *Style-Autocratic task:* These managers are concerned only with developing an efficient operation, who have little or no concern for people and who are quite autocratic in their style of leadership.

By using these four extremes as points of reference, every managerial technique, approach or style can be placed somewhere on the grid. Clearly (5, 5) managers have medium concern for production and for people. They obtain adequate, but not outstanding, morale and production. They do not set goals too high, and they are likely to have a rather benevolent autocratic attitude toward people.

The managerial grid is a useful device for identifying and classifying managerial styles, but it does not tell us why a manager falls into one part or another of the grid. To determine the reason, one has to look at underlying causes, such as the personality characteristics of the leader or the followers, the ability and training of managers, the organisation environment and other situational factors how leaders and followers act.

Leadership Continuum: The adaptation of leadership styles to different contingencies has been well characterized by Robert Tannenbaum and W. H. Schmidt, developers of the leadership continuum concept as per the Figures 1.5.2 and 1.5.3.

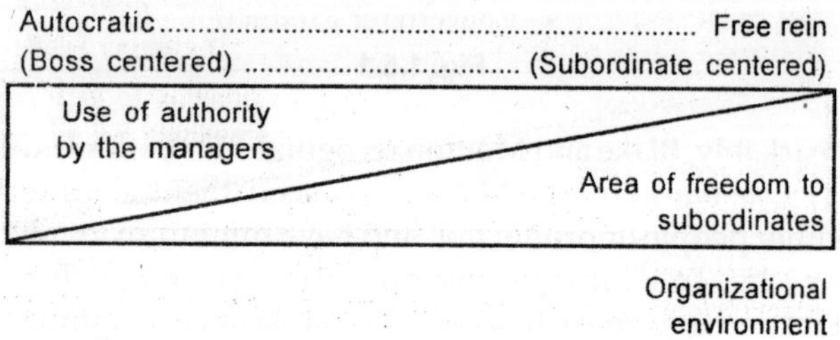

Fig. 1.5.2: Societal environment

They see leadership as involving a variety of styles, ranging from one that is highly boss centered to one that is highly subordinate centered. The styles vary with the degree of freedom a leader or manager grants to subordinates. Thus instead of suggesting a choice between the two styles of leadership- authoritarian or democratic – this approach offers a range of styles, with no suggestion that one is always right and another is always wrong.

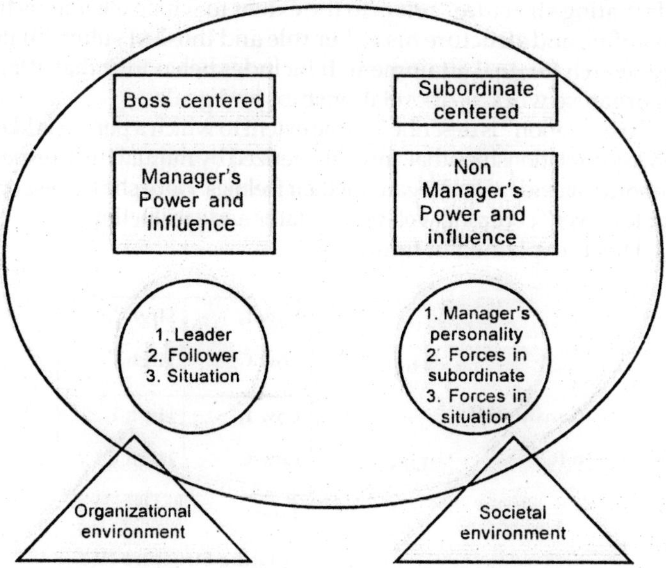

Fig. 1.5.3: Tannebaum's model of leadership

The continuum theory recognizes that which style of leadership is appropriate depends on

- The leader
- The followers
- and The situation.

In reviewing their continuum model in 1973, Tannenbaum and Schmidt placed circles around the model to represent the influences on style imposed by both the organisational environment and the societal environment. This was done to emphasize the open system nature of leadership styles.

Ohio State Studies

The most comprehensive and replicated of the behavioural theories resulted from research that began at Ohio State University in the late 1940s. The researchers sought to identify independent dimensions of leader behaviour. They narrowed the list into two categories that substantially accounted for most of the leadership behaviour described by subordinates. They called these two dimensions "initiating structure" and "consideration."

"Initiating structure" refers to the extent to which a leader is likely to define and structure his or her role and those of subordinates in the search for goal attainment. It includes behaviour that attempts to organise work, work relationships and goals.
"Consideration" is described as the extent to which a person is likely to have job relationships that are characterized by mutual trust, respect for subordinates ideas and regard for their feelings. He or she shows concern for follower" confront, well-being, status and satisfaction.

This is explained in figure 1.5.4

Consideration (C)	High	Low I_s Low C	High I_s High C
	Low	Low I_s Low C	High I_s High C
		Low	High

Initiating Structure (IS) →

Fig. 1.5.4

Extensive research based on these definitions found that leaders high in initiating structure and consideration tended to achieve high subordinate performance and satisfaction more frequently than those who rated low on either consideration, initiating structure or both. In conclusion, the Ohio State studies suggested that the high-high style generally resulted in positive outcomes but enough exceptions were found to indicate that situational factors needed to be integrated into the theory.

University of Michigan Studies

Leadership studies undertaken at the University of Michigan's Survey Research Centre, at about the same time as those being done at Ohio State, had similar research objectives, i.e. to locate behavioural characteristics of leaders that appeared to be related to measures of performance effectiveness.

The Michigan group also came up with two dimensions of leadership behaviour, i.e. employee-oriented and production oriented. Employee oriented leaders were described as emphasising interpersonal relations. The production-oriented leaders, in contrast, tended to highlight the task aspects of the job.

The conclusions arrived at by the Michigan researchers strongly favoured the leaders who were employee-oriented in their behaviour. Employee-oriented leaders were associated with higher group productivity and higher job satisfaction.

Scandinavian Studies

Researchers in Finland and Sweden reassessed the earlier two dimensions that capture essence of leadership behaviour. Their basic premise is that in a changing world, effective leaders would exhibit development oriented behaviour. These are leaders who value experimentation, seek new ideas and generate and implement change. The Scandinavian researchers added the third dimension-development orientation to the previous Ohio state data.

Situational Theories

Behavioural theories have had modest success in identifying consistent relationships between patterns of leadership behaviour and group performance. But what seems to be missing is consideration of the situational factors that influence success or failure. It is found that in a single organisation, there are two effective leaders but their styles are almost diametrically opposed. How can that be? This is because the two leaders work in different situations. The behavioural theories failed to take this into account. Situations change and leadership styles need to change with them. In this section, five important situational theories will be discussed. They are:

1. Fielder's Contingency Model.
2. Path Goal Theory.
3. Life Cycle Theory.
4. Leader-member Exchange Theory
5. Leader-participation Model.

1. Contingency Theory

The first comprehensive contingency model of leadership was developed by Fred Fielder. Fieldler's contingency model proposes that effective group performance depends on the proper match between the leader style of interacting with his/her subordinates and the degree to which the situation gives control and influence to the leader. Fielder developed an instrument, which he called the Least Preferred Coworker (LPC) questionnaire that purports to measure whether a person is task or relationship oriented. In a sense, Fielder model is an outgrowth of trait theory, since the LPC questionnaire is a simple psychological test. However, Fiedler goes significantly beyond trait and behavioural approaches by attempting to isolate situations, relating his personality measure to his situational classification, and then predicting leadership effectiveness as a function of the two.

Fiedler believes a key factor in leadership success is the individual's basic leadership style. For this purpose Fiedler created in LPC questionnaire. It contains 16 (sixteen) contrasting adjectives (such as pleasant-unpleasant, efficient-inefficient, open-guarded, supportive-hostile, etc.). The questionnaire asks the respondent to think of all the co-workers they have ever had and to describe the one person they least enjoyed working with by rating him or her on a scale of 1 to 8 for each of the 16 sets of concentrating objection. If the least preferred coworker is described in relatively positive terms (high LPC score), then the respondent is primarily interested in good personal relations with this coworker, and then relationship oriented. If the lest preferred coworker is seen in relatively unfavorable terms (Low LPC score), the respondent is primarily interested in productivity and thus would be labeled task oriented. About 16% of respondents score in the middle range. Such individuals can not be classified as either relationship oriented or task oriented and thus falls outside the theory's prediction. As a result, 84% belonged to section who score in either the high or low range of the LPC.

Fiedler assumes that an individual's leadership style is fixed. If a situation requires a task oriented leader and the person in that leadership position is relationship-oriented, either the situation has to be modified or the leader removed and replaced if optimum effectiveness is to be achieved.

After an individual's basic leadership style has been assessed through LPC it is now necessary to match the leader with the situation. Fiedler has identified three contingency dimensions that define the key situational factors and determine leadership effectiveness. These are:

1. *Leader-member relations:* The degree of confidence, trust and respect subordinates have in their leader. It is either good or poor.
2. *Task structure:* The degree to which the job assignments are categorized. It is structured or unstructured, i.e. high or low.
3. *Position power:* The degree of influence a leader has over power variables such as hiring, firing, discipline, promotions, salary increase, etc. It is either strong or weak. The facts are explained in Figure 1.5.5.

Leader Member relationship ⟶	Good				Poor			
Task structure ⟶	High		Low		High		Low	
Position power ⟶	Str-ong	We-ak	Str-ong	We-ak	Str-ong	We-ak	Str-ong	We-ak

Fig. 1.5.5

Fiedler's contingency model of leadership is presented as a graph, in which he compared relationship versus task oriented leadership styles in each of the eight situational categories. He concluded that task oriented leaders tend to perform better in situation that were very favourable to them and in situations that were very unfavourable. See Figure 1.5.6.

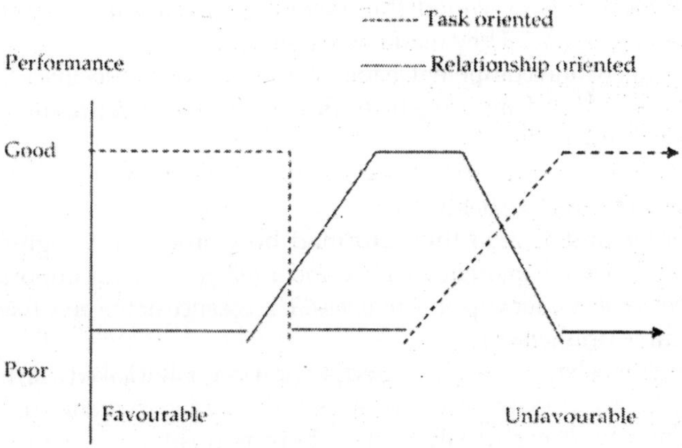

Fig. 1.5.6

	1	2	3	4	5	6	7	8
Leader-member relations	Good	Good	Good	Good	Poor	Poor	Poor	Poor
Task structure	High	High	Low	Low	High	High	Low	Low
Position power	Strong	Weak	Strong	Weak	Strong	Weak	Strong	Weak

So Fiedler would predict that when faced with a category 1, 2, 3, 7 or 8 situation task oriented leaders perform better. Relationship oriented leaders however perform better in moderately favourable situations in category 4, 5 and 6. Revision to contingency model- In 1987, Fiedler and an associate Joe Garcia reconceptualized the original contingency model of Fiedler. Specifically they tried to explain the process by which a leader obtains effective group performance. They called this reconceptualisation "Cognitive Resource Theory." They made two assumptions:

1. Intelligent and competent leaders formulate more effective plans, decisions and action strategies than less intelligent and competent leaders.
2. Leaders communicate their plans, decisions and strategies through directive behaviour.

Fiedler and Garcia then outlined how stress and cognitive resource such as experience, tenure and intelligence act as important influences on leadership effectiveness. The essence of the new theory gave three predictions.

1. Directive behaviour results in good performance only if linked with high intelligence in a supportive, non-stressful leadership environment.
2. In highly stressful situations, there is positive relationship between job experience and performance.
3. The intellectual abilities of leaders correlate with group performance in situations the leader perceives as non-stressful.

2. Path-Goal Theory

Developed by Robert House, path-goal theory is a contingency model of leadership that extracts key elements from the union state leadership research on initiating structure and consideration and expectancy theory of motivation.

The essence of the theory is that it is the leader's job is to assist his/her followers in attaining their goals and to provide the necessary direction and/or support to ensure their goals are compatible with the overall objectives of the group or organisation. The term path goal is derived from the belief that effective leaders clarify the path to help their followers to attainment of their goals and make the journey along the path easier by reducing roadblocks and falls.

According to path goal theory, a leader's behaviour is acceptable to subórdinate to the degree that it is viewed by them as an immediate source of satisfaction or as a means of future satisfaction. A leader's behaviour is motivational to the degree it (1) makes subordinate need satisfaction contingent on effective performance, and (2) provides the coaching, guidance, support and rewards that are necessary for effective performance. To test these statements, Robert House identified four leadership behaviours.

1. Directive
2. Supportive
3. Participative
4. Achievement-oriented.

In contrast to Fielder's view of a leader's behaviour, House assumes that leaders are flexible. Path goal theory implies that the same leader can display any or all of these behaviours depending on the situation. Path goal theory proposes two classes of situational or contingency variables that moderate the leadership behaviour outcome relationship.

1. Environmental contingency factors, i.e. task structure, formal authority system and work group.
2. Subordinate contingency factors, i.e. locus of control, experience and perceived ability.

Environmental factors determine the type of leader behaviour required if subordinate outcomes are to be maximized. Subordinate factors determine how the environment and leader behaviour are interpreted.

3. Life Cycle Theory

- Developed by Paul Hersey and Ken Blanchard, situational leadership is a contingency theory that focuses on the followers. Successful leadership is achieved by selecting the right leadership style which Hersey and Blanchard argue is contingent on the level of the follower's readiness or maturity.
- The emphasis on the followers in leadership effective reflects the reality that it is they who accept or reject the leader. Regardless of what the leader does, effectiveness depends on the actions of his/her followers. This is an important dimension that has been overlooked in most leadership theories. The term 'readiness' as defined by Hersey and Blanchard refers to peoples' ability and willingness to accomplish a specific task.
- Situational leadership uses the same two leadership dimensions that Fiedler identified, i.e. task and relationship behaviours. However, Hersey and Blanchard moved a step further by considering each as either high or low and then combining them into four specific leader behaviours: telling, selling, participating and delegating. They are described as:

1. **Telling:** High task, low relationship. The leader defines roles and tells people what how, when and where to do various tasks. It emphasizes directive behaviour (S_1).
2. **Selling:** High task, high relationship. The leader provides both directive and supportive behaviour (S_2).
3. **Participating:** Low task, high relationship. The leader and follower share in decision-making, with the main role of the leader being facilitating and communicating (S_3).
4. **Delegating:** Low task, low relationship. The leader provides little direction or support (S_A).

The final component in Hersey and Blanchard's theory is defining four stages of follower readiness:

R_1-People are both unable and unwilling to take responsibility to do something. They are neither competent nor confident.

R_2-People are unable but willing to do the necessary job tasks. They are motivated but currently lack the appropriate skills.

R_3-People are able but unwilling to do what the leader wants.

R_4-People are both able and willing to do what is asked of them.

Now the various components can be integrated in a graph. (Figure 1.5.7)

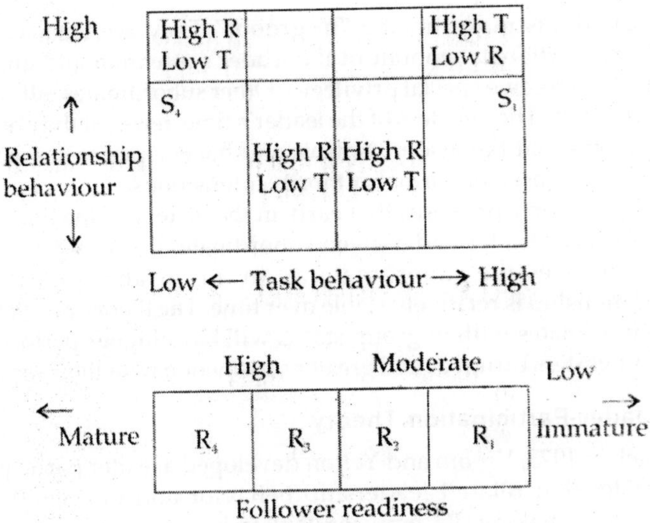

Fig. 1.5.7: Leader behaviours

As per the graph, as the followers reach high levels of readiness, the leader responds by not only continuing to decreases control over activities, but also by continuing to decrees relationship behaviour as well. At stage R_1, followers need clear and specific directions. At stage R_2, both high task and high relationship behaviour is needed. The high task behaviour compensates for the follower's lack of ability and the high relationship behaviour tries to get the followers psychologically to buy into the leaders decrease. R_3 creates motivational problems that are best solved by a supportive, non-directive, participative style. Finally at stage R_4, the leader does not have to do much because followers are both willing and able to take responsibility.

5. Leader-Member Exchange Theory

Almost all the leadership theories assumed that leaders treat all their subordinates in the same manner. But George Graen and his associates in their Leader-Member Exchange Theory noticed that leaders often act very differently toward different subordinates.

They argued that because of time pressures, leaders establish a special relationship with a small group of their subordinates. These individuals make up the "in group." They are trusted, get a disproportionate amount of the leader's attention and are more likely to receive special privileges. Other subordinates fall into the out group. They get less of the leader's time, fewer of the preferred rewards that the leader controls and have superior-subordinate relations based on formal authority interactions.

The theory proposes that early in the history of the interaction between a leader and a given subordinate, the leader implicitly categorizes the subordinate as an 'in' or an 'out' and that relationship is relatively stable over time. The theory predicts that subordinates with in group status will have higher performance ratings, less turnover and greater satisfaction with their superior.

Leader-Participation Theory

Back in 1973, Vroom and Yetton developed a leader participation model that related leadership behavior and participation to decision-making. Recognising that task structures have varying demands for routine and non-routine activities, these researchers argued that leader behaviour must adjust to reflect the task structure. Vroom and Yetton's model was normative because it provided a sequential set of rules that should be followed for determining the form and amount of participation desirable in decision-making, as dictated by different type of situations. The model was a complex decision tree incorporating seven contingencies, whose relevance could be identified by making "Yes" or "No" choices and five alternative leadership styles.

The model assumes that any of the behaviour may be feasible in a given situation:

1. AI : Autocratic I
2. AII: Autocratic II
3. CI: Consultative I
4. CII: Consultative II
5. GII: Group II.

In 1988, Vroom and Jago revised this model. The new model has the same five alternative leadership styles but expanded the contingency variables from 7 to 12. The revised model is very complex and sophisticated. The leader participation model confirms that leadership research should be directed at the situation rather than the person. It probably makes more sense to talk about autocratic and participative situations than about autocratic and participative leaders.

Further Readings

1. Keeth Davis, *Human Behaviour of Work*, New Delhi, Tata MacGraw Hill, 1981.
2. Eugene Jennings, "The Anatomy of Leadership", *Management of Personnel Quaterly*, Autumn, 1961.
3. Robert Tannon Baum and Warren H Schmidt, "How to choose Leadership. Pattern", *Harvard Business Review*, March-April, 1958.
4. R R Blake and J.S. Mouton, *The Management Grid*, Houston, Gulf Publishing, 1964.
5. Fred E Fielder, *A Theory of Leadership Effectiveness*, New York, McGraw Hill, 1967.

Chapter six

MOTIVATION

Motivation is a general term applying to entire class of drives, desires, needs, wishes and similar forces. Motivation is defined as the willingness to exert high levels of effort toward organisational goals, conditioned by the efforts ability to satisfy some individual need. While general motivation is concerned with effort toward any goal, the focus may be narrowed down to organisational goals in order to reflect our singular interest in work related behaviour. So the three key elements in the definition of motivation are:-

- Effort
- Organisational goals
- Needs.

The effort element is a measure of intensity. When someone is motivated, he/she tries hard. But high levels of effort are unlikely to lead to favourable job performance outcomes unless the effort is heading for in a direction that benefits the organisation. Effort that is aimed at and consistent with, the organisation's goals is the right kind of effort. Finally, motivation should be treated as a need satisfying process. A need means, some internal state that makes certain outcomes appear attractive. Here motivation involves a chain reaction. Felt needs give rise to wants or goals sought, which cause tensions (i.e. unfulfilled desire), which give rise to actions toward achieving goals which finally result in satisfying actions. See figure 1.61.

Needs ⟶ Give Rise ⟶ Wants ⟶ Which Cause ⟶ Tensions

↓

Satisfaction⟵which result in⟵ Actions ⟵ which give rise to

Fig. 1.6.1

The chain explanation is complex. In the first place, except for physiological needs such as hunger, needs are not independent of a person's environment. In the second place, the need want satisfaction chain does not always operate as simply as portrayed. Needs do cause behaviour, but needs also may result from behaviour. Satisfying one's need may lead to a desire to satisfy more needs.

Theories of Motivation

The theories of motivation can be discussed on two heads. They are:

Early Theories

The 1950s were a fruitful period in the development of motivation concepts. Three theories were formulated during this time, which although heavily attacked and now questionable in terms of validity are probably still the best known explanations for employee motivation. These are:

- Hierarchy of needs theory.
- Human Resource Model.
- Motivation Hygiene theory.

Motivation theories can also be classified as content theories, process theories and contemporary theories. In content theories, Maslaw's theories of needs theory, Hertzbarg's Two Factor Theory, Alderfer's ERG Theory and McClleland's Needs theory are included. In these theories, the guiding factors are fulfillment of needs. Process Theory includes Vroom's Expectancy Theory. In content theory and process theory -what motivate people to work? The answer is need and cognitive concepts respectively. And the contemporary theory is also linked with Equity theory.

Hierarchy of Needs Theory

One of the most widely mentioned theories of motivation is the hierarchy of needs theory put forth by Abraham Maslow. He saw human needs in the form of a hierarchy, ascending from the lowest to the highest, and he concluded that when one set of needs is satisfied, this kind of need ceases to be a motivator. Maslow's theory is based on the idea of prepotency of needs. Accordingly, he developed a scale on which at one end are lower order needs like physiological and security needs and at the other end higher order needs like self-actualisation needs. In between, there are middle order needs, i.e. social and self-esteem needs. Once the physiological needs are satisfied, then the need for other needs arise. These needs arise in a step by step process, each lower order need once satisfied, giving way for a unfulfilled higher order need.

The five needs of Maslow's model are:

1. *Physiological needs:* Physiological needs may be synonymous with the biological needs of the human beings like hunger, thirst, sex, etc. The grip of these needs on the human being is a strong that unless these needs are satisfied, there is no room for other needs.
2. *Security or safety needs:* These are the needs to be free from physical danger and of the fear of losing a job, property, food or shelter.
3. *Social, belongingness or love needs:* Since people are social beings, they need to belong, to be accepted by others. Human being not only loves but also wants to be loved by others.
4. *Esteem needs:* According to Maslow, once people begin to satisfy their needs to belong, they tend to want to be held in esteem both by themselves and by others. This kind of need produces such satisfaction as power, prestige, status and self-confidence.
5. *Self-actualisation needs:* Maslow regards this as the highest need in his hierarchy. It is the desire to become what one is capable of becoming to maximize one's potential and to accomplish something.

This is given in Figure 1.6.2.

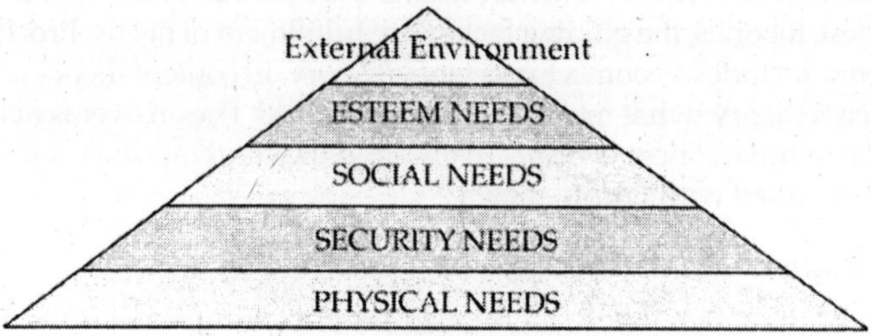

Fig. 1.6.2

It is questionable whether self-actualized persons are motivated or not. As Maslow emphasized, "they work, they try and they are ambitions even though is an unusual sense. For them, motivation is just character growth, character expression."

Characteristics of the basic needs: Maslow after discussing in detail the basic needs of humans and their hierarchical order, discusses a few characteristics of the basic needs.

1. The hierarchy is not rigid as it is implied theoretically which means there is no fixity in the hierarchy of needs. There is scope for deviations.
2. Hierarchy of needs is not watertight compartments. Satisfaction is relative term. Emergency of a particular need after satisfaction of a lower order need is not sudden, but a gradual phenomenon.
3. In an average person, need areas are more often unconscious than conscious.
4. The basic human needs and desires are the same irrespective of the societies and cultures they live in.
5. Human behaviour is multi-motivated and as such it is not influenced by a single variable like a need.
6. A satisfied man is not a motivator.
7. Further, there is overlapping of needs during their fulfillment at work situations as commented by David R Hampton. (See Figure 1.6.3).

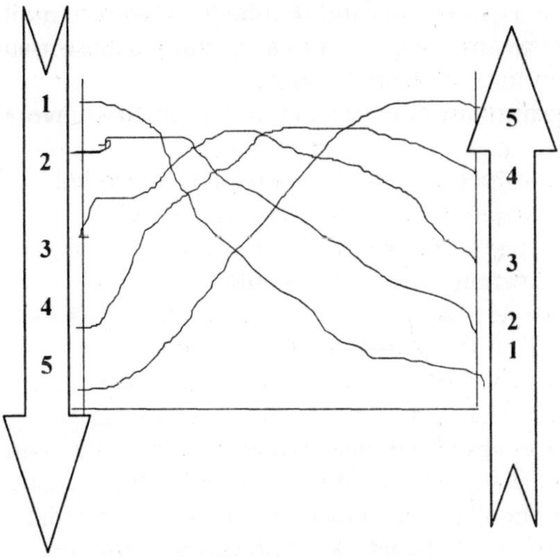

Concept Adopted from David R Hampton : 1981

Fig. 1.6.3: Overlaping of Needs: Maslow's Theory

Maslow's contribution is a signpost in social psychological research and he was a forerunner to many like Herzberg and Vroom. His theory of need hierarchy has had tremendous impact on modern management approach to motivation. In spite of the tremendous amount of research generated by Maslow's theory, theory has never been tested adequately as a complete theory.

Maslow's theory of need hierarchy was criticized mainly on the grounds of sophistication and validity of his research data and the order of hierarchy of needs. Some disapproved of that the needs from a lower order need to a higher order need not necessarily operate in the same order all the time. His concept of self-actualisation is criticized as vague, imprecise and too general. At times fulfillment of needs overlaps as higher order is to be fulfilled after lower order.

Mc Gregor Theories 'X' and 'Y': Human Resource Model:

Douglas McGregor proposed two distinct views of human beings; one basically negative labeled "Theory X" and the other basically positive labeled "Theory Y." After viewing the way in which managers dealt with employees, Mc Gregor concluded that a manager's view of the nature of human beings is based on a certain grouping of assumptions and that he/she tends to mold his/her behaviour towards subordinates according to these assumptions. The assumptions of theory 'X' are:

1. Average human being has an inherent dislike of work and will avoid it.
2. Hence most people must be corrected, controlled and directed and threatened with punishment to get them.
3. The average human being will avoid responsibilities and seek formal direction whenever possible.
4. Most people place security above all other factors associated with work and will display little ambition.

Traditionally known as carrot stick theory, theory 'X' of Mc Greger explains the consequence of a particular managerial strategy. The assumptions behind the theory treat man not only as an insecure beast, responding to the language of fear but as a man of dislike to all work under all circumstances. His conclusion is that, so long as the assumption of theory 'X' continue to influence managerial strategy, utilisation of the potentialities of the average human being is impossible.

Looking positively in the area of human needs and man's psychological quest for satisfaction of them as a wanting animal, McGregor formulates his theory 'Y', which offers a number of alternate assumptions for the integration of the individual and organisational goals. He has arranged his whole new set of assumptions about motivation and morale in a theory, which he prefers to call theory 'Y'. The assumptions are:

- The expenditure of physical and mental effort in work as natural as play or rest.
- Man will exercise self direction and self-control in the service of objective to which he is committed.
- Commitments to objectives are a function of the rewards associated with their achievement.
- The average human being learns under proper conditions not only to accept but to seek responsibility.
- Man more people are able to contribute creativity to the solution of organisational problems than do so.
- At present the potentialities of the average person are not being fully used.

Theory 'Y' leads to a preoccupation with the nature of relationship with creating an environment which will encourage commitment to organisational objectives and which will provide opportunities for the maximum exercise of initiative, ingenuity and self direction is achieving them. This theory recognizes interdependence of human organisations and participative management. The central principle in the assumption of theory Y is that integration of behaviors is the key process in management. Mc Gregor calls the theory Y as an open invitation to innovation.

Unfortunately, no evidence confirms that either set of assumptions is valid or that accepting theory X assumptions and steering one's actions accordingly will lead to more motivated workers.

Motivation: Hygiene Theory

The motivation hygiene theory, also known as Two Factor theory was proposed by Fredrick Herzberg. The theory identifies five strong determinants of the job satisfaction and five of job dissatisfaction, which are a totally different set of factors. See Figure1.6.4.

Hygiene factors	*Motivational factors*
1. Company policy and administration.	1. Achievement
2. Supervision	2. Recognition
3. Salary	3. Work itself
4. Interpersonal relations	4. Responsibilities
5. Working conditions	5. Advancement

Fig. 1.6.4

Herzberg found a duality of attitudes about work experience on the responses of workers on their jobs. Job experiences leading to favourable reactions most often were related to the context, in which the job was performed, i.e. the surrounding. As against this, factors causing unfavourable responses were found to be related to avoidance of discomfort. Herzberg labeled the factors associated with growth and task content of the job as "satisifiers." Factors associated with pain, avoidance and the surround of the job were labeled "dissatisfiers."

The factors identified as satisfiers which perform the role of motivators in job are as follows –

1. **Achievement:** The personal satisfaction of solving problems independently, completing a task and seeing the results of one's effort.
2. **Recognition:** Positive acknowledgement of the task completed or other personal achievement rather than generalized "human relations" expression of rewards.
3. **Work itself:** The task content of the job and relative interest, variety, challenge and freedom from boredom.
4. **Responsibility:** Being entrusted with full responsibility and accountability for certain tasks and having control over deciding how and when tasks are to be done.
5. **Advancement:** Advancement to a higher order of task to perform. The sense of the possibility for growth and advancement as well as the actual satisfaction from new learning.

On the other hand, the hygiene factors are potential dissatisfiers. Hygiene factors such as working conditions, company administration, salary, supervision, benefits and services are visualized as environmental elements that have little or no relationships to the motivation of specific job related behaviour. The motivating factors determine how an employee feels about his job, whereas hygiene factors only determine how a worker feels about his company. Herzberg has argued that an employee is either dissatisfied or not dissatisfied with hygiene factors and he is either satisfied or not satisfied with motivational job factors.

Again each set of factors are rarely involved in contributing to the other and each set is independent of each other. Dissatisfiers only produce short term changes in human actual and satisfiers produce long term attitudes. Herzberg calls hygiene factors as dissatisfiers and also maintenance factors whereas satisfiers are called motivators and growth factors. Therefore these two are made up of two uni- polar traits, each contributing very little to the other. The needs theory is reflected in figure 1.6.5

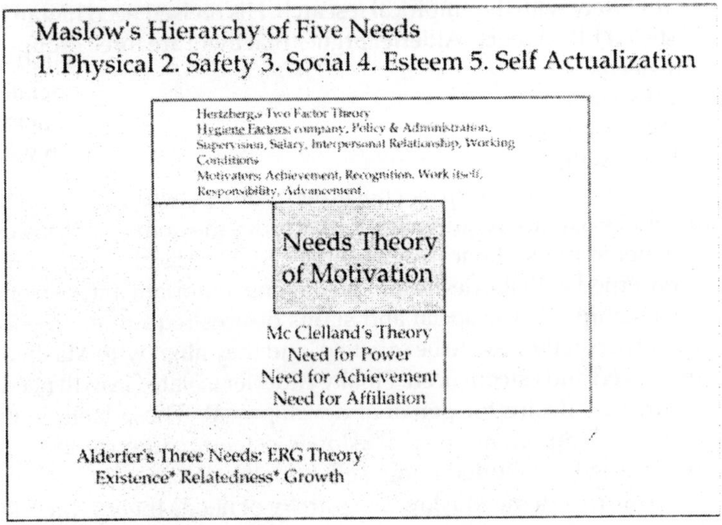

Fig. 1.6.5: Needs Theory of Motivation

Contemporary Theories

The early theories are well known but, unfortunately have not held up well under close examination. However all is not lot. A number of contemporary theories have one thing in common. Each has a reasonable degree of valid supporting documentation. They are called contemporary, not because they necessarily were developed recently, but because they represent the current state of the art in explaining employee motivation. The theories included in the list are:-

1. ERG Theory.
2. McClelland's Theory of Needs
3. Cognitive Evaluation Theory
4. Goal Setting Theory.
5. Reinforcement Theory
6. Equity Theory
7. Expectancy Theory.

ERG Theory

Clayton Alderfer has reworked Maslow's need hierarchy to align it more closely with the empirical research. His revised need hierarchy is labeled ERG theory. Alderfer argues that there are three groups of core needs"

E-Existence

R-Relatedness

G-Growth.

The existence group is concerned with providing our basic material existence requirements. It includes the items that Moslow considered physiological and safety needs. The relatedness group is concerned with the desire for maintaining important interpersonal relationships. These social and status desires require interaction with others if they are to be satisfied, and they align with Maslwo's social need and esteem need. Finally Alderfer isolate Growth needs, an intrinsic desire for personal development. These include the intrinsic component from Maslow's esteem category and the characteristics included under self-actualisation.

In contrast to the Maslow's hierarchy of needs theory, the ERG theory demonstrates that

1. More than one need may be operative at the same time, and
2. If the gratification of a higher level need is suppressed, the desire to satisfy a lower level need increases.

Maslow's need hierarchy is a rigid step like progression. ERG theory does not assume a rigid hierarchy where a lower need must be substantially gratified before one can move on. A person can, for instance, be working on growth even though existence or relatedness needs are unsatisfied or all the three need categories could be operating at the same time.

ERG theory also contains a frustration regression dimension. Maslow argued that an individual would stay at a certain need level until that need was satisfied. ERG theory counters by noting that when a higher order need level is frustrated, the individuals desire to increase a lower level need takes place. As for example, inability to satisfy a need for social interaction might increase the desire for more money or better working conditions. So frustration can lead to a regression to a lower need.

Further, a comparison of needs theory of Maslow, Herzberg and Alderfer is presented below in Figure 1.6.6.

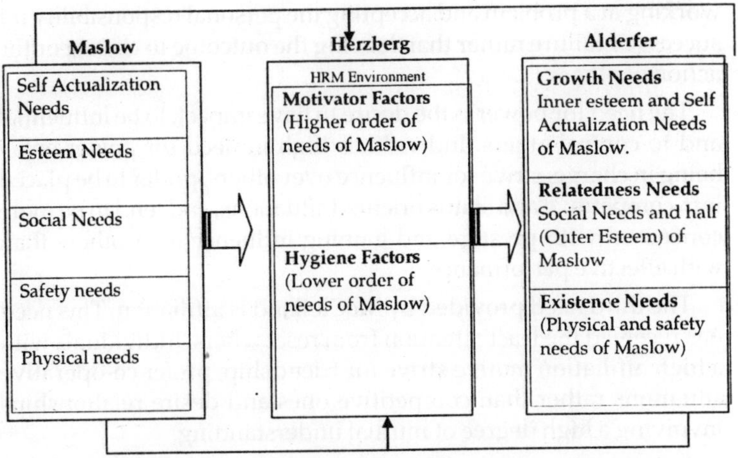

Fig. 1.6.6: Comparison of Needs Theories

McCleland's Theory of Needs

David McClelland and his association introduced three needs to achieve as a personality characteristic. These are important in organisational settings for understanding motivation.

McClelland's theory of needs focuses on three needs. They are:

1. **Achievement:** The drive to excel, to achieve in relation to a set of standards to strive.
2. **Power:** The need to make others behave in a way they would not have behaved otherwise.
3. **Affiliation:** The desire for friendly and close interpersonal relationships.

Some people strive for personal achievement rather than the rewards of successes. They have a desire to do something better or more efficiently than it has been done before. This drive is the achievement need. They seek situations where they can attain personal responsibility for finding solutions to problems, where they can receive rapid feedback on their performance they can tell easily whether they are improving or not, and where they can set moderately challenging goals. High achievers are not gamblers. They dislike succeeding by chance. They prefer the challenge of working at a problem and accepting the personal responsibility for success or failure rather than leaving the outcome to chance or the action of others.

The need for power is the desire to have impact, to be influential and to control others. Individuals high in need for power enjoy being in charge, strive for influence over others, prefer to be placed into competitive and status oriented situations, and tend to be more concerned with prestige and gaining influence over others than with effective performance.

The third need provided by McClelland is affiliation. This need has received the least attention from researchers. Individuals with a high affiliation motive strive for friendship, prefer co-operative situations rather than competitive ones and desire relationships involving a high degree of mutual understanding.

Individuals with a high need to achieve prefer job situations with personal responsibility, feedback and an intermediate degree of risk. When these characteristics are prevalent, high achievers will be strongly motivated. People with a high achievement need are interested in how well they do personally and not in influencing others to do well. The needs for affiliation and power tend to be closely related to managerial success. The best managers are high in their need for power and low in their need for affiliation. In fact a high power motive may be a requirement for management effectiveness.

Cognitive Evaluation Theory

Motivation theorists have generally assumed that intrinsic motivations such as achievement, responsibility and competence are independent of extrinsic motivators like high pay, promotions, good supervisor relations and pleasant working conditions. That is, the stimulation of one would not affect the other. But the cognitive evaluation theory suggests otherwise. It argues that when extrinsic rewards are used by organisations as payoffs for superior performance, the intrinsic rewards, which are derived from individuals doing what they like, are reduced. In other words, when extrinsic rewards are given to someone for performing an interesting task, it causes intrinsic interest in the task itself to decline. This theory contributed much to scholars like Harold Kelley, Lewin, Festinger, Bem and Heider.

Goal Setting Theory

In the late 1960's Edwin Locke proposed that intentions to work toward a goal are a major source of work motivation. That is, goals tell an employee what needs to be done and how much effort will need to be extended. The evidence strongly supports the value of goals. More to the point, we can say that specific goals increase performance, that difficult goals, when accepted, result in higher performance than do easy goals, and that feedback leads to higher performance than does non feedback.

Specific hard goals produce a higher level of output than does the generalized goal of "do your best." The specificity of the goal itself acts as an internal stimulus. If factors like ability and acceptance of the goals are held constant, we can also state that the more difficult the goal, the higher the level of performance. However it is logical to assume that easier goals are more likely to be accepted. But once an employee accepts a hard task, he will exert a high level of effort until it is achieved, lowered or abandoned.

People while do better when they yet feedback on how well they are progressing toward their goals because feedback helps identify discrepancies between what they have done and what they want to do. Feedback acts to guide behaviour. But all feedback is not equally potent. Self- generated feedback, where the employee is able to monitor his own progress has been shown to be a more powerful motivator than externally generated feedback.

In addition to feedback, three other factors have been found to influence the goals performance relationship. They are:

- Goal commitment,
- Self-efficacy and
- National culture.

Goal setting theory presupposes that an individual is committed to the goal that is, determined not to lower or abandon the goal. This is most likely to occur when goals are made public, when the individual has an internal locus of control and goals are self set rather than assigned. Self efficacy refers to an individual's belief that he is capable of performing a task. The higher the self efficacy, the more confidence is the ability to succeed in a task. So in difficult situations, we find that people with low self-efficacy are more likely to lessen their effort or give up altogether whereas those with high self efficacy will try harder to master the challenge. In addition, individuals high in self efficacy seem to respond to negative feedback with increased effort and motivation. Those low in self-efficacy are likely to lessen their effort when given negative feedback. Lastly goal setting theory is culture bound.

Reinforcement Theory

B. F. Skinner's Reinforcement theory is an offshoot of goal setting theory. Goal setting theory is a cognitive approach, proposing that an individual's purposes direct his action. In reinforcement theory, there is a behaviouristic approach, which argues that reinforcement conditions behaviour. Reinforcement theorists see behaviour as being environmentally caused.

Reinforcement theory ignores the inner state of the individual and concentrates solely on what happens to a person when he takes some action. Because it does not concern itself with what initiates behaviour.

Equity Theory

Equity theory advocated by J. Stacy Adam states that individuals compare their job inputs and outcomes with those of others and then respond so as to eliminate any inequities. Evidence indicates that the referent chosen is an important variable in equity theory. There are four referent comparisons an employee can use:

1. *Self-inside:* An employee's experiences in a different position inside his current organisation.
2. *Self-outside:* An employee's experiences in a situation or position outside his current organisation.
3. *Other inside:* Another individual or group of individuals inside the employees' organisation.
4. *Other outside:* Another individual or group of individuals outsides the employees organisation.

So employees might compare themselves to friends, neighbours, coworkers, colleagues in other organisations or past jobs they themselves had, which referent an employee chooses will be influenced by the information the employee holds about referents as well as by the attractiveness of the referent. This has led to focusing on three moderating variables.

- Gender
- Length of tenure
- Level in the education.

Based on equity theory, when employees perceive an inequity they can be predicted to make one of six choices:

1. Change their inputs
2. Change their outcomes.
3. Distort perceptions of self.
4. Distort perceptions of others.
5. Choose a different referent.
6. Leave the field.

Equity theory recognizes that individuals are concerned not only with the absolute amount of rewards they receive for their efforts, but also with the relationship of this amount to what others receive. They make judgments as to the relationship between their inputs and outcomes and the inputs and outcomes of others. Basing on one's inputs, such as effort, experience, education and competence, one compares outcomes such as salary level raises, recognition, and other factors. When people perceive an imbalance in their output-input ratio relating to others, tension is created. This tension provides the basis for negative motivation high labour turnover and absenteeism. So people strive for what they perceive as equity and fairness.

Expectancy Theory

One of the most widely accepted explanations of motivation is Vroom's expectancy theory. Expectancy theory argues that the strength of a tendency to act in a certain way depends on the strength of an expectation that the act will be followed by a given outcome and on the attractiveness of that outcome to the individual.

Expectancy theory pronounces that an employee is motivated to exert a high level of effort when he believes effort will lead to a good performance appraisal. A good appraisal will lead to organisational rewards like a bonus, salary increase or a promotion and the rewards will satisfy the employee's personal goals. The theory focuses on three relationships:

1. *Effort-performance relationship:* The probability perceived by the individual that exerting a given amount of effort will lead to performance.
2. *Performance-reward relationship:* The degree to which the individual believes that performing at a particular level will lead to the attainment of a desired outcome.
3. *Rewards-personal goals relationship:* The degree to which organisational rewards satisfy an individual's personal goals or needs and the attractiveness of those potential rewards for the individual. The explanation is given in Figure 1.6.7

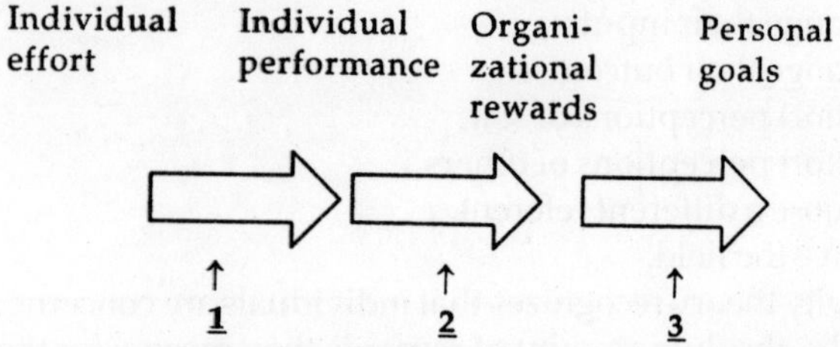

Fig. 1.6.7

Expectancy theory helps explain why a lot of workers are not motivated on their jobs and merely do the minimum necessary to get by. As a contingency model, expectancy theory recognizes that there is no universal principle for explaining everyone's motivations.

Chapter seven

COMMUNICATION

An effective communication system is an indispensable requirement of Information Technology savvy modern age management. Communication is the transfer of information from a sender to a receiver with the information being understood by the receiver. It always involves at least two people a sender and a receiver. One person alone cannot communicate, communication is what the receiver understands, not what the sender sends.

Chester Barnard viewed communication as the means by which people are liked together in an organisation to achieve a common purpose. Organisation can not exist without communication. If there is no communication, employees cannot know what their co-workers are doing management cannot receive information inputs and supervisors can not give instructions.

Purpose: In its broadest sense, the purpose of communication in an enterprise is to effect change to influence action toward the welfare of the enterprise. Especially communication is needed to:

- Establish and disseminate goods of an enterprise.
- Develop plans for their achievement.
- Organise human and other resources in the most effective and efficienct way.
- Select, develop and apprise members of the organisation.
- Lead, direct, motivate and create a climate in which people want to contribute.
- Control performance.

Process: Communication can be thought of as a process or flow. Communication problems occur when there are deviations in that flow. Before communication can take place, a purpose expressed as a message to be conveyed is needed. It passes between a source (sender) and a receiver. The message is encoded and is passed by way of some medium to the receiver who decades the messages initiated by the sender. The result is transference of meaning from one person to another.

Simply stated the communication process requires eight steps.
Step 1: is to develop an idea that the sender wishes to transmit. This step is represented by the sign. Sometimes seen on office or factory walls, that reads, "Be sure brain is engaged before putting mouth in gear."
Step 2: is to encode into suitable words, charts or other symbols for transmission. At this point the sender determines the method of transmission so that the words and symbols may be organised in suitable fashion for the type of transmission. For clarity see Figure 1.7.1.

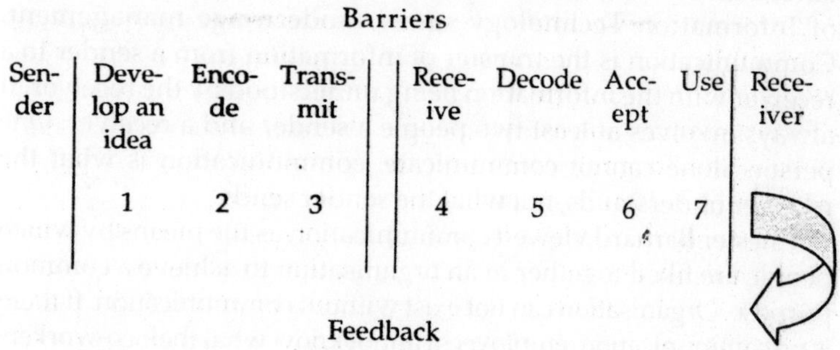

Fig. 1.7.1

Step 3: is to transmit it by the method chosen When the message is finally developed,

Step 4: In this step the initiative is transfereed to receivers who tune to receive the message.

Step 5: is to decode the message, so that it can be understood. The sender wants the receiver to understand the message exactly as it was sent.

Step 6: Once the receiver have obtained and decoded a message, they have the opportunity to accept or reject it, which is step 6.

Step 7: Is for the receiver to use the information. The receiver may discard it, perform the task as directed, store the information for future or do something else.

When the receiver acknowledges the message and responds to the sender, feedback has occurred. Feedback which is step 8 complete the communication loops. And each step is likely to be disturbed by noise.

Direction / Channels / Flow of Communication: Communication can flow vertically or laterally. The vertical dimension can be further divided into downward and upward directions.

Communication that flows from one level of a group or organisation to a lower level is a downward communication. When we think of managers communicating with subordinates, the downward pattern is the one we usually think of. It is used by group leaders, and managers to assign goals, provide job instructions, point out problems that need attention and offer feedback about performance. But downward communication does not have to be oral or face to face contact.

Upward communication flows to a higher level in the group or organisation. It is used to provide feedback to higher ups, inform them of progress toward goals and relay current problems. Upward communication keeps managers aware of how employees feel about their jobs, co-workers and the organisation in general. Managers also rely on upward communication for ideas on how thins can be improved. Some organisational examples of upward communication are performance reports prepared by lower management for review by middle and top management, suggestion boxes, employee attitude surveys, grievance procedures, etc.

When communication takes place among members of the same group, among members of work groups at the same level, among managers at the same level or among any horizontally equivalent personnel, it is described as lateral communication. Lateral or horizontal communications are often necessary to save time and facilitate coordination. Sometimes, these lateral relationships are formally sanctioned. Often they are informally created to short circuit the vertical hierarchy and expedite action. Further, there exists a third which is called 'Crosswise communication'. It includes Diagonal flow of information and also horizontal flow of information. A good deal of communication does not follow the organisational hierarchy. It crosses across the chain of command. This kind is used to speed of information flow to improve understanding and the co-ordinate efforts to acquire organisational objectives.

Communication Networks: Communication networks define the channels by which information flows. These channels are of two varieties, either formal or informal. Formal networks are typically vertical follow the authority chain, and are limited to task related communications. In contrast, the informal network usually better known as the grapevine- is free to move in any direction, skip authority levels and is as likely to satisfy group member's social needs as it to facilitate task accomplishments.

Generally there are four types of formal small group networks – chain, circle, wheel and all channels. See figure 1.7.2.

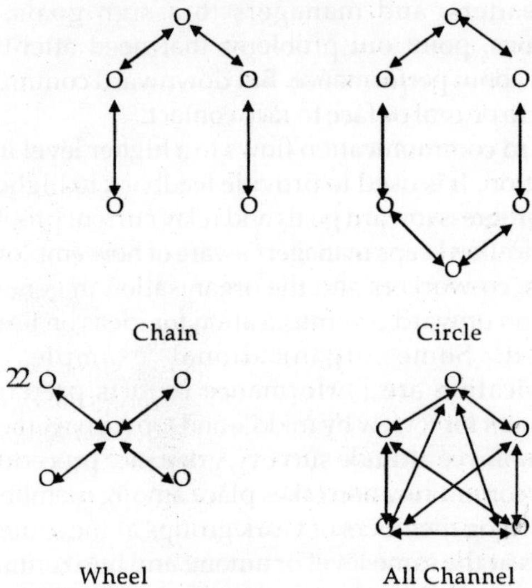

Fig. 1.7.2

The effectiveness of each network depends on the dependent variable. The structure of the wheel facilitates the emergence of a leader; the all channel network is best if it is concerned with high member satisfaction. And the chain is the best if accuracy is most wanted. So no single network is best for all circumstances. Moreover, another dimension to managerial communication exist- which is Informal communication. This informal network which is grapevine, has three main characteristics.

1. It is not controlled by management.
2. It is perceived by most employees as being more believable and reliable than formal communiqués issued by top management.
3. It is largely used to serve the self-interests of those people within it.

In fact grapevine is made of several informal communication networks that overlap and interact at a number of points. It cuts across rank or authority liens and follows any path horizontal, vertical, diagonal and zigzag. In addition to the social and informal communicational functions, the grapevine has work related functions also. It is much faster than the formal communication channel. Managers sometimes use it to spread information through planned leaks.

Keith Davis has studied the phenomenon of grapevines in the organisations and has identified four types of grapevine chains: Single stand, gossip, probability and cluster. See figure 1.7.3

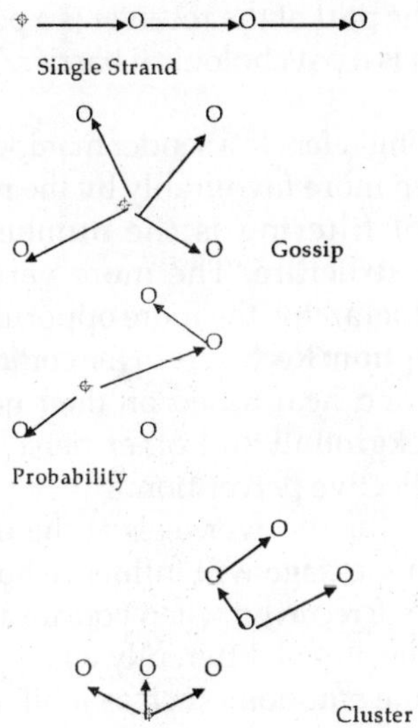

Fig. 1.7.3

In a single strand grapevine one person passes on information to another person who in turn passes on to another person and so on. It is quite inaccurate in passing information.

In a gossip grapevine one person gets some information and fells it to everyone he meets or talks to. This chain comes into play when some interesting but non job related information is being circulated.

In the probability chain an individual passes information to some others at random who in turn pass it on to some others. This is used when information is widely interesting but insignificant.

In the cluster chain, a person gives information to a select few who convey it some other selected few.

Barriers to Communication

Any factor that impedes the exchange of information between the sender and the receiver is a barrier to communication. These barriers may be overt and physical or covert and psychological or personal. The occurrence of noise in a machine room is a physical barrier, at that place and may be easily overcome by closing the machine or by moving it to another place. On the other hand poor language or understanding on the part of the receiver is a personal barrier and fear complex in him is a psychological barrier. The most common barriers are:

1. **Filtering:** Filtering refers to a sender manipulating information so it will be seen more favourably by the receiver. The major determinant of filtering is the number of levels in an organisation's structure. The more vertical levels in the organisation's hierarchy, the more opportunities for filtering.
2. **Selective perception:** Receivers in the communication process selectively see and hear based on their needs, motivations, experience, background and other personal characteristics. This is called selective perception.
3. **Emotions:** How the receiver feels at the time of receipt of a communication message will influence how he interprets it. The same message received when you are angry or distraught is likely to be interpreted differently when you are in a neutral position. Extreme emotions such as jubilation or depression are most likely to hinder effective communication.
4. **Language:** Words mean different things to different people. Age, education and cultural background are three of the more obvious variables that influence the language a person uses and the definitions he gives to words.
5. **Noise:** Noise in any factor that disturbs, confuses or otherwise interferes with communication. However totally noise free communication does not appear to be possible.
6. **Lack of planning:** Good communication seldom happens by chance. Too often people start talking and writing without first thinking, planning and stating the purpose of the message.
7. **Semantic distortion:** Another barrier to effective communication is semantic distortion, which can be deliberate or accidental. An advertisement that states, "we sell for less"

is deliberately ambiguous. It raises the question: Less than what?

8. **Loss by transmission and poor retention:** In a series of transmissions from one person to the next, the message becomes less and less accurate. Poor retention of information is rather serious problem.
9. **Distrust, threat and fear:** Distrust, threat and fear undermine communication. In a climate containing these forces, any message will be viewed with skepticism. Distrust can be the result of inconsistent behaviour by the superior, or it can be due to past experiences in which the subordinate was punished for honestly reporting unfavourable, but take information to the boss. In the light of threats whether real or imagined people tend to tighten up, become defensive and distort information.
10. **Information overload:** Information flow would help people overcome communication problems. But unrestricted flow may result too much information. People respond to information overland in various ways:
    - They may disregard certain information.
    - They make errors in processing it.
    - They filter information.
    - They may delay processing information.
    - Finally people respond to information overload by simply escaping from the task of communication.

Further Readings

1. William V. Haney, *Communication and Organisational Behaviour,* Homewood, III, Richard D Irwin, 1973.
2. Chester Barnard, *The Functions of Executive,* Cambridge, Harvard University Press, 1961.
3. American Management Association, *Ten Commandments of Good Communications,* New York, AMA, 1961.

Chapter eight

MANAGEMENT CONTROL

Control is an essential part of any organisation. The management process is incomplete without control function. But some people feel that organisational control as necessary nuisance a kind of costly managerial activity needed in the present world of uncertainty. The universal opinion, however, is that control is central to the success of any organisation.

There is a general sense that freedom is good and control is bad. But this is a misconception. In management, control has entirely different meaning. Control is the essence of good management. Control is concerned with ascertaining that planning, organising and directing functions result in attainment of organisational objectives. Controls precipitate bad decisions and their consequences and restore effectiveness and efficiency.

Precisely defined, control refers to the task of ensuring the desired results. Control is a process that guides activity towards some predetermined goal. It is defined as the regulation of work activity in accordance with predetermined plans as to ensure the accomplishment of organisational objective.

Principles

The discussion on the management of control is based upon certain rudiments or basic truths. These are referred to as principles. But these principles are understandably similar to those identified in discussions of the other managerial functions.

For everything, there should be an ideal standard. Standards are simply criteria of performance. They are the selected points in an entire planning programe at which measures of performance are made so that managers can get feedbacks. Again, the performance should be measured against the standards. The principle of 'critical point control' states that the effective control requires attention to those factors that are critical to evaluating performance against plans. There are many types of critical point standards such as, physical standards, cost standards, capital standards, revenue standards, program standards, intangible standards, goals and standards and strategies plans as control points for strategic control.

Characteristics

The major characteristics of control are:
- Control is an end function.
- It is a continuous process.
- Control is mainly forward looking.
- Control is all pervasive function.
- Control is a normative and positive force.
- Control guides behaviour.
- Control allows the organisation to cope with uncertainty.

Types

Depending on the time factor controls can be of 3 types:
1. Historical (Feedback)
2. Concurrent (Real time)
3. Predictive (Feed forward).

Feedback

Traditionally control was viewed as historical. It is because most of the control methods measure results after the performance. Income statements and position statements are examples of this type of control. Here control is seen as a *post mortem* of events the purpose of which is to improve in the future.

In a feedback control the measured activity has already occurred, and it is impossible to go back and correct performance to bring it up-to the standard. In stead correction must occur after the fact. In this out put is manipulated. Examples of feed back controls are disciplinary action, performance appraisal, interviewees, financial and budgetary results and final inspections. (See Figure 1.8.1).

Real Time

Concurrent control techniques immediately consider any problem and analyze it to take necessary and corrective steps before any major damage is done. Control chart is an example of this control. These controls are also known as steering control and occur while

Desired → performance ↑	Actual → Performance	Measurement of → actual performance	Comparison of actual performance against standards ↓
Implement-ation ← of corrections	Program of corrective action	← Analysis of causes of deviation	←Identification of deviations

Fig. 1.8.1

an activity is taking place. The navigator of an aircraft who adjusts the aircraft's movement is an example of concurrent control. When one drives a car, he must adjust the steering constantly, depending on the turns in the road, obstacles, changes in the terrain to keep ther vehicle upright and move towards destination.

Feed forward

Here the control system anticipates problems, the management encounters in future. Cash budget is an example of this type where the financial manager is in a position to estimate the next year's flow of cash. This control, attempts to anticipate problems or deviations from the standard in advance of their occurrence. It is thus a more aggressive, active approach to control, allowing corruptive action to be taken in advancement of the problem. Here manipulation is with the input not out put. The example is shooting a bird in the sky. Here the shooter has to fired ahead of birds position in sky to achieve the target. The requirements of feed forward control are:

- Make a though and careful analysis of the planning and control systems and identify the more important input variables.
- Develop a model of the system
- Take care to keep the model up to date.
- Collect data on input variables regularly and put them into the system.
- Regularly assess the variations of actual input data from planned for inputs and evaluate the impact on expected and results
- Take action.

Elements of Control

Organisational control aims at increasing efficiency and effectiveness by producing the desired results. In this process, recognition must be given to the people because; people are the key elements in the work place. It is vital in every organisation to know the reactions of employees for various types of controls imposed on them. The type of control to the exercised however depends on the work environment.

1. If the work environment is repetitive then the management relies heavily on mechanical control for getting the work done than on people.
2. In a highly varied and creative type of work environment, the control should be on co-operative lines with subordinates than on commands.
3. In work environment where task can not be watched constantly, measured precisely or specified in advance, the organisation must rely on subordinates for effective performance. To make control of subordinates attractive and effective, the following points are to be noted:
   - Quantitative standards should take account of feelings and uniqueness of each subordinate.
   - Human factor must be given consideration in addition to mechanical assets.
   - Goal setting must be participate and emphasizes self control as far as possible.

Requirements for Effective Control

To make the control, more effective, the following features are to be met with:

- Controls must be understandable.
- Controls must be flexible.
- Controls must be economical.
- Controls must be objective.
- Controls should recognize the importance of time element.
- Controls system should provide useful, understandable information.
- Controls should be forward looking.
- Controls should be selective.
- Controls should reflect the organisation structure and needs.
- Controls should lead to corrective action.

Further Readings

1. George R. Terry, *Principles of Management*, Homewood ILL, Richard D. Truin, 1988
2. Peter F Drucker, *The Practice of Management*, New York, Harper Brothers, 1974
3. Koontz O Donnell and Weihrich, *Principles of Management*, McGraw Hill, 1992
4. Billy E Goeta, *Management, Planning and Control*, New York, McGraw Hill, 1979.
5. Panl E Holden, LS Fish and Hnbert L Smith, *Top Management Organisations and Control*, New York, McGraw Hill.

Chapter nine

WORKERS PARTICIPATION IN MANAGEMENT (WPM)

The concept of participation[1], as a principle of democratic administration in an industry implies a share by rank and file in the decision-making process of an industrial organisation through their representatives at all the entire range of managerial action (V. G. Mehetra, 1966)

Workers participation in management (WPM) is defined and interpreted by many authorities in different ways. For example employers interpret it as the joint consultation prior to decision-making. Employees consider it as equivalent to co-decisions. According to Keith Davis[2], participation is near to the mental and emotional involvement of a person in a group situation which encourages him to contribute to group goals. It is a process by which authority and responsibility are shared with workers.

Features[3]

The main features of Workers Participation in Management are:

1. Participation means mental and emotional involvement rather than mere physical presence. It is more than consent or approval to managerial action.
2. WPM not as individuals but collectively as a group through their representation.
3. Workers participate in management is based on the worker invests his labour and ties his fate to his place of work.
4. WPM can be informal or formal. In both the cases, it is a system of communication and consultation where by employees expresses their opinions and contributes to managerial decision.
5. Workers participation should be chiseling wished from collective bargaining. Participation is based on mutual trust, information

sharing and problem solving. On the other hand collective bargaining is essentially based on power play, pressure tactics and negotiations.

6. There can be four levels of participation, i.e. shop floor, plant, department, corporate.
7. There are four degrees of participation, i.e. communication, consultation, co-determination and self-management.

Objectives[4]

WPM is recommended to achieve the following objectives:

- Increasing productivity for the general benefit of the enterprise, the employees and the community.
- Giving employees a better understanding of their, role in the working of the industry and of the process of production.
- Satisfying the workers urge for self-expression.
- Achieving industrial peace, better relations and increased cooperation in industry.
- Development of human personality.
- Development of leaders from within the industry.
- This WPM is inevitable in the industrial organisations.

Importance[5]

WPM has assumed great importance these days because of the following advantages:

1. **Reduced industrial unrest:** Industrial conflict is a struggle between two organised groups which are motivated by the belief that their respective interests are endangered by the self-interested behaviour of the other. Participation cuts at this very root of industrial conflict.
2. **Reduced misunderstanding:** Participation helps dispelling employees misunderstanding about the outlook of management in industry. These misconceptions would otherwise die hard and their damaging effect needs no explanation.
3. **Increased organisation balance:** If workers are invited to share in organisational problems, and to work towards common solutions, a greater degree of organisational balance occurs because of decreased misunderstanding and individual and group conflicts. Participation leads to increased misunderstanding throughout the organisation. People learn that others have also problems besides themselves.

4. **Improved communication:** It is seldom possible for managers to have knowledge of all alternatives and all consequences related to the decision which they must make. Because of the existence of barriers, much valuable information never reaches the managers. Participation tends to break to barriers and makes the information available to managers.
5. **Higher productivity:** Increased productivity is a possibility with the fullest cooperation between labour and management. Poor management relations do not encourage the workers to contribute anything more than the minimum desirable to retain their jobs.
6. **Increased commitment:** An important prerequisite for improving greater commitment is the individual's involvement and opportunity to express him. Participation allows individuals to express themselves at the work place rather than being absorbed into a complex system of rules, procedures and systems.
7. **Industrial democracy:** Participation helps to usher in an era of democracy in industry. It is based on the principle of recognition of the human factor. It tends to reduce class conflict between capital and labour.
8. **Development of individuals:** Participation enhances individual creativity and response to job challenges. If given the opportunity to question and suggest, instead of having to follow rigid set of instructions, the employee's natural ingenuity and ability are allowed expression.

Modes of Participation

Participation of workers in management is achieved by the following methods:

1. **Works Committee:** A works committee consists of equal number of representatives of both employees and the workers. It meets frequently for discussion on common problems of the workers and the management. After discussion joint decisions are taken and such decisions are binding on both parties. Matters like wage payment, bonus, training, discipline, etc. are discussed in and such meetings work committees are extremely popular in France and England. In India there is a statutory provision for the establishment of works committee under the Industrial Disputes Act, 1947.
2. **Joint Management Council:** Joint consultation scheme was started in UK with the formation of Whitely councils. Joint

consultation involves setting up of join committees represented by the workers and the management to discuss and give suggestions for improvement with regard to matters of mutual interest. The decisions of such committees are not binding on either party, yet they are implemented as they are arrived at mutual consultations.

3. **Collective Bargaining:** It is an industrial relations process in which employees through their elected leaders participate on equal basis with management in negotiating labour agreements, in administering the agreements and in redressing grievances of the workers.
4. **Co-partnership:** In copartner ship, workers are allowed to purchase share of the company and thus become its co-owners. In this way, they can participate in management of the company through their elected representatives on the Board of Directors. As share holders, the workers can also attend general meetings of share holders and exercise their voting rights.
5. **Worker-Director:** Should labour association with management result in a workers representative being given a seat on the board of directors? Many trade unionists have themselves pointed out such idea as illogical. In the countries where trade unions are very strong, the trade unions definitely reject the idea. This according to them would simply cause a confusion of roles and that the unfortunate work director would not be able to reconcile his position as a trade unionist representing the workers interest with him being a member of management. Once the worker Director identifies himself with the cause of management either at the top level or down the line, he can not act contrary to the management decision because of the principle of collective responsibility in the management.
6. **Suggestion Scheme:** Under suggestion scheme, the workers are encouraged to give their suggestions to the management on various administrative matters, and their suggestions are considered carefully and accepted, if found suitable. In addition rewards are also given to those who make constructive suggestions. For collecting suggestions of workers, suggestion boxes is kept in all departments. The workers may put their suggestions in writing into the box. The suggestions are collected every month and suitable decisions are taken jointly by a committee consisting of the representatives of workers and management.

7. **Grievance Procedure:** It also provides an opportunity to the workers to participate in decisions on matters affecting their interests. The model grievance procedure has three tier systems for settlement of grievances at the level of immediate supervisor, department head and bipartite grievance committee representing the management and the union. If the grievance committee is not able to redress the grievance, there is a provision for arbitration or appeal to the chief executive of the organisation.
8. **Quality Circle:** It is a unique concept which provides for voluntary participation by the workers in the direction of quality improvement and self development. Quality circle was first originated in Japan during 1962. The quality circles are relatively autonomous units usually led by a supervisor or a senior worker and organised as work units. The workers, who have a shared area of responsibility, meet weekly to discuss, analyze, and process solutions to ongoing problems.

Essentials for Effective WPM

It is suggested that to ensure effective WPM, the following conditions must be fulfilled:

1. **Democratic attitude of management:** The attitude of the management must be broad, progressive and democratic. It must be willing to associate the workers to discuss. the organisational problems freely and frankly with them and find joint solutions to the problems.
2. **Strong union:** There must be a strong and stable union in every enterprise to represent the workers in various forums of participation. The trade union leadership must be guided by the philosophy of co-operation in resolving the problems of the enterprise.
3. **Mutual trust and faith:** Existence of atmosphere of trust, faith, confidence and recognition is a must for co-operation between the workers and the management.
4. **Clarity of objective of WPM** – Management and workers must understand clearly the objectives of participation. Management should not take it as imposed liability and workers should not use it for expressing their grievances and demands only.
5. **Continuity:** It should be an on going process and should not be treated as one time affair. WPM should not be used merely as a fire-fighting instrument for handling industrial relations problem.

6. **Cordial industrial relations:** Labour-management relations in the enterprise should be cordial or at least there should be no tension in the relations. There should be no blockage of communication between them.
7. **Training in participation:** For successful participation of workers in management, it is necessary that the workers are sufficiently informed about participation programme in the enterprise and are given proper training in the field.

WPM in India

Regarding WPM, the Constitution of India makes provision that: the state shall take steps, by suitable legislation, or in any other way, to secure the participation of workers in the management of undertakings, establishments or other organisations engaged in any industry.

The Industrial Policy Resolution, 1956 stated that, "in a socialistic democracy, labour is a partner in the common task of development and should participate in it with enthusiasm."

The second five-year plan stressed the need for participation. The worker should be made to feel that in this own way; he is helping to build a progressive state.

The third five year plan suggested that the success or failure of an undertaking in an organisation is not the concern of management is not the concern of management alone. For the peaceful evolution of the economic system on a democratic basis, it is essential that WPM should be accepted as a fundamental principle.

Several study groups, seminars and conferences have been arranged to promote the idea of WPM. In 1956, a study group under the chairmanship of Mr. Vishnu Sahy, the then Secretary of Ministry of Labour, suggested the establishment of joint councils in Indian industries. The 15th Indian Labour Conference approved the suggestion.

In 1958, in a tripartite seminar in labour management co-operation, a scheme of joint management council is suggested. The Government of India set up a special unit in the Ministry of Labour to deal with all matters connected with the scheme of joint management council.

WPM gained momentum when Government of India introduced a scheme known as Nationalized Banks scheme. Under this scheme, two representatives of employees shall be elected on the Board of

Directors of each nationalized commercial bank. One representative will be from clerical and non supervisory cadre and the other from supervisory cadre. In 1981, the review of the scheme revealed that worker directors were ignorant of their role on the Board and many a time they were in conflict with the other Directors and Chairman. So the scheme was abolished by the Ministry of Finance. In 1975, Government of India announced a special scheme under Twenty Point Programme. Under this scheme, shop councils and joint councils were to be set up in mining and industrial undertakings employing 500 or more workers. Later on the scheme was extended to units employing 100 cores more workers.

Works Committee

Section 3(a) of the Industrial Disputes Act, 1947 provides for setting up works committee in all undertakings employing 100 or more workers. The works committee is to be composed of the equal number of workers and managements representative. The committee is expected to discuss matters of common interest and to promote measures for maintaining cordial relations between management and workers. The effectiveness of the work committee will depend on the following factors:

1. A more responsive attitude on the part of management.
2. Adequate support from unions.
3. Proper appreciation of the scope and functions of worker's committee.
4. Whole-hearted implementation of the recommendation of the works committee and
5. Proper coordination of the functions of the multiple bipartite institutions at the plant level now in vague.

Joint Management Council (JMC)

In the scheme of JMC it was suggested that the councils should be entitled to be consulted on certain specific matters. The management is expected to supply certain information to such councils. The councils should be constituted in units where 500 or more workers are working.

One important feature of JMC was that it was voluntary rather than obligatory in nature as was the case with the works committee. To be effective and manageable, the JMC should consist of equal number of representatives of employers and employees, not exceeding twelve in all at the same time number should not be less than six. The representatives of the union were to be appointed by the registered and well established union. In case more than one union, existed, the JMC was to be formed when unions among themselves agree as to the manner of representation. The function of the council were divided into three categories i.e. information sharing, consultative and administrative. To make the JMC successful, it is necessary that there must be provision for the recognition of one representative trade union in every organisation.

Shop Council and Joint Council Scheme

The main features of the scheme of participate management through shops council are:

1. Every industrial unit employing 500 or more workmen shall constitute a shop council for each department or shop or one council for more than one department or shop.
2. Employer's representatives must consist of persons from the unit concerned. Similarly, workers representation must be from those actually engaged in the department or shop concerned.
3. All decisions of shop council shall be on the basis of consensus. The decisions taken should be implemented by parties stated otherwise. A report of such implementation shall also be submitted to the council.
4. A shop council so formed shall function for a period of 2 years. It will meet as frequently as possible.
5. The chairman of the shop council shall be a nominee of the management and the vice chairman shall be elected by working members from amongst themselves.

Functions of shop council

- Assist management in achieving monthly/yearly production targets.
- Improvement of production, productivity and efficiency including elimination of wastage and optimum utilisation of machines capacity and man power.
- Specifically identify areas of low productivity and take necessary corrective steps at the shop level.
- To study absenteeism.
- Assist in safety measures.
- Assist in maintaining general discipline in shop.

- Physical conditions of working.
- Welfare measures.

Joint Councils

Joint councils are to be set up for the whole enterprise. The main features are:

- Members of the council must be actually engaged in the unit.
- Tenure of the council shall be two years.
- The chief executive shall be the chairman and vice chairman shall be the nominee of worker members of the council.
- Joint council shall meet at least once in a quarter.
- Every decision of the joint council shall be on the basis of consensus and not by a process of voting.
- The decision shall be binding upon both workers and management and shall be implemented within one month unless otherwise stated.

Functions of the Joint Council

The joint council shall deal with the following issues:

1. Optimum production, efficiency and fixation of productivity norms of man and machine for the unit as a whole.
2. Functions of a shop council which has a bearing on another council or the unit as a whole.
3. Matters remaining unresolved by shop councils.
4. The development of skills of workmen and adequate facilities of training.
5. The preparation of schedules of working hours and of holidays.
6. Awarding of rewards for valuable and creative suggestions made by workers.
7. Optimum use of raw materials and quality of finished products.
8. General health, welfare and safety measures.

Weakness of WPM in India

Broadly speaking, the schemes of WPM have failed in India. The reasons are:

1. There has been managerial resistance to workers participation schemes because they feel that workers are not competent to take decisions. The managers have been presented with little clear evidence that participation will really lead to increases in productivity and profitability in which they are truly interested.

2. A vast majority of workers in India are not strongly motivated to assume decision-making responsibility either directly or through representatives.
3. Under participative management, the employees representatives have to assume the dual role of spokesmen for the workers and the managers. Thus, employee's representatives are required to perform two incompatible roles–sharing managerial responsibility and leading the workers.
4. In India, more emphasis has been given to participation at the higher levels. That means active involvement is confined only to a few, and the creative potential of rank and file of workers is ignored.
5. Normally, worker's representatives are also active members of political parties. Many a time preference is given to political ends than to the interests of workers.
6. Workers participation schemes have been inspired and sponsored by the Government. There has been a lack of initiative on the post of management's and trade unions.
7. There have been labour laws which pervade virtually as areas of the work place.

From the above discussion, it may be said that constitutions in India have not been conducive to participative management. The trade union movement has not yet crystallized into a definite pattern. It is still dominated by politics and many of the trade unionists are social parasites who are out to fish in troubled waters. So long as this continues, workers cannot be expected to show the type of responsibility required to ensure the success of participative management.

Essentials for successful WPM

In order to make WPM successful, the following requirements should be fulfilled.

- There should be a progressive management in the enterprise which is conscious of its obligations and responsibilities to the owners of the business, the employees, the consumers and the country.
- A truly representative enlightened and strong trade union should come into being and should function on strictly constitutional lines.
- There should be unanimity between labour and management on the basic objectives of the organisation and a mutual recognition of their rights and obligations.

- Atmosphere of trust should be created on both sides. Unions should feel that management is not side tracking the effective union through a works committee. Management should equally realize that some of their know prerogatives are meant to be parted with.
- Both the workers and the management should be made conscious of the benefits of participation.
- One and only one union should be recognized in each industrial unit so that inter union rivalry should cease to play the disruptive role.

References

1. V. G. Mehtras, *Dismissal and Misconduct in Industry*, The National Institute of Labour Management, Bombay, 1971.
2. Kenith Davis, *Human Behaviour at Work: Dynamics of OB*, Tata McGraw Hill Publishing, New Delhi, 1975.
3. T. N. Chhabra and Suri, *op. cit.*
4. *Ibid.*
5. *Ibid*

Chapter ten

TRADE UNION MANAGEMENT

The trade union movement is an offshoot of industrialisation. The growth of modern industrial organisations involving use of modern technology and employment of large number of the workers has been followed by growth in trade unions throughout the world. This phenomenon has not only been observed in advanced countries of the world, but is also being witnessed in developing economies. The emergence of trade unionism is spontaneous and inherent in the growth of capitalism. The origin of trade unionism lies in he industrial revolution which disrupted the older way of life and created a new society forged by the shop, the factory, the mine and the industry.

Concept and Nature

Dale Yoder[1] has defined trade unionism as continuing, long-term association of employees formed and maintained for the specific purpose of advancing and protecting the interests of members in their working relationships. A trade union is a continuous association of workers which is formed with the purpose of protecting the interests of workers. According to Flippo,[2] "a trade union is an organisation of workers formed to promote, protect and improve, through collective action, the social, economic and political interests of its members."

From an analysis of the above definitions, the following features of trade union emerge:[3]

- It is an organisation formed by employees or workers.
- It is formed on a continuous basis. It is a permanent body and not a temporary one.
- It is formed to protect and promote all kinds of interests-economic, political and social of its members. The dominant interest with which a union is concerned is, however, economic.

- It includes federations of trade unions also.
- It achieves its objectives through collective action and group effort.

Thus a trade union is generally referred to as an organisation of orders. It is a voluntary democratic and continuing organisation of workers to protect their socioeconomic interests. In India section 2(h) of the Trade Unions Act, 1926 has defined union as, "only combination, whether temporary or permanent, formed primarily for the purpose of regulating the relations between the workmen and employers, or between workmen and workmen, or between employers and employers, or for imposing restrictive conditions on the conduct of any trade or business, and includes any federation of two or more trade unions."

Objectives[4]

Trade unions are essentially organisations for the protection and promotion of the interests of their members in particular and workers in general. The primary functions of trade unions are to protect the workers against the excesses committed by employers and to satisfy the needs of the workers. To be specific, however, the trade unions generally pursue the following broad objectives:

1. *Steady employment:* Steady employment is something which the employer by himself may not be able to guarantee to the workers. His ability to provide it is limited by the state of the market, which in large part is beyond his control. Achievement of this aspiration may thus involve workers in political action through their unions, for the maintenance of full employment.
2. *Rationalisation of personnel policies:* The economic security of an employee is determined not only by the level of wages and duration o his employment, but also by the management's personnel policies. If the decision of this type is the result of subjective evaluation and capriciousness, there is no security for the workers. If such decisions are, however, governed by statutory rules and rational policies, there is greater assurance of fair treatment and equal justice.
3. *Voice in decisions affecting workers:* The workers may successfully pressurize for higher wages. He may achieve a satisfactory rationalisation of personnel policies. But if the vital decisions as to the scale and schedule of production, introduction of labour saving devices, the closing or replication of plant, etc. remain outside the effective influence of workers, there is no real security for them. Each worker wants to know if the new machinery would

reduce him from a skilled operative to a machine attendant or a member of custodial force. He wants to know what his chances are for continued attachment to the company. The intervention of the union in such decisions of management is the only way by which the worker is able to achieve any degree of control over the affairs that concern him.

4. *Recognition and Participation:* Another objective that unions seek to achieve is winning recognition for the fact that they are equal partners with management in the task of production. This equality is something more than the equality at bargaining table. It is an intellectual quality.
5. *Gaining legislature enactments*: To provide legal sanctions to its demands, the unions attempt to get these framed in the form of Acts so that they become permanent features of the contact between the employers and the workers. For this purpose unions may take recourse of political action in terms of supporting any political party or forming their own political party.
6. *Miscellaneous services:* Modern trade unions also engage in providing educational, medical, recreational another facility for the development and welfare of their members and their families, if they have sufficient funds at their disposal.

Functions

For the achievement of the above mentioned objectives, the trade unions generally perform the following functions:

- Collective bargaining with the management to settle terms and conditions of employment.
- Advise the management on personnel policies and practices.
- Taking up the individual and collective grievances of the workers with the management.
- Work for achieving better say of workers in the management of affairs of the enterprise which influence the lives of the workers directly.
- Organising demonstrations, strikes, etc. to press the demands of the workers.
- Education of workers and their children.
- Welfare and recreational activities for their members.
- Representing of worker in various national and international forums.
- Securing legislative protection for the workers from the Government.

The functions performed by the trade unions may be broadly classified into three categories:

1. *Militant functions:* The chief purpose of the trade unions is to secure better conditions of work and employment. The unions also endeavour to secure some share in productivity gains and a greater share in the management. When the unions fail to accomplice these ends but the method of collective bargaining and negotiations, they adopt agitation methods and put up a fight with the management in the form of strike, boycott, gherao, etc. a situation that often turns into fierce antagonism.
2. *Fraternal functions:* A trade union is a fraternal association or a mutual benefit organisation supporting the members out of their own funds during the period of work stoppage due to a strike or lockout. It also provides financial assistance to the members during the period when they are unfit for work because of illness or employment injury or when they are temporarily unemployed.
3. *Political functions:* Many trade unions seek to improve the political status of the union, the leader, and the union members. They contest political elections and try to acquire political power.

Why do workers join Unions?

Workers or employees join trade unions for a variety of reasons though they may not be conscious of their motive of joining unions. These are:

- Economic benefits and better working conditions.
- A platform for self-expression.
- To get a check on arbitrary actions of management.
- For security reasons.
- Realisation of good employee-employer relations.
- For the creation of a sense of participation.
- Due to a sense of belongingness.
- Historical background factors also play a part in the disposition of employees to join a union.

Importance

In the modern industrial society, trade unions are a force in themselves. No managers of working organisations can ignore the influence of trade unions on the behaviour of their workforce and on the environment of management. As Yoder wrote, "unions are real; they affect the system and process of management."

Existence of strong trade unions is a precondition for industrial place and stability of the industrial economy. Decisions taken through the process of collective bargaining and negotiation between the employers and trade unions are bound to be respected both employers and workers. By insisting upon payment of standard rates of wages for their members, trade unions ensure efficient functioning of the industrial units. By organising fraternal functions, they improve the efficiency of workers. Effective trade unions are helpful in avoiding in articulate unrest of workers involving extensive absenteeism, frequent job changes / labour turnover, fighting, wondering from one plant or locality to another. Trade unions can play an important role in the planned economic development of a nation. They can help in the accelerated peace of economic development in many ways, more important of which are:

- By helping in the recruitment and selection.
- By inculcating discipline among the workforce.
- By enabling settlement of industrial disputes in a rational rather than erratic and chaotic manner.
- By helping social adjustments.
- By creating a committed industrial workforce.

Impact of Trade Union on Management

The existence of a union affects not only the overall organisation, but also the management in many ways. For the personnel manager the existence of a union means that all personnel decisions shall be subject to union's checks and controls. Apart from union's effects on policy making, there are several other areas which are affected by the existence of unions. These are:

1. Union policy affects the structure of laboraur employed. Though this factor is related to management decision, yet it also affects the overall organisation.
2. The existence of a union does affect the level of wages and the terms of their employment. A union may not tolerate unjust attitude of management with regard to payments of increments, overtime, promotion, paid vacations, leave, holidays, insurance plans, pension plans, medical reimbursement, etc.
3. A union's existence may affect the prices of the products manufactured by the organisation.
4. A union's policy in an organisation affects the position of individual workers in organisation.

5. It also affects industrial relations and industrial peace.
6. A union might also try to have control over scarce job opportunities. Generally union taken the stand that a fixed proportion of new jobs should be given to the blood relation of the existing employees of the organisation.

The presence of the union restricts management's freedom of action in many areas. In dealing with labour unions, it is important for the management to recognize that improved union management relations play a vital role in the success of an organisation.

In order to achieve their goals, trade unions may adopt any or a combination of the following methods:

1. *Methods of Mutual Insurance:* This method consists mainly of welfare activities conducted by trade unions for their members. Activities like medical aid, educational, credit facilities, sickness aid, etc. comes in the form of mutual insurance or mutual aid. These amenities and aids are provided out of the funds that its members contribute in the shape of membership subscriptions and donations, etc. Thus the effectiveness of this method is directly dependent upon the income of trade unions.
2. *Collective Bargaining:* Another method used by trade unions for improving the economic and social conditions of their members is collective bargaining. This is essentially a bipartite method under which trade union as a representative organisation of workers bargaining with the employers over the various issues such as terms and conditions of employment, wages, bonus, hours of work working conditions, welfare facilities, etc. and enter into agreement called collective agreement, with the employer.

Since individual worker is a weak bargainer, the method of collective bargaining is preferred. Bargaining may be made at the local level, at the regional level or at the national level.

3. *Legal Enactment:* Under this method, trade unions engage in political action for securing working and living conditions for the workers. This is done by exerting pressure for getting progressive labour laws passed by the legislature and to get them enforced properly. For getting protective and pro labour legislation passed by the legislatures, the unions send competent representatives of the workers to the Legislative Assembly and the parliament.
4. *Direct Action:* When the trade unions fail to achieve their goals by the above described methods, they resort to direct action. It is manifested in several forms like strikes, *gheraos*, *bandhs*, etc. Since

this method is harmful to all concerned in terms of loss of production, loss of wages, scarcity or non-availability of goods, etc. every effort should be made to avoid the us this weapon in the armory of trade unions. Evidently, what is required is cooperation and not conflict.

TRADE UNIONISM IN INDIA[5]

Backdrop

Trade Union activities in India began in the latter half of the 19th century with the foundation of modern industries. The construction of Railways was the first step in this direction and harbinger and forerunner of the modern Indian working class movement. Against the backdrop of India's freedom struggle and the emergence of the ILO, political ideologies greatly influenced the Indian Trade Union movement.

In 1890, N. M. Lokhandy established the Bombay Mill Hands Association, which is said to be the first trade union in India. Similar organisations were started in early years, such as:

- Amalgamated Society of Railway Servants of India and Burma (1897).
- Printers Union of Calcutta (1905)
- Postal Union in Bombay (1909)
- Kangar Hituardhak Sabha (1909)
- Social Service League (1911), etc.

Strikes were not unknown. In 1908, when B. G. Tilak was sentenced to eight years imprisonment, the textile workers of Bombay struck work for two weeks. But these unions were loose and sectarian organisations set up by social reformers rather than by workers. There was a remarkable growth of labour movement between 1904 and 1917 and several strikes were organised. But trade unions remained confined by and large to the upper ranks and educated sections of the working class.

Many factors came in the way of workers, building up protective organisations like trade unions. They are:

- Poverty and lack of employment.
- Diversities in every sphere.
- Exploitation of the situation by middlemen.
- Hostile environment.

The above factors delayed the growth of trade unions in India.

Political development like partition of Bengal, Swadeshi Movement helped the trade union movement. At the end of World War I growing economic hardships, the Russian revolution, establishment of ILO gave phillip to trade union movement. Beginning with the Home Rule League in 1915 and continuing through the Rowlatt Satyagaha in 1919, the national movement one again reached in crescendo in the Non-cooperation and Khilafat movement in 1920-22. It was in this context that there occurred a resurgence of working class activity in the years from 1919 to 1922. This situation was tailor made for the flowering of organised trade union movement in India.

The Madras Labour Union formed in 1918 by B. P. Wadia was a modern trade union organisation of India. Soon after that, two unions were formed in Bombay, one in Calcutta and four in Madras. In 1920, many more unions were organised in various parts of the country. These covered Railway men, dock workers, engineering workers, etc. The most important of these unions were the Majdur Mahajan, Railway Employee's Union, Mahatma Gandhi established Ahmedabad Textile Labour Association.

But the most important development was the formation of the AITUC in 1920. B. G. Tilak who had developed a close association with Bombay workers, was one of the moving spirits in the formation of ATUC, which had Lala Lajpat Rai, as its first President and Dewan Chaman Lal, as its General Secretary. The manifesto issued to the workers by the AITUC urged them not only to organise themselves but also to intervene in national politics. Between 1920 and 1922, the number of unions affiliated was 107. According to one estimate, the number of trade unions in 1924-25 was 167. But most of the trade unions were just strike committees which were formed for a strike and disappeared at its conclusion. The Gaya session of Indian National Congress (INC) decided to assist AITUC in organising workers. In 1926, Indian Trade Union Act was enacted, which gave legal status to trade unions.

AITUC remained the central organisation of the working class until independence. Its earlier leaders were N. M. Joshi, V. V. Giri, J. M. Sengupta, etc. M. N. Roy described the AITUC as a "strange conglomeration of nationalism, Utopianism and Reforms." Due to his pro-communism in 1929, a split occurred in AITUC. The moderate led by N. M. Joshi left AITUC to form AITUF. But the communists had differences among themselves resulting in another split in 1931, when communists formed Red Trade Union Congress

(RTUC). To facilitate unity in 1933, AITUF and railway unions amalgamated to form National Trade Union Federation (NTUF). In 1940, NTUF finally merged with AITUC. In 9141, the radicals in AITUC formed a new central federation called IFL.

After Independence, there was speedy growth in trade unions due to support from both the Government and the society at large. In 1947, moderates in AITUC separated and formed on the INTUC. Hindustan Mazdoor Sevak Sangha (HMSS) and ATLA became very active socialists broke away from INTUC and formed Hindustan Mazdoor Panchayat (HMP). HMP and IFL join together to form, Hindustan Mazdoor Sabha (HMS). A section of HMS formed UTUC in 1949. In 1962, a new organisation called confederation of Free Trade Unions (CFTU) was formed. In 1970 communists formed CITU. Old congressmen served themselves from the INTUC and formed the National Labour Organisation (NLO). Representatives of AITUC, INTUC and HMS established a National Council of Central Trade Unions (NCCTU) to provide a common platform for trade union activities. But the basic aim is to isolate CITU.

Features of Indian Trade Unions

1. Workers in India are unionized mainly on the basis of plants rather than on the basis of crafts. Craft unions are formed among non-industrial and professional workers, e. g. taxi drivers, teachers, journalists, etc.
2. The extent of unionisation is not uniform in all industries. Workers in some industries are better unionized than in others.
3. Most of the unions in India are small in size. So their financial condition is weak.
4. Unionisation is not limited to blue collar employees. White-collar workers are also getting into the union.
5. The primary unions are affiliated to a number of central unions.
6. There is very close link between trade unions and political parties.

Structure

The structure of unions refers to the basis on which unions are organised and to the pattern whereby the plant unions are linked to regional level or national level federations or unions.

Trade unions can be classified into three categories:

1. Craft unions
2. Industrial unions
3. General unions.

A craft union is an organisation of wage earners engaged in a single occupation. It may cover all workers engaged in a particular craft irrespective of the industries in which they are employed. An industrial union is organised on the basis of an industry rather than a craft. A general union is whose membership covers workers employed in different industries and crafts. General unions are not popular in India.

In India, trade unions have largely been organised by industry rather than craft. Although industrial unions have grown continuously, craft unions have also emerged here and there.

Problems of Trade Union Movement in India

The position of trade unionism in India is not very sound. In fact the trade union movement is wanting in many respects. This is because of the fact that the Indian trade unions of today suffer from many problems.

1. *Union growth:* Trade union activities are concentrated in large scale industry sector and there too in regard to manual labour only and mainly in bigger industrial centers. Hardly any trade union activity exists in small scale enterprises, domestic and agricultural labour. The degree of unionisation varies from industry to industry.
2. *Low membership:* The number of trade unions in India was increased considerably. But this has been followed by the declining membership per union. The average membership of all trade unions including both submitting returns and those not submitting returns is likely to be very low. This indicates the emergence of small sized unions in large numbers. This is due to the reason that any seven workers may form a union under the Trade Unions Act, 1926 and get it registered.
3. *Outside leadership:* Most of the trade unions in India have professional political leadership. The leadership is not rooted in the working class. The leadership of professional politicians is interested in exploiting workers for their political purposes. The interest of the working class is not protected by the political leaders. The political leadership is actually harmful to the cause of the working class. Strikes are prolonged by political leaders for personal prestige.
4. *Multiplicity of unions:* Multiplicity of grade unions is another problem. There at times as many as twenty unions in the same

plant. The existence of this phenomenon can be attributed partly to the labour laws.

5. *Inter and Intra union rivalry:* Due to the existence of multiple unions there occurs the problem of union rivalry. Unions try to play down each other in a bid to gain greater influence among workers. In the process they do more harm than good to the cause of unionism as a whole. Employers are given on opportunity to play unions against each other. They can refuse to bargain on the contention that there is not true representative union. Besides this, the workers, own solidarity is lost. Employers are able to take advantage of infighting between workers groups. Solution to this problem can be found in secret ballot vote.
6. *Absence of paid office bearers:* Majority of unions do not have whole time paid office bearers. Many union activists work on honorary basis. They devote only limited time and energy to trade union activities. The domination of political leaders is also due to the absence of full time union workers. The union office bearers are also not trained properly.
7. *Weak financial position:* The financial position of the trade units is very weak because their average yearly income is very low and inadequate. The subscription rates vary from union to union and are quite low in most of the unions. Under conditions of multiplicity of unions, unions interested in increasing their membership figures keep the subscription rate unduly low. As a result, the funds with the unions are inadequate and they can not undertake welfare programmes for their members.
8. *Subscription dues unpaid:* Large amounts of subscription dues remain unpaid by the workers. The names of constant defaulters continue to appear on the membership registers of most of unions. They are neither expelled nor cease to be member ipso facto, according to the union rules. Rules for expulsion of defaulting members are seldom invoked. Besides thus, unions do not have proper staff and organisation to collect subscription.
9. *Lack of interest:* In order to make the trade union movement succeed, the members of trade unions should take keen interest in the union affairs. They should understand what unionism is all about and what demands it makes on individual

members. They must feel the need to give the movement necessary support for a common cause. In India, a large number of workers have not joined any union. The attendance at the general meetings of the unions is very low. Under such circumstances, trade unionism cannot be expected to make much progress.

10. *Limited stress on welfare:* many unions in India undertake only limited welfare activities. They feel that their major activity is to fight with the employer for more wages and allowances. So workers are not attracted towards unions.
11. *Lack of public support:* The trade unions frequently resorts to strikes and demonstrations. They give limited attention to peaceful methods for the settlement of demands and disputes. The general public is affected due to strikes, go slow policy and other practices of unions. As a result, public support is not available to the unions.

References

1. D. Yoder, H. G. Henenan, J. G. Turnbull and C. Stone, *Handbook of Personnel Management and Industrial Relations,* McGraw Hill Book Co, New Delhi, 1958.
2. E. B. Flippo, *Principles of Personnel Management,* Mc Graw Hill Book, New York, 1986.
3. T. N. Chhabra and Suri, *Industrial Relations.*
4. *Ibid.*
5. *Ibid.*

Chapter eleven

CONFLICT MANAGEMENT

Conflict is a process that begins when one party perceives that another party has negatively affected, or is about to negatively affect, something that the first party cases about.

- The early approach to conflict assumes that all conflict was bad. Conflict was viewed negatively and it was used synonymously with such terms as violence, destruction and irrationality to reinforce its negative connotation. Conflict by definition was harmful and was to be avoided.
- The human relations approach argued that conflict was a natural occurrence in all groups and organisations. Since conflict was inevitable, the human relation school advocated acceptance of conflict.
- The interactions approach encourages conflict on the grounds that a harmonious, peaceful, tranquil, and cooperative group is prone to becoming static, apathetic and non-responsive to needs for change and innovation. So the major contribution of the interactionist approach, therefore is encouraging group leaders to maintain an ongoing minimum level of conflict enough to keep the group viable, self-critical and creative.

Whether a conflict is good or bad depends on the type of conflict. So, it is necessary to differentiate between functional and dysfunctional conflict. The interactionist view does not purpose all conflicts are bad. Rather some conflicts support the goals of the group and improve its performance. These are functional or constructive forms of conflict. Some conflicts hinder group performance or destructive forms of conflict.

So Conflicts are Constructive When

- Problems are brought out identified and clarified.
- Group think is avoided.

- Organisational lethargy is dissolved, creativity is promoted.
- More thought goes into ideas.
- Encourages group cohesiveness and provides for a system of check and balance in an organisation.

Conflicts are destructive when:

- Too much stress is created.
- Group decision-making is reduced to a feeble walk.
- Co-operation is replaced by infighting.
- Focus on short range goals at the cost of long range goals.
- Goals are distorted and resolution of conflict is viewed as win-lose rather win-win.

Process[1]:

The conflict process can be seen as comprising five stages. See Figure 1.11.1

Potential opposition or incompatibility	Cognition and personalization	Intentions
(1)	(2)	(3)
Anticipant conditions -communication	Perceived conflict Conflict Felt conflict	Conflict Handling intentions
	(5)	(4)
	Outcomes Increased group performance Decreased group performance	Behaviour Overt conflict - Party's behaviour - Other's reaction

Source: S.P. Robbins, organizational behaviour

Fig. 1.11.1

Step 1: The first step in the conflict process is the presence of conflicts that create opportunities for conflict to arise. They need not lead directly to conflict, but one of these conditions is necessary if conflict is to arise. These conditions may be communication, structure and personal variables. It is a myth that poor communication is the certainly not the source of all conflicts, although there is considerable evidence to suggest that problems in the communication process act of retard collaboration and stimulate misunderstanding. Semantic difficulties insufficient exchange of information and noise in the communication channel are all barriers to communication and potential antecedent conditions to conflict. The potential for conflict increases when either too little or too much communication takes place. Further, the channel chosen for communicating can have an influence on stimulating opposition. Some conflicts are structural in nature. Structure include variables such as size, degree of specialisation in the tasks assigned to group members, jurisdictional clarity, member goal compatibility, leadership styles, reward systems and the degree of dependence between groups. Personal factors are also potential sources of conflict. They include each persons, Indian value systems and the personality characteristics that account for individual idiosyncrasies and differences.

Step 2: If the conditions cited in step 1 negatively affect something that one party comes about, then the potential for opposition or incompatibility becomes actualized in the second stage. The antecedent condition can only lead to conflict when one or more of the parties are affected by and aware of the conflict for a conflict, perception is required. However, because a conflict is perceived does not mean it is personalized. It is at the felt level, when individuals become emotionally involved, that parties experience anxiety, tenseness, frustration or hostility.

Step 3: Intentions intervene between people's perceptions and emotions and their overt behaviour. These intentions are decisions to act in a given way. A lot of conflicts are escalated merely by one party attributing the wrong intentions to the other party. Additionally, there is typically a great deal of slippage between intentions and behaviour so that behaviour does not always accurately reflect a person's intentions. This is illustrated in Figure 1.11.2.

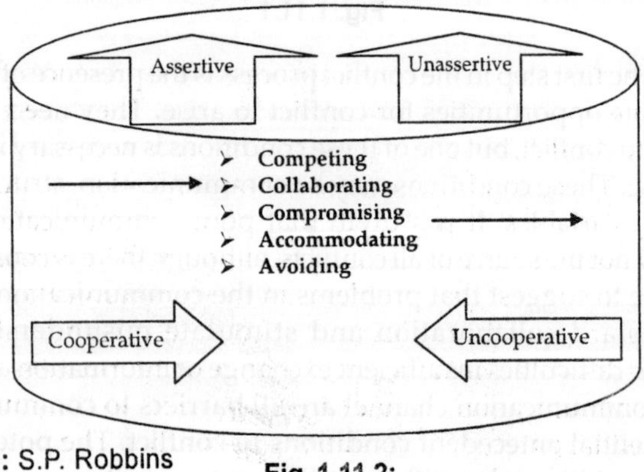

Source: S.P. Robbins

Fig. 1.11.2:

Using two dimensions, i.e. cooperativeness (the degree to which one party attempts to satisfy the other party's concerns) and assertiveness (the degree to which one party attempts to satisfy his own concerns) – five conflict handling intentions can be identified:

a. *Competing:* Assertive and un cooperative. A desire to satisfy one's interests regardless of the impact on the other party to the conflict.
b. *Collaborating:* Associative and cooperative. A situation where the parties to a conflict each desire to satisfy fully the concerns of all parties.
c. *Accommodating:* Unassertive and cooperative. The willingness of one party in a conflict to place the opponent interests above his own.
d. *Compromising:* Midrange of assertive and cooperative. A situation in which each party to a conflict is willing to give up something.
e. Avoiding means desire to withdraw from conflict.

Intentions provide general guidelines for parties in a conflict situation. They define each party's purpose. Yet people's intentions are not fixed. During the course of the conflict, they might change because of re-conceptualisation or because of an emotional reaction to the behaviour of the other party.

Step 4: At this stage conflicts become visible. The behaviour stage includes the statements, actions and reactions made by the conflicting parties. These conflicts behaviours are usually avert attempts to implement each party's intentions. But these behaviours have a stimulus quality that is separate from intentions. As a result of miscalculations or unskilled enactments, overt behaviours sometimes deviate from original intentions.

Step 5: The action reaction interplay between the conflicting parties result in consequences. These outcomes may be functional, in that the conflict results in an improvement in the group's performance or dysfunctional in that it hinders group performance.

Conflict Management[2]

Conflict may be harmful to an organisation but there are times when it is useful. It is for this reason that managers must learn to recognize the differences between constructive and destructive conflict situations. Conflict management is the use of resolution and stimulation techniques to achieve the desired level of conflict.

Conflict Resolution Techniques

1. Problem solving in face to face meeting of the conflicting parties for the purpose of identifying the problem and resolving it through open discussion.
2. Superordinate goals – Creating a shared goal that can not be attained without the cooperation of each of the conflicting parties.
3. Expansion of resources – When a conflict is caused by the scarcity of resources expansion of the resource can create a win solution.
4. Avoidance – Withdrawl from or suppression of the conflict.
5. Smoothing – Playing down of differences while emphasising common interests between the conflicting parties.
6. Compromise – Each party to the conflict gives up some thing of value.
7. Authoritative command – Management uses its formal authority to resolve the conflict and then communicates its desire to the parties involved.
8. Altering the human variable – Using behavioural change techniques such as human relations training to alter attitudes and behaviours that cause conflict.
9. Altering the structural variables – Changing the formal organisation structure and the interaction patterns of conflicting parties through job redesign, transfers, creation of coordinating positions, etc.

Conflict Stimulation Techniques

1. *Communication:* Using ambiguous or threatening messages to increases conflict levels.
2. *Bringing in outsiders:* Adding employees to a group whose backgrounds, values, attitudes, or managerial styles differ from those of present members.
3. *Restructuring the organisation:* Realising work groups, altering rules and regulations, increasing interdependence and making similar structural changes to disrupt the *status quo.*
4. *Appointing a devil's advocate:* Designating a critic to purposely argue against the majority positions held by the group.

References

1. S. R. Robbins, *Organisational Behviour*, PHI, New Delhi, 2008
2. *Ibid.*

Chapter twelve

TOTAL QUALITY MANAGEMENT (TQM)

Total Quality Management (TQM) refers to the deep commitment of an organisation to quality. Quality of products and services is an obsession and every step in the company's process is subjected to intense and regular scrutiny for ways to improve it. Almost every issue is subject to exploration and the process is a continuing one. Employees are provided with extensive training in problem solving, group decision-making and statistical methods.

TQM is a philosophy of management[1] that is driven by the constant attainment of customer satisfaction through the continuous improvement of all organisational processes. It replaces some of the traditional belies beliefs quality, i.e.

- High quality costs more.
- Quality can be improved by inspection.
- Defects cannot be eliminated completely.
- Quality is the job of the quality control personnel.

Principles[2]

After rejecting some traditional beliefs as mentioned above, TQM has adopted some new principles, such as.

1. Meet the customers' requirement on time the first time and 100% of the time.
2. Strive to do error free work.
3. Manage by prevention, not by correction.
4. Measure the cost of quality.

Features[3]

TQM is the latest mantra of management. In its essence TQM implies total commitment to quality. The essential features of TQM are:

1. Intense focus on the customer: The customer includes not only outsider who buy the organisations products or services, but also internal customers who interact and serve others in the organisation.
2. Concern for continual improvement: TQM is a commitment to never begin satisfied. 'Very good' is not good enough. Quality can always be improved.
3. Improvement in the quality of everything the organisation does-TQM uses a very broad definition of quality. It relates not only to the final product but how the organisation handles deliveries, how rapidly it responds to complaints, etc.
4. Accurate measurement: TQM uses statistical techniques to measure every critical performance variable in the organisation's operations. These performance variables are then compared against standards to identify problems, the problems are traced to their roots and the causes are eliminated.
5. Empowerment of employees: TQM involves the people on the line in the improvement process. Teams are widely used in TQM programme as empowerment vehicles for finding and solving problems.
6. Creation of a common company theme: TQM requires a common company theme to every service or product rendered by the company.
7. Improvement in communication: The communication process is improved in TQM. Every employee can communicate to everybody. For rapid communication process, channels are made barrier free. So use of modern technology is prescribed.
8. Bureaucracy to be reduced: For attainment of TQM, the role of bureaucracy must be reduced. Desegregation of public bureaucracies can only give quality service on every front. In the name of official secrecy, bureaucracy makes a wall between the people and the organisation. So de-bureaucratisation can ensure transparency and TQM.

Each of the principles of TQM calls for a new orientation and a broad perspective on the part of every employee. In the TQM, dispensation, almost everybody will be required to attend to every task, the ultimate goal begin the offer of better quality products or services. In fact TQM is a participative method because every employee in the organisation is involved and is expected to take responsibility for improving quality, everyday. It is a formal programme which involves direct participation by all employees. The programme seeks to achieve continuous process improvements so variability is constantly reduced. But it should be remembered that, the search for continual improvement crates a race without a finish line.

TQM is now accepted through the world and a dynamic process. To state it again TQM calls for continuous improvement of quality with cooperation of workers. In it there are three components – employee, quality product and services and customer satisfaction. Further, it is process of creating organisational culture. It is the concern of all managers but mainly planned by the top managers. TQM covers four stages during its march from its inception till today.

- Phase I (Quality Control) – Detection and rectification of defect, 1910-1930
- Phase II (Process Control) – Prevention of defects, 1930-1960
- Phase III (Product Improvement) – Manipulation at design stage, 1960-1980
- Phase IV (Creativity Improvement) - Creative innovation, 1980-

Benefits

The following are the benefits of TQM:

- TQM encourages innovation and creativity.
- It encourages production of quality products.
- It helps in providing satisfaction of customers.
- It provides good public images of corporations by providing high quality goods and services.
- Competitive advantage is established as wastages are minimum and profit increases.
- Employee feel elevated and motivated as the product of their enterprise is of high quality.

Implementation of TQM

W.E Deming, father of TQM, provided a formula for implementation of Total Quality Management. That is PDCA Cycle: Plan, Do, Check, Act, Cycle.

1. Plan—Laying down of policies and objectives
2. Check out methods to achieve objectives
3. Do—Training of workers to meet the requirement of TQM
   Start of New product by operating TQM

4. Check—Analyze the results and determine the result of non-performance.
5. Act—Prevent undesired effects in quality improvement. And suggest methods of design for future.

References

1. K.B. Asawsathappa, *Personnel and HRM*, Tata McGraw Hill, 2003
2. *Ibid.*
3. *Ibid.*

Chapter thirteen

STRATEGIC MANAGEMENT

There are different definitions of strategy. A comprehensive one refers to the determination of basic long-term objectives and of courses of action and allocation of resources to achieve these aims. Strategy is an important output of the planning process for any organisation. It is defined as a broad programme for defining and achieving an organisations objectives and the organisations response to its environment over time. After the World War II, many organisations and human institutions saw the light of the day, and a new concept strategic planning came into origin. A strategic plan is a broad grand plan. Those strategic plans constitute a separate management process called as strategic management. So then strategic management[1] is the management process that involves an organisation's engaging in strategic planning and then acting on those plans.

Dan Schendel and Charles Hofer gave a different definition of strategic management. They argued that structure of an organisation can be defined well if the attainment of objectives is added to policy and strategy. According to their definition there are four key aspects of strategic management.

- Goal setting
- Strategy formulation
- Administration
- Strategy Implementation

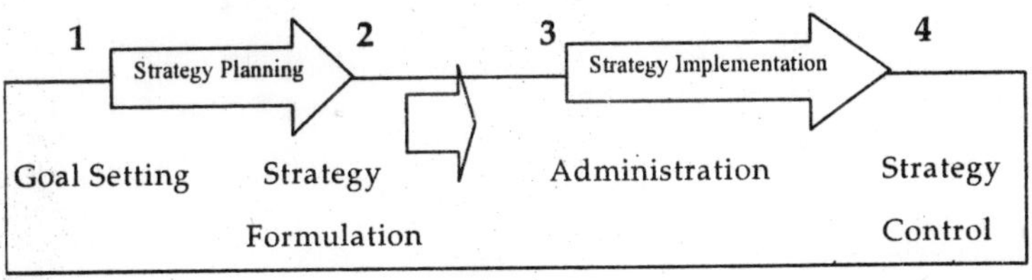

The first step in strategic management is the **setting of goals**. Once goals are set, a **strategy** is formulated which the second is set. The third step is the **administration** i.e. the task of achieving predetermined goals. The final step is **strategic control** which gives managers feedback on their progress. The first and second process constitutes strategic planning and the third and fourth step constitutes strategy implementation. Then strategic management is a disciplined way for managers to make sense of the environment in which their organisation operates and then to act.

As such strategic Management is that set of managerial decisions and actions that determines the longterm performance of an organization (S P Robbins Mary Coultor: 2003) And it involves eight - step process as explained below (Figure 1.13.1)

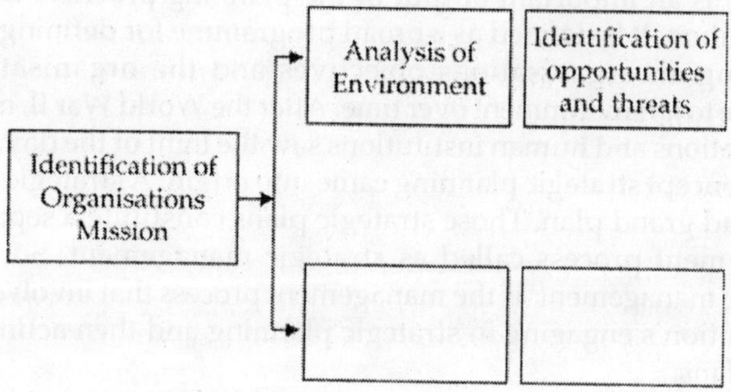

Fig. 1.13.1: Strategic Management Process

References

1. Stroner & Ors, *Management*, PHI, 1997

Chapter fourteen

MANAGEMENT OF CHANGE

Change is inevitable in life. Every individual and organisation should accept change as if, it is a way of life. More and more organisations today face a dynamic and changing environment that in turn, requires these organisations to adopt and then adopt. There are many forces that are acting as stimulants for change. These forces are changing nature of workforce, technology, economic hazards, competition, social trend and the global political scenario.

Managing Change[1]

Change means to make things different. Planned change means that is intentional and goal oriented. So it can be defined as a systematic attempt to redesign an organisation in a way that will help it adapt to changes in the external environment or to achieve new goals. It is mandatory for all the managers to improve their ability to manage change. Many large organisations have explicit change management programmes to increase the ability of the people throughout the organisation to anticipate and learn form the changes that are occurring. Then first the manager has to know the goal of change and source of change. There are two goals of planned change. First, it seeks to improve the ability of the organisation to adapt to changes in its environment. Second, it seeks to change employee behaviour. If an organisation is to survive, it must respond to changes in its environment. Since an organisation's success or failure is essentially due to the things its employee do or fail to do planned change is also concerned with changing the behviour of individuals and groups within the organisation. Managers must think planned change in its order of magnitude. First order change is linear and continuous. It implies no fundamental shift in the assumptions that organisational members hold about the world or how the organisation can improve its functioning. The second order change is multidimensional, multilevel, discontinuous, radical change in faring of assumptions about the organisation. Sources of change mean change agents. Change agents are the persons who act as catalysts and assume the responsibility for managing change activities.

Change Agents

The change agents can bring change in four categories:

- Structure
- Technology
- Physical setting
- People.

Changing structures involve making an alteration in authority relations, co-ordinations mechanisms, job redesign or similar structural variables. This might include a shift from a simple structure to a team based structure or the creation of a matrix design. Changing technology encompasses modifications in the way, work is processed and in the methods and equipments, used. Automation is a technological change that replaces people with machines. Changing the physical setting covers altering the space and layout refers to changes in employee attitudes, skills, ex-approaches, perceptions and behaviour.

Techniques to Managing Change[2]

There are some approaches or techniques to managing change. One such technique is Lewin's three step model. Organisations may be in a state of equilibrium, with forces pushing for change on one hand and forces resisting change by attempting to maintain the status quo on the other. Kurt Lewin expressed this phenomenon in his field force theory which suggests that an equilibrium is maintained by driving forces and restraining forces. Driving forces mean the forces that direct behaviour away from the status quo. Restraining forces mean the forces that hinder movement away from the *status quo*. In managing change, the tendency is to increase the driving forces.

Process of Change

The change process involves three steps:

1. Unfreezing

2. Moving
3. Refreezing.

Unfreesing creates motivation for changes. If people feel uncomfortable with the present situation, they may see the need for change. The second stage is the **moving**/changes itself. This change may occur through assimilation of new information, exposure to new concepts or development of a different perspective. The third stage, **Refreezing** stabilizes the change. Change to be effective has to be congruent with a person's self concept and values. If the change is incongruent with the attitudes and behavious of others in the organisation, chances are that the person will revert back to the old behaviour. Thus reinforcement of the new behaviour is essential.

Another approach is action research, which a change process is based on systematic collection of data and then selection of a change action based on what the analyzed data indicate. The process consists of five steps:

1. Diagnosis
2. Analysis
3. Feedback
4. Action
5. Evaluation.

The change agent often has an outsider in action research. It begins by gathering information about problems, concerns and needed changes from members of the organisation. The information gathered during the diagnostic stage is then analyzed. Action research includes extensive involvement of the change targets. That is the people who will be involved in any change programme must be actively involved in determining what the problem is and participating in creating the solution. So the third step is sharing with employees what has been found in first and second step. The employees with the help of the change agent develop action plans for bringing about any needed change. Finally consistent with the scientific under pinning of action research the change agent evaluates the effectiveness of the action plans.

Resistance to Change[3]

Organisations and other members, resist change. In a sense, this is position. It provides a degree of stability and predictability to behaviour. If there were not some resistance, organisational behaviour would take a characteristic of chaotic randomness. Resistance to change can also be a source of functional conflict.

Resistance to change does not necessarily surface in standardized ways. Resistance can be overt, implicit, immediate or deferred. It is easiest for management to deal with resistance when it is overt and immediate the implicit or deferred. Generally there are two sources of resistance, i.e. individual and organisational.

Individual resistance[4]

Individual sources of resistance to change reside in basic human characteristics such as perceptions, personalities and needs. There are five reasons why individuals resist change, i.e.

- Habit
- Security
- Economic
- Fear of the unknown
- Selective information processing.

Human beings are creatures of habit. Life is very multipart. It is not possible for the human being to consider the full range of options of the hundreds of decisions made everyday. To cope with this we rely on habits or programmed responses. When confronted with change, this tendency to respond in our accustomed ways becomes a source of resistance. People with a high need for security are likely to resist change because it threatens their feeling of safety. Another source of individual resistance is concerned with that changes will lower one's income. Changes substitute ambiguity and uncertainty for the known. Finally individuals shape their world through their perceptions. Once they have created this world, it resists change. So individuals are guilty of selectively processing information in order to keep their perceptions intact.

Organisational Resistance[5]

By nature, organisations are conservative. They actively resist change. Six major sources of organisational resistance are.

- Structural inertia.
- Limited focus of change
- Group inertia
- Threat to expertise
- Threat to established power relationships
- Threat to established resource allocations.

Organisations have built in mechanisms, to produce stability. The people who are hired into an organisation are chosen for fit. They are then shaped and directed to behave in certain ways. When an organisation is confronted with change, this structural inertia acts as a counter balance to sustain stability. Organisations are made up of a number of interdependent subsystems. One cannot change a particular subsystem without affecting the other. So limited changes in the sub-systems have positive impacts on the larger system. Even if individuals want to change their behaviour, group norms may act as a constraint. So here the group inertia resists change. Changes in organisational patterns may threaten the expertise of specialized groups. Any redistribution of decision-making authority can threaten long established power relationships within the organisation. The introduction of participative decision-making or self managed work team is the kind of change that is often seen as threatening by supervisors and middle managers. Those groups in the organisation that control sizeable resources often see change as a threat.

References

1. Stoner, *Management*, PHI, New Delhi, 1997.
2. S.P. Robbins, *Organisational Behaviour,* PHI, Pvt. Ltd, New Dlehi, 2006.
3. Koontz and Weihrich, *op. cit.*
4. S.P. Robbins, *op. cit.*
5. *Ibid.*

SUGGESTED READINGS

Gray Dessler, *Organisation and Management : A Contingency Approach,* Englewood Cliffs, NJ Printice –Hall, Inc., 1976

Gray Dessler, *Organisation and Management : A Contingency Approach,* Englewood Cliffs, NJ Printice –Hall, Inc., 1976

H. Levinson, " Management by Whose Objectives ? ", *HBR*, 48, Jul-Aug., 1970.

H. Simmon (1957) *Administrative Behaviour,* New York, Mcmillan.

H. G. Hicks and C. R. Gulett, *The Management of Organisations,* New York, McGraw-Hill, 1976.

H. G. Hicks and C. R. Gullett, *Organisations : Theory and Behaviour,* Tokyo McGraw-Hill,1975.

H.G. Hicks and C. R. Gullett, *The Management of Organisations,* Tokyo, McGraw Hill, 1976.

H. G. Hicks and C. R. Gullett, The Management of Organisations, Tokyo, McGraw Hill, 1976.

I. L. Janis, *Victims of Group Think,* Boston, Houghton Mifflin, 1973.

J. L. Gray and F. A. Starke, Organisational Behaviour, Ohio, Charles E. Merrill Co., 1977.

J. L. Gray and F. A. Starke, *Organisational Behaviour,* Charles E. Merril Pub. Co. Ohio, 1977.

John Kotter, *Organisational Dynamics: Diagnosis and Intervention*", Addison-Wesley Publishing Company, Inc. 1978.

Karl W. Deutsch, On Communication Models in the Social Sciences", *Public Opinion Quarterly,* 16, 1952.

L. Porter, E. E. Lawler and J. R. Hackman, *Behaviour in Organisations,* New York, McGraw Hill, 1975.

Larry E. Griener, Patterns of Organisational Change", *Harvard Business Review,* May-June, 1967.

Massie, Joseph L: *Essentials of Management,* New Delhi, Prentice Hall of India Pvt. Ltd., 1973.

P. F. Drucker, " Beyond the Stick and Carrot : Hysteria over the Work Ethic ". *Psychology Today,* Nov., 1973.

Payl Hersey and Kenneth Blanchard, *Management of Organisational Behaviour: Utilising Human Resources,* Prentice-Hall of India, New Delhi, 1982.

Rensis Likert, "The Human Organisation ", S. P. Robbins, *Organisation Theory*, NJ Prentice-Hall, 1983.

T. Herbert, *Dimensions of Organisational Behaviour*, New York, MacMillan 1981.

W. Warner Burke, Jock Fordyce, and Stanley Jacobson, " What is OD ? " *News and Reports from NTL Institute of Applied Behavioural Science*, Vol. 2, No. 3, June, 1968.

W. E. Reif, D. N. Ferrazzi and R. Evans Jr., " Job Enrichment : Who uses it and Why ? "*Business Horizons*, Vol. 17, No. 1 Feb., 1974.

Warren G. Bennis, "Organisation, Dinosaurs and Organisation Development", Organisational Behaviour: A Book of Readings, (ed), Keith Davis, *op. cit.*, Reading No. 37.

PART II

ORGANIZATIONAL BEHAVIOUR

Chapter one

ORGANIZATIOAL BEHAVIOUR: CONCEPT ANALYSIS

Learning Tips

- At the turn of the 20th century there was little concern for human aspects. The emphasis was on manipulation of workplace. For the first time the human side of work was paying attention with the work of mayo. Before discussing Organisational Behaviour, it matter of interest to define Organisation.
- An organisation is a consciously coordinated and structured social unit composed of two or more people that functions on a relatively continuous basis to accomplish a general and selected goals or set of goals. And Organisational Behaviour (OB) is the study and application of knowledge about how people as individuals and groups act with organisation. Thus to reiterate, OB can be defined as the understanding, prediction and management of human behaviour in organisation. It represents the behavioural aspect of management not the whole management. It attempts to provide skills to make managers of today-tomorrow effective. Figure 2.1.1 will exhibit organisation and Organisational Behaviour. And a detailed discussion of OB and its field of study will follow it.

Concept Analysis

Organisational Behaviour (OB) is the study and application of knowledge about how people an individuals and as groups act within organisations. It is a field of study that investigates the impact of individuals groups and structure on behaviour within organisations for the purpose of applying such knowledge toward improving organisations effectiveness. (Robbins, 2002)

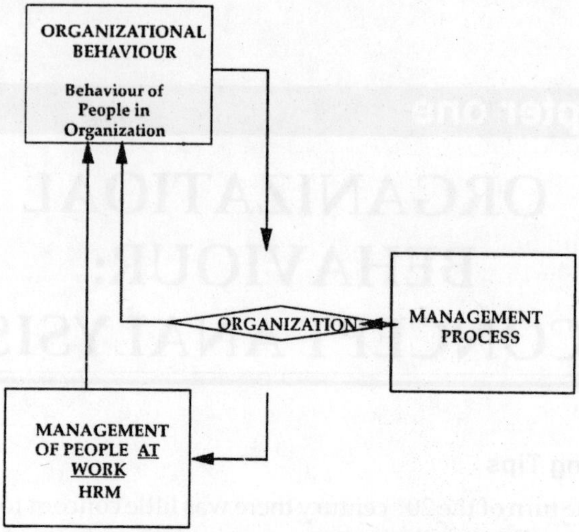

Fig. 2.1.1: Organisation

OB provides useful set tools at many levels of analysis. For example it helps managers look at the behaviour of individuals within an organisation. It also aids their understanding of the complexities involved in interpersonal relations, when two people interact. At the next level, OB is valuable for examining the dynamics of relationship within small groups, both formal teams and informal groups. When two or more groups need to coordinate their efforts, managers become interested in the inter-group relations that emerge. Finally organisations can also be viewed and managed as whole systems that have inter-organisational differences.

Goals of OB

The three primary goals of OB are typical of any science.

- The first is to describe, systematically how people behave under a variety of conditions. Achieving this goal allows managers to communicate about human behaviour at work using a common language.
- A second goal is to understand why people behave as they do. Managers would be highly frustrated if they could only talk about behaviours of their employees, but not understand the reasons behind those actions. Predicting future employee behaviour is another goal of OB. Ideally managers would have the capacity to

predict which employees might be dedicated and productive or which might be absent, tardily or disruptive on a certain day. This would allow them to take preventive actions.

- The final goal of OB is to control and develop some human activity at work. Since managers are held responsible for performance outcomes, they are vitally interested in being able to make an impact on employee behaviour, skill development, team effort and productivity. Managers need to be able to improve results through the OB can aid them in this goal.

Basics

The key elements in OB are people, structure, technology and the environment in which the organisation operates. When people join together in an organisation to accomplish an objective, some kind of structure is required. People also use technology to help get the job done, so there is an interaction of people, structure and technology. (See Figure 2:1.2)

People

People make up the internal social system of the organisation. They consist of individuals and groups and large groups as well as small

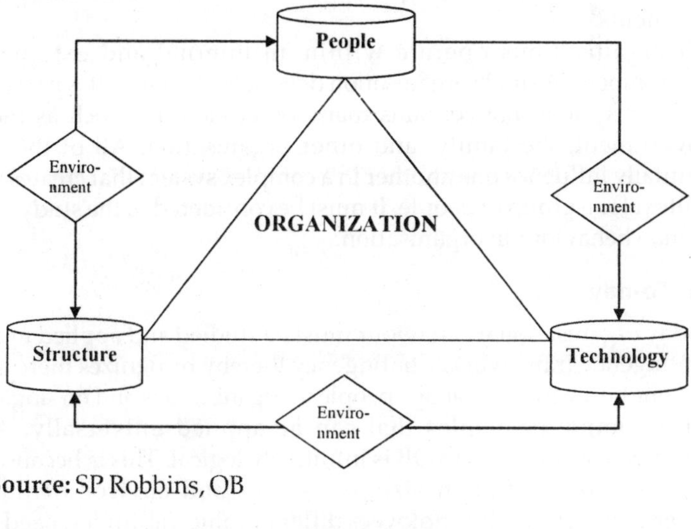

Source: SP Robbins, OB

Fig. 2.1.2

groups. There are unofficial, informal groups and more official formal ones. Groups are dynamic. They form, change and disband. The human organisation today is not the same as it was yesterday. People are living, thinking, feeling beings who work in the organisation to achieve their objectives. Organisations exist to serve people rather than people exist to serve organisation.

Structure

Structure defines the formal relationship of people in organisations. Different jobs are required to accomplish all of an organisation's activities. There are managers and employees. These people have to be related in some structural way so that their work can be effectively coordinated. These relationships create complex problems of cooperation, negotiation and decision-making.

Technology

Technology provides the resources with which people work and affects the tasks that they perform. They cannot accomplish much with their bare hands, so they build buildings, design machines, create work processes and assemble resources. The technology used has a significant influence on working relationships. The great benefit of technology is that it allows people to do more and better work but it also restricts people in various ways. It has costs as well as benefits.

All organisations operate within an internal and external environment. A single organisation does not exist alone. It is part of a larger system that contains many other elements such as the government, the family, and other organisation. All of these mutually influence one another in a complex system that creates a context for a group of people. It must be considered in the study of human behaviour in organisation.

OB To-day

Today organisational behaviour must be studied and applied in a contingency framework. Contingency thereby recognizes there is no "one best way" to manage people in organisations and no single set of simple principles that can be applied universally. A contingency approach to OB is intuitively logical. This is because organisations differ in size, objectives and environmental uncertainty. Similarly employees differ in values, attitudes, needs and experiences. So it would be surprising to find that there are universally applicable principles that work in all situations.

Further, it is to be noted that four r developmental trends enriched OB in India. (Pareek, 2004)

- The increase in the scope of applied behavioural sciences (ABS)
- Relaxing of boundaries between the behavioural sciences.
- Seeing the psychodynamic process as on integrating force for behavioural science research and application.
- Action research.
- Process – Process comprises the underlying human and behavioural dimensions of an organisation. Process – structure-content are interrelated.

Besides, optimistic factors in OB today are

- Characteristic attributed to women
- Strategy of appreciative enquire
- Planning changes driven by futuristic dream rather than analysis of past mistakes.
- Positive approach

FOUNDATIONS OF ORGANISATIONAL BEHAVIOUR (OB)

Although human relationships have existed since the beginning of time, the art and science of trying to deal with them in complex organisations is relatively new. In the early days people worked alone or in such small groups that their work relationships were easily handled. It has been popular to assume that under these conditions people worked in a Uptopia of happiness and fulfillment, but this assumption is largely a nostalgic reinterpretation of history. Human beings and organised activities have been around for thousands of years, but we need not go back beyond the 18th or 19th century to find OB's foundation. The discussion as to foundation of OB can be made under four heads:. (Robbins, 1996)

1. Early practices
2. Classical era
3. Behavioural era
4. OB to-day.

Early Practices

There is no question that hundreds of people helped to plant the 'seeds' from which the OB 'garden' has grown. Three individuals Adam Smith, Charles Babbage and Robert Owen have influenced in shaping the direction and boundaries of OB.

Adam Smith is cited by economists for his contributions to classical economic doctrine but his discussion in *The Wealth of Nations* published in 1776 included a brilliant argument on the economic advantages that organisations and society would reap from the division of labour. Smith concluded that division of labour raises productivity by increasing each worker's skills and dexterity, by saving time that is commonly lost in changing tasks and by encouraging the creation of labour saving inventions and machinery. Charles Babbage, a British mathematics Professor who expanded on the virtues of division of labour first articulated by Adam Smith. In this book *On the Economy of Machinery and Manufacturers*, published in 1832, Babbage added the following to Smith's list of the advantages of division of labour.

- It reduces the time needed for learning a job.
- It reduces the waste of material during the learning stage.
- It allows for the attainment of high skill levels.
- It allows a more careful matching of people's skills and physical abilities with specific tasks.

Robert Owen is important in the history of OB because he was one of the first industrialists to recognize how the growing factory system was demanding to workers. He chided factory owners for treating their equipment better than their employees. He criticized them for buying the best machines, but then proposed a utopian workplace that would reduce the suffering of the working class.

The Classical Era

The classical Covered the period from about 1900 to mid 1930s. It was during this time that the first general theories of management began to evolve. The classical contributors include F. V. Taylor, Henry Fayol, M. P. Follett, C. I. Bernard, etc.

Taylor sought to create a mental revolution among both the workers and management by identifying clear guidelines for improving production efficiency. He defined four principles of management called as scientific management:-

- Develop a science for each element of an individual's work.
- Scientifically select and then train, teach and develop the worker.
- Heartily cooperate with the workers so as to ensure all work is done in accordance with the principles of the science that has been developed.
- Divide work and responsibility almost equally among management and workers.

Administrative theory describes efforts to define the universal functions that managers perform and principles that constitute good management practice. The prolific contributor to administrative theory, Henri Fayol, proposed that all managers perform five management functions, i.e. planning, organising, commanding, coordinating and controlling. In addition, Fayol described the practice of management as something distinct from accounting, finance, production, distribution and other typical business functions. He argued that management was an activity common to all human undertakings in business, in government and even in the home. He formulated 14 principles of management such as division of work, authority, discipline, unity of command, unity of direction, order, subordination of individual interest to general interest remuneration, centralisation, scholar chair, equity, stability, initiative, spirit the crops.

Max Weber, a German sociologist developed a theory of authority structures and described organisational activity as based on authority relations. He was one of the first to look at management and OB from a structural perspective. Weber described an ideal type of organisation that the called bureaucracy. Bureaucracy was a system characterized by division of labour, hierarchy, detailed rules and regulations, impersonal relationships. He meant bureaucracy to be taken as a basis for theorising about work and how work could be done in large groups.

M.P. Follett and C.I. Bernard were two theorists who saw the importance of the social aspects of organisation. M. P. Follett was one of the earliest writers to recognize that organisations could be viewed from the perspective of individual and group behaviour. Individual potential, she argued remains only potential until released through group association. The managers job is to harmonize and co-ordinate group efforts. Follett's humanistic idea has influenced the way we look at motivation, leadership, power and authority today.

C.I. Bernard was influenced by Weber. But unlike Weber who had a mechanistic and impersonal view of organisations, Barnard Saw organisations as social systems that require human co-operation. He expressed his views in *The Functions of the Executive*. Barnard viewed organisations as made up of people who have interacting social relationships. Manager's major roles were to communicate and to stimulate subordinates to high levels of effort. Barnard argued that success depended on maintaining good relations with people and institutions outsides the organisation with whom the organisation regularly interacted.

Behavioural Era

The people side of organisations came into its own during the period we call the behavioural era. This era was marked by human relations movement and the wide spread application in organisations of behavioural science research.

In response to the growth of trade unionism at the turn of the century, some firms crated the position of welfare secretary. Welfare secretaries were supposed to assist workers by suggesting improvements in working conditions, housing, medical care, educational facilities and recreation. These people who were the fore runners of today's personnel or human resource management directors, acted as a buffer between the organisation and its employees.

Hugo Munsterberg created the field of industrial psychology with the publication of his text *Psychology and Industrial Efficiency* in 1913. He argued for the scientific study of human behaviour to identify general patterns and to explain individual differences. Munsterberg saw a link between scientific management and industrial psychology. Munsterberg suggested the use of psychological tests to improve employee selection the value of learning theory in the development of training methods and the study of human behaviour in order to understand what techniques are most effective for motivating workers.

The essence of human relations movement was the belief that the key to higher productivity in organisation was increasing employee satisfaction. In addition to Hawthrone studies, three people played important roles in conveying the message of human reactions, i.e. Dale Carnegie, Abraham Maslow and Douglas McGregor.

Without question, the most important contribution to the human relations movement within organisations behaviour came out of the Hawthrone studies undertaken at the western Electric Company's Hawthrone works in Cicero, Illinois. Scholars agree that Hawthrone studies had a large and dramatic impact on the direction of OB and management practice. Elton Mayo's conclusions were that behaviour and sentiments are closely related, group influences significantly affect individual behaviour, group standards establish individual worker output and money is a less factor in determining output than group standard, group sentiments and security. These conclusions led to a new emphasis on the human factor in the functioning of organisations and the attainment of their goals. They also led to increased paternalism by management.

The essential theme of Dale Carnegie's book *How to Win Friends and influence people* was that the way to success is through winning the co-operation of others.

Abraham Maslow proposed a theoretical hierarchy of five needs: Physiological, safety, social, esteem and self actualisation. From a motivation standpoint, Maslow argued that each step in the hierarchy must be satisfied before the next can be activated and that once a need is substantially satisfied, it no longer motivates behaviour. Moreover he believed that self actualisation, i.e. achieving one's fuel potential is the summit of a human beings existence.

Douglas McGregor best known for his formulation of two sets of assumptions Theory 'X' and 'Y' about human nature. Theory 'x' rests on an essentially negative view of people. It assumes they have little ambition, dislike work, want to avoid responsibility and need to be closely directed to work effectively. Theory 'Y' rests on a positive view of people. It assumes they can exercise self direction, accept responsibility and consider work to be as natural as rest or play. McGreger believed that theory 'Y' assumptions best capture the true nature of workers and should guide management practice.

Jacob Moreno formed an analytical technique called sociometry for studying group interactions. Members of a group were asked whom they liked or disliked and whom they wished to work with or not work with. Moreno's sociometry analysis has been used in organisations to create cohesive and high performing work teams.

B.F. Skinner established that behaviour is a function of its consequences. He found that people wild most likely engage in desired behaviour if they are rewarded for doing so. These rewards are most effective if they immediately follow the desired response and behaviour that is not rewarded or is punished is less likely to be repeated.

David McClelland tested the strength of individual achievement motivation by asking subjects to look at a set of somewhat ambiguous pictures and to write their own story about each subject. Based on these projective tests, McClelland found he was able to differentiate people with a high need to achieve from people with a low need to achieve. McClelland and his associates have successfully trained individuals to increase their achievement drive.

Leadership is one of the most important and extensively explored topics in OB. The work of Fielder on the subject is significant for its emphasis on the situational aspects of leadership as well as for its attempt to develop a comprehensive theory of leadership behaviour.

Frederick Herzberg sought an answer to the question: what do individuals want from their jobs? He concluded that people prefer jobs that offer opportunities for recognition, achievement, responsibility and growth. Managers who concern themselves with issues like company policies, employee pay, creating narrow and repetitive jobs and developing favourable working conditions might placate their workers but they would not motivate them. According to Herzbert if managers want to motivate their people, they should redesign jobs to allow workers to perform more and varied tasks.

J. Richard Hackman and Greg Oldham provided an explanation of how job factors influence employee motivation and satisfaction and would offer a valid framework for analysing jobs. Hackman and Oldham's research uncovered the core job dimensions- skill variety, task identity, task significance, autonomy and feedback. They found that among individuals with strong groom with needs, jobs that score high on these five core dimensions lead to high employee performance and satisfaction.

Components of OB

OB is an interdisciplinary science. Studying phenomena and process of organisation and its various components, is a matter of fact the components and their root disciplines are given below for clear understanding.

1. *Individual*
   - Motivation
   - Perception
   - Personality
   - Personal Effectiveness
   - Decision-making
   - Interpersonal Styles
   - Attitudes

   (The base discipline is psychology)
2. *Roles*
   - Role effectiveness
   - Leadership

- Work Motivation
- Role Stress
- Burnouts
- Coping Abilities

(The base discipline is psychology)

3. *Team*
   - Team Effectiveness
   - Interpersonal Communication
   - Conflict management
   - Consensus Building
   - Developing Collaborations

   (The base disciplines are sociology and psychology)
4. *Organisation*
   - Organisational Culture
   - Organisational Climate
   - Organisational Communication
   - Organisational learning
   - Organisational Change
   - Organisational Development

   (The base discipline is psychology)
5. *Context*
   - Power and Politics-Linked to Political Science
   - Cross Cultural Organisation- Linked to Anthropology
   - Sociocultural values - Linked to Anthropology

Necessarily OB is S-O-B-C paradigm where S stands for situation; O stands for Organisational participants; B stands for Behaviour ; C stands for consequences. Also it is theoretical micro concept of an organisation as given in the following chart.

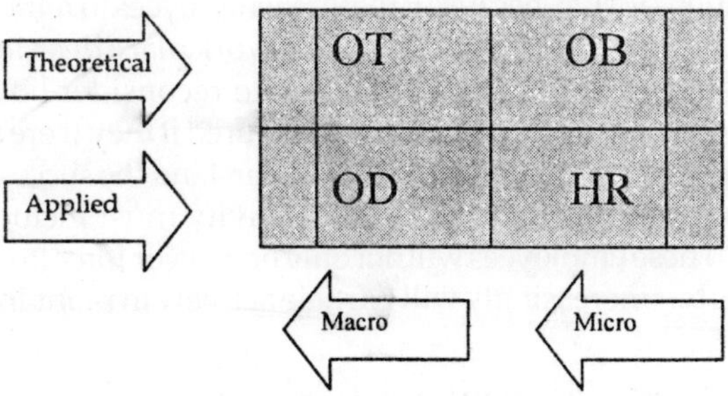

OT- Organisational Theory; OB- Organisational Behaviour; OD- Organisational Development; HR- Human Resources

Further OG is influenced by the following approaches.

- System Approach : Organisation's complex system related to its parts/unit
- Socio-technical System Approach: Technology would influence organisation
- Democratic Approach: Democracy at work place and human dignity/ Participation of actors
- Contingency Approach: Appropriate managerial behavioral capability in situations
- Interactive Approach : Cause and effect relationship /Constant Interaction

CONTEMPORARY CHALLENGES TO OB: Changing Context

There are a lot of challenges today for managers to use OB concept. Diversity in workforce, corporate restructuring and cost cutting, global competition, rapid change and innovation, information technology, etc. have no doubt changed the character of the challenges (Robbins, 1996 & Pareek, 2004)

1. Improving Quality and Productivity

More and more managers are confronting the challenges of improving quality and productivity. They have to improve their organisation's productivity and the quality of the products and services they offer. Towards improving quality and productivity, they are implementing programs like total quality management and reengineering. Total Quality Management (TQM) is a philosophy of management that is driven by the constant attainment of customer satisfaction through the continuous improvement of all organisational processes. TQM has implications for OB, because it requires employees to rethink what they do and become more involved in the work place decisions. The process of reengineering asks managers to reconsider how work would be done and their organisation structured if they were starting over. Today's contemporary managers understand the success of any efforts at improving quality and productivity must include their employees. These employees will not only be a major force in carrying out changes but increasingly will particle actively in planning those changes.

2. Improving People Skills

To cope with the day to day changing scenario, it is to be marked that one of the biggest challenge for the managers in organisation is to improve the skills of their employees. For this reason one has to give insights into specific skills, insights into own behaviour and then the behavour of others.

3. Managing Workforce Diversity

Diversity is of many forms. It is linked with bases of demography, culture, ideology religion, language, etc. It is important at all levels and care should be taken for leveraging diversity.

Workforce diversity is a broad challenge today. It means that organisations are becoming more heterogeneous in terms of gender, race, and ethnicity. It has important implications for management practice. Managers will need to shift their philosophy from treating everyone alike to recognising differences and responding to those differences in ways that will ensure employee retention and greater productivity-while at the same time, not discriminating. Diversity if positively managed, can increase creativity and innovation in organisations as well as improve decision-making by providing different perspectives on problems. When diversity is not managed properly, there is potential for higher turnover, more difficult communication and more interpersonal conflicts.

4. Globalisation

The world has now become a global village. In turn managers have to become capable of working with people from different cultures. Globalisation affects a manager's people skill in at least two ways. First, a manager is increasingly finding himself in a foreign assignment. He has always to cross the border of different countries, facing different needs, aspirations and attitudes. Secondly, even in his own country, he is going to find himself working with bosses, peers and subordinates who were born and raised in different cultures. What motivates a manager may not motivate others. Manager's style of communication may be straight forward and open by which others feel uncomfortable.

5. Empowering People

In many organisations, employees have become associates. There is no clear cut distinction between the roles of managers and workers. Decision-making is being pushed down to the operating level, where workers are being given the freedom to make choices about schedules, procedures and solving work related problems. In the name of participation now managers are going considerably further by allowing employees full control of their work. What is going on is that managers are embowering employees. They are putting employees in charge of what they do. And in doing so, managers have to learn how to give up control and employees have to learn how to take responsibility for their work and make appropriate decisions.

6. Innovation and Change

Today's successful organisations must foster innovation and master the art of change or they will become candidates for extinction. Victory will go to those organisations that maintain their flexibility, continually improve their quality and beat their competence to the market place with a constant stream of innovative products and services. An organisations employee can be the impetus for innovation and change or they can be a major stumbling block. The challenge for managers is to stimulate employee's creativity and tolerance for change. The field of OB provides a wealth of ideas and techniques to aid in realising these goals.

7. Coping with Temporaries

Managers have always been concerned with change. What is different now-a-days is the length of time between change implementations. Today change is an ongoing activity for most managers. Managing in the past could be characterized by long periods of stability, interrupted occasionally by short periods of change. Managing today would be more accurately described as long period of ongoing change interrupted occasionally by short periods of stability. The world that most managers and employees face today is one of permanent "temporaries." Today's managers and employees must learn to cope with temporariness. They have to learn to line with flexibility, spontaneity and unpredictability. The study of OB can provide important insights to better understand a work world of continual change, how to other some resistance to change and how best to create an organisational culture that thrives on change.

8. Declining Employee Loyalty

Corporate employees used to believe their employees would reward their loyalty and good work with job security generous benefits and pay increases. But now-a-days, in response to global competition, unfriendly takeovers and like, corporations began to discard traditional policies on job security-seniority and compensation. These changes have resulted in a sharp decline in employee loyalty. An important OB challenge will be for managers to devise ways to motivate workers who feel less committed to their employers while maintaining their organisations global competitiveness.

9. Improving Ethical Behaviour

Members of organisations are increasingly finding themselves facing ethical problems, situations where they are required to define right and wrong conduct. What constitutes good ethical behaviour has never been clearly defined. In recent years the distinction right from wrong has become more blurred. Employees see people all around them engaging in unethical practices. Managers and their organisations, are responding to this problem from a number of directions. Today's manager needs to create an ethically healthy climate for his employees, where they can do their work productivity and confront a minimal degree of ambiguity regarding what makes up right and wrong behaviour.

10. IT Development

It is an undeniable fact that Information Technological development is the key to information sharing to day. The greatest benefit of it is speedy decision-making. A greater accountability, accessibility, openness is assured. Obviously organisation becomes SMART organisation.

11. Outsourcing

A new concept in Human resource activity – outsourcing affect organisation Outsourcing is nothing but purchasing and selling of function or services form external sources. To meet the challenge organisations should be equipped with counter programmes.

12. Employees and Customer Redefined

Employees are empowered and they have become creative human resources. Likewise customers are enlightened enough to put pressure on organisations as to quality of product and service. Essentially, this changing profile of customers and people in enterprises are changing context of OB

13. Mangement of Privacy

In organisation two issues – Individual privacy and Group privacy – are to be upheld. This will enhance autonomy and reduce vulnerability of organisation (Calhan and Bies :2003 ; Westin :2003)

Further Readings

1. S.P. Robbins, *Organisational Behaviour*, PHI Pvt. Ltd, New Delhi, 2006
2. Gary Dressler, *Organisation and Management; A conlinserey Approach*, Prenlice Hall, 1976.
3. HG Hicks and CR Gullet, *The Management of Organisations*, McGraw Hills 1996.
4. Fred Luthans, *Organisational Behaviours*, McGraw Hill, New York,2000
5. L. Steven, McShane, *Organisational Behaviour*, Tata MacGraw Hill, 2000.

Chapter two

ORGANISATIONAL DESIGN

Organisation is a group of people working together cooperatively under authority toward achieving goals and objectives that mutually benefit the participants and the organisation. But organising is the process of arranging and allocating work, authority and resources among an organisation's members so they can achieve the organisation's goals. Different goals require different structures. So managers must match an organisation's structure to its goals and resources, a process called organisational design. Organisational design is the determination of the organisational structure that is most appropriate for the strategy, people, technology and tasks of the organisation. So the specific pattern of relationships that managers create in this process is called the organisation structure. Organisational structure is a framework that managers devise for dividing and coordinating the activities of members of an organisation.

Organising is an ongoing process. Strategies can change, organisational environments can change and the effectiveness, efficiency and economy of organisational activity do not always measure up-to what managers would like. So managers need to address six key elements[1] when the design their organisational structure.

1. **Work specialisation:** It is also called division of labour. It means the degree to which tasks in the organisation are subdivided into separate jobs. The essence of work specialisation is that, rather than an entire job being done by one individual, it is broken down into a number of steps, each step being completed by a separate individual. In essence, individuals specialize in doing part of an activity rather than the entire activity. Work specialisation also has its disadvantages. It tasks are divided into small, discrete steps, and if each worker is responsible for

only one step, then alienation and the absence of a sense, of control may easily develop.

2. **Departmentalisation:** Once job is divided through work specialisation, it is necessary to group these jobs together so common tasks can be coordinated. So departmentalisation is the grouping into departments of work activities that are similar and logically connected. There are four ways to achieve departmentalisation i.e.
   - By functions performed.
   - By the type of product the organisation produces.
   - On the basis of geography or territory.
   - The particular type of customers the organisation seeks to reach.
3. **Chain of command:** The chain of command or hierarchy is an unbroken line of authority that extends from the top of the organisation to the lowest level and clarifies who reports to whom. Authority and unity of command are two concepts generally interrelated with chain of command. Authority is the rights inherent in a managerial position to give orders and expect the orders to be obeyed. Unity of command means a subordinate should have only one superior to whom he is directly responsible. To facilitate coordination, each managerial position is given a place in the chain of command and each manager is a given degree of authority in order to meet his responsibilities.
   Time changes and so do the basic tenets of Organisation Design. The concepts of chain of command, authority and unity of command have substantially less relevance today because of advancements in computer technology and the trend toward empowering employees.
4. **Span of control:** It is the number of subordinates reporting directly to a given manager. It is important because, it determines the number of levels and managers an organisation has when the span becomes too large, employee performance suffers because supervisors no longer have the time to provide the necessary leadership and support. Small spans have their advocates. By keeping the span of control to 5 or 6 employees, a manager can maintain close control. But small spans have three major drawbacks, i.e.
   1. They are expensive because they add levels of management.
   2. They make vertical communication in the organisation more complex.

3. Small spans of control encourage overly tight supervision and discourage employee autonomy.

5. **Centralisation and decentralisation:** In some organisation's top managers make the decisions. Lower level managers carryout top management's directives. At the other extreme are organisations where decision-making is pushed down to those managers who are closet to the action. The former is centralized, where the latter is decentralized. Centralisation is the degree to which decision-making is concentrated at a single point in the organisation, while in decentralisation; decision discretion is rushed down to lower level employees. Consistent with recent management efforts to make organisations more flexible and responsive, there has been a marked trend toward decentralising decision-making.
6. **Formalisation:** It refers to the degree to which jobs within the organisation are standardized. If a job is highly formalized, then the job incumbent has a minimum amount of discretion over what is to be done, when it is to be done and how he should do it. Employees can be, expected always to handle the same input in exactly the same way, resulting in a consistent and uniform output. There are explicit job descriptions, organisational rules, clearly defined procedures, etc. when formalisation is law, job behaviours are relatively non-programmed and employees have a great deal of freedom to exercise discretion in their work. The degree of formalisation can vary widely between organisations and within organisations.

Types of Organisational Design[2]

Organisational Design is the decision-making process by which managers choose an organisational structure appropriate to the strategy for the organisation and the environment in which members of the organisation carry out the strategy. Organisational design thus has managers looking in two directions. Simultaneously inside their organisation and outside their organisation knowledge about organisational design has evolved over the past century. Initially, organisational design processes were concentrated on the internal workings of an organisation. The above described six elements have rich tradition in the history of management practice. But, gradually the new organisational design has been given more and more managerial attention giving rise to modern approaches to organisation design. The various approaches are types can be classified under the following lines:

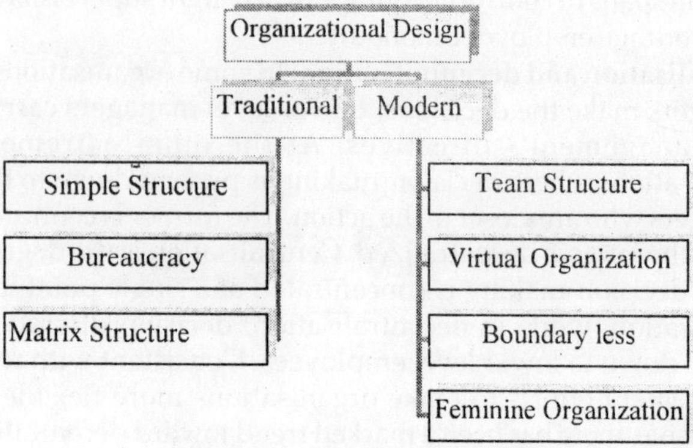

Fig. 2.2.1: Organisational design

Simple structure is a structure characterized by a low degree of departmentalisation, wide spans of control, authority centralized in a single person and little formalisation. Simple structure is not elaborated. It is a flat organisation, the strength of the simple structure lies in its simplicity. It is fast flexible, inexpensive to maintain and accountability is clear. One major weakness is that it is difficult to maintain in anything other than small organisations. It becomes increasingly inadequate as an organisation grows because its low formalisation and high centralisation tend to create information overload at the top.

The bureaucracy is characterized by highly routine operating tasks achieved through specialisation, much formalized rules and regulations, tasks that are grouped into functional departments, centralized authority, narrow spans of control and decision-making that follows the chain of command. The primary strength of bureaucracy lies in its ability to perform standardized activities in a highly efficient manner.

Another popular organisational design is the matrix structure. The matrix combines two forms of departmentalisation i.e. functional and product. The strength of functional departmentalisation lies in putting like specialists together, which minimizes the number necessary, while it allows the pooling and shoring of specialized resources across products. Its major disadvantage is the difficulty of coordinating the task of diverse functional specialists so their activities are completed, on time and within budget. The most structural characteristics of the matrix is that it breaks the unity of command concept. Employees in the matrix have two bosses their functional department managers and their product managers. Therefore, the matrix has a dual chain of command. The strength of the matrix lies in its activity to facilitate co-ordination when the organisation has a multiplicity of complex and interdependent activities. The matrix reduces bureau pathologies. It facilitates the efficient allocation of specialists. The major disadvantageous of the matrix structure lies in the confusion it crates, its prosperity to foster power struggles and the stress it places on individuals.

The primary characteristics of the team structure are that it breaks down departmental barriers and decentralizes decision-making to the level of the work team. Team structures also require employees to be generalists as well as specialists.

Virtual organisation is a small core organisation that outsourcers major business functions. In structural terms, the virtual organisation is highly centralized, with little or no departmentalisation. It stands in sharp contrast to the typical bureaucracy that has many vertical levels of management and where control is sought through ownership. The major advantage to the virtue organisation is its flexibility.

Jack Welch coined the term 'boundary less organisation.' It means an organisation that seeks to eliminate the chain of command have limitless spans of control and replace departments with empowered teams. By removing vertical boundaries, management flatness the hierarchy status and rank are minimized. The organisation looks more like a silo than a pyramid. Cross hierarchical teams, participate decision-making practices and the use of 360° appraisal are some techniques to break down vertical boundaries. Functional departments create horizontal boundaries. The way to reduce these barriers is to replace functional departments with cross functional teams and to organise activities around processes. When fully operational, the boundary less organisation also breaks down barriers to external constituencies and barriers created by geography. Globalisation, strategic alliances, customer organisation linkages are some of the techniques that reduce external boundaries. The one common technological thread that makes the boundary less organisation possible is networked computers. They allow people to communicate across intra organisational and inter organisational boundaries.

Feminine organisation is an organisation characterized by humanistic treatment of individuals, non opportunism, careers defined through service to others, commitment to employee growth, creation of a caring community and power sharing. People are treated as individuals, with individual values and needs, rather than as occupants of offices. Relationships are seen as possessing value in them, not just as formal means to the achievement of organisational goals. Whereas organisation members in a bureaucracy define career success in terms of promotions, acquisition of power and pay increases, organisation members in the feminine model measure success in terms of service to others. Feminine organisations create extensive personal growth opportunities for their members. Members become closely bound in a community sense. In the feminine organisation, information is generously shared. Feminine model may be more effective in organisations that are essentially managed by and for women.

References

1. S.P. Robbins, *Organsational Behaviour*, PHI Pvt. Ltd, New Delhi, 2006
2. Ibid.

Chapter three

ORGANISATIONAL CULTURE

Organisational Culture[1] refers to a system of shared meaning held by members that distinguishes the organisation from other organisations. In other words, it is a set of important understandings, such as norms, values, attitudes and beliefs shared by organisational members.

There are seven primary characteristics than in aggregate, constitutes the essence of organisational culture:

1. **Innovation and risk taking:** The degree to which employees are encouraged to be innovative and take risks.
2. **Attention to detail:** The degree to which employees are expected to exhibit precision, analysis and attention to detail.
3. **Outcome orientation:** The degree to which management focuses on results rather than on the techniques and processes used to achieve these results.
4. **People orientation:** The degree to which management decisions take into consideration the effect of outcomes on peoples within the organisation.
5. **Team orientation:** The degree to which work activities are organised around teams rather than individuals.
6. **Aggressiveness:** The degree to which people are aggressive and competitive rather than easy going.
7. **Stability:** The degree to which organisational activities emphasize maintaining the *status quo* in contrast to growth.

Each of these characteristics exists on a continuum from low to high organisational culture is concerned with how employees perceive the characteristics of an organisation is culture, not with whether or not they like them. It is a descriptive term and it differentiates from that of job satisfaction, which is evaluative.

Organisational culture represents a common perception held by the organisations members. The individuals with different backgrounds or at different levels in the organisation will tend to describe the organisations culture in similar terms. Many organisations have also some subcultures within a dominant culture. A dominant culture expresses the core values that are shared by a majority of the organisations members. Care values mean the primary or dominant values that are accepted throughout the organisation. Subcultures tend to develop in large organisations to reflect common problems, situations or experiences that members face. These subcultures are likely to be defined by department designations and geographical separation. If organisations had no dominant culture and were composed only of numerous subcultures, the value of organisational culture as an independent variable would be significantly lessened because there would be no uniform interpretation of what represented appropriate and inappropriate behaviour. It is the shared meaning aspect of culture that makes it such a potent device for guiding and shaping behaviour.

There are strong and weak cultures also and strong cultures have a great impact on employee behaviour and are more directly related to dipping turnover. In a strong culture, organisations core values are both intensity held and widely shared. The more members who accept the core values and the greater their commitment to those values, the stronger the culture is. A strong culture will have a great influence on the behaviour of its members because the high degree of sharpness and intensify creates an internal climate of high behavioural control. A strong culture demonstrates high agreement among members about what the organisation stands for. A strong organisational culture increases behavioural consistency. The stronger an organisations culture the less management need be concerned with developing formal rules and regulations to guide employee behaviour.

Models of Organisational Culture (OC)—Frameworks For Study

I. Power Model

- Autocratic Culture: Focus on Proper Protocol
- Bureaucratic Culture: Focus on Rules, Regulations and Procedures
- Technocratic Culture: Focus on Perfection
- Entrepreneurial culture: Focus on Result and Customer Satisfaction
- Democratic Culture : Focus on Participation in Decision-making

II. Hofstedes : His Four Dimensions For Organisational Culture

- Individualism Vs Collectivism
- Uncertainty Vs. Avoidance
- Power Distance
- Masculine Vs. Feminist

III. Martin: Three Dimensions for Organisational Culture

- Integrated Level: Common characteristics in groups
- Differentiated level: Different characteristic in different sub-groups
- Fragmented Level: Contradictions and confusions in the groups. (Martin, 1992 in Panda & Gupta, 2001)

Functions of Organisational Culture

The functions organisational culture can be discussed from two angles, i.e. both positive and negative. Positively it performs a number of functions within an organisation.

- It has a boundary defining role that is it creates distinctions between one organisation and others.
- It conveys a sense of identity for organisational members.
- Culture facilitates the generation of commitment to something larger than ones individual self interest.
- It enhances social system stability.
- Culture serves as a sense making and control mechanism that guides and shapes the attitudes and behaviours of employees.

Culture boosts organisational commitment and increase the consistency of employee behaviour. These are clearly benefits to an organisation. From an employees stand point, culture is valuable because it reduces ambiguity.

Dysfunctional Aspects

Nevertheless there are some dysfunctional aspects of culture as given below:

1. It is a barrier to change. It is a liability where the shared values are not in agreement with those that will further the organisations effectiveness. When the environment is undergoing rapid change, the organisations entrenched culture may no longer be appropriate.
2. Culture is a barrier to diversity hiring new employees who because of race, gender, ethnic or other differences are not like

the majority of the organisations members create a paradox. Management wants new employees to accept the organisation's core culture values. But at the same time, management wants to openly acknowledge support for the differences these employees bring to the work place strong cultures put considerable pressure on employees to conform. They limit the range of values and styles that are acceptable obviously this creates a dilemma.

3. Organisational culture is a barrier to mergers and acquisitions. Historically the key factors that management looked at in making merger or acquisition decisions were related to financial advantages. But in recent years, culture compatibility has become the primary concern.

Winding up

An organisation's current customs, traditions and general way of doing things are largely due to what it has done before and the degree of success it has had with those attempts. This leads to the ultimate source of an organisation's culture. Once a culture is practiced within the organisation environment it is the employees to maintain it by adding a set of similar experiences. Selection practices, actions of top management and socialisation methods are three forces to play particularly important part in sustaining a culture. Culture is transmitted to employees in a number of forms, the most potent being stories, rituals, materials symbols and language.

Reference

1. S.P. Robbins, *Organisational Behaviour*, PHI, New Delhi, 2006.

Chapter four

ORGANISATIONAL CHANGES

Change is alien to organisational life. Yet it is inevitable. To put it in other words, it is the only constant in life. Every individual and organisation should accept change as if; it is a way of life. More and more organisations today face a dynamic and changing environment that, in turn, requires these organisations to adopt and then adopt. There are many forces that are acting as stimulants for change. These forces are changing nature of workforce, technology, economic hazards, competition, social trend and the global political scenario.

Dimensions of OC

Organisational Change is a multifaceted phenomenon. A number of dimensions exit as to it.

- It is a sequential process.
- In it there is the role of Corporate management, consultant for chance, Organisational counterpart, and Implementation Team and chief implementer to put into practice and Task force to complete the task.
- Several factors of Implementation

Fullen & Pomfret (1977) recommended four ways of Implementations:

A. Innovation, B. Strategy and Tactics, C. Characteristics of Adopting Units, D. Characteristics of Macro socio-political units. Also it is marked that the implementation is an intricate process and requires a great amount of attention to 1. Planning, 2. Monitoring, 3. Action, 4. adoption, and Support. Word Bank Document (1997) highlighted planning, phasing, process, strategies and monitoring for the implementation of change.

Obviously, Implementation Team, minimum control, review and feedback, sharing of information, action, adoption, support of – training, resources, top management, link and net work and commitment are basic requirement of change in organisation.
A model to elaborate implementation is given below in Figure 2.4.1 for better clarity of understanding.

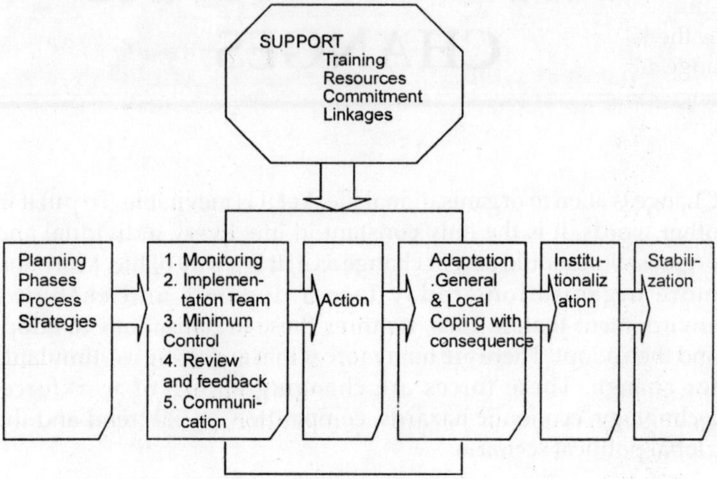

Fig. 2.4.1

Source: This model is taken from Uday Pareek, 2004 p. 478.

Managing Change[1]

Change means to make things different. Planned change means that is intentional and global oriented. So it can be defined as a systematic attempt to redesign an organisation, in a way that will help it adapt to changes in the external environment or to achieve new goals. It is mandatory for all the managers to improve their ability to manage change. Many large organisations have explicit change management programmes to increase the ability of the people throughout the organisation to anticipate and learn from the changes that are occurring. Then first the manager has to know the goal of change and source of change. There are two goals of planned change. First it seeks to improve the ability of the organisation to adopt to changes in its environment. Second, it seeks to change employee behaviour. If an organisation is to survive, it must respond to changes in its environment. Since an organisations success or failure is essentially due to the things its employees do or fail to do, planned change also is concerned with changing the behaviour of individuals, and groups within the organisation. Manager must think planned change in its order of magnitude. First order change is linear and continuous. It implies no fundamental shift in the assumptions that organisation members hold about the world or how the organisation can improve its functioning. The second order change is multidimensional, multi level, discontinuous, radical change in framing of assumptions about the organisation. Sources of change mean change agents. Change agents are the persons who act as catalysts and assume the responsibility for meaning change activities. The change agents can bring change in four categories.

1. Structure
2. Technology
3. Physical setting
4. People

Changing structures involve making an alteration in authority relations, coordination mechanisms, job redesign or similar structural variables. This might include a shift from a simple structure to a team based structure or the creation of a matrix design. Changing technology encompass modifications in the way work is processed and in the methods and equipment used. Automation is a technological change that replaces people with machines. Changing the physical setting covers altering the space and layout arrangements in the workplace. Changing people refers to changes is employee attitudes, skills, expectations, perceptions and behaviour.

Approaches to Management of Change[2]

There are some approaches or techniques to managing change. One such approach is Lewin's three step model. Organisations may be in a state of equilibrium, with forces pushing for change on one hand and forces resisting change by attempting to maintain the *status quo* on the other. Kurt Lewis expressed this phenomenon in his field force theory which suggests that an equilibrium is maintained by driving forces and restraining forces. Draining forces mean the forces that direct behaviour away from the *status quo*. Restraining forces mean the forces that hinder movement away from the *status quo*. In managing charge, the tendency is to increase the driving forces. The change process involves three steps:

1. Unfreezing

2. Moving
3. Refreezing.

Unfreesing creates motivation for change. If people feel uncomfortable with the present situation, they may see the need for change. The second stage is the change itself. This change may occur through assimilation of new information, exposure to new concepts or development of a different perspective. The third stage refereeing stabilizes the change.

Change to be effective has to be congruent with a person's self-concept and values. If the change is incongruent with the attitudes and behaviours of others in the organisation, chances are that the person will revert back to the old behaviour. Thus reinforcement of the new behaviour is essential.

Another approach is action research with is a change process based on systematic collection of data and then selection of a change action based on what the analyzed data indicate. The process consists of five steps.

1. Diagnosis
2. Analysis
3. Feedback
4. Action
5. Evaluation.

The change agent is often on outsider in action research. It begins by gathering information about problems, concerns and needed changes from members of the organisation. The information gathered during the diagnostic stage is then analyzed. Action research includes extensive involvement of the change targets. That is the people who will be involved in any change program must be actively involved in determining what the problem is and participating in creating the solution. So the third step is sharing with employees what has been found in first and second step. The employees with the help of the change agent develop action plans for bringing about any needed change. Finally, consistent with the scientific underpinnings of action research the change agent evaluates the effectiveness of the action plans.

Resistance to Change[3]

Organisations and their members resist change. In a sense, this is positive. It provides a degree of stability and predictability to behaviour. If these were not some resistance organisational behaviour would take on characteristics of chaotic randomness.

Resistance to change can also be a source of functional conflict. Resistance to change does not necessarily surface in standardized ways. Resistance can be avert implicit, immediate or deferred. It is easiest for management to deal with resistance when it is overt and immediate. The greater challenge in managing resistance that is implicit or deferred. Generally there are two sources of resistance i.e. individual resistance and organisational resistance.

Individual resistance[4]: Individual sources of resistance to change reside in basic human characteristics such as perceptions, personalities and needs. There are five reasons why individuals resist change, i.e.

- Habit
- Security
- Economic
- Fear of the unknown
- Selective information processing.

Human beings are creatures of habit. Life is very complex. It is not possible for the human being to consider the full range of options for the hundred of decisions, made everyday. To cope with this we rely on habits or programmed responses. When confronted with change, this tendency to respond in our accustomed ways becomes a source of resistance. People with a high need for security are likely to resist change because it threatens their feeling of safety. Another source of individual's resistance is concern that changes will lower ones income i.e. economic factors. Changes substituted ambiguity and uncertainty for the known. Finally individuals shape their world throughout their perceptions. Once they have created this world it resists change. So individuals are quality of selectively processing information in order to keep their perceptions intact.

Organisational Resistance[5]: By nature, organisations are conservative. They actively resist change. The major sources of organisational resistance are:-

- Structural inertia
- Limited focus of change
- Group inertia
- Threat to expertise
- Threat to established power relationships or Fear of loss of Power
- Threat to established resource allocations. Or Fear of inadequate resources
- Vested Interest

- Fear of over load of work
- Fear of large scale disturbances
- Fear of Obsolesce
- Indifference of Top Management.

Organisations have built in mechanisms to produce stability. The people help in building stability. The people who are hired into an organisation are chosen for fit. They are then shaped and directed to behave in certain ways. When an organisation is confronted with change, this structural inertia acts as a counter balance to sustain stability. Organisations are made up of a number of interdependent subsystems. One can not change a particular subsystem with out affecting the other. Even if individuals want to change their behaviour, group norms may act as a constraint. So here, the group inter resists change changes in organisational patterns may threaten the expertise of specialized groups. Any redistribution of decision-making authority can threaten long established power relationships within the organisation. The introduction of participative decision-making or self managed work teams is the kind of change that is often seen as threatening by supervisors and middle managers. Those groups in the organisation that control sizable resources often see change as a threat.

How to Overcome Resistance to Change?

There are six techniques are suggested for change agents in dealing with resistance to change. They are:

a. Proper education and good communication.
b. Participation or integrating employees in decision-making process.
c. Offering facilitation and supportive effort like counseling therapy, new skill training, etc.
d. Negotiating the situation tactfully.
e. Clever manipulation after analysing the situation properly.
f. Coercion or application of direct threat or force on the resisters.

References

1. Struner & Ors, *Management*, PHI, 1997
2. S.P. Robbins, *Organisational Behaviour*, PHI, New Delhi, 2006
3. Koontz and Weihrich, *Essentials of Management*
4. SP Robbins, *Organisational Behaviour*, PHI, New Delhi, 2006.
5. *Ibid*.

Chapter five

ORGANISATIONAL DEVELOPMENT

Organisation Development is a mode of introducing planned change in an organisational setting. Often the connotation has been used very widely. Sometimes in the mid 1940s training programmes began to take a different perspective. Instead of concentrating of skill development in operational matters, management experts developed a feeling that if successful performance and decision-making in organisation can be optimized the inter-actional attitudes and habits of the individuals, who compose the organisation could be changed. They termed this change as a change in organisational climate. The trend to emphasise improves interpersonal relations as a means of Organisational Development (OD). In essence OD is both an educational strategy and on implemented course of action which focuses attention on the whole culture of an organisation in order to bring about a planned change.

OD is a collection of planned change interventions, built an humanistic democratic values that seek to improve organisational effectiveness and employee well being. Bennis has stated that, "OD is a response to change, a complex educational strategy intended to change the beliefs, attitudes, values and structure of organisations so that the can better adopt themselves to new technology markets and challenges and the dizzying rate of change itself. It aims at developing the organisation into an organic system as a contrast to the mechanical system." According to Wenderall French,[1] 'OD refers to a long range effort to improve an organisations problem solving capabilities and its ability to cope with changes in its external environment with the help of external or internal behavioural scientist consultants or change agents as they are sometimes called." According to Blake and Mouton,[2] "OD is a systematic way of introducing change based on a structural model for thinking, progressing in a programmatic sequence of steps from individual learning to organisation application, focused upon those silent and often negative attributes of culture which dictate action that so frequently contradict business logic, with emphasis on confronting and resolving conflict as a pre-requisite to valid problem solving and employing a variety of techniques of organisational study and self learning to bring about the necessary change."

To this a better definition of OD has been forwarded by Uday Pareek. OD is a planned effort initiated by process specialist(s) to help an organisation develop its diagnostic skills, coping capabilities, linkage strategies and a culture of mutuality (Pareek, 2004). Necessarily it is an method of inculcating planned and process oriented change in an organisation. To repeat it again, dimensions to OD as per Pareek are the following :

- A Planned effort
- Initiated by Process Specialists
- Diagnostic skills
- Coping capabilities
- Linkage strategies
- Culture and mutuality.

Characteristics[3]

The chief characteristics of OD are:

- It is an educational strategy which attempts to bring about a planned change.
- It relates to real organisational problems instead of hypothetical classroom cases.
- It uses sensitivity training methods and emphasizes the importance of experimentally based training.
- Its change agents are almost external consultants outside of the organisation.
- External change agents and internal organisation executives establish a collaborative relationship involving mutual trust and influence and jointly determine goals.
- External change agents are humanists seeking to establish a social and altruistic philosophy within an organisation.

Importance

OD values human and organisational growth, collaborative and participative processes and a spirit of inquiry. The following points identify the values in most OD efforts.

- *Respect for people:* Individuals are perceived as being responsible, conscientious and caring. They should be treated with dignity and respect.
- *Trust and support:* The effective and healthy organisation is characterized by trust authenticity, openness and a supportive climatic.
- *Power equalisation:* Effective organisations de-emphasize hierarchical authority and control.
- *Confrontation problems* should not be swept under the rug. They should be openly confronted.
- *Participation*: The more that people who will be affected by a change are involved in the decisions surrounding that change, the more they will be committed to implementing those decisions.

Goals[4]

OD seeks to change the organisational environment in which a manager works. It aims at the improvement of the total system to ensure that the full potential of a manager's ability is utilised, and there is a sustained change in his behaviour which is conducive to a better organisational performance. The goals of OD are:

1. To develop self-renewing, viable system which can be organised in a variety of ways, depending on the tasks that are to be performed?
2. To increase the level of trust and support among an organisation's members.
3. To create an environment in which authority assigned role is augmented by authority based on knowledge and skill.
4. To increase the openness and authenticity of communications laterally, vertically and diagonally.
5. To increase the openness and authenticity of communications laterally, vertically and diagonally.
6. To optimize the effectiveness of both the stable and the temporary systems through which much of an organisation's work is accomplished by built in and continuous improvement mechanisms.
7. To move towards high collaboration and low competition between inter dependent units.
8. To create conditions in which conflict is effectively management.
9. To reach the point where decisions are taken on the basis of an information source rather than an organisation's role.

10. To enhance the identification of members and group with the organisation as a whole.
11. To assist managers in setting challenging but realistic goals for themselves.

So, the goals of OD are linked to the following actors and the components of OD are:

• The Person	Individual
• The Inter-person	Individual Competition
• Team	Groups
• Inter-teams	Interface between Groups
• Organisation	Stability to cope with Individual team Interact with environment, and interface with environment.

OD Techniques

Some techniques are suggested for brining about change. These are:

- Sensitivity training
- Survey feedback
- Process consultation
- Team building
- Inter-group development

In sensitivity training, training groups seek to change behaviour through structured group interaction. It is also called laboratory training or T-Group training. Members are brought together in a free and open environment in which participants discuss themselves and their interactive processes. The objective of T-group is to provide the subjects with increased awareness of their own behaviour and how others perceive them. In survey feedback questionnaires used to identify discrepancies among members perceptions. Discussion follows and remedies are suggested. Everyone in an organisation can participative in survey feedback. In process consultation, consultant gives client insights into what is going on around the client, within the client and between the client and other people, identifies processes that need improvement. Team building utilises high interaction among team members to increase trust and openness. Team building can be applied within groups or at the inter-group level where activities are interdependent. A major area of concern in OD is the distant. A major area of concern in OD is the dysfunctional conflict that exists between groups. As a result this has been a subject to which change efforts have been directed. Inter-group development seeks to change the attitudes, stereotypes and perceptions that groups have of each other.

References

1. W.L. French and Don Hellregial, *Personal Management and Organisation Development; Fields in Transition*, Houghton Mifflin, Boston, 1971.
2. R. Bloke and J. S. Mouton, *Building a Dynamic Corporation through Grid Organisation development*, Addison Wesley, Readings, 1969.
3. C.B. Mamoria, *Personnel Management*, Himalaya Publishing House.
4. W.L. French, *op. cit.*

SUGGESTED READINGS

For Part One : Organisation Behaviour

Culhan M. J. and R. J. Bies(2003) Consumer Privacy: Balancing Economic and Justice Considerations'. *Journal of Social Issues*, 59(2) pp 232-342.

D. N. Dhanagare, (2003) ' Globalisation: Towards an Alternative view. Sociological Bulletin, 52(1) pp 4-31.

Fred Luthans (2002) OB New York, MCGraw-Hill.

Gray Dessler, *Organisation and Management : A Contingency Approach*, Englewood Cliffs, NJ Printice –Hall, Inc., 1976

H. Levinson, " Management by Whose Objectives ? ", *HBR*, 48, Jul-Aug., 1970.

H. Simmon (1957) *Administrative Behaviour*, New York, Mcmillan.

H. G. Hicks and C. R. Gulett, *The Management of Organisations*, New York, McGraw-Hill, 1976.

H. G. Hicks and C. R. Gullett, *Organisations : Theory and Behaviour*, Tokyo McGraw-Hill 1975.

H. G. Hicks and C. R. Gullett, The Management of Organisations, Tokyo, McGraw Hill, 1976.

H. G. Hicks and C. R. Gullett, The Management of Organisations, Tokyo, McGraw Hill, 1976.

I. L. Janis, Victims of Group Think, Boston, Haughton Mifflin, 1973.

J. L. Gray and F. A. Starke, *Organisational Behaviour*, Ohio, Charles E. Merrill Co., 1977. W. e. Reif, D. N. Ferrazzi and R. Evans Jr., " Job Enrichment : Who uses it and Why ? "*Business Horizons*, Vol. 17, No. 1 Feb., 1974.

J. L. Gray and F. A. Starke, *Organisational Behaviour*, Charles E. Merril Pub. Co. Ohio, 1977.

John Kotter, *Organisational dynamics : Diagnosis and Intervention*, Addison-Wesley Publishing Company, Inc. 1978.

Karl W. Deutsch, "On Communication Models" in the Social Sciences", Public Opinion Quarterly, 16, 1952.

L. Porter, E. E. Lawler and J. R. Hackman, Behaviour in Organisations, New York, McGraw Hill, 1975.

Larry E. Griener, " Patterns of Organisational Change", *Harvard Business Review*, May-June, 1967.

Massie, Joseph L: *Essentials of Management*, New Delhi, Prentice Hall of India Pvt. Ltd., 1973.

P. F. Drucker, " Beyond the Stick and Carrot: Hysteria over the Work Ethic ". *Psychology today*, Nov., 1973.

P. N. Khandwalla (ed) (1988), *Development : A New Role for the Organisational Science*, ND, Sage.

Payl Hersey and Kenneth Blanchard, *Management of Organisational Behaviour : Utilising Human Resources*, Prentice-Hall of India, New Delhi, 1982.

R. A. Swanson and E. F. Holton (2001) *Foundations of Human Resource Development*, San Fransisco.

Rensis Likert, *The Human Organisation* ,

S. P. Robbins, *Organisation Theory*, NJ Printice-Hall, 1983.

T. Herbert, *Dimensions of Organisational Behaviour*, New York, MacMillan 1981.

Udai Pareek (2002) *Effective Organisations: Beyond Management to Institution Building*,Oxford & IBA

- (2004)Understanding Organisational Behaviour, Oxford

W. Warner Burke, Jock Fordyce, and Stanley Jacobson, " What is OD ? " *News and Reports* from NTL Institute of Applied Behavioural Science, Vol. 2, No. 3, June, 1968.

Warren G. Bennis, "Organisation, Dinosaurs and Organisation Development", *Organisational Behaviour: A Book of Readings*, (ed), Keith Davis, op. cit., Reading No. 37.

PART III

HUMAN RESOURCE MANAGEMENT

Chapter one

HRM: CONCEPT ANALYSIS

Learning Tips

- Concept of Human Resource Management
- In, on and out of Human Resource in the Organisation, More clearly it deals with Human Resource Planning, Job, Analysis, Recruitment and selection. So far as continuities of HR are concerned orientation, promotion, transfer, training, performance management and Management Development are discussed.
- Only salary administration and retirement and fringe benefits are not explained here.
- Besides employer-employee relations, Human Resource Audit, HRIS, and future of HRM are analysed in brief.

Meaning and Definition

Human Resource Management (HRM) is a management function that helps managers to recruit, select, train and develop employees for an organisation. Obviously, HRM is concerned with the people's dimension in organisations or management of people at work. It is a series of integrated decisions that form the employment relationship; their quality contributes to the ability of the organisations and the employees to achieve their objective. It is concerned with the people dimension in management. Since every organisation is made up of people, acquiring their services, developing their skills, motivating them to higher levels of performance and ensuring that they continue to maintain their commitment to the organisation are essential for achieving organisational objectives. This is true, regardless of the type of organisation-government, business, education, health, recreation or social action. Again HRM is the planning, organising, directing and controlling of the procurement, development, compensation, integration, maintenance and separation of human resources to the end that individual organisational and social objectives are accomplished. So the core points in HRM are:[1]

1. Organisations are not mere bricks, machineries or inventories. They are people. It is the people who staff and manage organisations.
2. HRM involves the application of management functions and principles. The functions and principles are applied to acquisitioning, developing, maintaining and remunerating employees in organisations.
3. Decisions relating to employees must be integrated. Decisions on different aspects of employees must be consistent with other human resource decisions.
4. Decision made must influence the effectiveness of an organisation. Effectiveness of an organisation must result in betterment of services to customers in the form of high quality products supplied at reasonable costs.
5. HRM functions are not confined to business or administration only. They are applicable to non-business organisations too.

Thus, HRM refers to a set of programmes, functions and activities designed and carried out in order to maximize both employee as well as organisational effectiveness.

Scope

The scope of HRM is indeed vast. All major activities in the working life of a worker from the time of his or her entry into an organisation until he or she leaves – come under the purview of HRM. See Figure 3.1.1 for details.

Specifically, the activities of HRM are HR planning, job analysis and design, recruitment and selection, orientation and placement, training and development, performance appraisal and job evaluation, employee and executive remuneration, motivation and communication, welfare, safety and health, industrial relations and the like. For the sake of convenience all these functions can be categorized into seven sections:

- Introduction to HRM
- Employee hiring
- Employee and executive remuneration
- Employee motivation
- Employee maintenance

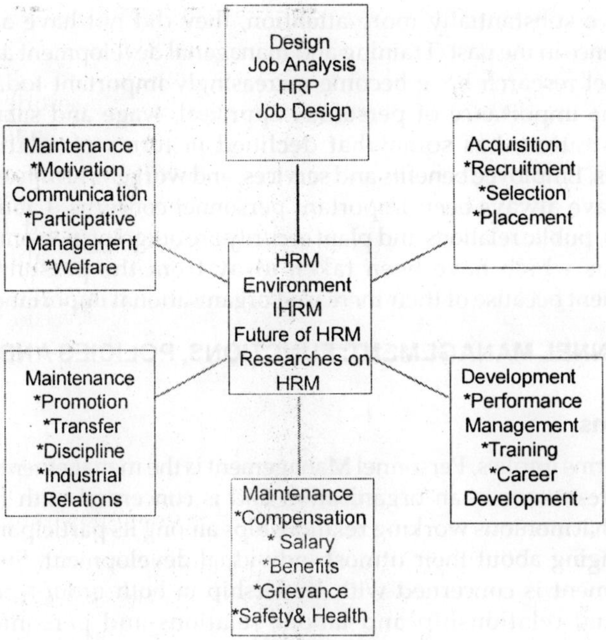

Fig. 3.1.1

- Industrial relations
- Prospects of HRM.

Changing scope

The scope of IIRM has changed somewhat over the last few decades. However this change has been relatively slow in comparison to the changes in other areas of business, management and administration. Sikula observes: "Changes definitely are taking place in HRM. Some personnel subfunctions seem to be breaking away from personnel, others seem to be new sub area while still others seem to be changing only in terms of their relative emphasis and degree of importance." Many of these changes depend on the size of an organisation in which the personnel function occurs, the managerial personnel philosophies, the growing importance of the functions, the changing organisational demands, employee needs and societal concerns. Managerial and organisational development, manpower planning, organisational planning are incoming areas, i.e. they are now going to receive substantially more attention, they did not have any prominence in the past. Training and managerial development and personnel research have become increasingly important today, while the importance of personnel appraisal, wage and salary administration, has somewhat declined in terms of relative emphasis. Employee benefits and services, and worker's health and safety have always been important personnel concerns. Labour relations, public relations and plant security are outgoing personnel sub-areas which have been taken away from the personnel department because of their increased organisational importance.

PERSONNEL MANAGEMENT: FUNCTIONS, POLICIES AND ROLES

Functions

As the terms implies, Personnel Management is the management of human resources in an organisation and is concerned with the making harmonious working relationships among its participants and bringing about their utmost individual development. Such management is concerned with leadership in both groups and individual relationship and labour relations and personnel management. In fact personnel management undertakes all those activities which are concerned with human elements or relations as well as with material elements in an organisation. Whatever may be the functions, the main objective is to bring together expertise in a scientific way and to create attitudes that motivate a group to achieve its go a economically, effectively and speedily.

Classification of Functions[2]

Broadly speaking experts have generally classified the functions into two major categories, such as a) managerial functions, b) and operative functions. Others have classified functions as general and specific functions and yet others as personnel administration function and Industrial Relations functions. So the classification of functions has been discussed as given below:

(a) General and Specific Functions.

Under General type of functions, the personnel management is required

- to conduct personnel research.
- to assist in programmes of personnel administration.
- to develop appraisal plans.

- to launch education and training programmes.
- to develop a competent workforce.
- to establish and administer varied personnel services delegated to personnel department.

Under specific functions, the personnel management may involve the areas of employment, safety, wage and salary, benefit schemes, community relations, advice and counseling the employees.

(b) Personnel Administration and Industrial Relations Functions

- Personnel Administration function relate to the function of managing people from the lower to the upper level of the organisation and embraces policy determination as well as implementation of policies by the personnel at lower levels.
- Industrial Relations functions on the other hand are not directly related to the function of managing people but refer to interactions between the management and the representatives of the unions.

(c) Functions classified on the basis of Capacities

This classification has been adopted by Saltonstall. According to him, although personnel management's functions is the staff function. It also performs three roles:

- He performs a line function not only because he directs the work in his own department but also in some service functions. Such as recruitment, administration of benefits, the plant canteen and allied activities.
- He functions as a coordinator of personnel activities, in so far as he controls the functions of other departments.
- He performs a typical staff functions in the form of assisting and advising the line personnel to solve their problems.

(d) Functions according to the Degree of Authority

Dale Henning and French made an interesting observation that, "the personnel man as described in text books and journals is like – Abominable snowman" much talked about but seldom seen. They have classified their function into three categories:

- Area of maximum authority, e.g. direction of pay roll calculations, orientation procedure, transfer, rules, etc.
- Area of combined use of authority and persuasion e.g., establishment of disciplinary procedure, inter-departmental data

gathering, determining the number of participants in a training programme, etc.

- Area of maximum persuasion, are salary changes under the rules of the plant, employment of individuals, initiating disciplinary action, etc.

Functions of personnel management can be discussed under two broad heads, i.e.

- Managerial Functions
- Operative Functions.

Managerial Functions

Management is a multipurpose action which has three pieces of work, two of which are directly related to 1) personnel managing a business; 2) Managing managers, and managing workers; and 3) the work. Thus a personnel manager is a manager and as such he must perform the basic functions of management. He exercises authority and leadership over other personnel. His functions involve POSDCORB, i.e. planning, organising, staffing, directing, co-ordination, Reporting and budgeting.

1. Planning: Planning is a predetermined course of action. According to Allen, "it is a trap laid to capture the future." Terry is of the view that, "Planning is the foundation of most successful actions of the plans, strategies, programmes, policies, procedures and standards needs to accomplish the desired organisation objectives. In fact planning today avoids crisis of tomorrow. The two most important features of planning are research and forecasting. These two are inter-related. Forecast is possible only as a result of research. Personnel management should be able to predict trends in wages, in labour market, in union demands, in other benefits and in personnel policies and programmes. The task of forecasting personnel needs in relation to changes in production is extremely important, both for employees and management.

2. Organising: After a course of action has been determined, an organisation established to carry it out. This is done by designing the structure of relationships among jobs personnel and physical factors. An organisation is the wedding of authority and responsibility, because, in its essentials, it consists of the assignment of specific functions to designated persons or departments with authority to have them carried out, and their accountability to management for the results obtained. It seeks to achieve the maximum return with minimum effort by decentralisation, whereby the power of decisions is brought down as near as possible to the individual concerned. How far this can be done will depend upon the top management's philosophy and appreciation of the benefits of delegation and decentralisation.

3. Directing: Directing the subordinates at any level is a basic function of the managerial personnel. According to McGregor, "Many managers would agree that the effectiveness of their organisation would be at least doubled if they could discover how to tap the unrealized potential present in their human resources." Directing is involved with getting persons together and asking them to work willingly and effectively for the achievement of designated goals. Directing deals not only with the dissemination of orders within an organisation units and departments, but also with the acceptance and execution of these orders by the employees. The decisions are taken by the top management, but only after consultation with the personnel department. A review or checking of the safety installments, wage rate ranges, disciplinary action and general wage changes are all the responsibility of the personnel department. Final action is taken only when the green signal has been obtained from it.

4. Coordinating: Coordinating refers to balancing, timing and integrating activities in an organisation, so that a unit of action in pursuit of a common purpose is achieved. Coordination in the management of personnel takes place at all levels, from the top management through to the supervisor and those for whom he is responsible. The personnel department has to coordinate the tasks of developing, interpreting and reviewing personnel policies, practices and programmes, such as safety programmes, employee benefits, job evaluation, training or development and communication. These activities are generally put into operation by and through the line people, but it is the personnel department which follows them through, unifies them, and checks to see how they work.

5. Controlling: Controlling is the act of checking, regulating and verifying whether everything occurs in conformity with the plan that has been adopted, the instructions issued and the principles established. It is greatly concerned with actions and remedial actions. It is through control that actions and operations are adjusted to predetermined standards and its basis is information in the hands of the managers. By check, analysis and review, the personnel department assists in realising the personnel objectives. Auditing training programmes, analysing labour turn over records, directing morale surveys, conducting separation interviews, interviewing new employees at stipulated intervals comparing various features of the programmes with other organisation programmes in the area, industry and nation – these are some of the means for controlling the management of personnel. This monitoring process provides management with actual performance information for comparison with predetermined performance standards. If there are unavoidable deviations from the planned performance, corrective action can be taken immediately.

Operative Functions

The operative function of personnel management is concerned with the activities specifically dealing with procuring, developing, compensating and maintaining an efficient workforce. These functions are also known as service functions.

1. The procurement function is concerned with obtaining of a proper kind and number of personnel necessary to accomplish an organisation goal. It deals specifically with such subjects as the determination of manpower requirements, their recruitment, selection and placement, induction follow-up, transfers, lay offs, discharge and separation, etc.
2. The development functions are concerned with the personnel development of employees by increasing their skill through training so that job performance is properly achieved. Drafting and directing training programmes for all levels of employees, arranging for their on the job, office and vestibule training, holding seminars and conferences, providing for educational and vocational counseling and appraising employee potential and performance are under taken under this function.
3. The compensation function is concerned with securing adequate and equitable remuneration to personnel for their contribution to the attainment of organisational objectives, functions related to wage surveys, establishment of job classifications, job descriptions and job analyses, merit ratings, the establishment of wage rates and wage structure, wage plans and policies, wage

systems, incentives and profit sharing plans, etc. fall under this category.

4. Integration function deals with the integration of human resources with organisation and to cope with inevitable conflicts that ensure. Integration is concerned with the attempt to effect a reasonable reconciliation of individual, societal and organisation interests. It rests on the premise that significant overlapping of interests do exist in the organisation in such programmes as job enlargement, job evaluation, variable compensation plans. The greater the overlap, the more productivity would coincide with employee satisfaction. The organisation often expects things from employees that they would prefer to avoid. For this reason, organisations have disciplinary action programmes as well as some freedom to do away with the services of particular employees.
5. The maintenance function deals with sustaining and improving the conditions that have been established. Specific problems to maintain the physical conditions of employees and employee service programmes are the responsibility of the personnel department.

IIPM'S Concept:[3] The Indian Institute of Personnel Management (IIPM), Calcutta classifies the functions of personnel management into following categories:

- Improvement of industrial relations.
- Promotion of joint consultation.
- Helping management to formulate a labour policy and improving communication between management and employees.
- Advising the management on the fulfillment of statutory obligations relating to safety, health, and welfare of the employees.
- Improving factory amenities and welfare provisions, and
- Advising the management on the training and further education of employees.

In sum, IIPM is of he view that all those functions which are concerned with the human element in industry, as distinct from the mechanical elements, may be categorized into three classes—welfare activities to labour or personnel aspects and industrial relations aspects.

Functional Areas of Personnel Management: On the basis of the various functions which the personnel management generally undertaken, the functional areas of personnel management may be set forth as below:

1. Organisational planning, development and task specialisation.
2. Staffing and employment.
3. Training and development.
4. Compensation, wage and salary administration.
5. Motivation and incentives.
6. Employee services and benefits.
7. Employee records
8. Labour or industrial relations, and
9. Personnel Research and Personnel Audit.

Policies[4]

The dictionary meaning of 'policy' is a 'plan of action' and that 'plan' is a policies. According to Flippo, "policy is a man-made rule of pre-determined course of action that is established to guide the performance of work toward the organisation objectives. It is a type of standing plan that serves to guide subordinates in the execution of their tasks." According to Calhoon, "personnel policies constitute guides to action. They furnish the general standards or bases on which decisions are reached. Their genesis lies in an organisation's values, philosophy, concepts and principles."

Thus personnel policies refer to principles and rules of conduct which formulate, redefine, break into details and decide a number of actions that govern the relationship with employees in the attainment of the organisation objectives. Personnel policies are the key stone in the arch of management and the life blood for the successful–functioning of the personnel management because, without these policies, there can not be any lasting improvements in labour management relations. Personnel policies are the statements of intention indicating an agreement to a general course of action. It also indicates specifically what the organisation purposes to do and thus suggests the values and view points which dominate the organisations actions, Further, it is a positive declaration and a command to an organisation.

Aims and Objectives: A management's personnel policy should have two types of objectives, general and specific. The statement of general objectives should express the top management's basic philosophy of human resources and reflect its deep underlying convictions as to the importance of people in an organisation and of the management activity which deals with people, i.e. personnel administration. The statement of specific objectives should refer to the various activities of personnel administration connected with staffing, training, developing, wage and salary administration, motivation, employee services and benefits, employee records, labour relations and personnel research.

The aims of personnel policies are:

- To enable an organisation to fulfill or carry out the main objectives which have been laid down as the desirable minima of general employment policy.
- To ensure that its employees are informed of these items of policy and to secure their cooperation for their attainment.
- To provide such conditions of employment and procedures as well enable all the employees to develop a sincere sense of unity with the enterprise and to carry out their duties in the most willing and effective manner.
- To provide an adequate, competent and trained personnel for all levels and types of management.
- To protect the common interests of all the parties and recognize the role of trade unions in the organisation.
- To provide an efficient consultative service which aims at creating mutual faith among those who work in the enterprise?
- To establish the conditions for mutual confidence and avoid confusion and misunderstanding between the management and the workers.
- To provide security of employment to workers.
- To provide an opportunity for growth within the organisation.
- To identify the work and accomplishment of the employees by offering non-monetary incentives.

In brief, personnel policies should respect human dignity and personnel integrity, ensure fair treatment for all, irrespective of caste, creed or colour and offer reasonable social and economic security to employees.

Need for personnel policy: The need for formulating personnel policy is basically two fold, i.e. to have a formal statement on corporate thinking which will serve as a guideline for action, and to establish consistency in the application of the policies over a period of time so that each one in the origination gets a fair and just treatment.

Organisations should have personnel policies as they ensure the following benefits.

- The basic need and requirements of both an organisation and its employees require deep thought. The management is required to examine its basic convictions as well as give full consideration to practices in other organisations.

- Established policies ensure consistent treatment of all personnel throughout an organisation. Favoritism and discrimination are thereby minimized.
- A certainty of action is assured even though the top management personnel may change.
- Because they specify routes towards selected goals, policies serve as standard or measuring yards for evaluating performance.
- Sound policies help to build employee enthusiasm and loyalty.
- They set patterns of behaviour and permit participants of plan with a grater degree of confidence.

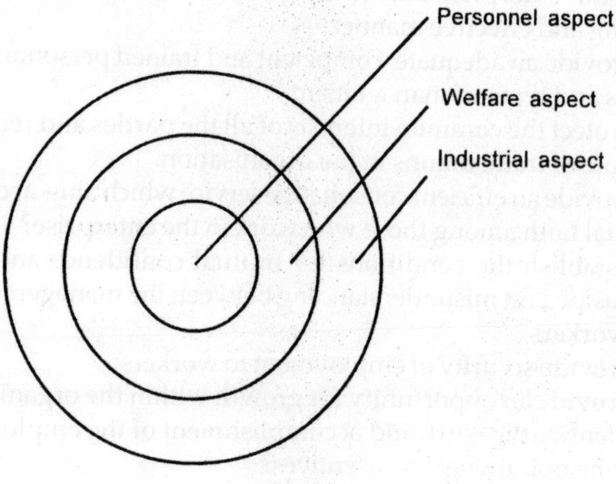

Fig. 3.1.2

Dimensions of Personnel Management

As given in Figure 3.1.2 above the following are the different dimensions of Personnel management.

1. *Personnel aspect:* It covers recruitment, selection, placement, training, compensation, etc.
2. *Welfare aspect:* It deals with working conditions, amenities and benefits.
3. *Industrial aspects:* Union management relations, Collective Bargaining and grievance handling are the aspect of this area.

Principles: In designing personnel policies, the management must balance the needs, goals, objectives and values of both the employers and the employees. Since these policies are rules of conduct, they are based on the following principles:

1. Put the right man in the right place.
2. Train everyone for the job to be done.
3. Make the organisation to co-ordinate to get the work done.
4. Supply the right tools and the right conditions of work.
5. Give security with opportunity incentive, recognition.
6. Look ahead, plan ahead for more and better things.

In brief, the principles should ensure that equity and justice are accorded to all the employees, that wages and salaries are adequate and fair, that every employee has scope for development to the limit of his capabilities, that fairness is guaranteed in maintaining the discipline and that these principles are followed without discrimination against any grade of employees.

Origin and Source of Personnel Policies: Policies stem from a wide variety of places and people. They are not created in a vacuum but are based on a few principal sources, which determine the content and meaning of policies. These are:

- The past practice of an organisation.
- The prevailing practices among sister concerns in the neighborhood and throughout the country in the same industry.
- The attitudes, ideals and philosophy of the Board of Directors, top management and middle and lower management.
- The knowledge and experience gained from handling day to day personnel problems.
- Employee's suggestions and complaints.
- Collective bargaining programs.
- State and national legislation.
- Changes in the country's economy.
- International forces.
- The culture of the plant and its technology, its business environment, its social and political environment.
- The extent of unionism.
- The attitudes and social values of labour.
- Social responsibility of the organisation toward the public and
- The goals of the organisation

Role: In the modern era, the personnel management typically performs a variety of roles, such as the roles of conscience, of a counselor, a mediator a company spokesman, a problem solver end a change agent. It performs many miscellaneous roles in accordance with the needs of a situation, such as: See Figure 31.3

1. The conscience role is that of a humanitarian who reminds the management of its moral and ethical obligations to its employees.
2. The personnel manager plays the role of a counselor to whom the employees frequently go for consultation and with whom they discuss their marital, health, mental, physical and career problems.
3. As a mediator he plays the role of a peace maker, offering to settle, and the disputes that may arise among individuals or groups.
4. The personnel manager has always been a frequent spokesman for or representative of the company because he has a better overall picture of his company's operations.
5. The personnel manager also acts as a problem solver with respect to the issues that involve HRM and overall long range organisational planning.
6. He works as a change agent within the organisation because he is best suited to introduce and implement major institutional changes.
7. He helps line managers learn to detect and solve its own problem.

Personnel role	*Welfare role*	*Clerical role*	*Legal role*
a. Advisory b. Manpower planning - recruitment -selection c. Training and Development d. Measurement of assessment of individual and group behaviour	a. Research in personnel and organizational problems b. Managing services- canteens, grain shops, create transport cooperatives etc. c. Group dynamics - Group counseling -Motivation -Leadership -Communication	a. Time keeping b. Salary and wage administration c. Maintenance of records d. Human Engineering - Man machine relationship	a. Grievance handling b. Settlement of disputes c. Handling disciplinary actions d. Collective bargaining e. Joint consultation

Fig. 3.1.3: Role of personnel management

The functions and roles of Personnel Management are very comprehensive and varies and are determined and influenced by such factors as the size, nature and location of organisation, business or industry, its short and long, term objectives, nature of industry and product, market conditions, economic, cultural and political and legal environment, the structure of the executive and administrative officers, the mental makeup of the personnel managers and the overall organisational philosophy of business.

The role of personnel management is ever expanding and is strengthened by greater interest shown in human relations problems by specialists such as behavioural scientists, industrial engineers, social psychologists, labour and legal advisors, industrial and computer technologists all of whose researchers have enriched the field of personnel management, its functions and changed their nature making them wide and humanitarian.

Emerging Role: It has been rightly apprehended that there are dangers of the personnel manager giving way to the new specialists who are coming up the experts in Information Technology, in the management of research and development, and in manpower planning, unless the personnel manager tries and acquires advance knowledge of and prepares for the change. He should, therefore concern himself with the following major areas of change which are up-and-coming.

- Changing composition of workforce, with the white collar gradually becoming a dominant group.
- Growing unionisation among the workforce is greatly increasing their strength to demand increasing participation in decision-making activities influencing their interests.
- Increasing role of government in acting protective legislation to bring about a balance in the interests and rights of the participants in the organisation.
- Revolution in information technology and other technological innovations, which might adversely affect the interests of the workforce and their occupational mobility.
- Rapidly changing jobs and skills requiring long range man power planning
- Increasing concern of many firms for accepting greater social responsibility.

In all these areas of change, personnel management people would need more training, retraining, mid career retraining. They also can not afford to neglect the "bread and butter" problems of day to day personnel administration.

Personnel Management and HRM

A subtle difference exits as to Personnel Management and Human resource management. A M Sharma explained the distinction and William B Werther Jr and Keith Davis pointed out the HRM objectives and function. These are noted below (Sharma, 2003 and Werther and Ors). See Table 3.1.1.

Table 3.1.1

Personnel management	*HR management*
1. Personnel function is an independent function	1. Human Resource system is a subsystemof a larger system.
2. There are several subfunctions under personnel function.	2. Human Resource system also deals with various functions of HR components.
3. The main task of personnel management is to respond effectively to the demands (coping role)	3. The main task of Human Resource system is to develop enabling capabilities.
4. Personnel management has the main responsibilities for personnel matters.	4. All managers share the responsibilities of human resource management.
5. The main responsibilities of personnel management relate to salary, job administration and management of people and their development.	5. The responsibilities of Human Resource system relate to people element and process of the organization.
6. The major attention of personnel management is on personnel administration or management.	6. The major attention of Human Resource System is on developing people and their competencies.
7. Personnel system and procedures should be designed to achieve maximum efficiency.	7. HR system and procedures should be designed of process values to reduce human wastage.

Additionally, William B Werther, Jr and Keith Davis pointed out the HRM objectives and functions.

HUMAN RESOURCE MANAGEMENT: RISING TRENDS

During the last decade, significant changes have taken place in the social, economic, technological, and political environment of administration. However the recent spate of changes in the

Table 3.1.2: HRM objectives and functions

1. Societal objectives	1. Legal compliance 2. Benefit 3. Union-Management 4. Personnel objectives
2. Organisational objectives	1. Human Resource Planning 2. Employee relatives 3. Selection 4. Training and Development 5. Appraisal 6. Placement 7. Assessment
3. Functional Objectives	1. Appraisal 2. Placement 3. Assessment
4. Personnel Objectives	1. Training and Development 2. Appraisal 3. Placement 4. Compensation 5. Assessment

(Source : William B. Werther Jr. and Keith Davis, Human Resources and Personnel Management, P.15.)

economics of the world by the creation of World Trade Organisation (WTO), economic liberalisation and trend towards globalisation have brought many opportunities and threats for the changes, rather they have to design and execute innovative mechanisms of developing skills and competencies of human resources to prepare them to accept the emerging challenges including:

- Revolution in information technology having far reaching impact on every sub-systems of business and creating need for building up 'knowledge capital'.
- Advancement of technology leading to obsolescence of present skills and techniques.
- Development of new technologies which will provide cutting edge to the organisations adopting new technology.
- Economic and industrial policy changes leading to though competition from multinational cooperation's.
- Changing international environment leading to free flow of goods and services throughout the world.
- Changing profile of workforce.

- Increased number of mergers and acquisitions leading to redundancy of thousands of workers.
- Increased pressure on organisations to contract out the various services like house keeping, security gardening and para clinical.
- Changing needs and expectations of customers rendering the existing processes and products obsolete.

The above trends will have a tremendous force on the tasks of future HRM professionals who will have to act as change agents or change facilitators. They will have to build up "learning organisations" having the capacity and capability to learn from experimentation, past experiences and experiences of others and transfer the learning to all human resources for greater organisational effectiveness.

The trends in HRM can be discussed from two angles, i.e. external and internal. External forces include political legal, economic, technological and cultural. Internal factors include unions, organisation culture and conflicts, professional bodies, etc.

Political-Legal: There may be greater Government interference in business in the near future to safeguard the interests of workers, consumers and the public at large. Government's participation in trade, commerce and industry will also pose many challenges before management. The government may restrict the scope of private sector in certain areas in public interest or it may open to the private sector certain areas which were earlier reserved for the public sector. Further, there may be new avenues of cooperation between the government and private sector. In fact, there may be more and more joint sector enterprises. The Government will also like to see that the interests of workers in industrial enterprises are adequately protected.

Many changes are taking place in the legal framework within which the industrial relations system in the country is now functioning. It is the duty of HRM professionals to fully examine the implications of these changes and bring about necessary adjustments within the organisation so that greater utilisation of human resources can be achieved. This, indeed, is and would remain a major challenge for the HRM. In fact, in the wake of the national approach in consonance with the egalitarian national aspirations, it is the responsibility of the HRM professionals to anticipate the changes and prepare the organisation to face them without any breakdown in its normal functioning.

Economic: Economic environment refers to all those economic forces which have a bearing on the HR function. Growth strategy, industrial production, agriculture, population, national and per capita income money and capital markets, suppliers, competitors, customers and industrial labour are the components of the economic environment. For the HR department, suppliers are those who provide human resource to an organisation. Employment exchanges, universities, colleges, training institutions, consulting firms, competitors and the like are the sources that supply human resources. Competition plays a significant role in some of the HR functions and activities. As the number of organisations competing for human resources increases, so does the importance of the staffing function and its appraisal and compensation activities. If several companies make job offers to one individual, the organisation with more attractive terms and conditions will win. When employees with particular skills are hard to obtain, the organisation may need to groom its own employees through well managed HR planning programmes coordinated with training and development activities. Customers have their own influence on a company's personnel functions.

Globalisation: National policies are being influenced significantly by extra-national forces on a variety of economic, social and labour matters. Problems and decision in one part of the world affect prospects in other parts of the world and shape the events and institutions elsewhere too. International debt and cross-national inequities are limiting the sovereignty of independent nations to act decisively even on matters concerning their own nations.

The WTO regime has emphasized on the removal of quantitative restrictions on international trade and the lowering of the tariff walls. This made several Indian business organisations feel the pain involved in adjusting to the emerging global market demands. Further event of Sept. 11 and following recession had their adverse shock on the Indian business and industry. There was decline in growth rate in several segments of the manufacturing sector in India.

Globalisation impinges, on HRM because 1) it contributes to structural changes resulting from new forms of organisation of work and production within and between firms ; 2) it subjects national labour markets to increased pressures from foreign economic influences. The impact of globalisation can be observed from the following trends:

- Integration of economies.
- Global benchmarking for highest quality of products.
- Change in management style.
- Radical change in the focus of public enterprises.
- Increase in inequities.

Technological Advances: With the changes coming in the wake of advanced technology, new jobs are created and many old jobs become redundant. There is a general apprehension of large scale unemployment. In the competitive world of today, industry cannot hope to survive for long with the old technology. The problem of unemployment resulting from modernisation will be solved by properly assessing man power needs and training of redundant employees in alternate skills. This is a difficult process are it may hurt some people but there is no escape. Thus change and modernisation have to be accepted if industry has to grow and develop. To be specific HRM Environment, Globalisation, HRM Litigations, Political, Technology, Business Environment, Changing Workforce and Economical Factors are the figuring trends of HRM as given in figure 3.1.6.

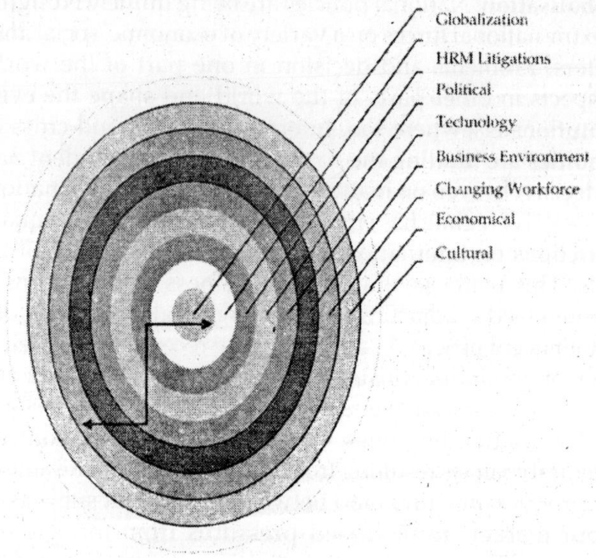

Fig. 3.1.6

Cultures Forces: Culture refers to the complex whole which includes knowledge, belief, art, morals, laws, customs and other capabilities and habits acquired by an individual as a member of a society. But how does culture influence the HRM. In the first place, culture creates the type of people who become members of an organisation. Culture prepares people along particular lines, tending to put a personality stamp upon them. When people with different cultural background promote, own and manage organisations, they themselves tend to acquire distinct cultures. Secondly the attitude of workers towards work is the result of their cultural background. Thirdly, time dimension which influences HRM, has its roots in culture. Finally work ethics, achievement needs and effort reward expectations, which are significant inputs determining individual's behaviour are the results of culture.

Unionisation: A trade union may be understood as an association of workers or management formed to protect their own individual interests. The role of a union is too well known. All HR activities recruitment, selection, training, compensation, IR and separations are carried out in consultation with union teachers. The role of unions becomes pronounced when a new wage agreement needs to be signed.

The trade unions have developed a negative and unreasonable attitude of:

- As holding the management responsible even for the wrong and willful actions of workers.
- Utilisation of the trade union platform for promotion of self interest by a few trade union and political leaders instead of opposing the wrongs done by the management against the organisation as well as the workers.
- Opposing any change by management.
- Misperceived role conflict in supporting constructive and positive actions of management while representing the workers in joint management council and collective bargaining.
- As balance between reward and contribution. Changes in workforce police (a) Mores in education level–The governments of various countries are taking steps to eradicate illiteracy and increase the education level of their citizens. Educated consumers and workers will create very tough task for the future managers.
- Change in skill level–The rapid pace of globalisation has resulted in the need for more and more skilled workers in certain sectors

like chemicals, information technology, biotechnology, pharmaceuticals, etc. Modernisation has increased the demand for highly skilled and technological empowered workers.

- Knowledge worker–The use of modern technology and the new management styles has resulted in the need for 'knowledge workers' who are multi skilled.
- Age group and aspiration of workers – Workers today belong to younger generation whose aspirations are different from those of the earlier generations. Today's workers want to progress in their life and have an ideal about the life style they want to lead. The workers are becoming more aware of their higher level needs and this awareness would intensify further among the future workers.

Environmental Challenges: HRM Initiatives

To start, the environmental challenges are the forces external to the organisation. They, essentially in turn, influence organisational performance. But it is a fact that, they are largely beyond managements' control. Therefore, the leader in Utkal University need to monitor the external environment constantly for analysing TOWS (threats, opportunities, weakness and strengths). Additionally, the organisational executive must also quickly react to challenges. To this seven important environmental challenges exist. They, too, are also changing rapidly. The rising use of Internet, workforce diversity, globalisation, new legislations, evolving work, family roles, skill shortages, and the rise of service sector have a bearing on Human Resource Management (Meja, 2003). Obviously, the factors affecting HRM functions/ activities in 21st Century are the following.

1. **Impact of technology:** Technological upgradation is the need of modern day organisation. Everything in office is now computer savvy. Internet and e-mail is now part of official jargon. Office automation, paper-less office are the new slogan of work place. This technological change in turn brings new skills, down sising, collaborative work, and internet revolution.
2. **Impact of TQM:** Quality has became an most applicable word. Simply it means something is better than something else. Total Quality Management is way of creating an organisational culture committed to the continuous improvement of skills, teamwork, processes, product and services quality and

customer satisfaction. Virtually, TQM is linked to every aspect of organisational life. (W. Walter, 1986).

To put succinctly, TQM centres round four components- Do it right the first time (rather than making and correcting mistakes) be customer oriented, make continuous improvement and build team work and empowerment. In organisation Total Quality HRM approach relates to caring for people. Naturally, to get people to care about quality, one has to care about people. Employees' involvement has become key to TQM. Further, this TQM's primary focus is on continuous improvement and on going incremental change.

3. **Economic challenges:** Economic condition has a positive impact on HRM activities. To match this down sising is necessary. Organisations which failed to recognize these economic compulsions may have to be thrown out of gear in the market place Scooter India Ltd. and HMT are two examples. Further SBI undertook Voluntary Retirement Scheme (VRS) to dealing overstaff in wake of computerisation of branches.
4. **Impact workforce diversity** Workforce diversity in the field of HRM signifies that people in organisations are from varied age group, gender, race, ethnicity. With the reservations of job for Schedule Caste, Scheduled Tribes, Other Backward Classes women, physically disabled 'men at work' are changing. Women employees today compose of a major share of the workforce. In 2000, 75% of employed men had employed wives. This figure is 54% in 1980 (Meja, 2003). This trend is rising. And by 2050, workforce will be a mix of General Caste, Scheduled Caste, Scheduled Tribes, Socially and Economically Backward Class, Other Backward Class, Muslims, etc. Certainly this will be a real challenge to Manager's role in future.
5. **Employees retaining and internet:** Employees retaining is a major problem. In the era of globalisation with the advent of internet, e-learning reaches employees everywhere. It is an enabler for HR practitioners and Human Resources. Employees are gathering HRM information. Employees being offered more leave the organisation. So, to say internet affects employees retaining.

   The pervasive impact of Internet on HR can be summarized as

   1. People acquired greater written communication skills through the use of email.

2. Interment is creating an open labour market. As such web information facilitates jobs and hiring decisions.
3. Labour turnover is rising as employees are aware of facilities and incentives available with competition.
4. Traditional 'paper and pencil' learning is being replaced by e-learning as it reaches and touches employees everywhere at any time.
5. Manager's operational techniques are quickly and effectively available to HR world.

6. **Rapid change:** Many organisations face rapid change. For survival and prosperity they have to adapt to quick and effective changes. Human resources are almost key to an effective organisational system. And they are affected to a greater degree in either positive or negative direction. Naturally, this rapid change creates job stress. This may at times leads to work place violence. And support mechanism if developed, can reduce this syndrome.
7. **Globalisation**: The dramatic challenge to HR is globalisation. It adds fuels for competition both at local global arena. Further it is fuelled by the Internet usages. It has far reaching implications on HRM. They are:
   1. Assimilation of global work culture.
   2. Alliance with global institutions for better productivity
   3. A mixed workforce.
8. **Legislations and decision of Apex Court** : HR activities are more or less affected by enactment of new social legislations and judgement by Apex court. At times HR are getting benefits and at times they are at trouble. The prime responsibility of these two is to minimize complaints. Supreme Courts decision on sexual harassment is a point here to note. As such it is unthinkable that any HR practices and issues faced by employees is not affected by Government regulations. Prohibition of child labour is a case to be reckoned with. Moreover, legislation has also deep influence on HR function. In the field of reservation the role of legislature is paramount. Consequently, it touches HR issues to great extent. For example presently UPA Govt. is thinking of extending the reservations to private organisations. Similar are the other effects of judgements of Apex Court and High Courts so far as HR is concerned.

9. **New Evolving Work and Role of Family:** In the new work culture both husband wife are earning. This trend is gaining momentum day by day. Simultaneously women are facing double burden both at home and work place. On average they are devoting 42 hrs per work of average to official work and 30 hours at home to family work. In comparison men spent less hours in home towards household work and rearing of children. To deal with this phenomenon, "family friendly" programmes, "child-care" and elder care referral services, flexi-work are introduced. However in Indian scene these facilities are not practiced at great length.
10. **Competitive advantage:** For survival competitive advantage is necessary in terms of cost and quality. In University scenario cost of the education and quality of education shall be the symbol of growth. Evidently this has a direct link with the well being of the HR of the organisation. Controlling cost, improving quality, decentralized decision-making, downsising, organisational re-engineering/restructuring are necessary for dramatic transformation of the organisation. In one word, organisational restructuring needs effective management of human resources, as it involves staffing demands, work flows, training needs, compensation requirement, etc.

HRM: The Concept

Before analysing the concept of HRM it is pertinent to discuss about the features of a healthy organisation. (Fordyce and Weil: 1981), Ghosal, Piramal and Bartlett: 2000) and High Performance System.[3] In the main, the features of healthy organisation are:

1. *Clear objectives:* The institutions should have clear objective or mission.
2. *Trust:* The leader manager tries to build trust between employees and management.
3. *Problems solving approach:* The management tries to solve problems of organisation including problems of Human Resources instead of multiplying the same.
4. *Team play:* The management should encourage team play as to planning and performance.
5. *Collaboration:* The feature of collaboration and conflict resolution is of prime importance. This will lead to conflict management in the organisation for smooth sailing of the boat of HR practices.

6. *Learning and relationship:* Modern organisations are learning one. Workers are learning workers. Hence learning is the sign of growing organisations. Likewise, this will help in building interpersonal relationship for a healthy human relation.
7. *Speedy and open communication:* Communication is the nerve of an organisation. It links the organisational purposes with human resources, stake holders and customers.

   As such speedier and open the communication the delivery system of the organisation is up to the mark and is performance savvy.
8. *Effective control for compliance:* Moreover, the organisation is sound if its control system is effective and efficient, thereby it wields compliance.
9. *A high degree of commitment:* Commitment of the HR is the index of performance. In healthy organisation there is high degree of commitment. People identify themselves with the organisation. In other words the employees are thinking the organisation as their own.
10. *Consistency:* Temporariness and inconsistency are the signs of deceased organisation and decaying. On the contrary consistency is the hallmark of a developing organisation.
11. *Innovativeness:* Competence moves the organisation a step forward. Additionally innovativeness adds to competence. Obviously without innovativeness the organisation can not survive in the age of competitive world.

Moreover, the discussion of organisation – in which HR practices perform –will be incomplete if the paradigm of High Performing work system will not be discussed. To start with, it is said effective HRM practices have touching effect on the performance of the unit. As a matter of fact that features of HPWS (High Performance Work System) are noted below.

- Large number of highly qualified applicants for each strategic position.
- The use of validated selection and promotion models/ procedures.
- Extensive training and development of new employees.
- The use of formal performance appraisal and management.
- The use of multi source (360 degree) performance appraisal and feedback.
- Linkage of merit increases to formal appraisal process.
- Above market compensation for key positions.

- High percentage of entire workforce included in incentive systems.
- High differential in pay between high and low performers.
- High percentages of HR activities spent on outsource activities (e. g. recruiting, payroll).
- High percentage of workforce working in self-managed team based work.
- Low percentage of employees covered by Union contract.
- Relatively low number of employees per HR professional.
- High percentage of jobs filled from within.

In reality, HPWS is a healthy grand for effective HR management. Also in this context the effectiveness of HR system is to be judged. Prior to that it is central to explain the dimensions of HR. HRM is a medium through which goals of both human resources and the concerned organisations are met. To put in again, HRM is management of man at work. So the process is concerned with the effective fulfillment of the mission of the organisation by procuring, developing and maintaining competent and skill workforce. So the pattern of HRM is concerned with.

- Acquisition of Human Resources through hiring (Recruitment and Selection).
- Development of Human Resources by training.
- Maintenance of Human Resource (Transfer, Promotion, Performance management, Grievance and compensation, etc.).
- Relational Management of Human Resources. (Relationship between employees and management).

To put it in other term the domain of HRM is linked to

1. *Reward system:* Rewarding for best performance to motivate Human Resources.
2. *Organisation decision:* Designing structure for defining job and job positions.
3. *Staffing:* Staffing deals with putting right people at right work at right time.
4. *Performance management and appraisal:* It deals with the evaluation part of Human Resources for effective control and productivity.
5. *Employees training and development:* Prepare the employees of the organisation to meet the future challenges of globalisation, new work, information technological development and needs of changing structures

6. The same facts as to HRM can also be presented in a different way. Total Human Resource practices are connected with HR environment and Human Resource Information System (HRIS). In this area the other included parameters are staffing, training, performance management, compensation, career planning and labour relation.

Also for better clarify the environment of whole gamut of Human Resource Development are:

- Human Resources Planning
- Hiring-Recruitment and Selection
- Training
- Performance Appraisal
- Compensation
- Promotion
- Transfer
- Discipline
- Grievance Handling
- Employees Participation
- Employees Welfare
- Employee-Employer Relatives

And it is to be marked there are three important 'C' for effective Human Resource Development. They are:

- Competence - Competence of Human Resource to deal with competitive advantage in the 21st century.
- Commitment - Involvement to work and organization for development.
- Culture - Culture of the organization is the milestone and insignia of its appreciation and acceptance by customers.

In this connection HRD process developed by P. Suba Rao[4] is presented here in figure 3.1.6

In it the important components are extential, empathetic, coping process, building process and growth process. The first three are connected with people in "individual" capacity. The last two are related to "Group" and "Organisation as a Whole" respectively. Extential component deals with HR dimensions of career planning, performance appraisal and job evaluation. Empathetic component is connected with compensation, conflict and co-operation of Human Resources. Besides, coping process has an intimate link with stress management a scenario blocking the development and growth. Building process- The group dynamics is connected with

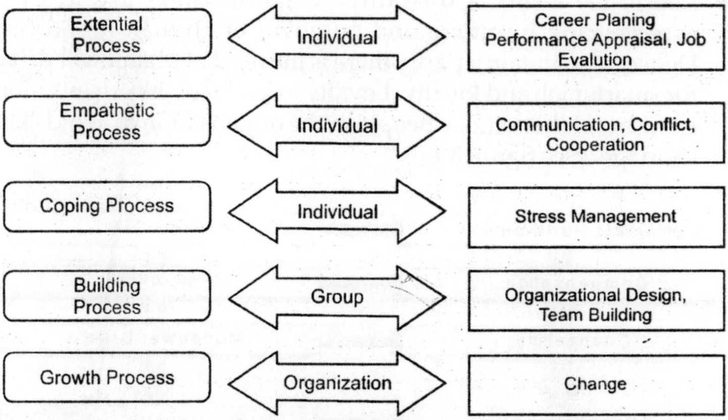

Fig. 3.1.6: HRD process

Source: P. Suba Rao (2005), Essentials of Human Resources Management and Industrial relations, Himalaya Publishing House, Mumbai

organisational design, team work and team building, the key to organisations survival. Additionally 'change' factor is inevitable and noticeable in any type of organisation. So growth component is changes in the organisations.

All these components can be called HRD climate as it prepares congenial atmosphere for development. The parameters, the same discussed factors in another set are:

- *Worker participation:* Employees participation in management and decision-making.
- Compensation – Pay package and fringe benefits to employees to boost motivation.
- *Counseling:* Providing skilled and technical advice for career development and planning.
- *Recreational:* Work overload is a common phenomenon in this competitive world. Stress from overburden is ruling at work place. Obviously, providing some recreational measures is good for Human Resources and the organisation.
- *Training:* Skill development and IT upgradation of employees are made through training.
- *Promotion:* To emulate motivation at work promotions are provided to employees. As such they are constantly climbing up in career ladder without being stagnant.

- *Manpower drive:* Constantly organisations are always experiencing incoming and outgoing of Human Resources. Hence, to maintain a parity there is the need of Manpower drive for smarter job and loyalty. Loyalty to leader of the organisation is the bond that retains people in the organisation to avoid skill shortage. (See figure 3.1.7)

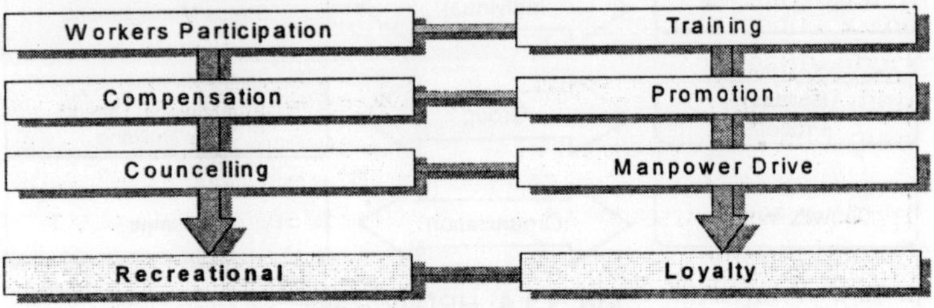

Fig. 3.1.7: HRD climate parameters

Amazingly, in the organisational setting Managers and HR heads are performing the role of performers. In a recent High Performance workforce study 2007, Global Management Consultancy firm for Accenture, reported in *Times of India,* (on 40 Indian CEOs and Human Relation Department Heads) it is pointed out that HR is their most critical workforce (Globally HR's is ranked No. 7 in the packing order of importance). And they are of the opinion that there was deep dissatisfaction with HRS Performance (Malkani, Accentuare). "In an adequacy vs expectations survey across different workforces like rules, manufacturing, research and development, HR etc HR performed the worst. Study explained that there is a gap between CEO's potential and actual achievement by HR function. In effect, all the organisations are "fishing in the same pond creating a severe talent crunch." So to develop new appropriate metric to track HR for workforce performance is a major issue. Another difficult situation in the HR area is the retention and leadership development. In this context the effectiveness of HR is put in figure 3.1.8 for a better clarity on the issues posed.

HRM : Its Functions

HRM is people dimension in organisation. It is pervasive in nature. Above and beyond, its orientation is related to action part of the organisation, people and development of the organisation. So far

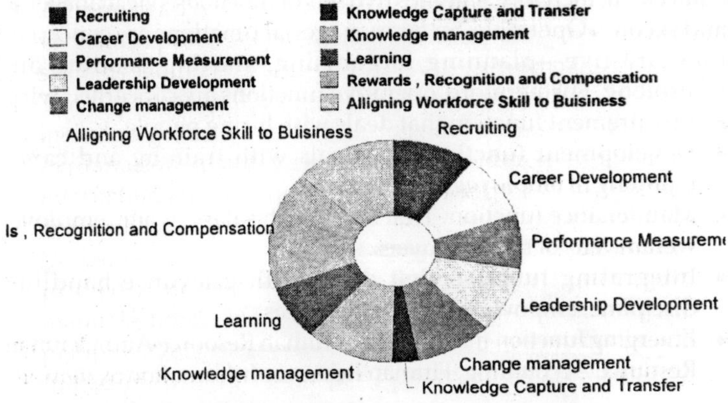

Fig. 3.1.8: Effectiveness of HR in percentage

Source: Higher performance stud TOI/14 Aug. 2007

as employees dimension is concerned it touches personnel welfare and industrial aspect, to put it again. The very objectives of HRM are:

1. To help the organisation to reach its goals.
2. To improve the skills and abilities of the workforce effectively.
3. To provide the organisation with well trained and well motivated employees.
4. To increase to the fullest the employee's job satisfaction and self-actualisation.
5. To develop and maintain a Quality of Work Life (QWL).
6. To communicate HR policies to all employees.
7. To be ethically and socially responsive to the needs of the society.

Additionally, VSP Rao also identified 8 areas of HR practices that touches Human Resources.

- Attracting and retaining talent.
- Training people for challenging roles.
- Developing skills and competencies.
- Promoting team spirit.
- Developing loyalty and commitment.
- Improving job satisfaction.
- Enhancing standard of living.
- Generating new employment opportunity.

HRM signifies "a set of activities in all organisations intended to influence the effectiveness of human resources and organisations"

(Glucek). It, therefore, signifies two sets of functions: one managerial, and second: Operative. So far managerial functions are concerned they are five—planning, organising, staffing, leading and controlling. Furthermore, operative functions are concerned with

- Procurement function that deals with hiring people.
- Development function that deals with training and career planning of employees.
- Maintenance function: That deals with salary, wage, employee welfare, etc. of the employees.
- Integrating function that deals with grievance handling, discipline, empowerment of employees.
- Emerging function that concerns Human Resource Audit, Human Resource Accounting, Human Resource Information System, etc.

Human Resource Manager: Multifaceted Roles

Human Resource Manager's role is multifaceted and multi dimensional namely administrative, operational and strategic (Rao, 2005).

Accordingly administrative roles of human resource manager comprise of policy making, advising, housekeeping, counseling, welfare and legal consultation. Secondly, operational roles of HR manners deals with recruiting talent, training HR, motivating HR, Co-ordination, mediating and champions the causes of employees. Thirdly, HR manager acts as a change agent, a facilitator and s/he is a strategic partners.

Evidently it is the manager /HR manager who performs a key role in influencing HR for fulfillment of organisational role. In this context comes the leadership dimension of HR manager. To be specific there is subtle difference between leader and manager which can be known from Figure 3.1.9.

LEADER	*MANAGER*
Innnovates	Administers
Focus on People	Focus on System/ Structure
Inspires Trust	Relies on Control
Long range Perspective	Short range View
Accepts challenges	Accepts Status Quo
Leadership is doing the right thing	Management is doing things right

Fig. 3.1.19: Manager equations

Essentially, role of the leaders in HRM environment is of prime importance. As to this 'Leader' word is expanded as : L-Listener; E-Energetic; A-Adaptive; D-Decision Maker; E-Effective; R-Reliable. The mantra of leader is 'DO' means act. And a leader is known by 3 PS and 10 Cs. Hence 3Ps are positive thinking, positive feeling and positive action. Above all 10 Cs features of leadership are : Character, Caring, Committed, Confident, Communicative, Creative, Competitive, Constant, Courageous, and Charismatic. (See Figure 3.1.10).

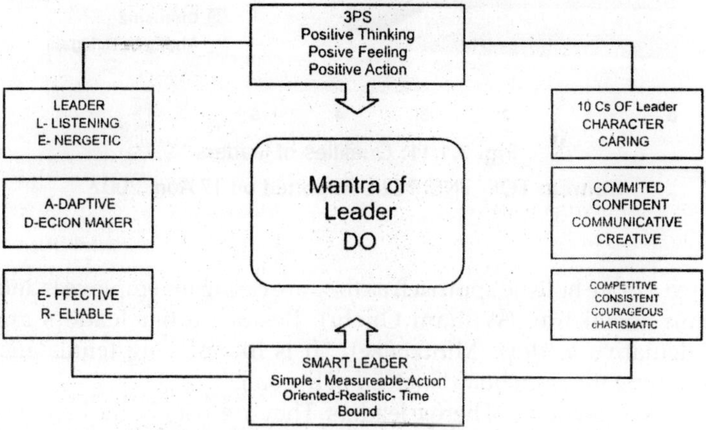

Fig. 3.1.10: Leadership-features

To add to the qualities of good leader, Figure 3.1.11 may be referred. As such the qualities are honesty, efficiency, ability to inspire, education, can carry people along, courage of conviction, willingness to learn, vision, fairness, charisma and ability to change (*TOI*: 17 Aug. 07).

With these qualities a leader is a SMART one – where S stands for simple; M stands for Morale: A stands for Accountable; R stands for Responsive and T stands for Transparency. For graphical representation of 3Ps, 10 Cs the figure 3. 9 above may be referred to. Besides, it is matter of interest to put here XYZ of Leadership (See a report in *Times of India*, dated 25, August 2007). Enforcer leaders (Theory x Leader) are necessary to man X type of people (Greger) who are disciplined to work. To man Y type of people who are self directed, Empowering Leaders are the right choice. (Theory Y leaders: Mac Greger). Further Holistic leaders (Theory Z leaders)

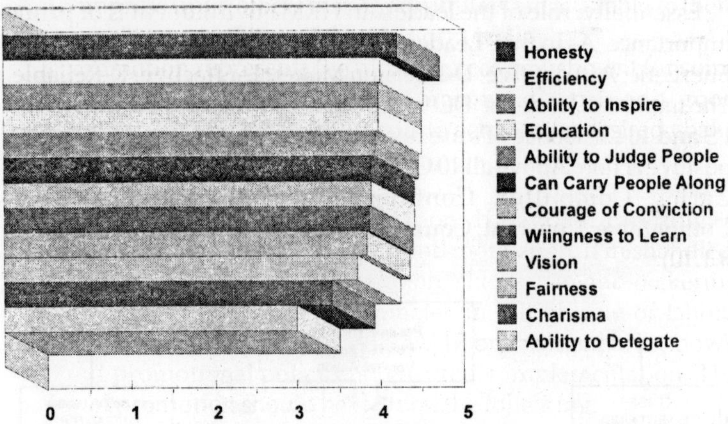

Fig. 3.1.11: Qualities of leaders

Source: TOI - TNS POLL Reported on 17 Aug. 2007

have a more holistic approach as they are caring for employees and their social life. (William Ouchi). Besides other leaders are Calculative leaders (Mintzberg). "It is like playing tennis and watching the Scoreboard instead of the ball."

Next category is of heroic leaders. They are just like the hero of a drama. They create a lot of noise; and before it is know they vanish from the scene. Mintzberg called these high decibel leaders as "Pretended artists", being the most dangerous one. Last one is charismatic leaders. It is noted that often charisma is confused with competence and for that matter organisations are to pay heavy prices (Rakesh Khurna: Harvard Business School).

More to the point, the four 'Ms' referred by dean of Leadership Gurus (Warren Bennis and Burt Nanus: Leaders: 1985) are the competencies of leaders for sailing the ship of organisation. They are:

- Management of Attention: To have a vision.
- Management of Meaning: Ability to communicate the vision for sharing.
- Management of Trust: Ability to perform consistently.
- Management of Self: Knowledge of this strength and weakness.

For graphical presentation (See Figure 3.1.12)

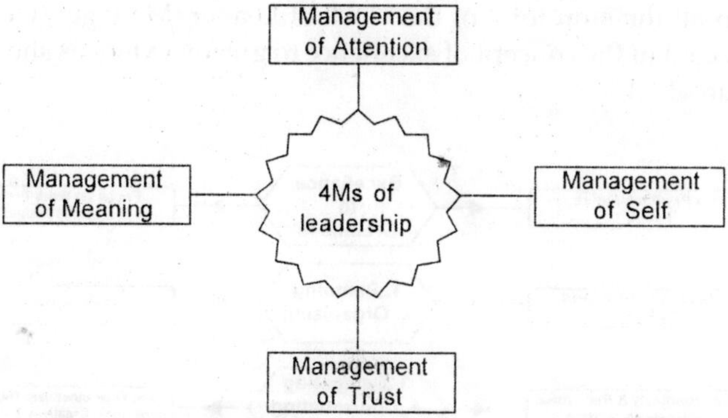

Fig. 3.1.12: 4Ms of good leadership
Source: Warren Bennis and Burt Nanus, Leadership:1985

In essence, Leaders are more and more caring to employees' needs. They, in effect, fulfill the wants of Man and Women workforce in the organisation. For better clarity a comparison chart prepared by K. A. Knownch (1995) is presented in Figure 3.1.12 under head "What People Want." Accordingly, number one want for men and woman are interesting work and appreciation by Leader-Manager. Necessarily, there is the need of caring leader to look after the needs of the people. To this the *Leader Wisdom* of Robbin Sharma is of great help. (See Figure 3.1.13).

Fig. 3.1.13: What people want: Contrast male and female
source: K.A. Kownch (1995)

Rank	*Male*	*Female*
I	Interesting work	Appreciation
II	Appreciation interesting work	
III	Feeling of being employee	Feeling of being employee
IV	Good ways	Job security
V	Job security	Good ways
VI	Promotion	Promotion
VII	Good working condition	
VIII	Loyalty to employee	Loyalty to employee
IX		
X	Sympathetic help	Good working condition

In all the sum total of the work of Leader/Manager/CEOs is reflected in the concept of excellence to greater extent as shown in Figure-3.1.13.

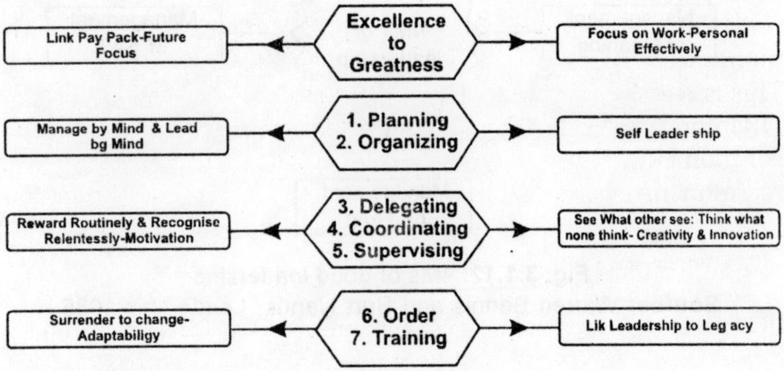

Fig. 3.1.13: Leader wisdom: Robin sharma

Emerging Paradigm: Challenges of HRM

Apart from that before analysing the areas of HR practices it is matter of interest and compulsion to put here few new facts. One such is emerging paradigm and challenges of HRM. True, the future of HRM is more demanding. In this domain another term Human Resource Development is used. The former is maintenance of HR while the latter is pro-active programme of organisation to prepare workforce for the future challenges. So to put the challenges that HR practices are facing today (Pandey: 1999) are : (a) Tomorrow's Organisation's aim is to be bench marker- 'out performer'. So the slogan is 'Outperform or die'. For this there is the need systems adaptability and preparedness with new talents to face the fast changing strategies. So talents hunt, focus on knowledge building and skill developments are major issues. The strategies are at HR practices, workplace level and at value commitment level. In this regard the study of Bhandarker (2003) is of much help.

Second challenge is linked to bond between vision, mission, and value of the organisation with Human Resource Management.

Next challenges are certain mismatch in the areas of reward and punishment system, closed or controlled performance appraisal system, career planning, capability and competence building, effective communication, performed. Leadership, cadre management, absence of grievance handling mechanism, uncongenial working condition, half-hazard or no counseling system and finally shortage of skilled HR practitioners are among other pressing challenges.

Additionally Information technological development brought monumental, dramatic and significant changes in the HR practices. This is related to Human Resource Management System HRMS/ HR Information System (HRIS). As an integrated and comprehensive solution HRMS extends its helps in the HR practices areas such as recruitment, payroll maintenance, training, performance evaluation and measurement. So to say HRMS links HR planning with Organisations' performance.

More particularly, management of HR information, automation of certain HR process like employees information and management application tracking and HR acquisition, outsourcing and talent management system (Recruit to Retain) are the effective uses of HRIS in modern day organisation (Krishna).

Besides, capability and talent management building organisational ethos, knowledge and residence management are other important challenges that cripple organisation. Therefore, the steps to build organisational ethos, as per Pareek (2003) are opinion, co-operation, trust, autonomy, productivity, authenticity, confrontation and experimentation (OCTAPACE). This is required for talent utilisation and management (David-Ringwood: 2002). And in this context, it is important to build organisational ethos for effective transitional management of transformations and achieving excellence. For this there is the need of high level commitments on the part of employees and employer (Walton: 1985).

As well, knowledge management is of prime necessity in the area of man management. It deals with a set of processes. Knowledge process falls under five headings: creating, showing, sourcing mapping and measuring. Side by side there is the compulsion of nescience management. Identifying the degree of 'nescience' is a step further to evaluate talents. Ignorance is wider than knowledge. Always ignorance is displaced by knowledge and then ignorance in new wide areas. Promoting new option is the key to manage ignorance (David: 2003) and ignorance management is control to talent development-two sides of a coin. Four basic principles are there to master ignorance management. They are the principles of (1) deferment (2) prematurely, (3) irrelevance, and (4) Waste. (David: 2003).

More to the point, two approaches exist as to manage knowledge. One 'people track' and two "IT tracks." The first focuses on the management of people through assessing, changing and improving individual skill. The second IT track put stress on management of information. More and more knowledge management is linked to explicit knowledge know how. Essentially, it aims at value additions to the organisations through improvement and innovations. Necessarily it is a process of growing intellectual capital (Stewart: 1997).

Certainly, HR role is primary in knowledge management through the use of informative management tools. More and more knowledge management among HR is a collaborative effort and initiative. In this respect there are certain social learning enables to effect knowledge management (Murty). They are:

- Positive communicative climate
- Goal Alignment
- Enabling workplace design
- Team based morale
- Socialising
- Constructive Performance Management
- Effective leadership
- Valuing skill, reward and recognition strategies
- Timely Induction programmes.

These enables create congenital atmosphere for facilitating knowledge management in organisation. As a result of knowledge workers are created with expertise, skill and training. SKA- Skill, Knowledge and Ability are the keys to HR development. In the 21st century an encouraging trend is, knowledge workers constitute a major portion of the workforce in comparison to 20th century. Ann Andrews calculated in the knowledge age 2% of the working population will work on land, 10% will work in industry and rest will be knowledge workers (Wikipedia: org/knowledge worker).

No doubt management of knowledge workers is a challenging job for HR manager. Knowledge workers are central to excellence of the organisation. The areas in which HR people finds it difficult in managing knowledge workers are : (1) Recruiting (2) Retaining with the help of Hire Smart People and then Alone (HSPALTA) Approach (Davenport).[3] (3) Developing creativity amongst them. In this context, the role of HR is to be examined. To find a place in the age of competitive advantage with cutting edge technology, performance improvement of HR is the only way out. HR practices play a great role in accomplishing the aim. As such knowledge management and HRM are left and right hand of organisational structure. "To be is to learn, to learn is to know and to know is to win" (Davenport). Obviously win-win situation is only through management of knowledge workers and challenging job of HR practices. Some HR practices that manage knowledge workers are:

- Efficient hiring procedures.
- Appropriate retention programmes with promotion pay packages and incentives.
- Motivating knowledge workers by rewards.
- Congenial working conditions with flexibility and autonomy.
- Provision for knowledge sharing through workshop, seminars and effective communication.
- Provision for fringe benefits in commensurate with new life style like family care, child care, etc.
- Training to improve creativity and competence.
- Counseling to solve career problems.
- Encouraging decision-making.

Thus, HR practices provide a good ground for grooming of knowledge workers. Contrary lack of initiative to manage knowledge worker by HR manager also affects the organisation and hinders growth and development. "Brain Drain" is the inevitable result of inefficient knowledge management by HR managers.

Skill Management: It is the ongoing process of assessing and updating skill. It provides a structural approach to develop individual and collective skill. Form this, individual employees, lime managers and organisations executives are benefited. And in this endeavour HR managers' role is quite central and important.

Time Management: Comprises of tools for planning and scheduling time. Its main purpose it so enhance the effectiveness and efficiency of human resources in organisation. The other name of time management is self-management. (Srivastav and K. Ghosh).

In nutshell, the greatest HR challenges shall be in the areas of:

- Development of openness and transparency.
- Building ethos and culture.
- Diversity management.
- Balancing organisational goal with HRD system.
- Development of leadership.
- Re-engineering HRD.

- Creating horizontal organisation.
- HR outsourcing.
- Initiation of interactive process for change.
- Creating learning organisations.

Regarding the trends in HR effectiveness a report concerning. Evaluating Human Capital and the Human Resources Function by Mike Haffenden, Andrew Lambert and David Creelman is to be referred. It is more related to evaluating the role of HR and advocating of latest trends in evaluation. According Haffenden prescribed four relatively measures in HR metrics (Donaldson).

1. Efficiency
2. Effectiveness
3. Talent
4. Breakthrough.

To add to the foregoing analysis competency mapping in Performance Management is of matter of interest. Competency mapping generally, is for enhancing HR performance. There are various models MBTI - Myers Briggs Type Indicator to map different possible combinations of personalities say extraverts and introverts.

- Managerial Assessment of Proficiency (MAP) : Computerized practical exercise.
- Thomas Disc Profiling (by William Marston) Based on interaction; D-Dominance, I-Influence, S-Steadiness and C-Compliance.
- Kundu Introversion Extraversion Inventory (KIEI)- Measurement of Adult behaviour.

Human Resource Capability Model

The model can be used by HR people to focus on their development needs. The excerpts are from website HRCP model- (adopted from website). The model has five Features.

Knowledge Brining HR to Business

- Uses specialist knowledge to advise and develop.
- HR related policies and practices and to influence.
- Organisational and individual performance and behaviour at work.

HR related policies and processes

- Continually builds knowledge and expertise.
- Understands current HR approaches, tools and technology.

- Actively stays upto date with organisational guidelines and processes.

Organisational dynamics

- Understands the culture of the organisational and its impact on HR policies and processes.
- Has an appreciation of corporate governance and strategically uses this information.
- Understands the interplay between organisational structure and culture.
- Understands the points of influence in the organisation.

Development and reward systems

- Is alert to and understands where organisations stand in the market.
- Knows what makes the organisation an employer of choice.
- Has a detailed knowledge of current HRD thinking and applications to maximize the potential of staff.

CREDIBILITY- Having an Influential Seat at the Table

- Is well respected, influences and makes a positive impression on others, behaves with integrity, walk the talk and thinks quickly on one's feet.

Is influential and persuades others

- Makes a positive impression and engenders confidence.
- Influence attitudes and opinions and gains agreement to plans and ideas.
- Negotiates and resolves conflict.
- Effectively communicates across audiences.

Acts as a strong role model

- Acts with integrity, has high ethical standards and upholds values.
- Models high standards of behaviour through own actions.
- Inspires trust by treating all individuals fairly.
- Makes fair decisions and stands by agreements made.
- Is resilient and shows courage.

Is analytically agile

- Demonstrates strong analytical skills in diagnosing issues and trends.

- Anticipates problems and initiates effective responses.
- Assesses and priorities issues.
- Thinks laterally.
- Thinks quickly on one's feet.

ALIGNMENT – Connecting HR with the Business

Though knowledge and understanding of the business, integrates HR initiatives with and helps to shape corporate strategy.

Scans and reads the business

- Takes responsibility for learning about, and being alert to, changes in the business.
- Maintains business knowledge through frequent interaction with people in the workplace.
- Reads and translates the organisations business to others.

Integrates HR initiatives with business plans

- Identifies and sets HR priorities within the context of business plans.
- Presents strong business cases for HR initiatives
- Blends both a strategic and operational focus in providing advice and delivering results.

Contributes to and supports corporate strategy

- Translates Government and organisational expectations of performance and direction into business context.
- Works to support and shape long term organisational goals.
- Works with line areas to promote and facilitate the integration of people issues into the business plan.

PERFORMANCE – Achieving High Quality Business Results

Applies business acumen to HR decisions

- Approaches HR issues from a strategic business perspective.
- Understands the implications of business plans.
- Understands financial and budgetary implications.
- Understands and uses business analysis and evaluation tools.
- Demonstrates effective project and contract management skills.

Drives for results and manages risk

- Anticipates situations, assess the probable impact, weighs options and plans accordingly.

- Is energetic and takes personal responsibility to deliver on agreed outcomes.
- Accesses best resources to get the job done.
- Maintains high performance even when under pressure.
- Is prepared to stand one's ground in the best interest of the organisation.

Evaluates outcomes

- Continually monitors HR initiatives to maintain consistency with business outcomes.
- Evaluates outcomes, considers business implications and integrates results into the performance improvement cycle.
- Assesses the added value of implemented HR initiative.

RELATIONSHIPS – Partnering with the Business

Facilitates positive working relationships, mentors, others and focuses on client needs.

Creates and maintains partnerships

- Establishes and maintains good relationships across the organisation.
- Collaborates with clients to formulate and implement HR initiatives.
- Fosters open and frank discussion of issues with others.

Focuses on other's needs

- Understands and focuses on the needs of people and the organisation.
- Accommodates and adapts to different circumstances and audiences.
- Demonstrates an interest in and understanding of the views of others.

Coaches and develops others

- Enables others to make the best use of their talents.
- Empowers others to take initiative and solve problems.

INNOVATION- Bringing Ideas to the Business

Prepares people for new challenges, makes change happen, seeks and facts on opportunities and improves and enhances the way we do things.

Prepares people for change

- Proactively explains and supports change initiatives.
- Demonstrates a clear sense of one's own role as an enabler of change.
- Builds a shared enthusiasm and purpose for change.
- Supports individuals to mange change.

Seeks out and acts on opportunities

- Continually looks for ways to enhance and create methods to achieve business outcomes.
- Seeks, evaluates and integrates better practices within the organisation.
- Champions innovative ideas and projects.

Is flexible and explores options

- Critically evaluates and explores alternatives to the way things are done.
- Helps others to find creative ways around obstacles.
- Is open to new ideas.
- Seeks and encourages ideas from others.

References

1. E.B. Flippo, *Principles of Personnel Management*, McGraw Hill Book, New York, 1980.
2. C.B. Mamoria *Personnel Management*, Himalaya Publications, Bombay, 1996.
3. *Ibid*.
4. E. B. Flippo, *op. cit*.

Further Readings

1. J. Bernardin, *Human Resource Management*. An Experimental Approach, Tata McGraw Hill, New Delhi, 2003.
2. L.R. Gornez Megia, Ors, *Managing Human Resources*, Pearson Education, New Delhi, 2003
3. Robert Aushin, *Managing Knowledge Eorkers*, Harvard Business School, 2006
4. Mark Forster, *Do it Tomorrow and Other Secrets of Time Management*, Hodder and Stoughtin Religious, 2006
5. S.P. Handley, *Workforce Engagement*, Frederic Jacobs, 2007.

Chapter two

HUMAN RESOURCE PLANNING

"Manpower Planning" and "Human Resource Planning" are synonymous terms. In the past, the phrase manpower planning was generally used but now the emphasis is on human resource planning, which has broader base. Human resource or manpower planning is the process by which a management determines how an organisation should move from its current manpower position to its desired manpower position. Through planning, a management strives to have the right number and right kinds of people at the right places, at the right time, to do things which result in both the organisation and the individual receiving the maximum long range benefit.

Coleman has defined human resource or manpower planning as "the process of determining manpower requirements and the means for meeting those requirements in order to carry out the integrated plan of the organisation."

Stainer defines planning as, "strategy for the acquisition, utilisation, improvement and preservation of an enterprise's human resources. It relates to establishing job specifications or the quantitative requirements of jobs determining the number of personnel required and developing sources of manpower."

Thus, it will be noted that manpower planning consists in projecting future manpower requirements and developing manpower plans for the implementation of the projections. This planning is not rigid or static. It is amenable to modification, review and adjustments in accordance with the needs of an organisation or the changing circumstances.

As such Manpower planning or Human Resource Planning (HRP) deals with 3Rs – Right employees in Right Job at Right time. It is based on HR demand and HR supply. It tries to assess the need of workforce in an organisation. The very objectives of HRP are to forecast HR requirement; to cope with changes; to use existing manpower productivity and to promote employees in a systematic manner (Overman; 1999). And the benefits of HRP are it helps in preparing a pool of talent; in reducing cost of organisation/ in preparing successive plans (Baytos: 1984) and in preparing employees for the future needs. The process of HRP consists of:

1. Forecasting the demand of employees.
2. Preparing supply forecasting/manpower inventory.
3. Determining the gap between demand and supply.
4. Formulating HR plans and policies.

On the whole with HRP recruitment plan, redeployment plan, retaining plans are being made. And for HRP, there is also the need of job analysis for the effective planning.

Need for HRP

Human Resource Planning is deemed necessary for all organisations for one or the other of the following reasons:

- To carry on its work, each organisation needs personnel with the necessary qualifications, skills, knowledge, work experience and aptitude for work. These are provided through effective manpower planning.
- Since a large number of persons have to be replaced who have grown old, or who retire, die or become incapacitated because of physical or mental ailments, there is a constant need for replacing such personnel. Otherwise, the work would suffer.
- HRP is essential because of frequent labour turnover which is unavoidable and even beneficial because it arises from factors which are socially and economically sound such as voluntary quits, discharges, marriage, promotions or factors such as seasonal and cyclical fluctuations in business which cause a constant ebb and flow in the workforce in many organisations.
- In order to meet the needs of expansion programmes, HRP is unavoidable.
- The nature of the present workforce in relation to its changing needs also necessitates the recruitment of new labour. To meet the challenge of a new and changing technology and new techniques of production, existing employees need to be trained or new blood injected in an organisation.
- Manpower planning is also needed in order to identify areas of surplus personnel or areas in which there is a shortage of

personnel. If there is a surplus, it can be redeployed and if there is shortage, it may be made god.

Factors affecting HRP

HRP is influenced by several factors. The most important of these are:

1. **Type and strategy of organisation:** The type of organisation is a very much important determinant, because it is involved with production process, number and type of staff needed and the supervisory and managerial personnel required. Primarily the organisation is either proactive or reactive in HRP. It can either decide to carefully anticipate the needs and systematically plan them to file them for in advance, or it can simply react to needs as they arise. Similarly the organisation decides the breadth of the plan. The organisation must also decide upon the formality of the plan. Finally, the organisation must make a decision on flexibility the ability of HR Plan to anticipate and deal with contingencies. No organisation likes high level of uncertainty. Organisations seek to reduce uncertainty by planning, which includes forecasting and predicting possible future conditions and events.
2. **Organisational Growth Cycles and Planning**: The stage of an organisation's growth can have considerable influence on HRP. Small organisations in their early stage may not have personnel planning. Need for planning is felt when the organisation enters the growth stage. HR forecasting becomes essential. Internal development of people also begins to receive attention in order to keep up with the growth. A mature organisation experiences less flexibility and variability. Growth slows down. The workforce becomes more formalized and less flexible and innovative. Issues like retirement and possible retrenchment dominate planning. Finally in the declining stage, HRP takes a different focus. Planning is done for lay off, retrenchment and retirement.
3. **Environmental Uncertainties**: HR managers really have opportunity to operate in a stable and predictable environment. Political, social and economic changes affect all organisations. HR planners deal with environmental uncertainties by carefully formulating recruitment, selection and training and development policies and programmes.

4. **Time Horizon:** It is another factor affecting personnel planning on one hand, there are short term plans spanning six months to one year. On the other hand, there are long-term plans which spread over three to twenty years. The exact time span however depends on the degree of uncertainty prevailing in an organisation's environment.
5. **Quality of Information:** The information used to forecast personnel needs originates from a multitude of sources. A major issue in personnel planning is the type of information which should be used in making forecasts closely related to the type of information is the quality of data used. The quality and accuracy of information depend upon the clarity with which the organisational decision makes have to define their strategy, organisational structure, budgets, production schedules, etc.
6. **Nature of Job:** Personnel planers must consider the nature of jobs being filled in the organisation. Job vacancies arise because of separations, promotions, and expansion strategies.
7. **Off Loading the Work:** Several organisations off load part of their work to outside parties either in the form of sub-contracting. Off loading is a regular feature both in the public sector as well as in the private sector. Most organisations have surplus labour and they do not want to worsen the problem by hiring more people.

HRP Process[1]

The process of HRP is one of the most crucial, complex and continuing managerial functions. It embraces organisation development, management development, career planning and succession planning. It is a multi step process including: (as given in Figure 3.2.1).

- Organisational objectives & polices.
- HR demand forecast.
- HR supply forecast.
- HR programming
- HR implementation.
- Control & Evaluation.

Organisational Objectives & Policies: HRP should be based upon organisational objectives. Specific requirements in terms of number and characteristics of employees should be derived from the organisational objectives. Objectives are defined by the top management and the role of HRP is to serve the overall objectives by ensuring availability and utilisation of human resources. Once the organisational objectives are specified, communicated and understood by all concerned, the HR department must specify its objectives with regard to HR utilisation in the organisation. (Refer Figure 3.2.1).

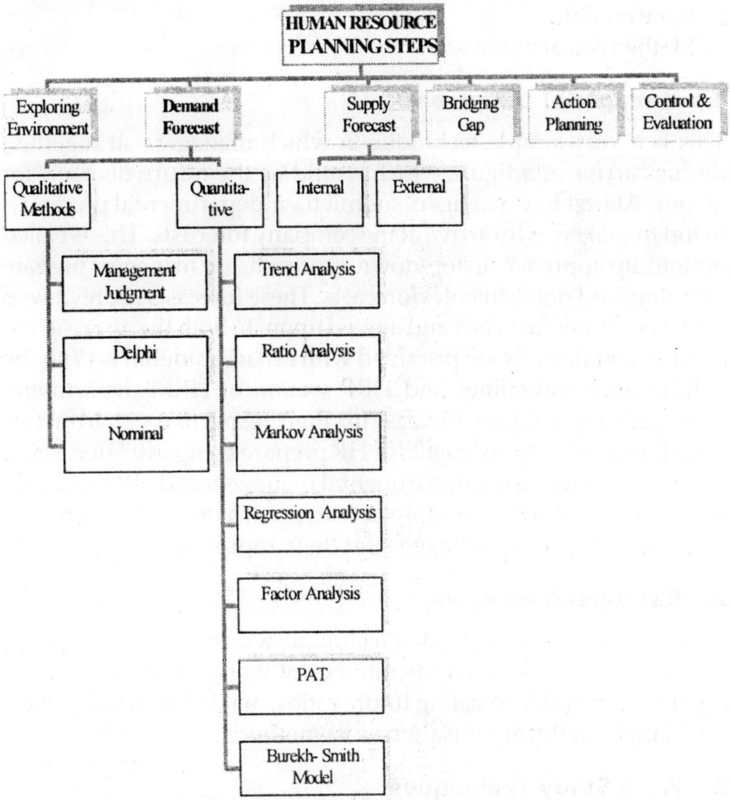

Fig. 3.2.1

HR Demand Forecast: Demand forecasting is the process of estimating the future quantity and quality of people required. The basis of the forecast must be the annual budget and long term corporate plan, translated into activity levels for each function and department. Forecasting considers several factors like competition, economic climate, laws and regulatory bodies, change in technology, social factors, budget, production level, organisational structure, employee separation, etc.

There are many Forecasting techniques such as:

1. Managerial judgment.
2. Ratio trend analysis
3. Work study techniques
4. Delphi technique
5. Flow models
6. Mathematical models.

1. Managerial Judgment

This is a very simple technique in which managers sit together, discuss arrive at a figure which would be the future demand for labour. At first line managers submit their departmental proposals to top managers who arrive at the company forecasts. This is called bottom-up approach. In top-down approach, top managers prepare company and departmental forecasts. These forecasts are reviewed with departmental heads and agreed upon. In both the approaches, departmental heads are provided with broad guidelines. With the help of such guidelines and HRP section of HRM department, managers, can prepare forecast for their respective departments. Simultaneously top managers of HR prepare company forecasts. A committee comprising departmental managers and HR managers will review the two sets of forecast; arrive at a unanimity, which is then presented to top managers for their approval.

2. Ratio-trend Analysis

This is the quickest forecasting technique which involves studying past ratios e. g., between the number of workers and sales in an organisation and forecasting future ratios, making some allowance for changes in the organisation or its methods.

3. Work Study Techniques

It can be used when it is possible to apply work measurement to calculate the length of operations and the amount of labour required. Starting with the production budget, budgets of productive hours are compiled using standard hours for direct labour. The standard hours per unit of out put are then multiplied by the planned volume of units to be produced to give the total number of planned hours for the period. This is then divided by the number of actual working hours for an individual operator to show the number of operators required. Allowance will have to be made for absenteeism and idle time.

4. Delphi Technique

Delphi technique solicits estimates of personnel needs from a group of experts, usually managers The HRP experts act as intermediaries, summarize the various responses and report the findings back to the experts. The experts are surveyed again after they receive this feedback. Summaries and surveys are repeated until the experts opinions begin to agree. The agreement reached is the forecast of the personnel needs.

5. Flow Models

The simplest flow model is called the Markov model, which the forecasters will determine the time that should be covered, establish categories, called states to which employees can be assigned, count annual movements among states for several time periods and estimate the probability of transitions from one state to another based on past trends. Demand is a function of replacing those who make a transition. There are many alternatives to the Markov model. One is semi Markov model which takes into account not just the category but also the tenure of individuals in each category. Another is vacancy model which predicts probabilities of movement and number of vacancies. Markov analysis is advantageous because it makes sense to decision-makers.

6. Mathematical Models

Mathematical models are used in human need forecasting too. One widely used model is

$$E_n=[(Lagg_n)+G]^{1/x}/Y$$

Where E_n =Estimated level of personnel demand in 'n' planning years.

Lagg=Aggregate level of current business activity.

G=Total growth in business activity anticipated through period 'n'

X=Average productivity improvement anticipated from today through

Planning period 'n'

Y=a conversion figure relating today's overall activity to personnel required.

The main purpose of this model is to predict E_n, the level of personnel necessary in 'n' periods.

HR Supply Forecast: Supply Forecasting measures the quantity of human resources that is likely to be available from within the organisation. Forecasts are based on:

1. *An analysis of existing resources:* The existing employees are analyzed by occupation, level of skill, status and length of service. Movements in ratios between, for example, direct and indirect staff would be studied to provide guidance on trends and to indicate where future changes might result in supply problems.
2. *An analysis of wastage:* The rates at which different categories of employees are leaving, to produce forecasts of future replacement requirements. The incidence of wastage in different areas and occupations and the reasons for leaving should also be examined as a guide to any action required reducing losses.
3. *An assessment of changes in conditions of work and absenteeism:* The hours available in the future will obviously be affected by changes in standard hours of work, overtime policies, the length and timing of holidays, shift systems, retirement policy, and the policy for employing part timers. The scope for work sharing should also be considered, that is, one job being split between two or possibly even more people, on the basis of one person doing the work for part of the day and another person or persons taking over the job for the rest of the day.
4. *Forecasting the output of training schemes:* These would include apprentices, and other full time training courses. The output forecast would take account of natural wastage during the training period, bearing in mind that wastage often increases quite considerably at the end of an apprenticeship, unless steps are taken to encourage ex-apprentices to stay.

HR Programming: Once an organisation's personnel demand and supply is forecast, the two must be reconciled or balanced in order that vacancies can be filled by the right employees at the right time. HR programming therefore assumes greater importance.

HR Plan Implementation: It is the action planning which decides how many human resource targets should be achieved and what needs to be done to deal with problems of major technological change, redundancy or high wastage. The main elements are:

1. The recruitment plan which will set out:

- The numbers and types of people required and when they are needed.
- Any special supply problems and how they are to be dealt with.
- The recruitment programme.

2. The human resource development plan, which will show:

- The number of trainees required and the programme for recruiting or training them.
- the number of existing staff who need training or retraining and the training programme.
- the new courses to be developed or the changes to be made for existing course.

3. The retention plan which will describe the actions required to reduce avoidable wastage under the following headings:

- Pay problems.
- Employees leaving to further their career.
- Employees leaving because of conflict.
- Induction crisis.
- Shortage of labour.
- Changes in working requirements.
- Losses of unstable recruits.

4. The redevelopment plan which will set out programmes for transferring or retraining existing employees:

5. The Redundancy plan, which will indicate:

- The extent to which surpluses of people can be absorbed by natural wastage.
- Who is to be redundant, where and when?
- The scope for encouraging voluntary redundancy and the inducements that needs to be offered.
- The plans for redevelopment or retraining, where this has not been covered n the redevelopment plan.
- The steps to be taken to help redundant employees find new jobs.
- The policy for declaring redundancies and making redundancy payments.

The programme for consulting with unions or staff associations and informing those affected.

Control and Evaluation: It represents the final phase in the HRP process. The HR plan should include budgets, targets, and standards. It should also clarify responsibilities for implementation and control and establish reporting procedures which wilt enable achievements to be monitored against the plan.

Essentials for Successful HRP: There are at least eight pre-requisites for successful HRP:

1. HRP must be recognized as an integral part of corporate planning. The planner of HR must therefore, be aware of corporate objectives.
2. Backing of top management.
3. HR responsibilities should be centralized in order to coordinate consultation between different management levels.
4. Personnel records must be complete, up-to-date and readily available.
5. The time horizon of the plan must be long enough to permit any remedial action.
6. The techniques of planning should be those best suited to him data available and the degree of accuracy required.
7. Plans should be prepared by skill levels rather than by aggregates.
8. Data collection, analysis, techniques of planning and the plans themselves need to be constantly revised and improved in the light of experience.

References

1. L.K. Asnia Thappa, *Personnel Management*, Tata McGraw Hill, New Delhi, 2003.
2. RL Mathis; JH, Jackson, *Human Resource Management*, South Western College, Publishiers, 2003
3. J.M. Ivancevich, *Human Resource Management*, Irwin McGraw Hill, New York; 2003.
4. Gary Dressler, *Human Resource Management*, Pearson, New Delhi, 2002.

Chapter three

JOB ANALYSIS AND WORK DESIGN

Human Resource Planning and Organisational Development have cherished an intimate relationship with Job Analysis. A job may be defined as a collection or aggregation of tasks, duties and responsibilities which as a whole, is regarded as a regular assignment to individual employees, and which is different from other assignments. In other words, when the total works to be done is divided and grouped into packages, we call it a job.

Job analysis is a procedure by which relatable and pertinent information is obtained about a job. It is a detailed and systematic study of relevant information relating to the operations and responsibilities of a specific job. After a job has been defined, it is analyzed, i.e. each task is described in detail. Job Analysis is a procedure or process of getting appropriate information about jobs, especially what the worker does, how he gets it done, why he does it, skill, education and training required, relationship to other jobs, physical demands, environmental conditions, etc. In other words, it refers to the anatomy or framework of the job. It is a complete study of job, embodying every known and determinable factor, including the duties, responsibilities involved in its performance, the conditions under which the performance is carried on the nature of the task, the qualities required in the worker and such conditions of employment as pay, hour, opportunities and privileges. It also emphasizes the relation of one job to others in the organisation.

Utility of JA as described in Figure 3.1.1 are:

- Human Resource Planning
- Recruitment
- Selection & Placement
- Training

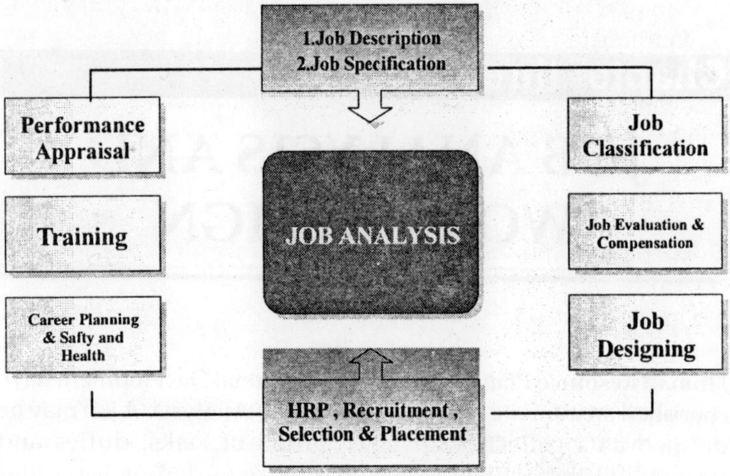

Fig. 3.3.1: Purpose and Uses of Job Analysis[1]

- Career Planning
- Safety and Health
- Performance Appraisal
- Job Evaluation
- Job Classification
- Job Designing.

Further, from another angle purpose and utility of JA is analyzed. To start with, a comprehensive JA programme is an essential ingredient of sound personnel management. It is the major input to forecasting future human resource requirements, job modifications, job evaluation, determination of proper compensation and the writing of job descriptions. The information provide by JA is useful, if not essential, in every phase of employee relations.

1. **Organisation & Manpower Planning:** It is helpful in organisational planning for it defines labour needs in concrete terms and coordinates the activities of the workforce and clearly divides duties and responsibilities.
2. **Recruitment & Selection:** By indicating the specific requirements of each job, it provides a realistic basis for the hiring training, placement, transfer and promotion of personnel.
3. **Wage & Salary Administration:** By indicating the qualifications required for doing a specified job and the risks and hazards

involved in its performance, it helps in salary and wage administration. JA is used as a foundation, for job evaluation.

4. **Job Re-engineering:** JA provides information which enables us to change jobs in order to permit their being manner by personnel with specific characteristics and qualifications. It takes two forms, i.e., industrial engineering and human engineering. Industrial engineering activity is concerned with operational analysis, motion study, work simplification methods and improvements in the place of work and its measurement. Human engineering takes into consideration human capabilities, both physical and psychological and prepares the ground for complex operations of industrial administration, increased efficiency and better productivity.
5. **Employee Training and Management Development:** JA provides the necessary information to the management of training and development programmes. It helps to determine the content and subject matter of training courses. It also helps in checking application information, interviewing weighing test results and in checking references.
6. **Performance Appraisal:** It helps in establishing clear cut standards which may be compared with the initial contribution of each individual.
7. **Health and Safety:** It provides an opportunity for identifying hazardous conditions and unhealthy environmental factors so that corrective measures may be taken to minimize and avoid the possibility of accidents.

Contents of JA[2]

This fact has been explained in figure 3.3.2 & 3.3.3 See next page

Then it is obvious that job analysis is usually a clear indication of a job description and job specification. See Figure 3.3.3A.

Steps in JA

There are five basic steps required for doing a Job Analysis:

1. *Collection of background information:* According to Terry, "the make up of a job, its relation to other jobs and its requirements for competent performance are essential information needed for a job evaluation. This information can be had by reviewing available background information such as organisation charts, class specifications and existing job descriptions which provide a starting point from which to build the revised job description.

1. Job identification	:	Its title including code number
2. Chief characteristics	:	Its location, physical setting, suppression, union jurisdiction, hazards and discomforts.
3. What the typical worker does	:	Specific operation and tasks that makeup an assignment, their relative timing and importance, their simplicity, complexity, the responsibility or safety of others for property, funds, confidence and trust.
4. Which materials and equipment, a worker uses	:	Metals, plastics, grains, yarns, milling machines, punch presses and micrometer.
5. How a job is performed	:	Nature of operation i.e. lifting, handling, cleaning, washing, feeding, removing, drilling, driving, etc.
6. Required personnel attributes	:	Experience, training, physical strength, coordination, physical demand, mental capabilities, aptitudes, social skills etc.
7. Job relationship	:	Experience required opportunities for advancement, patterns of promotions, essential cooperation, direction, or leadership.

Figure 3.3.2

Job description	Job specification
A statement containing items such as:	A statement of human qualifications necessary to do the job. It contains items such as:
• Title	• Education
• Location	• Experience
• Job summary	• Training
• Duties	• Judgment
• Machines, tools, equipment	• Initiative
• Materials and forms used	• Physical efforts
• Supervision given or received	• Responsibilities
• Working conditions	• Communication skills
• Hazards	• Emotional characteristics
	• Unusual sensory demands

Source: K. B. Aswasthappa, *Personnel and HRM*, Tata McGraw Hill, 2003.

Figure 3.3.3: Job analysis

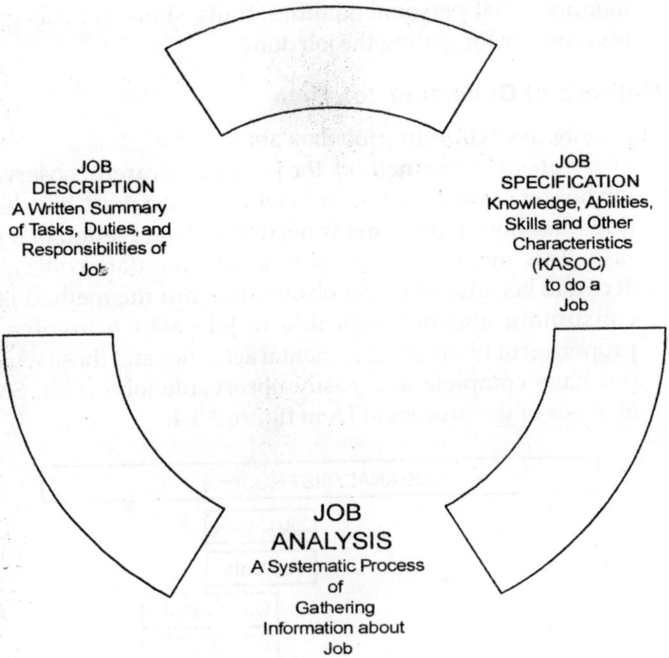

Figure 3.3.3A

2. *Selection of representative position to be analyzed:* Since the analysis of all jobs would be time consuming flow representatives positions should be analyzed.
3. *Collection of job analysis data:* Job data on features of the job required employee qualifications and requirements should be collected either from the employees who actually perform a job, or from other employees who watch the workers doing a job and thereby acquire knowledge about it, or from the outside persons, known as the trade job analysts who are appointed to watch employees performing a job.
4. *Developing a job description:* The information collected is to be developed in the form of a job description. This is a written statement that describes the main features of the job as well as the qualifications/ activities which the job incumbents must possess.
5. *Developing a job specification:* The last step is to convert the job description statements into job specifications, i.e. to specifically

mention what personal qualities, traits, skills and background is necessary for getting the job done.

Methods of Collecting Job Data

The methods of collecting job data are:

1. *Observation:* In this method, the job analyst careful observes the job holder at work and records what he/she does, how he/she does and how much time is needed for completion of a given task. This method is very simple and the data collected are accurate because of direct observation but the method is time consuming and in applicable to jobs which involve high properties of unobservable mental activities and those which do not have complete and easily observable job cycles. See the analysis of the process of JA in figure 3.3.4.

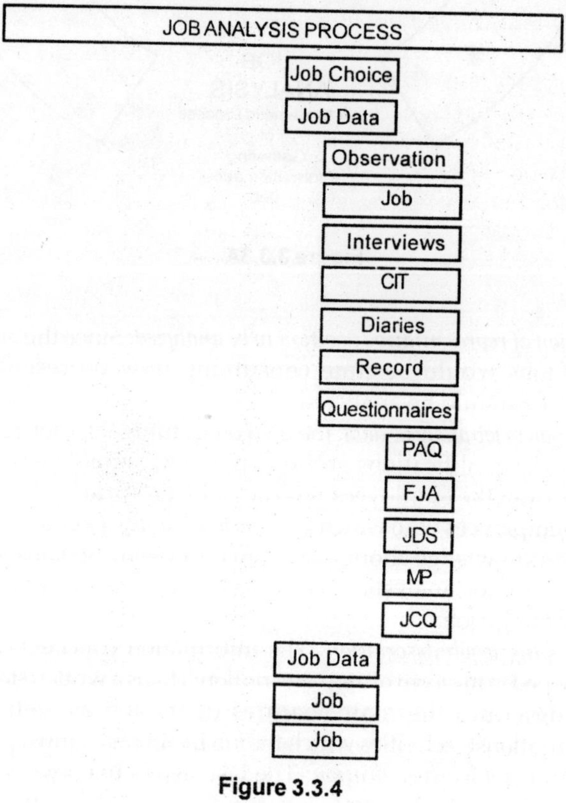

Figure 3.3.4

2. *Interview:* In this, the analyst interviews the job holder and his/her supervisor to get information about the job. Usually a structured interview form is used to record the information. During the interview the analyst must make judgments about the information to be included and its degree of importance. The interview method is also time consuming.
3. *Questionnaire:* Job holders fill in the given structured questionnaire, which are then approved by their supervisors. The filled in questionnaire offer enough data on jobs. Standard questionnaires are available or they may be prepared for the purpose by the analyst. The questionnaires method has its own advantages and limitations. The major advantage is that information on a large number of jobs can be collected in a relatively short period of time. The method helps save time and the staff required carrying out the programme. But the accuracy of the information obtained through the questionnaire leaves much to be desired. Job analysis work requires specialized knowledge and training.
4. *Checklists:* A checklist is similar to questionnaire but the response sheet contains fewer subjective judgments and tends to be either yes-or-no variety. Checklists can cover as many as 100 activities and job holders tick only those tasks that are included in their jobs. Preparation of a checklist is a challenging job. The specialists who prepare the checklist must collect all relevant information about the job concerned. When a checklist has been prepared for a job, it is sent to the job holder. He/she is asked to check all listed tasks that he/she performs and indicate the amount of time spent on each task as well as the training and experience required to be proficient in each task. The checklist thus answered, will be the basis for tabulating job related data.
5. *Technical conference:* In this method, services of supervisors who possess extensive knowledge about a job are used. It is from these experts that details about the job are obtained. Here a conference of supervisors is used. The analyst initiates dissuasion which provides details about jobs.
6. *Diary method:* This method requires the job holders to record in detail their activities each day. If done faithfully, this technique is accurate and eliminates errors caused by memory lapses. But this is time consuming.

The methods described above are not mutually exclusive. None of them is universally superior. The best results can be obtained from a combination of these methods.

Some quantitative techniques are also used for collecting job data. Some of them are:

a. *Position Analysis Questionnaire (PAQ):* PAQ contains 194 job elements on which a job is created depending on the degree to which an element is present. The primary advantage of PAQ is that it can be used to analyze almost every job.
b. *Management Position Description Questionnaire (MPDQ):* It is a highly structured questionnaire containing 208 items relating to managerial responsibilities, restrictions, demands and other miscellaneous position characteristics.
c. *Functional Job Analysis (FJA):* It is a worker oriented job analytical approach which attempts to describe the whole person on the job.

WORK /JOB DESIGN (JD)[3]

The logical sequence to job analysis is job design[2]. Job design is the process of deciding on the content of a job in terms of its duties and responsibilities, on the methods to be used in carrying out the job, in terms of techniques, systems and procedures, and on the relationships that should exist between the job holder and his/her superiors, subordinates and colleagues. Thus JD involves three steps:

1. Specification of individual tasks.
2. Specification of the method(s) of performing each task, and
3. Combination of tasks into specific jobs to be assigned to individuals.

Step 1 and 3 determine the content of the job, while step 2 indicates precisely how the job shall be performed. While designing a job, requirements of the organisation and individual needs of the job holder must be considered.

JD is affected by organisational, environmental and behavioural factors. A properly designed job will make it productive and satisfying.

Organisational Factors

Organisational factors include:

- Characteristics of task
- The flow of work
- Economics which is concerned with designing and shaping jobs to fit the physical abilities and characteristics of individuals so that they can perform their job effectively.
- Work practices.

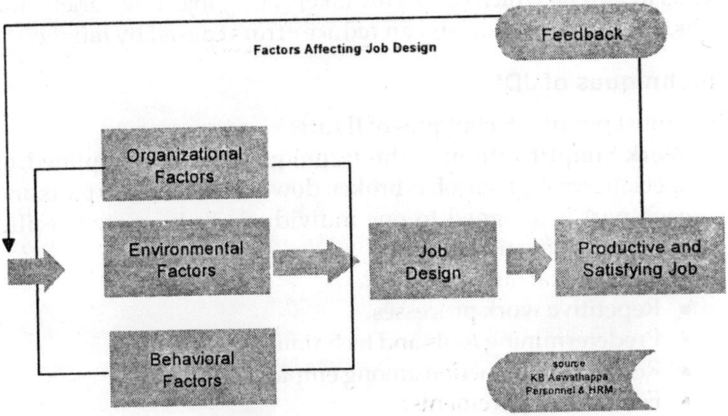

Fig. 3.3.5: Factor affecting JD

Environmental Factors: Environmental elements affect all activities of HRM and JD is no exception. The factors that have a bearing on JD are employee abilities and availability, and social and cultural expectations. Efficiency consideration must be balanced against the abilities and availability of the people who are to do the work. Literacy, knowledge and awareness among workers have improved considerably, so also their expectations from jobs. Hence, jobs must be designed to meet the expectations of workers. When designing jobs for international operations, uniform designs are almost certain to neglect national and cultural differences. Hours of work, holidays, vacations, rest breaks, religious beliefs, management styles, and worker sophistication and attitudes are just some of the predictable differences that can affect the design of jobs across international borders. Failure to consider these social expectations can create dissatisfaction, low motivation, low quality of work life, etc.

Behavioural factors: Behavioural factors have to do with human needs and the necessity to satisfy them. Higher level needs are more significant in this context. Individuals must receive meaningful feedback about their performance, preferably by re-evaluating their own performance and defining the feedback. Autonomy is being responsible for what one does. It is the freedom to control one's responses to the environment. The absence of autonomy can cause poor performance. Lack of variety may cause boredom. Boredom leads to fatigue which causes mistaken. So by injecting variety into jobs, personnel specialists can reduce errors caused by fatigue.

Techniques of JD[4]

The most popular techniques of JD are:

1. **Work Simplification:** In this technique, the job is simplified, or specialized. A given job is broken down into small sub parts and each part is assigned to one individual. To be more specific, work simplification involves
   - Mechanical facing of work.
   - Repetitive work processes.
   - Predetermining tools and techniques.
   - Restricted interaction among employees.
   - Few skill requirements.

   Work simplification is done so that the less trained and less paid employees can do these jobs. Wok simplification is adopted when job designers feel that jobs are not specialized enough.
2. **Job Rotation:** Job rotation implies movement of employees from job to job. Job remains unchanged, but incumbents shift. With job rotation, a given employee performs different jobs but more or less jobs of the same nature. Job rotation is likely to increase intrinsic reward potential of a job because of different skills and abilities needed to perform it. It may be stated that job rotation may not have much impact on employee enthusiasm and efficiency. According to Herzberg, job rotation is merely, "substituting one zero for another zero."
3. **Job Enlargement:** Job enlargement involves expanding the number of tasks or duties assigned to a given job. It is naturally opposite to work simplification. Adding more tasks or duties to a job does not mean that new skills and abilities are needed to perform it. There is only horizontal expansion. Herzberg was right when he said that job enlargement is "adding zero to zero." Job enlargement is usually resisted by employees.
4. **Job Enrichment:** Job enrichment seeks to improve both task efficiency and human satisfaction by building into people's jobs, quite specifically, greater scope for personal achievement and recognition, more challenging and responsible work and more opportunity for individual advancement and growth. An enriched job will have more responsibility and autonomy, more variety of tasks and more growth opportunities. The employees

do more planning and controlling with less supervision but more self-evaluation.

5. **Self-Directed Teams:** A self-directed work team is an intact group of employees who are responsible for a whole work process or segment that delivers a product or service to an internal or external customer. Team members work together to improve their operations, handle day to day problems and plan and control their work. Highly effective teams are composed of groups of committed individuals who trust each other, have a clear sense of purpose about their work are effective communicators within and outside the team, make sure that everyone in the team is involved in decisions affecting the groups and follow a process that helps them plan, make decisions and ensure the quality of their work.
6. **High Performance Work Design:** It is a means of improving performance in an environment where positive and demanding goals are set. It starts from the principle of autonomous group working and develops an approach which enables groups to work effectively together in situations where the rate of innovation is high. Operational flexibility is important and there is, therefore, the need for employees to gain and apply new skills quickly with minimum supervision. In most organisations, which are caught up in the morale of bureaucracy, such high performance work design does not work.

References

1. C.B. Mamoria, *Personnel Management*, HPH, 1996.
2. *Ibid.*
3. K. Aswasthappa, *Personnel Management and HRM*, Tata McGraw Hill, 2003.
4. *Ibid.*

Chapter four

RECRUITMENT

Recruitment forms are the first stage in the process which continues with selection and ceases with the placement of the candidate. It is the next step in the procurement function, the first being the manpower planning. Recruitment is understood as the process of searching for and obtaining applicants for jobs, from among whom the right people can be selected. So recruitment is the process of finding and attracting capable applicants for employment. It is a collection of qualified aspired job candidates. The process begins when new recruits are sought and ends when their applications are submitted. The result is a pool of applicants from which new employees are selected.

Purposes and Importance

The general purpose of recruitment is to provide a pool of potentially qualified job candidates. The purposes are to:

- Determine the present and future requirements of the organisation in conjunction with its personnel planning and job analysis activities.
- Increase the pool of job candidates at minimum cost.
- Help increase the success rate of the selection process by reducing the number of visibly, under-qualified job applicants.
- Help reduce the probability that job applicants, once recruited and selected will leave the organisation only after a short period of time.
- Meet the organisation's legal and social obligations regarding the composition of its workforce.
- Begin identifying and preparing potential job applicants who will be appropriate candidates.
- Increase organisational and individual effectiveness in the short term and long-term.
- Evaluate an effectiveness of various recruiting techniques and sources for all types of job applicants.

Recruitment represents the first contact that a company makes with potential employees. It is through recruitment that many individuals will come to know a company and eventually decide whether they wish to work for it. A well planned and well managed recruiting effort will result in high quality applicants, whereas a haphazard and piecemeal effort will result in mediocre ones. The recruitment process should inform qualified individuals about employment opportunities, create a positive image of the company, provide enough information about the jobs so that applicants can make comparisons with their qualifications and interests, and generate enthusiasm among the best candidates so that they will apply for the vacant positions.

Factors Affecting Recruitment

All organisations, whether large or small, do engage in recruiting activity, though not to the same extent. This differs with:

- The size of the organisation.
- The employment conditions in the community where the organisation is located.
- The effects of past recruiting efforts which show the organisation's ability to locate and keep good performing people.
- Working conditions and salary and benefit packages offered by the organisation which may influence turnover and necessitate future recruiting.
- The rate of growth of organisation.
- The level of seasonally of operations and future expansion and production programmes.
- Cultural, economic and legal factors.

Recruitment Process

Recruitment refers to the process of identifying and attracting job seekers so as to build a pool of qualified job applicants. The process comprises five steps which are inter- related.

1. **Recruitment planning:** Planning involves the translation of likely job vacancies and information about the nature of these jobs into a set of objectives or targets that specify the number and type of applicants to be contacted. Organisations always plan to attract more applicants than they will hire. Some of these contacted will be uninterested, unqualified or both. The type of people depends on the tasks and responsibilities involved and the qualifications and experience expected.

2. **Strategy development:** In this step some important decisions are to be taken. Organisation must decide whether to hire less skilled employees and invest on training and education programmes, or they can hire skilled labour and professionals.

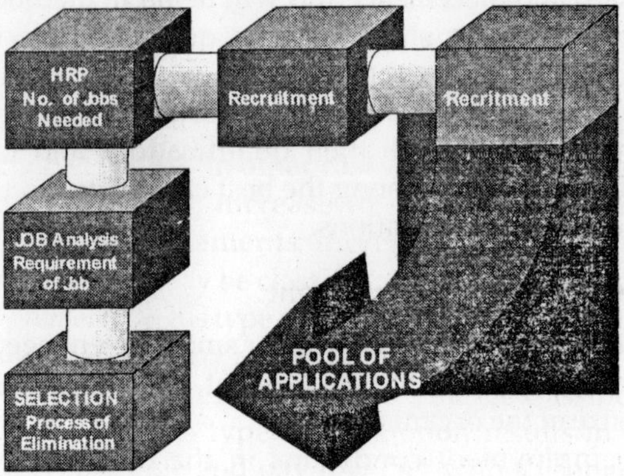

Fig. 3:19

The second decision is regarding methods used in recruitment and selection. The advent of computers had made it possible for employers to scan national and international applicant qualifications. The next decision is for the organisation to look into labour markets to reduce costs. Generally, companies look in to the national market for managerial and professional employees, regional or local markets for technical employees and local markets for clerical and blue collar employees. The next important problem for the organisation is regarding methods or sources of recruitment. Internal recruitment seeks applicants for positions from those who are currently employed. Internal sources include:

- *Present Employees:* Promotion and transfers from among the present employees can be a good source of recruitment.
- *Employee References:* Employees can develop a good prospects for their families and friends by acquitting them with the advantage of a job with the company, furnishing cards of introduction, and even encouraging them to apply.
- *Former Employees:* Some retired employees may be willing to come back to work on a part time basis, or may recommend some one who would be interested in working for the company.

- *Previous Applicants:* Although not truly an internal source, these who have previously applied for jobs can be contacted by mails a quick and in expensive way to fill an unexpected opening.

External sources far outnumber the internal methods. Specifically, sources external to an organisation are professional or trade associations, advertisements, employment exchanges, college/university/institute placement services, walking and writing, consultants, contractors, displaced persons, radio and television, acquisition and mergers and competitors. But both the internal and external sources have its advantages and disadvantages. The worth main points are:

Internal Recruitment

Advantages	*Disadvantages*
1. It is less costly	1. It perpetuates the old concept of doing things
2. Organizations have better	2. It abets raiding
3. Employee motivation and morale increases	3. Politics play a crucial role
	4. Morale problem for those not promoted.

External recruitment

Advantages	*Disadvantages*
1. Benefits of new skills, new talents and new experiences	1. Better morale and motivation is denied
2. Compliance with reservation	2. It is costly
3. Scope for annoyance, jealousies and heart burn area voided	3. Chance of creeping in false positive and false negative errors
	4. Adjustment of new employees to the organizational culture takes longer time

Whatever be the source of recruitment, the job seekers must submit application forms seeking employment. These applications shall be supplied by the employer (called Application Banks) or the applicants may be expected to prepare their own application forms and submit on or before the expiry of the stipulated date. An effective recruiting strategy must determine when to look decide on the timing of events besides knowing where and how to look for job applicants.

3. **Searching:** Once a recruiting plan and strategy are worked out the search process begins. It involves two steps. The first step is source activation. This means that no actual recruiting takes place until line managers have verified that a vacancy does exist

or wild exist. If the organisation has planned well and done a good job of developing its sources and search methods, activation soon results in a flood of appellations. The applications received must be screened. Those who pass have to be contracted and invited for interview. Unsuccessful applicants must be sent letters of regret. The second step in the searching process concerns communication. Here the organisation is in jeopardy. On one hand, they want to do whatever they can to attract desirable applicants. On the other, they must resist the temptation of over selling their virtues. In selling the organisation, both the message and the media deserve attention. Message refers to the employment advertisement. With regard to media, it may be stated that effectiveness of any recruiting message depends on the media.

4. **Screening:** The selection process will begin after the applications have been scrutinized and short listed. The purpose of screening is to remove from the recruitment process, at an early stage, those applicants who are visibly unqualified for the job. Effective screening can save a great deal of time and money. Care must be exercised however, to assure that potentially good employees are not lost and that women and minorities receive full and fair considerations and are not rejected without justification. The techniques used to screen applicants vary depending on the candidate sources and recruiting methods used.
5. **Evaluation and control:** Evaluation and control is necessary as considerable costs are incurred in the recruitment process. Questions should always be asked as to whether the recruitment methods used are valid and whether the recruitment process itself is effective. Statistical information on the cost of advertisements, time taken for the process, and the suitability of the candidates for consideration in the selection process should be gathered and evaluated.

The recruitment process has the objective of searching for and obtaining applications from job seekers in sufficient numbers and quality. Keeping this objective in mind, the evaluation might include.

- Return rate of applications sent out.
- Number of suitable candidates for selection.
- Retention and performance of the candidates selected.
- Cost of the recruitment process
- Time lapsed data.
- Evaluation of recruitment methods include :

- Number of initial enquiries received which resulted in completed application forms.
- Numbers of candidates at various stages of the recruitment and selection process.
- Number of candidates at various stages of the recruitment and selection process.
- Number of candidates recruited.
- Number of candidates retained in the organisation after six months.

Essentials of a Good Recruitment Policy

The recruitment policy of an organisation must satisfy the following conditions:

- It should be in conformity with its general personnel policies.
- It should be flexible enough to meet the changing needs of an organisation.
- It should be so designed as to ensure employment opportunities for its employees on a long term basis so that the goals of the organisation should be achievable.
- It should match the qualities of employees with the requirements of the work for which they are employed, and
- It should highlight the necessity of establishing job analysis.

The nature and extent of the recruitment programme depends on a number of factors including the skills required, the state of the labour market, general economic conditions and the image of the employer. An enterprise which has a reputation of paying for wages, providing good employee benefits and taking interest in employee welfare activities would attract a large number of applicants than it needs without making any extra recruiting effort.

Re-Hiring: U Turn in HR Practice

In fact re-hiring was an unhealthy and unacceptable practice. But presently, organisations are considering the cases of employees who left for a better job. On the job applications of the 'Left-outs' employees HR managers are formulating re-hiring policy. This has dual benefits- for employees and for organisations as both are familiar with the expectations of each. This trend is gaining ground to control attrition. In this connection the points of re-hiring of ex-employees are"

- 2nd Innings: People work with one organisation; quit the job either on dissatisfaction or for better career growth prospects. This is not applicable to dismissed/ terminated cases.
- Boomeranging work: HR experts termed this as 'boomeranging' and also stamped it as a "Smart recruitment strategy."
- Back with A Bang: Undoubtedly, re-hiring is an intelligent 'practice', with no guarantees of repeating of part mistakes in quitting.

Today's corporates the Freedback Ventures. Xerox India Ltd.,, etc. are practicing this re-hiring policy for providing second chance to their former employees. They gained more experience, wisdom and maturity for better work. On the contrary 'boomeranging' helps in culting the cost of training. Besides, it ensures branding and clarity on both sides by bringing diverse experiences to the organisation. (Yasmi Taj: *TOI*: 2007)

Further Readings

1. M. Armstong, *A Hand Book of Human Resource Management*, Bachees, 2006.
2. CD Fisher, et al. *Human Resource Management*, Houghton Mifflin Co. Boston, 1997.
3. David A Decenz and S.P. Robbins, *Personnel Human Resource, Management* Prentice Hall of India, New Delhi, 1989.
4. Edwin B Flippo, Personnel Management Gin Ed, MacGraw Hill, NY, 1984.

Chapter five

SELECTION

Selection is the process of picking individuals out of the pool of job applicants with requisite qualifications and competence to fill jobs in the organisation. It is the process of differentiating between applicants in order to identify those with greater chances of success in a job.

Recruitment and selection are the two crucial steps in the HR process and are often used interchangeably. There is however, a fine distinction between the two. While recruitment refers to the process of identifying and encouraging prospective employees to apply for jobs, selection is concerned with picking the right candidates from a pool of applicants. Recruitment is said to be positive in its approach as it seeks to attract as many candidates as possible. Selection on the other hand is negative in its application in as much as it seeks to eliminate as many unqualified applicants as possible in order to identify the right candidates.

While formulating a selection policy, due consideration should be given to organisational requirements as well as technical and professional dimensions of selection procedures. Yoder and others have suggested goals, technological issues, cost factors, extent of formality, etc. In other words, an effective selection policy must assert the 'why' and 'what' aspects of the organisational objectives.

Essentials of a Selection Procedure

The selection procedure adopted by an organisation is mostly tailor made to meet its particular needs. The through nets of the procedure depend upon three factors:

- Nature of selection whether faulty or safe, because a faulty selection affects not only the training period that may be needed, but also results in heavy expenditure on the new employee and the loss that may be incurred by the organisation in case the job occupant fails on his job.

- The policy of the company and the attitude of the management adopt a practice to hire more than the actual number needed with a view to removing the unfit persons from the jobs.
- The longer the probation period, the greater the uncertainty in the minds of the selected candidate about his future.

1 The hiring process can be successful, if the following preliminary requirements are satisfied :

- Some one should have the authority to hire. This authority comes from the employment requisition as developed by an analysis of the work load and workforce.
- There must be some standard or personnel with which a prospective employee may be compared, i.e. there should be available before hard, a comprehensive job description and job specifications as developed by a job analysis.
- There must be a sufficient number of applicants from whom the required number of employees may be selected.

Steps in Selection Procedure

There is no short cut to an accurate evaluation of a candidate. The hiring procedures are, therefore, generally long and complicated. Many employers make use of such techniques and pseudo sciences as phrenology physiognomy, astrology, graphology, etc., while coming to hiring decisions. However in modern times these are considered to be unreliable measures.

The following is a popular procedure though it may be modified to suit individual situation.

- Reception or preliminary interview or screening.
- Application Blank – A fact finder that helps in learning about an applicant's background and life history.
- A well conducted interview to explore the facts and get at the attitudes of the applicant and his family to the job.
- A physical examination health and stamina.
- Physiological testing to explore the surface area and get an objective look at a candidate's suitability for a job.
- A reference check.
- Final selection approval by manager and communication of the decision to the candidate.

Barriers to Effective Selection[1]

The main objective of selection is to hire people having competence and commitment. This is often hurdled because of certain impediments. They are:

1. **Perception:** Our inability to understand others accurately is probably the most fundamental barrier to selecting the right candidate. Our views are highly personalized; as a result we all perceive the world differently. Our limited perceptual ability is obviously a stumbling block to the objective and rational selection of people.
2. **Fairness:** Fairness in selection requires that no individual should be discriminated against on the basis of religion, region, race or gender. But the low numbers of women and other less privileged sections of the society in middle and senior management positions and open discrimination on the basis of age in job advertisements and in the selection process would suggest that all the efforts to minimize inequity have not been very effective.
3. **Validity:** It is a test that helps predict job performance of an incumbent. A test that has been validated can differentiate between the employees who can perform well and those who will not. However a validated test does not predict job success accurately.
4. **Reliability:** A reliable method is one which will produce consistent results when repeated in similar situations.
5. **Pressure:** Pressure is brought on the selectors by politicians, bureaucrats, relative, and friends to select particular candidates. (Aswathappa: 2003)

Approaches to Selection

There is a tendency to prefer host country citizens to man overseas operations. So it is imperative to know approaches of selection.

1. **Ethnocentric approach:** In this approach, staffing decisions are made at the organisations head quarters. Subsidiaries have limited autonomy, and key jobs at home and abroad are filled by employees from the head quarters. Nationals from the parent country dominate the organisation at home and abroad.
2. **Polycentric:** Each subsidiary is treated as a distinct national entity with local control over operations. However the head quarters control key financial targets and investment decisions. Subsidiaries are managed by local citizens, but the key jobs remain with staff from the parent country.
3. **Regiocentric:** Here control within the group and the movement of staff are managed on a regional basis reflecting the particular disposition of business and operations within the group.

Regional managers have greater discretion in decisions. Movement of staff is largely restricted to specific geographical regions.

4. **Geocentric:** In this case, business strategy is integrated thoroughly on global basis. Staff development and promotion are based on ability, not nationality such organisations are uncommon.

Reference

1. CB Mamoria, *Personnel Management*, HPH, 1996.

Further Readings

1. E.H. Burack and Robert Smith, *Personnel Management-A Human Resource Systom Approach*, West Publishing Cost Panel, 2000.

Chapter six

INDUCTION, PROMOTION, AND TRANSFER

INDUCTION

Induction, or orientation or indoctrination is a technique by which a new employee is rehabilitated into the changed surroundings and introduced to the practices, policies and purposes of the organisation. In other words, it is a welcoming process the idea is to welcome a newcomer make him feel at home and generate in him a feeling that his own job, however small is meaningful and has a significance as a part of the total organisation.

Objectives[1]

When a newcomer joins an organisation, he is an utter stranger to the people, work place and work environment. He may feel unsecured, shy and nervous. The first few days may be anxious and disbursing ones for him. One may have anxiety caused by not following the usual practices prevalent in the organisation or the haphazard procedures, or lack of information. These may develop discouragement, disillusionment or defensive behaviour. Induction leads to reduction of such anxieties, dispels the irrational fears of present employees, and hold colleagues responsible for assisting the newcomers so that the may feel confident.

There is another reason for effective induction. It helps minimize what might be called the reality shock some new employees undergo. This reality shock is caused by the incompatibility between what the employees expect in their new jobs and the realities they are confronted with. The newcomer may expect:

- Opportunities for advancement
- Social status and prestige
- Responsibility

- Opportunities to use special attitudes and educational background.
- Challenge and adventure.
- Opportunity to be creative and original.
- Lucrative salary.

But when the expectations are often fulfilled and therefore result in frustrating experiences for new employees, experiences of which include jobs with low initial challenge, inadequate feedback and inadequate performance appraisals. This result is reality shock orientation can help overcome this problem by providing for more realistic expectations on the part of new employees and more understanding on the part of the supervisors.

Finally the purpose of induction is to introduce the new employee and the organisation to each other, to help them become acquainted, and to help them accommodate each other. The newcomer is explained what is expected of him and for this, he is explained the rules, regulations, policies and procedures that directly affect him. He is made aware of how his job fits into the overall operation of the organisation, his own duties and responsibilities, and to who is should look for when he has any problem.

Procedure

An organisation has an obligation to make integration of the individual into the organisation as smooth and anxiety free as possible. Whether that is achieved through a formal or informal placement orientation programme depends on the size of the organisation and the complexity of the individuals' new environment. Many organisations develop formal orientation programmes. These might include a tour of the offices or plant, a tack about the history of the organisation and short discussion with a representative of the personnel department who will describe the organisation's benefit plans. Other organisations may utilise an informal orientation programme which might include being assigned to another senior employee who will not only introduce the new worker to other workers but show him other things too.

There is no model induction procedure. Each organisation develops its own procedures as per it needs. But the procedure should basically follow these steps:

1. The new person needs time and a place to report to work.
2. It is very important that the supervisor or the immediate boss meet and welcome the employee to the organisation.

3. Administrative work should be completed. Such items as vacations, probationary period, medical absences, suggestion systems should be covered.
4. The departmental orientation can be conducted. This should include a get acquainted task, introduction to the department, explanation of the functions of the department, and job instruction and to whom he should look for help when he has any problem.
5. Verbal explanations are supplemented by a wide variety of printed material, employee hand books, flayers, employee manuals, house journals, picture stories, comics and cartoons, pamphlets, etc. along with short guided tour around the plant.

Induction programmes usually cover things like employee compensation benefits, personnel policies, employees daily routine, company organisations and operations and safety measures and regulations. Orientation is generally provided on the following :

1. The significance of the job with all necessary information about it including job training and job hazards.
2. The company, its history and products, process of production and major operations involved in his job.
3. Structure of the organisation.
4. Employees own department and job and how they fit into the organisation.
5. Relations between foremen and personnel department.
6. Company policies, practices, objectives and regulations.
7. Personnel policy and sources of information.
8. Terms and conditions of service, amenities and welfare facilities.
9. Rules and regulations governing hours of work and overtime, safety, and accidents prevention, holidays and vacations, methods of reporting tardiness absenteeism.
10. Grievance procedure and discipline handling.
11. Social benefits and recreation services.
12. Opportunities, promotions, transfers, suggestion schemes and job stabilisation.

Typical Techniques

A typical induction programme should consist primarily of three steps:

1. *General orientation by the staff of the personnel department:* It gives the necessary general information about the history and operations of the firm – the purpose of which is to help an employee to build some pride and interest in the organisation. Information is also given on specific employee services such as pension, health and welfare plans, safety programmes, etc.
2. *Specific orientation by the job supervisor or his representative*: Here induction is specific and requires skill on the part of the foreman. The employee is shown the department and his place of work, introduced to other employees, informed of the location of the bathrooms, lavatories, canteens and time clock and told about the organisations specific practices and customs. The purpose of specific induction is to enable an employee to adjust himself to his work and environment.
3. *Follow up orientation by either the personnel department or the supervisor*: This induction takes place some time within one week to six months from the time of the initial hiring and orientation. It is conducted either by a foreman or a specialist. Its purpose is to find out whether the employee is reasonably well satisfied with him. The employee may be asked whether his hours of work and his pay are as represented to him before employment, how he feels about his boss, how he feels about his fellow workers and whether he has any suggestion to make for changes in the induction procedure or in other company practices. The interviewer records the answers as well as his own comments on the employees' progress. Through personal tasks, guidance and counseling, efforts are made to remove the difficulties experienced by the newcomer.

Problems of Induction

An induction programme can go wrong for a number of reasons. The HR department should try to avoid such errors. Some of them are:

1. Supervisor which is entrusted with the job is not trained or is too busy.
2. Employee is overwhelmed with too much information in a short time.
3. Employee is overloaded with forms to complete.
4. Employee is given only menial task that discourage job interest and company loyalty.

5. Employee is asked to perform tasks where there are high chances of failure that could needlessly discourage the employee.
6. Employee is pushed into the job with a sketchy orientation under the mistaken belief that "trial by fire" is the best orientation.
7. Employee is forced to fill in the gaps between a broad orientation by the HR department and a narrow orientation at the departmental level.
8. Employee is thrown into action too soon.
9. Employee mistakes can damage the company.
10. Employee may develop wrong perceptions because of short periods spent on each job.

PROMOTION

"Promotion" is a term which covers a change and calls for greater responsibilities and usually involves higher pay and better terms and conditions of service and therefore, a higher status or rank. According to Scott and Clothier, "A promotion is the transfer of an employee to a job which pays more money or one what carries some preferred status."

A promotion may be defined as an upward advancement, of an employee in an organisation to another job, which commands better pay/wages, better status/prestige, and higher opportunities/challenges, responsibility, and authority, better working environment, hours of work and facilities, and a higher work.

Purposes[2]

The purposes of promotion may be outlined as follows:

- To motivate employees to higher productivity.
- To attract and retain the services of qualified and competent people.
- To recognize and reward the efficiency of an employee.
- To increase the effectiveness of the employee and of the organisation.
- To fill up higher vacancies from within the organisation.
- To build loyalty, morale and a sense of belongingness in the employee.

- To impress upon others that opportunities are available to them too in the organisation, if they perform well.

A promotion represents the ultimate accomplishment for some employees. Many achieve it through hard work and good performance. A few follow short cuts to achieve the desired goal.

Principles[3]

Promotion is a double edged weapon. If handled carefully, it contributes to employee satisfaction and motivation. If mishandled, it leads to discontentment, frustration, skepticism and bickering among the employees and culminates in a high rate of labour turnover. It is the responsibility of the HR department to lay down a sound promotional policy and ensure its implementation. The policy of promotion should be clear on the following:

1. The management must make it clear whether to fill up higher positions by internal promotions or recruit people from outside. Generally speaking, top positions in an organisation are filled through external recruit meat. The lower positions, however, are filled up by promotions from within.
2. When it has been decided to fill up higher positions with promotions, a further decision on determining the basis of promotion should be made by the management. The basis of promotion may be seniority or merit or both.

If seniority is the basis for promotion, an employee with the longest period of service will get promoted, irrespective of whether he or she is competent to occupy a higher post or not.

A promotion on the basis of seniority has merits and demerits. The merits are:

- It is easy to administer.
- There is less scope for subjectivity or arbitrariness in fixing seniority.
- Labour unions welcome seniority based promotions.
- Seniority and experience go hand in hand and therefore it is right and proper to make promotions on this basis.
- Subordinates are more willing to work under on older boss who has given many years of service to the company.
- Loyalty is rewarded.

The demerits are:

- Seniority is no indication of competence.

- In spite of judicial pronouncement, there is no single criterion for fixing the seniority of an employee.
- Young and competent people get frustrated and might leave the organisation.

The merits of promotion by competence are:

- Efficiency is encouraged, recognized and rewarded.
- Competent people are retained because better prospects are open to them.
- Productivity increases.

The disadvantages of promotion by merit are:

- Discontentment among senior employees.
- Scope for favoritism.
- Loyalty and length of service are not rewarded.
- Opposition from union leaders.

3. Another point to be made clear about the policy of promotion is whether to promote employees against vacancies or non-vacancies. In many organisations, employees are promoted on a non-vacancy basis after they complete a minimum period of service. Such promotions are time bound and not based on vacancies or merit.
4. A promotion policy should establish a well defined promotion chart showing that can go up to what level in the organisation. The promotion chart is highly useful to the management because it clears any suspicion which the employees may have and enables the aspirants to make them eligible for promotion.
5. Frequent promotions are inadvisable from the point of view of the employer and the employees. Frequent changes in the assignments of individuals make them stagnate in their jobs and their responses to change get stilted and the initiative that they take to keep themselves abreast of new developments diminishes over the years.
6. A promotion should be preceded by a job analysis, and performance appraisal. A job analysis is essential to know what the job demands from its incumbent. Employee assessment, in the other hand, enables the management to know whether the employee in question can match the requirements of the job.
7. The promotion policy should be discussed with labour unions, and their acceptance should be obtained in the form of an agreement.

8. When promotions are made on the basis of competence, openings for promotion should be displayed prominently at several places to enable interested people to apply.

Types

A promotion involves an increase in status, responsibilities and pay. But in certain cases, only the pay increases and the other elements remain stagnant. In other cases, the status only increase without a corresponding increase in pay or responsibilities. Depending on which elements increase and which remain stagments, promotions may be classified into following types:-

1. *Horizontal promotion:* This type of promotion involves an increase is responsibilities and pay and a change in designation. But the employee concerned does not transgress the job classification.
2. *Vertical promotion:* This type of promotion results in greater responsibility, prestige and pay together with a change in the nature of the job.
3. *Dry promotions:* Dry promotions are sometimes given in lieu of increases in remuneration. Designations are different but no change in responsibilities.

TRANSFER

A transfer involves a change in the job of an employee without change in responsibilities or remuneration. Yoder and his associates have defined transfer as "a lateral shift causing movement of individuals from one position to another involving any marked change in duties, responsibilities, skills needed or compensation." A transfer is a horizontal or lateral movement of an employee from one job section, department, shift, plant or position to another at the same or another place where his salary, status and responsibility are the same.

Edwin B. Flippo[4] advocates a transfer deals with a change in the job accompanied by a change in the place of job, of an employee without change in responsibilities and salary/ remuneration. It differs from promotion where increase in pay and responsibility are there. Further promotion is few in career path, where transfers are many- the best example being service in banking sector. Transfers may be for administrative reasons that imply benefit to organisation. Moreover, transfers may be for correcting the mistakes of the employees in the organisation.

In effect, shortage of staff at a place, conflict management between supervisor and supervised, balancing of surplus, break the monotony of employees and sorting out of family related and health problems are the causes of transfers. Obviously, to tackle transfers organisations are framing transfer policies. Time frame for transfer is an important criterion-which is known to its employees. Factors like authority to transfer, reasons for transfers, performance of the employees are also other guidelines of transfer policy. Generally, such transfer takes different shapes:

- Production Transfer – purpose is to balance surplus staff.
- Replacement Transfer – To avoid laying of senior people.
- Versatile Transfer – To make people competent and skill in multi faceted areas.
- Shift Transfer – Sharing of work in shifts.
- Remedial Transfer – Transfer is to break the monotony and solve other problems.

Purposes[5]

Transfers are generally made to build up a more satisfactory work team and to achieve the following purposes:

1. To satisfy such needs of an organisation as may arise out of a change in the quantity of production, fluctuations in work requirements and changes in the organisational structure, the introduction of new lines of production, the dropping of existing product lines, the reallocation of or reduction in the workforce due to a shortage or a surplus in same section so that lay offs may be avoided, filling in of the vacancies which may occur because of separations or because of the need for suitable adjustments in business operations.
2. To meet an employees own requests when he feels uncomfortable on the job because of his dislike of his boss or his fellow workers or because better opportunities for his future advancement do not exist there, or because family circumstances, which may compel him to change the place.
3. To make use of proper the services of an employee when he is not performing satisfactorily and adequately and when the management feels that he may be more useful or suitable elsewhere, where his capacities would be better utilised.
4. To increase the versatility of the employee by shifting him from one job to another so that he may have ample opportunities for gaining a varied and broader experience of work.

5. To adjust the workforce of one plant with that of another, particularly when one is closed down for reasons beyond the control of the employer.
6. To replace a new employee by an employee who has been in the organisation for a sufficiently long time.
7. To help employees work according to their convenience so far as timings are concerned.
8. To penalize the employee, transfers are also done, under which either a difficult trade union activist or infringer may be transferred to a remote branch where he cannot continue his activities.
9. Transfer for the maintenance of a tenure system. Here the employees hold a certain job for a fixed tenure but he is made to move from job to job with a view to enabling him to acquire a variety of experience and skills and also to ensure that he does not get involved in politically informal groups.

Transfer Policy

Every organisation should have adjust and imperial transfer policy which should be known to each employee. The responsibility for effecting transfers is usually entrusted to an executive with power to prescribe the conditions under which requests for transfers are to be approved.

For successful transfer policies it is necessary to have a proper job description and job analysis. Cases should be taken to ensure that frequent or large scale transfers are avoided by laying down adequate selection and placement procedures for the purpose. A good transfer policy should

- Specifically clarify the types of transfer and the conditions under which these will be match.
- Locate the authority in some officer who may initiate and implement transfers.
- Indicate whether transfers can be made only within a sub unit or also between departments, division.
- Indicate the basis for transfer.
- Decide the rate of pay to be given to the transferee.
- Intimate the fact of transfer to the person concerned well in advance.
- Be in writing and duly communicated to all concerned.
- Not be made frequent and not for the sake of transfer only.

References

1. C.B. Mamoria, *Personnel Management*, HPH, 1996
2. C.B. Gupta, *Human Resource Management*, S. Chand & Sons, New Delhi, 2001.
3. CB Gupta, *op.cit.*
4. Edwin B. Flippo, *Personnel Management*, 4th edn. McGraw Hill, New York, 1984.
5. C.B. Mamoria, *op. cit.*

Further Readings

1. W.B. Werther and K. Davis, *Human Resource Management*, New York, McGraw Hill, 2003.
2. W.F. Cascio, *Managing Human Resources*, Tata McGraw Hill, New Delhi, 2004.

Chapter seven

TRAINING AND DEVELOPMENT

Training in organisation is for individual development and organisational development. Every organisation needs to have well trained and experienced people to perform the activities that have to be done. If the current or potential job occupant can meet this requirement, training is not important. But when this is not the case it is necessary to raise the skill levels and increases the versatility and adaptability of employees. As the jobs become more complex, the importance of employee development also increases. In a rapidly changing society an organisation must commit resources if it is to maintain available and knowledgeable workforce.

Training, education and development are three terms frequently used. Training is a process of learning a sequence of programmed behaviour. It is application of knowledge. It gives people an awareness of the rules and procedures to guide their behaviour. It attempts to improve their performance on the current job. Development is a related process. It covers not only those activities which improve job performance but also those which bring about growth of the personality, help individuals in the progress towards maturity and actualisation of their potential capacities so that they become not only good employees but better men and women. Training a person for a bigger and higher job is development. Education is the understanding and interpretation of knowledge. It does not provide definitive answers, but rather it develops a logical and rational mind that can determine relationships among pertinent variables and thereby understand phenomena. Education is most important qualities of mind and character and understanding of basic principles and develops the capacities of analysis, synthesis and objectivity. Usually, education is outside the scope of an organisation functions.

For knowledge management, skill upgradation and relationship development training is imperative. Training helps/prepares organisations to face future challenges in the era of 21st century. True training and development are used interchangeable. But there is subtle difference between these two. The focus of training is current job while that of development is current job and future job. Orientation of training is active and that of development is pro-active. Further scope of training and development are individual employees and work groups respectively. Time frame of training is immediate. Time frame of development is long-term. Along with the goal of training is fixing of current skill deficit.
On the contrary the goal of development is preparation of future demand of work. See table- 3.7.1.

Table 3.7.1: Training versus development

	Training	*Development*
Focus	Current Job	Current job, future jobs
Scope	Individual employees	Work group or organization
Time frame	Immediate	Long term
Goal	Fix current skill deficit	Prepare for future work demands

Training, therefore, prepares an employee to do his present job efficiently and to prepare for future higher job. (Fitzgerald: 1992). Necessary training builds SKA—Skill, Knowledge and Ability—for the job. It is helpful both for the organisation and the people. Training may be skill training; refresher training, cross-functional training, creative training, team training, diversity training, and literacy training (Rao, 2005). Further, training may be administered through Job Institution-Training (JIT), coaching, mentoring, job rotation, apprenticeship training. Besides, on-the-job training there is off-the job training. The methods of off-the job training are vestibule training, role playing, lecture, conferences, etc.

Obviously, training is the basic and strong mechanism of HRD which contributes directly to the individual development (Bansal, 1991). Empowerment of people with appropriate knowledge is the training result. It is a fact that there are certain basic assumptions about training as reflected in Table 3.7.1. Training has undergone a sea change. On line training is now introduced. The training in transition is analyzed by K. S. Gupta: (Gupta, 2000) which is placed below in Table 3.7.2.

Table 3.7.2: Basic assumptions about training

Assumption about the organization	*Assumption about people*
Organization has objectives that it wants to achieve for the benefit of all stakeholders or members, including owners, employees, customers, supplies and neighbours	People have aspirations, they want to develop, learn new abilities and use them
These objectives can be achieved only through harnessing the abilities of its people, releasing potential and maximizing opportunities for development	In order to learn and use new abilities people need appropriate opportunities resources and conditions
Hence people must know what they need to learn in order to achieve organizational goals	Hence to meet people's aspiration, the organization must provide effective and attractive learning sources and ambience.

Source: Ojha, 2000

Table 3.7.3: Transition in training

Transition	*New order*
The knowledge acquired by participants through training lead to action	Motivation and skills acquired through training lead to action. Skills are basically acquired through practice
Trainees use to learn what trainers impart. Learning as a function simply depends on the capacity of the trainees and the ability of the instructors to teach	The complexity of the learning function depends on the motivation and capacity of trainees, principles of trainee groups, training methods, behaviour of trainers and climatic condition of training institution
Training function is exclusively limited to training establishment itself. It functions in a waterlight compartment and begins and ends with specific training programme	Responsibility of training lies with three basic groups like-trainees organizations, trainees and training establishment. It consists of a preparatory and pre-training phase and a subsequent post-training phase. All phases contribute equally to success of a training programme
Objective of training is more provision oriented than need oriented	Objective of training totally depends upon the felt need of workers

Source: Gupta, 2000

In reality the present day training is a "New Avatar" in the age of LPG era with organisation being High Performance work system and learning organisation. More and more employees are undergoing a "Learning Process rather than a training process." There are two types of learning models are traditional (Pedagogical model; two modern Andragogical model) developed by Malcom. S. Knowles. The details is placed in Table 3.7.4.

Table 3.7.4: Pedagogy Vs. Andragogy Models

Concept/Process	*Pedagogy*	*Andragogy*
Learner	Dependent on teacher	Increasingly self directing
Readiness to learn	Uniform by age level and curriculum	Develops from life task
Learner's experience	To be built later	Rich resource for learning process
Orientation to learning	Subject centered	Task or problem centered
Motivation	Tense, authority oriented, formal	Relaxed, warm, collaborative informal
Setting of learning objectives	By teachers	By mutual negotiation between learner and facilitators
Learning process	Transmittal techniques and assigned readings	Inquiry, independent study and experimental technique
Evaluation	Created by teacher against norms	By learner, learning validated by peers
Learning responsibility	On the teacher	On the learner

[Source: Kannan, 2000]

Training and development deal with the design and learning for better work in the organisations. In some organisations 'training' is replaced by 'learning'.

It is true, there are challenges to training. Is the training is a solution to the problem? Are the purposes of training are clear? Is training fruitful? Is the training a good investment? The answers to the questions varied from organisation to organisations depending on HR Manager, environment and trainees itself. Whatever may be the fact training of HR is must for development of the both organisation and employees. Side by side to improve managerial performance, upgradation of knowledge and skill training is imparted to managerial positions under Executive Development programmes.

Need for Training[1]

The need for the training of employees would be clear from the observations written below:

1. *To increase productivity:* Instruction can help employees increase their level of performance on their present assignment. Increased human performance often directly leads to increase operational productivity and increased company profit.
2. *To improve quality:* Better informed workers are less likely to make operational mistaken. Quality increases may be in relationship to a company product or service or in reference to the intangible organisational employment atmosphere.
3. *To help a company fulfill its future personnel needs of organisations* that have a good internal educational programme will have to make less drastic manpower changes and adjustments in the event of sudden personnel alternatives.
4. *To improve organisational climate:* An endless chain of positive reactions results from a well planned training programme. Production and product quality may improve; financial incentives may then be in supervisory pressures ensured and base pay rate increase result.
5. *To improve health and safety:* Proper training can help prevent industrial accidents. A safer work environment leads to more stable mental attitudes on the part of employees.
6. *Obsolescence prevention:* Training and development programmes foster the initiative and creativity of employees and help to prevent manpower obsolescence, which may be due to age, temperament or motivation, or the inability of a person to adopt himself to technological changes.
7. *Personal growth:* Employees on a personal basis gain individually from their exposure to educational experiences. Again management development programmes seem to give participants a wider awareness, an enlarged skill and enlightened entrusted philosophy and make enhanced personal growth possible.

It may be observed that, the need for training arises from more than one reason.

a. An increased use of technology introduction.
b. Labour turnover arising from normal separations due to death or physical incapacity, for accidents, disease, superannuation, voluntary retirement, promotion within the organisation and change of occupation.
c. Need for additional hands to cope with an increased production of goods and services.
d. Employment of inexperienced, new or badly labour requires detailed instruction for an effective performance of a job.
e. Old employees need refresher training to enable them to keep abreast of the changing method, techniques, etc.
f. Need for enabling employees to do the work in a more effective way, to reduce learning time, reduce supervision time, reduce waste and spoilage of raw material and produce quality goods, and develop their potential.
g. Need for maintaining the validity of an organisation as a whole and raising the morale of its employees.

Training Cycle

Key areas of training activities, training responsibilities, training cycle and model training process are also given by A. M Sharma in a different tone (Sharma: 2003):

Training Activities are

- Identification of training and development needs.
- Provision of training schemes of groups with common needs.
- Provision of internal training cases.
- Assessment of external training facilities.
- The evaluation of training activities.
- The management of training staff.

Additionally, the training "responsibilities" are:

- Setting the training policy.
- Analysis of training needs.
- Overall planning and coordination of training.
- Preparation of long-term training plan.
- Design, implementation and evaluation of training programmes.
- Financing the training activities.
- Selection of trainees
- Selection of trainers.

And the training cycle is given below in Figure 3.7.1

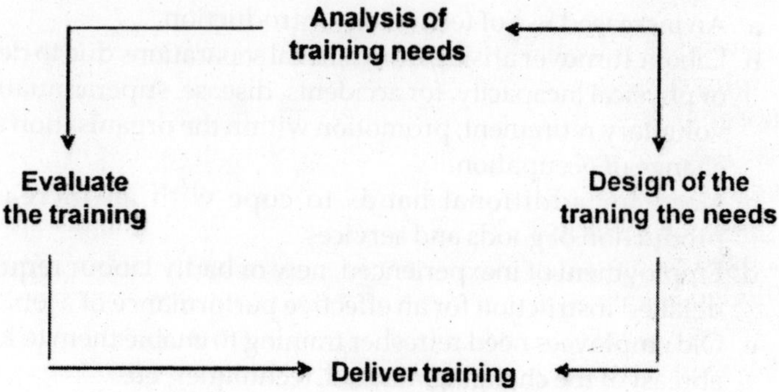

Fig. 3.7.1

Source: A.M. Sharma Personnel and Human Resource Management, 2003, Himalaya Publishing House.

To add this model of training process is reflected below for better appreciation. (Figure 3.7.2)

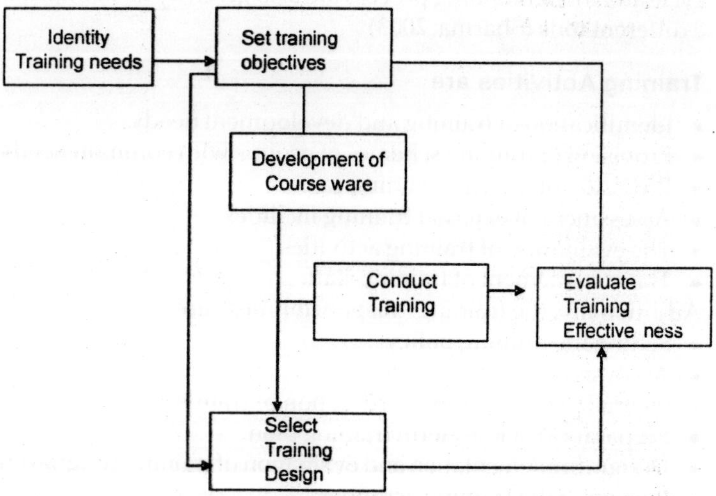

Fig. 3.7.2

Source: A. M. Sharma, HPH, 2003

Importance[2]

Training is the keystone of sound management, for it makes employees more effective and productive. It is actively and thoroughly connected with all the personnel or managerial activities. It is an primary part of the whole management programme, with all its many activities functionally inter related.

There is an ever present need for training men so that new and hanged techniques may be taken advantage and improvements effected in the old methods, which are woefully inefficient.

Training is a practical and vital necessity because, apart from the other advantages, it enables employees to develop and rise within the organisation, and increase their market value, earning power and job security. It enables management to resolve sources of friction arising from parochialism, to bring home to the employees the fact that the management is not divisible. It moulds the employees' attitudes and helps them to achieve a better cooperation with the company and a greater loyalty to it. The management is generated in the sense that higher standards of quality are achieved, a satisfactory organisational structure is built up, authority can be delegated and stimulus for progress applied to employees. Training, moreover, heightens the morale of the employees, for it helps in reducing dissatisfaction, complaints, grievances and absenteeism, labour turnover. Further, trained employees make a better and economical use of materials and equipment, therefore wastage and wastages are lessened, and the need for constant supervision is reduced.

Principles[3]

Since training is a continuous process and not a one shot affair, and since it consoles time and entails much expenditure, it is necessary that a training programme or policy should be prepared with great thought and care, for it should serve the purposes of the establishment as well as the needs of employees. Moreover, it must guard against over training, use of poor instructions, too much training in skills which are unnecessary for a particular job, imitation of other company's training programmes, misuse of testing techniques, inadequate tools and equipment and over reliance on one single technique.

A successful training programme presumes that sufficient care was been taken to discover areas in which it is needed most and to create the necessary environment for its conduct. The selected trainer should be one who clearly understands his job and has professional expertise, has an aptitude and ability for teaching, possesses a pleasing personality and a capacity for leadership is well versed in the principles and methods of training, and is able to appreciate the value of training in relation to an enterprise.

Certain general principles should be considered while organising a training progamme. For example:

1. Trainees in work organisations tend to be most responsive to training programmes whey they feel the need to learn. The individual who perceives training as the solution of problems will be more willing to enter into a training programme than will the individual who is satisfied with his present performance.
2. Learning is more effective where there is reinforcement in the form of rewards and punishments. In other words, after an action, if satisfactory is received, the action will be repeated. If no satisfaction is received, the action will not be repeated.
3. In the long run, awards tend to be more effective for changing behaviour and increasing ones learning than punishments.
4. Rewards for the application of learned behaviour are most useful when they quickly follow the desired performance.
5. The larger the reward for good performance following the implementation of learned behaviour, the greater will be the reinforcement of the new behaviour.
6. Negative reinforcement through application of penalties and heavy criticism following inadequate performance, may have a disruptive effect upon the learning experience of the trainee than positive reinforcement.
7. Training that requests the trainee to make changes in his values, attitudes and social beliefs, usually achieves better results if the trainee is encouraged to participate, discuss and discover new, desirable behaviour norms.
8. The trainee should be provided with feedback on the progress he is making in utilising the training he has received. The feed back should be fast and frequent.
9. The development of new behaviour norms and skills is facilitated through practice and repetition.
10. The training material should be made as meaningful as possible because if the trainee understands the general

principles underlying what is being taught, he will probably understand it better than if he were just asked to memorize a series is isolated steps.

Training process

Organ ization objectives and strategies (1)
↓
Assessment of Training needs (2)
↓
Establishment of training goals (3)
↓
Devising Training programme (4)
↓
Implementation of Training programmes (5)
↓
Evaluation of Results (6)

The first step in the training process in an organisation is the assessment of its objectives and strategies. An organisation assess the strengths and weaknesses of its human resources only after analysing the product of the organisation, quality of the product and future improvement programme of the products or services rendered.

The second step in training process is needs assessment. Needs assessment exposes prevailing problems and the challenges to be met in the future through training and development. Needs assessment occurs at too levels, i.e. group and individual. An individual needs training when his/her performance meets the trend of deficiency. The problem of performance deficiency caused by absence of skills or knowledge can be remedied by training. Faulty selection, poor job design, uninspiring supervision or some personal problem may also result in poor performance. Transfer, job redesign, improving quality of supervision or discharge will solve the problem. Assessment of training needs occurs at the group level too. Any change in the organisations strategy necessitates training of groups of employees. Training can also be used when high scrap or accident rates low morale and motivation or other problems are diagnosed.

The third step in the training process is the establishment of training and development goals. Without clearly set goals, it is not possible to design a training and development programme and after it has been implemented, there will be no way of measuring its effectiveness. Goals must be tangible, verifiable and measurable.

The fourth step is the devising training and development programme. In this programme, trainees, trainers, methods and techniques of training must be properly identified. Trainees should be selected on the basis of self nomination, recommendations of supervisors or by the HR department itself. Trainers may include immediate supervisors, co-workers, and members of the personnel staff, specialists, outside consultants, industry associations or academicians. A multitude of methods of training are used to train the employees. Training techniques represent the medium of imparting skills and knowledge to employees. Among the most commonly used techniques are lectures, films, audio cassettes, case studies, role playing, video tapes and simulations. The level of learning must be decided in designing training and development programme. There are three basic levels at which inputs like education, skills can be taught. At the lowest level, the employee must acquire fundamental knowledge. This means developing a basic understanding of a field and becoming acquainted with the languages, concepts and relationships involved in it. The goal of the next level is skill development. The highest level aims at increased operational proficiency. This involves obtaining additional experience and improving skills that have already been developed. All the inputs of training can be offered at the three levels. How effectively they are learned depends on several principles of learning like employee motivation, practice opportunities, reinforcement, feedback, etc. Finally the place of conducting training and development programme is to be considered. Typically, basic skills are taught at the job, and basic grammar skills are taught on the site. Much of interpersonal and conceptual skills are learnt off the site.

The fifth step in the training process is the implementation of training programme. In fact, this step is problem packed. In the first place, most managers are action-oriented and frequently say they are too busy to engage in training efforts. Secondly, availability of trainers is a problem. Training and development requires a high degree of creativity. Training programme should be scheduled without maintaining gap in regular work. Programme implementation involves deciding the location and organising training and other facilities, scheduling the training programme, conducting the programme and monitoring the progress.

The final step in the process is the evaluation of results. The main objective of evaluating the training programme is to determine if they are accomplishing specific training objectives, i.e. correcting performance deficiencies. Training programmes should be evaluated to determine their cost effectiveness. Credibility of training and development is greatly enhanced when it is proved that the organisation has benefited tangibly from it. Evaluation specialist must be clear about the goals and purposes of evaluation. Evaluation must be continuous and specific. Evaluation must be based on objective methods and standard.

Training Methods/Techniques

The forms and types of employee training methods are inter- related. It is difficult, if not impossible, to say which of the methods or combination of methods are multifaceted in scope and dimension and each suitable for a particular situation. Care must be used in adapting the technique/method to the learner and the job. An effective training technique generally fulfills these objectives, provide motivation to the trainee to improve job performance, develop a willingness to change, provide for the trainees active participation in the learning process, provide a knowledge of results about attempts to improve it and permit practice when appropriate.

Classification of training methods

On the job training (OJT) | Demonstration and examples | Apprenticeship | Others

Vestibule | Simulation

Classroom method or off the job training

Lectures | Conference | Case study | Role playing | Programme instruction

---

Source: C. B. Mamoria, Personnel Management

Every employee gets some On-the Job Training (OJT), when he joins an organisation. Trainees earn as they learn under the watchful edges of a master. Under this technique, an employee is placed in a new job and is told how it may be performed. It is chiefly concerned with developing in an employee a bank of skills and habits consistent with the existing practices of an organisation, and with orienting him to his immediate problems. There are variety of OJT methods, such as coaching, under study, job rotation and special assignments. The main advantage of OJT is that the trainee learns on the actual equipment in use and in the true environment of his job. It is highly economical since no additional personnel are required for training. The trainee learns the rules, regulations and procedures by observing their day to day applications. The principal disadvantage of OJT is that instruction is often highly disorganised and haphazard and not properly supervised.

Vestibule training is a classroom training which is often imparted with the help of the equipment and machines which are identical with those in use in the place of work. This technique enables the trainee to concentrate on learning the new skill rather than on performing an actual job. It is a very efficient method of training semi-skilled personnel; particularly when many employees have to be trained for the same kind of work at the same time. This training is given in the form of lectures, conferences, case studies, role playing and discussion.

In the demonstration method, the trainer describes and displays something, as when he teaches an employee how to do something by actually performing the activity himself and by going through a step by step explanation of why and what he is doing. Demonstrations are very effective in teaching because it is much easier to show a person how to do a job than to tell him to gather instruction from the reaching material. Demonstrations are often used in combination with lectures, pictures, text materials, discussion, etc. Teaching by example is effective in mechanical operations or interpersonal relationships for job duties and responsibilities for informal group standards, supervisory expectations, etc.

Simulation is a technique which duplicates, as nearly as possible the actual conditions encountered on a job. Simulation techniques have been most widely used in aeronautical industry. Trainee interest and employee motivation are both high in simulation exercises because the actions of a trainee closely duplicate real job conditions. This training is essential in cases in which actual OJT might result in a serious inquiry, a costly error, or the destruction of valuable materials or resources. It is for this reason that the technique is a very expensive one.

For training in crafts, trades and in technical areas, apprenticeship training is the oldest and most commonly used method, especially when proficiency in a job is the result of a relatively long training period of two years to three years for persons of superior ability and from four years to five years for others. The field in which apprenticeship training is offered are numerous. A major part of training time is spent on the job productive work. Each apprentice is given a programme of assignments according to a predetermined schedule, which provides for efficient training in trade skills. The merits of this method are many. A skilled workforce is maintained. Immediate returns can be expected from training. The workmanship is good. The hiring cost is lower because of reduced turnover and lower production costs.

Classroom method is also called off the job training. It means that training is not a part of everyday job activity. The actual location may be in the company classrooms or in places which are owned by the company or in connection with the company. This method consists of lectures, conferences, group discussions, case studies, role playing, programme instruction and T. Group training. Lectures are regarded as one of the simplest ways of imparting knowledge to the trainees, especially when fact, concepts or principles, attitudes, theories and problem solving abilities are to be taught. Lectures are formal organised talks by the training specialist, the formal superior or other individual specific topics. Then main advantage of the lecture system is that it is simple and efficient and through it more material can be presented within a given time than by any other method. But the system violates the principle of learning by doing. It is a one way communication. Again a clear and vigorous verbal presentation requires a great deal of preparation for which management personnel often lack the time. The untrained lecturers either rumple or pack for too much information in the lecture, which becomes unpalatable to the listener. In the conference method, the participating individuals confer to discuss points of common interest to each other. A conference is basic to most participate group centered methods of development. It is a formal training, conducted in accordance with an organised plan, in which the leader seeks to develop knowledge and understanding by obtaining a considerable amount of oral participation of the trainees. Learning is facilitated by building up on the ideas contributed by the conferences. The conference is ideally suited for the purpose of analysing problems and issues and examining them from different view points. It is an excellent method for the development of conceptual knowledge and for reducing dogmatism and modifying attitudes because the participants develop solutions and reach conclusions, which they often willingly accept. But it is limited to a small group of persons, because larger groups often dishearten the active participation of all the conferences. The progress is usually slow because all those desiring to speak on a point are generally allowed to do so. Consequently, irrelevant issues easily creep in. The seminar or group discussion method is also useful in certain circumstances. The person in charge of the seminar distributes in advance the material to be analyzed in the form of required readings. The seminar compares the reactions of trainees, encourages discussion, defines the general trends and guides the participants to certain conclusions. The case study method or the learning by doing was first developed in 1880 by Christopher Langdell at the Harvard Law schools. The method is based upon the belief that managerial competence can best be attained through the case study, deliberation and discussion of performance cases. The case is a set of data, written or oral miniature description and summary of such data that present issues and problems calling for solutions or action the part of the trainee. When the trainees are given cases to analyze, they are asked to identify the problem and to recommend tentative solutions for it. This method offers to the trainees matter of reflection and bring home to them a sense of the complexity of life as opposed to theoretical simplifications of and practices in the decision-making process. It diagnoses and deals with real life situations. In case study method, the trainee is expected to master the facts, become acquainted with the content of the case, define the objectives sought in dealing with the issues in the case, identify the problems in case and uncover their probable causes, develop alternative courses of action, select the alternative that is most in keeping with the stated objectives. This method promotes analytical thinking and develops a persons problem solving. It encourages open mindedness and serves as a means of integrating the knowledge obtained form different basic disciplines. The method is accepted by everyone for it deals with detailed descriptions of real life situations. The role playing method was developed by Moreno. He coined the terms 'role playing,' role reversal,' 'socio-drama,' psychodrama and a variety of specialized terms, with emphasis on learning human relations skills through practice and insight into one's own behaviour and its effect upon others. It has been defined as a method of human interaction which involves realistic behaviour in the imaginary situations. In role playing, trainees act out a given role as they would in a stage play. Two or more trainees are assigned parts to play before the rest of the class. These parts do not involve any memorisation of lines or any researchers. The role players are simply informed of a situation and of the respective roles they have to play. In role playing method, human sensitivity and interactions are stressed. The knowledge of results is immediate. It brings about desired changes in behaviour and attitudes. The method of programmed instruction is teaching by the machine method. It involves a sequence of steps which are often set up through the central panel of an electronic computer as guides in the performance of a desired operation or series of operation. It incorporates a pre-arranged, proposed, or desired course of proceedings pertaining to the learning or acquisition of some specific skills or general knowledge. A programmed instruction involves breaking information down into meaningful units and then arranging these in a proper way to form a logical and sequential learning programme. The programme involves, presenting question, facts or problems to the trainees instantly receives feedback on the basis of the accuracy of his answers. In this method the trainees learn at their own place. The materials to be learned are broken down into small units. Immediate feedback is available. Active learner participation takes place at each step in the programme. There is a high level of learner motivation. Another method is T-group training. It is also a sensitivity training. This usually comprises association, audio visual aids and planned reading programmes. Members of a professional association receive training by it in new techniques and ideas pertaining to their own vocations. Through a regular supply of professional journals and informal social contacts or gatherings, members are kept informed of the latest development in their particular field planned and supervised reading programmes are conducted. Technical publications and the latest journals are kept in the library for the use of the trainees. Retraining programmes are also arranged for employees who have long been in the service of an organisation.

Barriers to Effective Training

The major hindrances which can make a training programme ineffective are:

1. *Management commitment is lacking and uneven:* Most organisations do not spend on training. The rank and file workersare ignored. This must change for as a result of rapid technological change, combined with new approaches to organisational design; workers are required to learn new skills. In an increasingly competitive environment, the ability to implement rapid changes in products and technologies is often essential for economic viability.
2. *Aggregate spending on training is inadequate:* Organisations spend negligible proportions on training. Worse still, budget allocation to training is the first item to be cut when an organisation faces a financial crunch.
3. *Educational Institutions breed graduates lacking in skills:* This is the reason why organisations must spend vast sum of money to train workers in basic skills.
4. Large scale poaching of trained workers is also a barrier.
5. Organisations one downsising and delay ring in order to from their workforces. But there is no help to workers.

Essentials for Effective Training

The training programmes can be made effective and successful if the following hints are considered:

- Specific training objectives should be outlined on the basis of the type of performance required to achieve organisational goals and objectives. An audit of personnel needs compared with operational requirements will help to determine the specific training needs of individual employees.
- Attempt should be made to determine if the trainee has the intelligence, maturity and motivation to successfully complete the training programmes.
- The trainee should be helped to see the need for training by making him aware of the personal benefits he can achieve through better performance.
- The training programme should be planned so that it is related to the trainees' previous experiences and background.
- Attempts should be made to create organisational conditions that are conducive to a good learning environment. It should be

made clearly why changes are needed. Any distractions in the way of training environment should be removed.

- If necessary, a combination of training methods should be selected so that variety is permitted and as many of the senses as possible are utilised.
- It should be recognized that all the trainees do not progress at the same rate. Therefore, flexibility should be allowed in judging the rates of progress in the training programme.
- If possible, the personnel involvement or active participation of the trainee should be got in the training programme. He should be provided with opportunity to practice the newly needed behaviour norms.
- As the trainee acquires new knowledge skills or attitudes and applies them in job situation he should be significantly rewarded for his efforts.
- The trainee should be provided with regulation constructive feedback concerning his progress in training and implementation of the newly acquired abilities.
- The trainee should be provided with personal assistance when he encounters learning obstacles.

References

1. C.B. Mamoria, *Personnel Management*, HPH, Bombay, 1996
2. *Ibid.*
3. *Ibid.*

Further Readings

1. R.Lynton and U. Pareek, *Training for Development*, Sage Publications, New Delhi, 2002.
2. R.A. Neo, *Employee Training and Development*, Burr Ridge, II, McGraw Hill Irwin, 1999.
3. A.C. Hamblin, *Evalualion and Control of Training*, McGraw Hill, 1974.

Chapter eight

CAREER PLANNING AND CAREER DEVELOPMENT

The term 'career' does not have a precise definition. It has come to mean the progress of an individual in a few of work throughout the employable years of his life. Sometimes it means deviation to a specialty. The recent trend in public administration and management is however, to have a career system for the employees in which young persons are carefully selected and work at various levels in an organisation throughout their working life. This will be possible only if the career system provides satisfying opportunities of advancement to the employees.

Career planning and development are concepts encompassing events which affect the promotion or progression of an individual. Career management is the process which enables an organisation to meet its current and projected manpower requirement through provision of opportunities of advancement for its employees. It aims at optimising the effectiveness of human resources of the organisation through planned development of their knowledge skills and potentialities. Career planning refers to planned and systematized progression of events and developments in the field of work or vocation of an individual during the service period of his life. Some careers may be only vaguely identified. But the basic characteristics of a career are–

- Some objective criteria to identify it.
- Some job titles.
- Some kind of viable progression through objectivity
- Continuity over a considerable length of time.

Objectives

The objectives of career development are much wider. It is also meant to better serve the organisation.

1. To secure right man at the right time in the right place.

2. To increase employee satisfaction by developing their skill and full potential.
3. To strengthen the organisation by enabling it to retain good employees.

In short, the main objective of the career development is to ensure the growth of the organisation and the individuals in a harmonious way.

Career development means to provide all conditions conducive to the development of the persons once recruited in the organisation. So that they can realize their full potential and occupy higher positions in the organisation and ultimately reach the top position in the organisation or outside it. It may be noted that for the top positions we have to accept the possibility of a person going outside the organisation to reach his full potential of growth. The idea, however, remains that the employees will remain in the organisation for a long time and the organisation should create a environment in which the employees can work for the benefit of the organisation as well as realize their own growth potential.

Steps for Career Development

Keeping in view the observations about the need for creating a congenial atmosphere in the organisation for the career development of the employees the following steps can be identified:

1. **Selection:** One of the important conditions for the development of employee is that they should get the work of their liking. This will happen only when the employees are selected for the jobs which suit their abilities and temperaments. In other words, they should have both the ability and willingness to perform the job.
2. **Training:** For the growth and development of the natural potential of the employees, it is necessary that they should receive in-service training at regular intervals. The employees are directly recruited young on the basis of general qualifications. They have therefore to receive on the job induction training to prepare them for their actual job. As they go up the organisation, the requirements of their jobs change and it is necessary to prepare them for these assignments. In service training is the real instrument to achieve this end.
3. **Mobility:** Nothing develops an employee more than to get an idea of the whole system of which he is a part. It is partly achieved b training and partly by mobility in the organisation. It means

what employees may be given an opportunity of working in a number of positions without sacrificing the needs of the jobs.

4. **Promotion:** Promotions are rewards for serving the organisation. These rewards should be planned to act as effective incentives to the employees to put in their best performance. For this purpose the promotions should come at reasonable intervals, neither too early nor too late. It is also necessary to have proper rules for promotion in which absolute impartiality should be observed.
5. **Proper personnel policies and practices:** To maintain the morale of the employees it is necessary for the organisation grades. Other important areas of attention would be transfer, disciplinary matters, etc. In all these personnel practices the organisation has to be fair and just and also appear to be so. Every one should clearly know where he stands in the framework of the organisation's personnel policies.

Career Planning for Career Development[1]

Career development is an incessant unremitting and never-ending process. The organisation must continue to assess its present and emerging needs in respect of personnel. The type and number of new jobs required will indicate the needs in respect of recruitment, training, promotion, etc. The organisation should prepare, exclude and all the time up to date a career development plan for its employees. The various steps in the process of planning for career development are:

1. **Analysis of personnel situations:** The first step in the planning for career development is to analyze the present personnel situation of the organisation. This provides data for the projection of future needs in respect of various personnel functions. To assess the present situation, following information may have to be collected:
   a. Existing number of employees, their qualifications, training, age, experience, etc.
   b. Various levels of administration and the number of employees in each.
   c. Span of control within the organisation.
   d. Facilities of training available within the organisation and outside it.
   e. Any shortage of personnel presently being felt along with the required qualifications.

2 **Future projection of the personnel needs:** On the basis of past trends and the present situation, future requirements of personnel

may be projected. To make these projections more reliable, care must be taken to include personnel needs on account of any expected and unusual developments and for starting of new line of activities.

3. **Identification of career needs:** On the basis of these projections the organisation can work out the future requirements of the personnel. They can also work out in detail the promotional needs of the existing staff as well as the staff to be recruited in future. This assessment needs to be done very carefully so that the recruitment of the new staff can be planned to suit the career development needs of all the staff.
4. **Selection of priorities:** Since it may not be possible to meet all the career development needs of the organisation. Some priorities may have to be laid down for the purpose.

Development of Career Plans

On the basis of the information gathered and priorities laid down a career development plan should be prepared which should provide for-

1. **Recruitment:** Based on the assessment of personnel needs, it should be worked out how many of the posts will require fresh recruitment and at what levels and at what time. Steps should be worked out after taking into account the vacancies caused by promotion retirement, etc.
2. **Training:** Having reviewed the existing skills of the employees and having assessed their future skill needs, a plan should be prepared for providing them adequate training to fill the gaps. It will have to be laid down how many employees will require to be trained in which skills and in which institutions. Again action has to be initiated to make arrangement with these institutions for training the employees.
3. **Promotion:** Nothing affects the morale of the employees more than the delay in the legitimate promotions. It is therefore necessary that on the basis of the assessment made, the promotions should be planned accordingly. The promotion procedure takes its normal time. The organisation should keep in view this procedural time requirement while planning for promotion.
4. **Study:** In case the employees require some special kind of training which necessitates their absence from work over a long period of time adequate arrangements should made for their study. The career development plans should provide for all the related personnel functions, while making these arrangements.

5. **Preparation of action plan:** On the basis of planning mentioned above, the organisation has to prepare an action plan to put into practice the ideas developed in the planning process. A separate section has to be created for this purpose. The action to be taken by each individual has to be worked out in detail and a time schedule has to be given to every one. The central direction of the action plan has to be undertaken by the special section in the headquarters.

Implementation of Career Plan

The purpose of career development is to attract and retain men and women of taken and ambition in the employment. To establish good career service and to attract the best talent in the service, certain essentials are to be observed. These are:

- There should be equality of opportunity for the citizens to enter the public service.
- There should be equal pay for equal work.
- There should be equal opportunity for promotion and advancement promotion should be based upon merit.
- There should be security and stability of job.
- The work culture must ensure job satisfaction.

Significance

Career development helps the organisation in more than one way. It adds to the effectiveness of the personnel administration, besides being essential to cope with changing needs. The significance is:

- It guarantees looked-for talents i.e. right people for the changing staffing requirements of the organisation.
- It attracts and retains highly talented personnel.
- It ensures equal opportunity for minorities and women.
- It removes employees' dissatisfaction by providing opportunities of advancement and better prospects.

As such benefits of career development system for employees and organisation are provided below as given by Z B Lelbowitz, C Farren and B L Kaye. (Z. B. Lelbowitz ors:1986)

Benefits of Career Development

The benefits of career development system for managers, emoloyees and Organisation are provided by Z B Lelbowitz and others. (Lelbowitz and Ors: 1986). They are L See Table 3. 7)

Table 3.8.1: Benefits of career development system

Managers	*Employees*	*Organization*
1. Increased skill in career	Helpful assistance with career decisions	Better use of managing own employees skills.
2. Greater retention of valued employees	Enrichment of present job and increased job satisfaction	Dissemination of information at all organizational level
3. Bettercommunication between manager and employee	Better communication between employee and manager	Better communi- within the organisation as a whole
4. More realistic staff development	More realistic goals planning and expectations	Greater retention of valued employees
5. Productive performance appraisal discussions.	Better feedback on performance.	Expanded public image as a people developer
6. Greater understanding of the organisation	Current information on the firm and the future	Increased effectiveness of personnel system
7. Enhanced reputation as a people developer	Greater personnel responsibility for career	Greater clarification of goals of the organisation

Source: Z. B. Lelbowitz, C. Farren and B. L. Kaye, Desi

Barriers: There are some barriers on the way of career development. They are:

- The first hurdle is the requirement of local residence for a particular job. Only local people are appointed to some jobs. It hinders promotion opportunities because a talented person may not be a local resident.
- Sometimes promotions of employees are made only in the department in which they are serving. It restricts the area of promotion of public officials.
- There is a widespread feeling that there are no incentives for efficiency in government jobs. This factor has also discouraged many talented persons from seeking public service career.

Career planning simply means planning of holding job during one's work life. Edwin B. Flippo defined a career as a sequence of separate but related work activities that provides continuity, order and meaning in a person's life. Career planning is associated with number of terms (Wrether and Davis). A career path is a sequential pattern of jobs that forms a career. And the career goals are the future positions one strives as part of one's career. As such career planning is the process employees select career goals and the career path to reach the goals. In this connection comes the terms of career development and career management. Career development is those personal improvement one undertakes to achieve in a personal career plan. (Beach). And career management is the process of designing and implementing career goals, career plans and strategies to enable the organisation to satisfy HR needs while allowing the individuals to achieve their career goals. (French and Bell Jr. 1978).

In brief, it can be said career planning and development are concepts encompassing events which affect the promotion or progress of an employee. And the very objective of career development is to ensure the growth of the organisation and the individuals in a harmonious way. In the area of career planning, therefore, the role of HR manager is noteworthy. Here Table 3.6 may be referred to as to career management and HR management Activities (Walker, 1980).

Table 3.8.2: Career Management and HR management activities

Career Management	*Human Resource Planning Issues*
Recruitment	
Attracting a flow of applicants	Knowing/ influencing the supply of talent available Use of agencies or search firms
Defining hiring requirements	Defining staffing needs Defining bona fide job requirements
Selection	Providing realistic information to recruits
Induction and orientation	Validation of selection process Straightening of the learning curve
Placement	Minimization of early turnover
Defining job requirements and career paths	
Inventories and placement systems	How to define professional and managerial job requirements and job families/career paths.
Job posting and bidding	What to put into an inventory and how o put it to use

Contd.

Contd.

Selection procedures	How much emplovee involvement is desired/appropriate
Fast-trac k programs	Valuation of internal selection procedures and practices
Management succession programs	Managing accelerated career progress for high potential employees
Relations	Minimizing disruptive effects of relocations, controlling relocations.
Training and development	
Individual career planning	Equipping employees with tools to do their own effective career planning.
Training needs analysis	Managing raised expectations.
Program design and development	Defining training and development needs objectively.
Research and evaluation	Weighting alternative approaches for meeting these needs.
	Evaluating the costs, benefits, and quality of programs.
Recruitment and alternatives	
Terminations	Policies and philosophy regarding reverse or lateral career steps
Retirements	Policies governing terminations and ensuring legal compliance.
Demotions and transfers	Effecting flexible retirement policies and practices

Source: J.W. Walker, *Human Resource Planning*, New York, McGraw-Hill, 1980, p. 250.

Reference

1. SL. Goel, *Administration, Theory and Practice*, Deep & Deep, New Delhi, 2003.

Chapter nine

MANAGEMENT DEVELOPMENT

The manager is the dynamic, vibrant, energetic, self motivated land forceful element in an enterprise. The caliber and performance of managers will largely determine the success of an enterprise. If the organisation wants to improve the quality of its managers, it must expend money and effort and introduce imaginative and systematic development schemes for them in which managers they play a crucial role. All organisations need to devote great attention to the continuous supply of their future managers, both functional and general. The major and more elusive task of management development is to mould and fashion the behaviour component into a virile and unmixed weapon of enterprise achievement. The secret of effective management lies in vitality, a conceptual attitude of mind concerned with profitable results matched by determination and integrity in management and managers.

Managerial Functions Consist of Three Key Tasks

- The maintenance and operation of the organisational communication with a view to translating the broad organisational goals into detailed working purposes and providing feedback on progress on the problems of achievement.
- The maintenance of the viability of an organisation.
- The maintenance of faith in the superiority and desirability of achieving the organisational aims.

For the discharge of these functions, it is essential and appropriate that men with certain qualities are appointed. These qualities are:

- Donation by organisational personality.
- Adherence to corporate morality and code of conduct in official actions.
- Possession of general abilities.
- Specialized knowledge and ability.

Characteristics of Managers

Management development process would be better understood if the main characteristics of managers are noted. The successful manager has the following characteristics:

- He moves rapidly from job to job.
- He is flexible, realistic and sensitive to the complexities of his work environment.
- He earns his spurs by handling critical assignments.
- He engages in anticipatory socialisation at each stage he copies the values of those who are a step above him.
- He is not necessarily an organisation conformist.

Management development is an educational process utilising a systematic and organised procedure by which managerial personnel learn conceptual and theoretical knowledge for general purposes. These purposes concern: productivity, quality, human resource planning, morale, indirect compensation, health and safety, personnel growth, etc.

Purpose or Objectives[1]

Management development is an attempt at improving an individuals managerial effectiveness through a planned and deliberate process of learning. For an individual this means a change through a process of planned learning. This should be the common and significant aim of development attempts from the point of view of the trainer and the trainee in an organisational setting.

The change in the individual must take place in those crucial areas which can be considered as output variables:

1. Knowledge change
2. Attitude change
3. Behaviour change
4. Performance change and
5. End operational results.

The success of development effort to be marked as effective depends upon the following inputs:

1. Trainee's personnel characteristics, such as his intelligence and motivation to learn.
2. His actual learning efforts.

These two variables are influenced by

- Formal organisational
- Leadership climate and
- Cultural features

The organisational aims of management development are to secure the following valuable end results.

- Improvement in technical performance.
- Improvement in supervision and leadership at each level.
- Improvement in inter departmental cooperation.
- Highlighting individuals' weaknesses.
- Attracting good men.
- Facilitating sound promotion from within policies and practices.
- Ensuring that the qualifications of key personnel become better known.
- Creating reserves in management ranks.
- Making an organisation more flexible by an increased versatility of its members.
- Improving organisation structure.
- Stimulating junior executives to do better work.
- Broadening key men in the middle cadre.

In sum management development aims at securing management improvement in the short run.

It may be summed up that the primary objectives of executive or management development are:

- To provide adequate leaders.
- To increase the efficiency of performance.
- To serve as a means of control in operations.
- To train managers for higher assignment who show potential for growth.
- To prepare them for adaptation to changes environment, ideological and technological.
- To develop a unity of purpose and improve morale.

The causes of management development programmes are thus:

1. The rapid rate of technological and social change in society has necessitated the training of manners so that they may cope with these developments.
2. The introduction of automation, intense market competition from foreign countries, the growth of new markets in the under-developed countries, enlarged participation of labour in management and greater interest by the public and the government in the actions of the businessmen have all led to the need for the development of managerial personnel.
3. Increased recognition by business and industrial leaders of the social and public responsibilities of management has necessitated the development of managerial personnel.

4. The increased size and complexity of most organisations require trained managers.
5. The frequent labour management strives have necessitated the services of trained personnel.
6. The change in socio-economic forces, including changes in public policy and the concepts of social justice, industrial democracy, problems of ecology, ekistics (problems of human settlements), ergonomics (problems of working environment) and cultural anthropology (problem of fitting machines to men) – all these demand increasing attention of the management for decisions in these diverse fields.

Management Development Process[6]

According to Dooher and Marquis, the stages involved in a management development programme are:

- Organisational planning
- Programme targeting.
- As curtaining key positions requirements.
- Managerial appraisal.
- Replacement of skills inventories.
- Planning individual development programmes.
- Appraising existing programmes.

Since the object of management development is to influence and modify the behaviour of the managers in operation, it is necessary that in training a management development programme for specified managerial group, the following points should be involved.

- Identify the pattern of behaviour at which the programme is aimed at which it seeks to influence and modify.
- Identify the causes, the impulses, horizontally up and down the enterprise which lend to give rise to the pattern of behaviour.
- Identify the nature of exposure.
- The programme must take care to throw impulse into the system in a manner that generates the urge to behaviour changes from within the trainee manager by the process of evolving rather than an imposition from outside.

The essential components or steps of a management development programme are:

1. **Looking at organisations objectives:** The objects tell, where we are going and will develop a framework from which the manager needs can be determined.

2. **Ascertaining development needs:** It calls for organisational planning and forecast of its needs for present a comprehensive job description, job specification and job analysis.
3. **An Appraisal of present management talent:** It is made with a view to determining qualitatively the type of personnel that is available within an organisation itself. The performance of a management individual is compared with the standard expected of him. His personal traits are also analyzed so that a value judgment may be made of his potential for advancement.
4. **A management manpower inventory:** It is prepared for the purpose of getting complete information about each management individual's bio-data and educational qualifications, the results of tests and performance appraisal. This information is generally maintained on cards, one for each individual.
5. **Planning of individual development programme:** It is undertaken to meet the needs of different individuals, keeping in view the differences in their attitudes and behaviour and in their physical, intellectual and emotional qualities. The weak and strong points of an individual are known from his performance appraisal reports, and on the basis of these, tailor made programmes are framed and launched. Such programmes give due attention to the interests and goals of the subordinates as well as the training and development opportunities which exist within an organisation.
6. **Establishment of training and development programmes:** This job is done by the personnel department. A comprehensive, and well conceived programme is generally prepared, certain concentrated brief courses. Such courses may be in the field of human relations, time and motion study, creative thinking, memory training, decision-making, leadership, etc.
7. **Evaluating development progammes:** The evaluation is any attempt to obtain information on the effects of a training programme and to assess the value of training in the light of that information. The evaluation discloses the relevance of programmes to an organisation it needs. It reveals whether programmes have contributed to the effectiveness of an organisation and whether programmes need to be continued or replaced by other relevant activities which might aid in the achievement of organisation's goals.

Organisation Climate for Management Development

Management development cannot take place unless a favourable climate for it is created at the top which extends down through each level of the organisation. It may come to a stand still if encouragement is not available to the persons concerned. If the growth stops at the middle management, it is impeded at that level, and then the first line management and non supervisory employees too suffer. Therefore, the creation of a proper organisational climate is a must for the success of any development programme.

By organisational, climate is meant the circumstances or conditions in which the management guides the development and growth of the people at all levels by training, counseling, delegation and communication.

In order that a proper development climate is crated, it must be borne in mind that:

- Development is learning rather than a teaching process. The burden for final growth rests on the individual.
- Growth takes place through a striving process in which objectives are set high and tasks involve stretching.
- Development takes place largely by building on the strength of the people rather than by a concentration on the elimination of weakness.
- A feeling of confidence in and approval of the process of development must be generated among those who are to be affected by it.
- At all levels, a genuine faith in development is necessary, a belief that people can and will with proper goals and encouragement do better.
- All concerned must, with an open heart and mind, be willing to welcome and accept any change in a point of view .

To develop a proper management climate, it is vital to pay a vigorous and constant attention to the administration of a development programme. There must be a comprehensive and coordinated planning and the plan should be communicated to all those who have to administer and function under the programme. A plan should apply first to the top so that management at that level may, by its own efforts, set an example for personnel development.

Essentials for the Success of Management Development Programme

The management development programme should be based in a definite strategy which should spell out the type, coverage and objectives of the programme. The multi-tier supervisory and management development programme should start from the first time supervisor and go all the way up to the top management.

A management programme should not only be looked upon as something meant for the limping horses in the organisation. It should be for the high fliers as well. In view of knowledge explosion and the consequent threat of managerial obsolescence, such programme should be meant for everyone in an organisation and not just for the weak ones.

The training division should not be a dumping ground for people found to be unsuitable for other jobs. It should be manned by a group of smart and successful managers drawn from various functional areas and disciplines. A multidisciplinary approach should be emphasized in training programmes rather than the purely personal flavour that is often found in them.

For the development of management, it is essential for the top management to promote a culture:

- For learning and gaining knowledge.
- For guest of excellence.
- For the tolerance of mistakes.
- For striving to maintain a balance and an equity.
- For the discovery of self and others.

The programme should be prepared well in advance and should contain decisions about instructional methods and development approaches to be used and have a provision for expertise and the necessary support systems, and should be based on the policy of promoting a proper utilisation of trained executives, their knowledge and techniques in the management of the operations of an organisation.

Management development programmes may be made fruitful by circulating the following materials among the participants:

- Newsletter conveying information about corporate affairs.
- Copies of takes given by management personnel.
- Excerpts from well written and informative articles.
- Copies of minutes of meetings distributed among those who were not present.

When these matters are discussed by a group, new plans and improved procedures often emerge.

Regarding techniques and methods of management development, we have discussed in length in techniques and methods of training. The methods and techniques both on the job and off the job, which we have discussed in the chapter training, are also same for the management development programmes.

Administering a Management Development Programme[7]

While administering the programme, due consideration should be given to the following points:

1. An management development programme should support a systematic career planning for managerial personnel, otherwise the frustrated trainees might seek opportunities elsewhere and the whole investment made in training programmes would go waste.
2. Management development does not comprise involvement in a series of structured courses, but there should also be an active interaction between the trainee and the management.
3. Training programme should cover as far as possible, every manager, capable of showing potential for growth.
4. The entire programme should be properly planned. The trainees should take part in it.

References

1. C. B. Mamoria, *Personnel Management,* Himalaya Publishing, Bombay, 1996.
2. *Ibid.*
3. *Ibid.*
4. S.R. Goel, *Personnel Administration.*
5. C.B. Mamoria, *Personnel Management,* HPH, 1996.
6. H. Koontz, *Appraising Managers as Managers,* McGraw Hill Book, New York, 1971.

Further Readings

1. DT. Hall, *Career in Organisations* Santa Monica, Goodyear, 1976.
2. S. Sullivan et al, *Careers in the Next Millennium,* HRM Review, 8. 1998.
3. J. Green Hans, *'Career Management,* Fort Worth TX Dryden, 1987.
4. HJ. Bernardin, J.E Russel, *Human Resaurce Management,* New York, McGraw Hill, 2002.

Chapter ten

PERFORMANCE APPRAISAL

Once the employee has been selected, trained and motivated, he is then appraised for his performance. Performance appraisal is the step where the management finds out how effective it has been at hiring and placing employee. If any problems are identified, steps are taken to communicate with the employee and to remedy them. Performance evaluation or appraisal is the process of an employee or a group of employees on a given job and his potential for future development. It consists of all formal procedures used in working organisations to evaluate personalities, contributions and potentials of employees.

According to Flippo[1] "Performance appraisal is the systematic, periodic and an impartial rating of employees' excellence in matters pertaining to his present job and his potential for a better job." So it is the process of obtaining, analysing and recording information about the relative worth of an employee. Performance Appraisal is a process of consisting of a series of steps. It is the systems examination of an employee's strengths and weaknesses in terms of the job. It is scientific or objective study. Again it is a continuous process, wherein the evaluations are arranged periodically according to a definite plan.

Objectives

The main objectives of employee assessment are:

- To provide feedback to employees so that they come to know where they stand and can improve their job performance.
- To provide a valid database for personnel decisions concerning placements, pay, promotion, transfer, punishment, etc.
- To diagnose the strengths and weaknesses of individuals so as to identify further training needs.

- To provide coaching, counseling, career planning and motivation to subordinates.
- To develop positive superior-subordinate relations and thereby reduce grievances.
- To facilitate research in personnel management.
- To test the effectiveness of recruitment, selection, placement and induction programmes.

Process

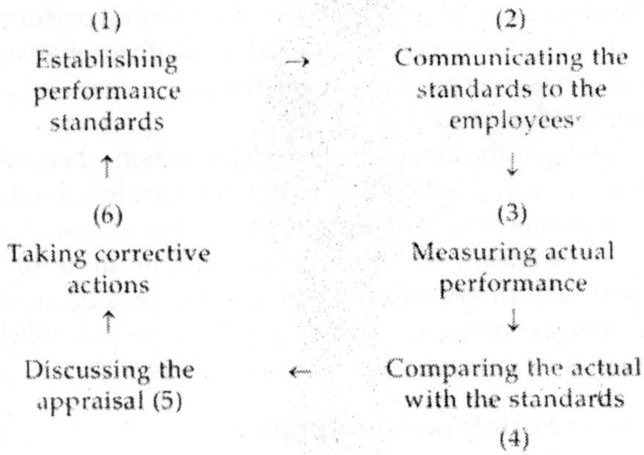

Broadly speaking, the process of evaluation begins with the establishment of performance standards. At the time of designing a job and formulating a job description, performance standards are usually developed for the position. These standards should be clear and not vague and objective enough to be understood and measured. These standards should be discussed with the supervisors to find out which different factors are to be incorporated, weights and points to be given to each factor and these then should be indicated on the appraisal form, and later on used for appraising the performance of the employees.

The second step is to communicate these standards to the employees, for the employees left to themselves, would find it difficult to guess what is expected of them. To make communication effective feedback is necessary from the subordinate to the manager satisfactory communicated by the manager has been received and understood in the way it was intended.

The third step is the measurement of performance. To determine what actual performance is, it is necessary to acquire information about it. We should be concerned with how we measure and what we measure. Four sources of information are frequently used to measure actual performance, i.e. Personal observation, statistical reports, oral reports and written reports.

The fourth step is the comparison of actual performance with standards. The employee is apprised and judged of his potential for growth and advancement. Attempts are made to note deviations between standard performance and actual performance.

The fifth stage, in which the results of appraisal are discussed periodically with the employees, where good points, weak points and difficulties are indicated and discussed so that performance is improved. The information that the subordinate receives about his assessment has a great impact on his self-esteem and on his subsequent performance.

The final step is the initiation of corrective action when necessary. Immediate corrective action is of two types. One is immediate and deals predominately with symptoms. The other is basic and delves into causes coaching and counseling may be done or special assignments and projects may be set, persons may be deputed for formal training courses, and decision-making responsibilities and authority may be delegated to the subordinates.

Problems in Performance Appraisal[2]

The ideal approach to performance evaluation is that in which the evaluator is free from personal biases, prejudices and idiosyncrasies. This is because when an evaluation is objective, it minimizes the potential capricious and dysfunctional behaviour of the evaluator which may be detrimental to the achievement of the organisational goals. Inequities in evaluation often destroy the usefulness of the performance system, resulting in inaccurate, invalid appraisals, which are unfair too.

There are many significant problems in performance appraisal. They are:

1. **Errors in rating:**
   a. Leniency of severity: It means either loose or strict. Leniency or severity on the part of the rater makes the assessment subjective. Subjective assessment defeats the very purpose of performance appraisal.
   b. *Central tendency:* It means average rating. This occurs when employees rated near the average or middle of the scale. The attitude of the rater is to play safe. This safe playing attitude

stems from certain doubts and anxieties which the raters have while assessing the rates. Naturally the raters use such expressions as 'satisfactory' and average to describe the performance of the rates.

c. *Halo effect:* It occurs when on aspect of an individuals performance influences the evaluation of the entire performance of the individual. In an organisation, an halo error occurs when an employee who works late constantly might be rated high on productivity and quality of output as well as on motivation.
d. *Stereo typing:* It means ago, sex, caste and religion affects the raters attitude towards the rate, not an actual outcomes or behaviour.
e. *Primary and regency effects:* The rater's ratings are heavily influenced either by behaviour exhibited by the ratee during the early stages of the review period (primacy) or by outcomes exhibited by the ratee near the end of the review period (regency).
f. *Perceptual set:* This occurs when the rater's assessment is influenced by previously held beliefs. For example, if the supervisor has a belief that employees hailing from one particular region are intelligent and hard working, his subsequent rating of an employee hailing.
g. *Performance dimension order:* Two or more dimensions on a performance instrument follow or closely follow each other and both describe or rotate to a similar quality. The rater rates the first dimension accurately and then rates the second dimension similar to the first because of their proximity. If the dimensions had been arranged in a significantly different order, the ratings might have been different.
h. *Spillover effect:* This refers to allowing past performance appraisal ratings to unjustifiably influence current ratings. Past ratings, good or bad, result in similar rating for the current period although the demonstrated behaviour does not deserve the rating, good or bad.
i. *Status effect:* It refers to over rating of employees in higher level job or jobs held in high esteem, and under rating employees in lower level job(s) held in load esteem.

2. **Lack of reliability:** Sometimes rater's stability and consistency cannot be maintained as a result the incoming men rater

evaluates the employee in a different manner. So lack of reliability also brings problem in performance appraisal.

3. **Incompetence:** Performance appraisal should be a conscious effort. The rater must be trained enough to have some competence and knowledge about the evaluation procedure of the ratee. Lack of competence and knowledge creates great disorder in the appraisal process.
4. **Negative approach:** Performance appraisal should not be a fault finding process. Such negative approach will hamper the very objective of the appraisal and also the organisation.
5. **Multiple objectives:** Multiple objectives of the organisation sometimes distort the performance appraisal. Multiple objectives force the rater to change the procedure frequently.
6. **Resistance:** Resistance from the side of employees or trade unions is now the biggest hurdle in performance appraisal process. The fear of loosing the job after the process is the main cause behind.

Methods of Appraisal

There are many methods for the evaluation of the employees. The methods can be classified into two, i.e. traditional and modern methods.

Traditional	*Modern*
1. Confidential report	1. Assessment centre
2. Essay method objectives (MBO)	2. Management by
3. Rating scales Rating Scale (BARS)	3. Behaviourally Anchored
4. Check lists	4. Psychological appraisals
5. Forced choice	
6. Forced distribution	
7. Critical incident	
8. Field Review	
9. Group Appraisal	
10. Ranking	
11. Paired comparison	
12. Cost accounting	

Source: K. B. Ashwathappa, *Personnel and HRM*

Traditional

1. *Confidential report:* Confidential records are maintained mostly in government departments. Called the Annual Confidential

Report (ACR, the approach have 14 items, i.e. leadership, attendance, self expression, ability to work with others, initiative, job knowledge, ability to understand new material, ability to reason, originality and resourcefulness, areas of work that suits the person best, judgment, integrity, responsibility and any defect. Twelve of these are filled on a four point grade scale (excellent, good, fair poor). For integrity, there is a special instruction from management. The system is highly secretive and confidential.

2. *Essay method:* In the essay method, the rater must describe the employee within a number of broad categories, such as -
   - The rater's overall impression of the employees performance.
   - The promotion ability of the employee.
   - The jobs that the employee is now able to perform.
   - The strengths and weakness of the employee.
   - The training and development assistance required.

   The strength of the essay method depends on the writing skills and analytical ability of the rater. However many raters do not have good writing skills. The essay method can consume much time. It also depends on the memory power of the rater.
3. *Rating scales:* This is the simplest and most popular technique. A typical rating scale comprises of a job related performance criterion such as dependability, initiative, output, attendance, attitude, cooperation, etc. Each scale ranges from excellent to poor. The rater checks the appropriate performance level on each criterion, and then computes the employees total numerical score.
4. *Checklists:* Under this method, a checklist of statements on the tariffs of the employee and his job is prepared in two columns – i.e. a 'yes' and a 'no'. All the rater should do is tick the 'yes' column if the answer to the statement is positive and in column 'no' if the answer is negative. After ticking off against each item, the rater forwards the list to the HR department, where the actual assessment of the employee takes place.
5. *Forced choice:* In this the rater is given a series of statements about an employee. These statements are arranged in blocks of two or more and the rater indicates which statement is most or least descriptive of the employee. This approach is known as the forced choice method because the rater is forced to select statements which are readymade.

6. *Forced distribution*[3]: The method operates under an assumption that the employee performance level conforms to a normal statistical distribution.

   The major weakness of the forced distribution method lies in the assumption that employee performance levels always conform to a normal distribution. In organisations that have done a good job of selecting and retaining only the good performers, the use of forced distribution approach would be unrealistic.
7. *Critical incident:* This method of employees' assessment has generated a lot of interest these days. The approach focuses on certain critical behaviour of an employee that makes all the difference between effective and non effective performance of a job. Such incidents are recorded by the superiors as and when they occur. One of the advantages of the critical incidents method is that the evaluation is based on actual job behaviour.
8. *Field review:* This is an appraisal by someone outside the assesse's own department, usually someone from the corporate office or the HR department. The outsider review employee records and holds interview with the ratee and his superior. This method is used for making promotional decision at the managerial level.
9. *Group appraisal:* Under this method, employees, are rated by an appraisal group, consisting of their supervisor and three or four other supervisors who have some knowledge of their performance. The supervisor explains to the group, the nature of his subordinate's duties. The group then discusses the standards of performance for that job, the actual performance of the job holder and the causes of their particular level of performance, and offer suggestion for future improvement if any.
10. *Ranking:* It is the oldest and simplest method of performance appraisal, by which the men and his performance are considered as an entity by the rater. The relative position of each man is tested in terms of his numerical rank. This is the simplest method of separating the most efficient from the least efficient any relatively easy to develop. But the greatest limitation is that in practice it is very difficult to compare a single individual with human beings having varying behaviour traits.

11. *Paired comparison:*[4] Under this method, the appraiser compares each employee wit every other employee, one at a time. For example, there are five employees named A, B, C, D, and E. Technological performance of A is first compared with the performance of B and a decision is made about whose performance is better. Then A is compared with C, D and E in that order. The same procedure is repeated for other employees. The number of comparisons can be calculated with the help of the formulae N (N-1)/2, when N stands for the number of employees to be compared.
12. *Cost accounting:* This method evaluates performance from the monetary returns the employee yields to the organisation. A relationship is established between the cost included in keeping the employee and benefit of the organisation derives from him. Performance of the employee is then evaluated based on the established relationship between the cost and the benefit.

Modern

1. *Assessment centre:* The purpose of this method is to test candidates in a social situation, using a number of assessors and a variety of procedure. The most important feature of assessment center is job related simulations. Under this method evaluators join together to judge performance of employees in several situations with the use of a variety of criteria. It is used mostly to help select employees for the first level supervisory positions. In this method, the use of situational exercises are in basket exercise, business game, role playing incident and leaderless group discussion. Evaluators are drawn from experienced managers with proven ability at different levels of management. They evaluate all the employees both individually and collectively.
2. *MBO*[5]: It is evolved by Peter F Drucker. MBO is potentially a powerful philosophy of managing and an effective way for operational in the evaluation process. It is described as a process whereby the superior and the subordinate managers of an organisation jointly identify its common goals, define each individual major areas of responsibility in terms of results expected of him and use these measures as guides for operating the unit and assuring the contributions of each of its members. MBO has an objective in itself. The objective is to change behaviour and attitudes towards getting the job done.

Although MBO has something of an area of mystery about it, it really is a fairly simple procedure. It consists of five basic steps-setting the organisation goal, joint goal setting, performance review, establishment of major check posts to measure progress and feedback.

Thus under MBO programme an employee and his supervisor meet and together define, establish and set certain goals which the employee would attempt to achieve within the period of prescribed time. They also discuss the ways and methods of measuring employee progress.

So MBO is an important performance tool. It has certain advantages, which are:

- MBO helps and increases employee motivation.
- Managers are more likely to compete with themselves than with other managers.
- MBO results in a means ends chain.
- MBO reduces role conflict and ambiguity.
- MBO provides more objective appraisal criteria.
- MBO forces and aids in planning.
- MBO identifies problems better and early.
- MBO identifies performance deficiencies.
- MBO helps the individual manager to develop personal leadership in this context the Matrix Model of Phillips India is presented below which is adopted from K Prasad's book, Getting The Right People.

High	2 Employees (problems)	3 Star
Low	1 Separation planned	4 Citizen solid

Fig. 3.10.1: Matrix model of phillips

(Adopted from K. Prasad's *Getting the Right People*, Macmillan, 2001)

1. Employees with low performance are given chance to improve. If they failed they are to be separated.
2. People with high potential and with low performance are called problem employees. Attempts have been made to improve their performance. In about 20%, there is failure which amounted to separation.

3. Employees have high potential and they are high performer; so called 'star performer'.
4. People are high performer and with low potentials. They are called solid citizen. They are given training to improve potentiality and capabilities.

3. BARS – Behaviourally Anchored Rating Scales, some times called behaviourally expectation scales, are rating scales whose scale points are determined by statements of effective and ineffective behaviours. They are said to be behaviourally anchored in that the scales represent a range of descriptive statements of behaviour varying from the least to the most effective. BARS have the following features:
   - Areas of performance to be evaluated are identified and defined by the people who will use the scales.
   - The scales are unshared by descriptions of actual job behaviour that, supervisors agree, represent specific levels of performance. The result is a set of rating scales in which both dimensions and anchors are precisely defined.
   - All dimensions of performance to be evaluated are based on observable behaviours and are relevant to the job being evaluated since BARS are tailor made for the job.
   - Since the raters who will actually use the scales are actively involved in the development process, they are more likely to be committed to the final product.

   BARS were developed to provide results which subordinates could use to improve performance. Superiors would feel comfortable to give feedback to the rates. Further, BARS help overcome rating errors.
4. *Psychological appraisal:* Large organisations employ full time industrial psychologists. When psychologists are used for evaluations, they assess an individual's future potential and not post performance. The appraisal normally consists of in-depth interviews, psychological tests, discussions with supervisors and a review of other evaluations. The psychologist then writes an evaluation of the employees intellectual, emotional, motivational and other work related characteristics that suggest individual potential and may predict future performance.

   Employees Appraisal or Performance Appraisal is a method to measure the performance of employee in terms of variables like cost, time, quality and quantity. Its history can be traced back to FW Taylor's time and motion study. No doubt it is essential for training and development and particularly for career development of the employee. Particularly, Performance Appraisal is a timely and regular measurement and review of workforce performance in the organisation. The very purpose is to:

- Provide feedback to the employees on their performance.
- Provide opportunity for analysing the shortcomings and for development pinpoint the training/learning needs of the employees
- Enable the organisation to award, reward and punishment.
- Fix HR decision as to salary, promotion, increment, transfer and disciplinary action.

Though, traditionally it is treated as a closed control mechanism, but it is used as a technique of employees development. No more it is past-oriented activity, job evaluation or identifying the wrongs. It is future oriented in educating the poor performers; it is a method to standardize how well one can do a job and it rectifies the wrongs through learning process.

To put succinctly, it is a process of three steps – one, setting work standard; two, evaluating workforce's performance as per standard; three, offering feedback to employees for remedial action as to low performance.

Moreover, performance appraisal serves five useful purposes (Candy, Carson: 1996 and Smither (ed): 1998). They are:

1. Performance appraisal helps in compensation decisions.
2. It serves as an aid to promotion decisions.
3. It provides guidelines for training and development of the employees.
4. If offers feedback to employees, so that they can move in their career path.
5. It acts as an additional tool for personal development.

Essentially Performance Appraisal has double benefits- employer and employees' perspectives. The appraisal factors may differ from organisation to organisation (Mamoria, 2000).

They are :

- Ability to plan, delegate, control and coordinate
- Knowledge of jobs
- Costs and result consciousness
- Power of expression and communication
- Decision-making
- Comprehension

- Use of discussion and judgment
- Resourcefulness and industry
- Cooperation
- Habit of listening
- Interpersonal relations/sociability
- Leadership
- Courage to disagree and to reason tactfully
- Organising ability
- Ability to run meeting
- Attitude to work
- Loyalty
- Initiative and creativity
- Dependability
- Quality of work
- Intelligence
- Integrity
- Personality
- Tidiness
- Attendance
- Work output
- Drive.

Further the appraisers are supervisors, peers, subordinates and there is also the concept of self-appraisal, outsourcing and consultants. Generally appraisal is made at the end of the year (Calender/Financial). To add to it D. A. Decenzo, S. P. Robbins (2004), W. F. Casio (2003) examined in details the steps of appraisal process. Accordingly the steps are:

a. Establish performance standard
b. Communication of the standard
c. Measure actual performance
d. Evaluation of performance with standard
e. Taking corrective action

And the performance appraisal methods is divided into three categories (Grote, 2000, Rao, 2005).

Performance Management Models : K Prasad

As to this two Performance Management models are presented by K. Prasad – one is performance linked HR Sub system and other is Performance Management Self Renewing Cycle in figure 3.10.2 and 3.10.3 respectively below.

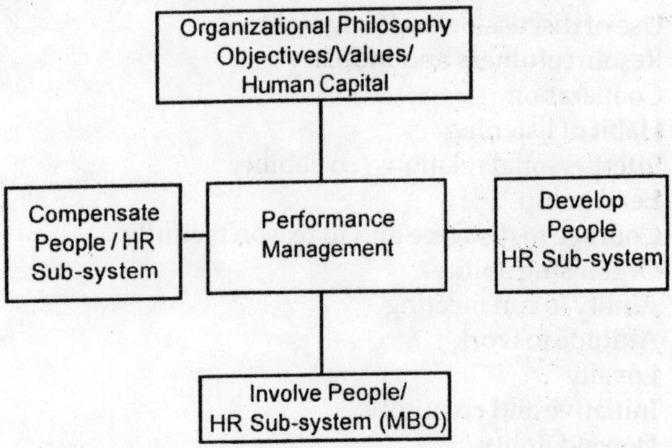

Fig. 3.10.2: Performance Linked HR Sub-System

Source: K. Prasad (2005), Strategic Human Resource Management, Macmillan, New Delhi)

1. **Individual Evaluation Methods**

• Confidential Report	- Used in Govt. organization; A descriptive report.
• Essay Evaluation	- Rater's views are reflected as to strength and weakness.
• Critical incidents	- Exposure to statement of ineffective and effective behaviour
• Check lists	- With yes/no option.
• Graphic rating scale	- Rating by scores.
• Behaviorally anchored Rating scale	- Performance Dimensions in rating scale
• Forced choice method	- Rating with closed choice to eliminate biasness.
• Management by objectives (MBO)	- Goal setting and appraisal programmes.

2. **Multiple – Person Evaluation Methods**
   - Ranging
   - Paired comparison
   - Forced Distribution
3. **Other Methods**
   - Group Appraisal
   - Human Resource Accounting
   - Assessment Centre
   - Field Review.

In performance management, an innovative multi rater method 360 degree Appraisal is designed. By it an employee is rated by supervisor, subordinates, peers and customers/ clients. Obviously, this multi-source approach provides an insight how people around employee see his/her performance. In 21st century most organisations are using 360 degree feedback as a part of their performance management programme and development process. In comparison to traditional one- annual appraisal by boss, more appreciation for 360° degree appraisal as a part of staff appraisal and development initiative. Principal merits of this multirater method are:

- Employees can know much to his/her self as colleagues perceive them.
- It enriches personal effectiveness for better work and for healthy organisation.
- It provides for open culture as there is showing of feedback.

On the whole 360° ratings add to competence and excellence.

Modern concept [6] 360° Appraisal

Usually performance appraisal is done by the superior of the employee. But now-a-days, the approach to performance appraisal has been changed. It is called 360° appraisal in which involved the appraisal by superiors, subordinates, peers and customers.

References

1. E.B. Flippo, *Principles of Personnel Management*, McGraw Hill Book, New York, 1980.
2. K.B. Ashwathappa, *Personnel and HRM*, Tata McGraw Hill Publication. 2003.
3. *Ibid.*
4. *Ibid.*
5. S. George Odiorne, *Personel Administration by Objectives*, Richard, D Irwin, New York, 1971.
6. C.B. Gupta, *Human Resource Management*, S. Chand & Co, New Delhi, 2001.

Chapter eleven

EMPLOYMENT RELATIONS: COLLECTIVE BARGAINING

Collective bargaining is the process in which representatives of two groups, i.e. employers and employees meet and attempt to negotiate an agreement which specifies the nature of future relationship between the two. According to Beach, "collective bargaining is concerned with the relations between unions representing employees and employers. It involves the process of union organisation of employees, negotiation, administration and interpretation of collective agreements covering wages, hours of work and other conditions of employment, engaging in concerted economic action and dispute settlement procedures."

Collective bargaining is the term used to describe a situation in which the essential conditions of employment are determined by a bargaining process undertaken by representatives of a group of workers on the one hand and of one or more employers on the other. According to Flippo[1] "collective bargaining is a process in which the representatives of a labour organisation and the representatives of business organisation meet and attempt to negotiate a contract or agreement, which specifies the nature of employee-employer union relationship."

A manual issued by the ILO in 1960 defines collective bargaining as "negotiations about working conditions and terms of employment between an employer a group of employers or one or more employer's organisations, on the one hand, and one or more representative worker's organisations, on the other with a view to reaching an agreement."

So collective bargaining involves negotiations, drafting, administration and interpretation of documents. It is between the employers and the union representing their employees with regard to their joint understanding as to wages, hours of work and other terms and conditions of employment. An effective collective bargaining pre-supposes the existence of two competent agencies of

1. Able management
2. Organised trade union and that too with an open mind to understand and appreciate the stand of each other.

On the basis of structural arrangements, collective, bargaining may be classified into two broad categories:

1. Single employer bargaining and
2. Multi-employer bargaining. Single employer bargaining takes place between one company and either one union and more than one union where there are several unions at different plants. Multi-employer bargaining signifies collective bargaining between the employers' federation and the workers of an industry represented by the federation of all the trade unions. This type of bargaining may take place at local, regional or industry level.

Features

The essential features of collective bargaining are:

- It is a collective process.
- It is a continuous process.
- It is a flexible and dynamic process.
- It is a method of partnership of workers in management It is a way to establish industrial democracy.
- It is based on give and take approach and not in take or leave approach.
- It is an attempt in achieving and maintaining discipline in industry.
- It is an effective step in promoting industrial jurisprudence.

Significance[2]

Collective bargaining not only includes negotiation, administration and enforcement of the written contracts between the employees and the employers, but also includes the process of resolving labour management conflicts. Thus collective bargaining is legally and socially sanctioned way of regulating in the public interest the forces of power and influence inherent in organised labour management groups. The role of collective bargaining for solving the problems arising at the plant and industry levels has been widely recognized.

Labour legislation and the machinery for its implementation prepare a framework according to which industrial establishments should operate. Collective bargaining helps to promote co-operation and mutual understanding between the workers and the management. It provides a framework for deciding the terms and conditions of employment without resort to strikes and lockouts and without the intervention of outsiders.

1. **Importance to Employees**
   a. Collective bargaining develops a sense of self respect and responsibility among the employees.
   b. Collective bargaining increases the strength of the workers. Their bargaining capacity as a group increases.
   c. Collective bargaining increases the morale and productivity of employees.
   d. It restricts management's freedom for arbitrary action against the employees.
   e. Effective collective bargaining machinery strengthens the trade union movement.
2. **Importance to Employers**
   a. The workers feel motivated as they can task to the employers on various matters and bargain for higher benefits.
   b. It is easier for the management to resolve issues at the bargaining table rather than taking up complaints of employee individually.
   c. Collective bargaining promotes a sense of job security among the employees and thereby tends to reduce cost of labour turnover to management, employees as well as the society at large.
   d. Collective bargaining opens up the channels of communication between the top and the bottom levels of the organisation which may be difficult otherwise.
3. Importance to society
   a. Collective bargaining can facilitate industrial peace in the country.
   b. Collective bargaining results in the establishment of a harmonious industrial climate which supports the pace of a nation's effort towards economic and social development since the obstacles to such development can be largely eliminated or reduced.

c. The exploitation of workers by the management can be checked.

Function

Over the past few decades, collective bargaining has come to accepted as a process of decision-making and a mechanism for balancing the power between the employers and the employees. In the process collective bargaining performs three important functions.

1. Technique of long run social change

Collective bargaining in its broader aspect is not confined only to the economic relations between employers and employees. In fact it is a technique whereby an inferior social class or group carries on a never slackening pressure for a bigger share in the social sovereignty as well as for more welfare, security and liberty for its individual members. Social change consists of the alteration of pattern of actions and interactions and also a simultaneous change in the norms, values, cultural products and symbols. Thus when viewed as a process of social change, collective bargaining encompasses more than the direct clash between employers and unions. It refers to the rise in the political and social power achieved by workers and their organisations. With gradual rise in social and political power, workers gain greater recognition and ability to assert against employees.

2. Peace treaty or temporary truce

Collective bargaining may be viewed as a struggle between two opposing powers which is smoothened by the compromises. Compromise represents a state to which each side is prepared to descend from the original stand. This recording from original position may come about in two major ways:

a. *Compromise with combative aspects:* When combative aspects of parties are in operation, the outcome of struggle depends on the parties' relative strength. The inherent strength of each side is its ability to withstand strike. This is partly an economic matter. The ability to withstand strike also depends on such non-economic factors as loyalty of workers to union and their willingness to make personal sacrifices to support its goals the degree of loyalty is affected by the presence of any factionalism within the union.

   The settlement between the two parties when finally reached, with or without strike, is a compromise. The extend to which each side is willing to accept less than its original bargaining demands depends, in part, on how strong it feels relative to its opponent. The compromise then is a temporary truce with neither side being completely satisfied with the results.

b. *Compromise without combative aspects:* Not always as in the above case, the compromise is the culmination of continuous struggle and antagonistic attitudes. Instead a majority of contracts are reached without a strike the trace is signed before either opponent fires a shot. A tranquil stability is achieved in the process of controlling economic change. That is the union starts first of all to make changes and improvements in its relations with the employers.

3. Industrial Jurisprudence

Collective bargaining creates a system of industrial jurisprudence. It is a method of introducing civil rights in industry, that is, of requiring that management be conducted by rules rather than arbitrary decisions. It establishes rules which define and restrict the traditional authority exercised by management.

Process

The bipartite collective bargaining process usually starts with a charter of demands being presented to the management by the unions on behalf of their constituent members. A fresh chatter is submitted upon the expiry of an earlier agreement. If there is an existing agreement between management and union, as is often the case then till the fresh agreement is signed, the provisions of the existing agreement would continue till it expires.

Before the actual negotiations begin, both the management and the union groups go through several intra organisational bargaining. The management will have to settle a set of internal policy issues, relating to the concessions they would make, the wages they would pay and the changes that they would like to effect as obviously thee are areas of wide divergence. Again the balance between viability of the firm, in terms of profits and labour costs needs to be reconciled. An organisation has competing interests to content with in that it has to cater to all the share holders, the employees and the consumers. The share holders expect profits and higher dividends, the employees expect higher wages and the firm has to deliver quality products at a competitive price to survive and enhance its image. Internal strategies have to focus on reconciling these interests and fix priorities for the demands of the several groups from time to time.

Moreover, some important aspects such as the cost implications of the unions' demands and its effect on profits, viability of the firm, and the escalation of prices of its goods and services have also to be considered by the management group. Besides, in many cases, some managerial prerogatives may be questioned. Gathering of comparative data from firms in the region and industry, in terms of practices and percentage wage increase negotiated in the recent. Past, is necessary too. Some firms take a policy decision to maintain leadership roles while others opt for middle level positions and finally others opt for the lower rungs. Each of these approaches will necessitate certain postures at the negotiating table depending on the way the case is agreed to defend the chosen strategy.

Similarly, the union team having gone through an intra-organisational political exercise decides upon their strategy and priorities so as to present a united front at the negotiating table. Gathering of data, once again, would be the first step towards formulating the charter of demands. The various groups categories, such as skilled, semi skilled and unskilled workers, will each want to maintain and further their differentials amongst each other. The quantum therefore needs to be reconciled by the union representatives without alienating the several groups.

They also work out quantum of wage increase and other welfare measures in preparing the charter of demands. Problem areas either in terms of multiple employee grievances. Therefore, there is a great onus on the part of the union executive to keep in direct touch with the rank and file members in order to ascertain their views and needs.

Essentials of Successful Collective Bargaining

Collective bargaining is an institutionalized representative process. It involves an exercise in graceful retreat from original position, a retreat without seeming to retreat to compromise. As such, it is a complex process, involving psychology, politics and poker. It is a process of tough minded economic calculus and horse trading. To make collective bargaining successful, following conditions must be satisfied.

- Strong and stable union is essential for the successes of collective bargaining.

- The recognition by the management of the representative trade union as a bargaining agent is of paramount significance.
- The bargaining machinery must be efficient and permanent. No ad hoc arrangements are satisfactory for the simple reason that bargaining is a continuing process.
- There has to be a greater emphasis on mutual accommodation rather than conflict or uncompromising attitude. Conflicting attitude does not lead to amicable labour relations. It may foster union militancy as the union reacts by engaging in pressure tactics.
- If collective bargaining has to be fully effective, a favorable political climate must exist. The government must be convinced of bargaining's positive contribution. If encouraging attitude of government exists, it does everything to facilitate bargaining process such as providing machinery for the settlement of disputes mediation and conciliation.
- The procedures must be developed to ensure that negotiators have full authority to bind their constituents. If bargaining representatives have to refer constantly back to their respective organisations, it makes bargaining process most ridiculous and ineffective, because parties known by experience that bargaining team is only a show piece and not the real authority.

References

1. E.B. Flippo, *Principles of Personnel Management*, McGraw Hills Books, New York, 1980
2. CD Miller, HW Form, *Industrial Sociology*, Harper and Row, New Delhi, 1964.

Chapter twelve

HUMAN RESOURCE AUDIT (HRA)

An audit is properly speaking, an examination and verification of accounts and records. Human Resource Audit refers to an examination and evasion of policies, procedures and practices to determine the effectiveness of human resource management. In other words, human resource audit or periodical reviews of the effectiveness of a management are concerned with:

- The measurement of the effectiveness of personnel programme and activities, and
- The determination of what should or should not be done in the future as a result of such measurement.

Objective[1]

The objectives of a personnel audit are:

- To review the whole system of management programmes in which a management develops, allocates and supervises human resources in an organisation with a view to determining the effectiveness of these programmes.
- To seek explanations and information i.e. to get answers to questions, "why did it happen?" and "what happened?"
- To evaluate the extent to which line managers have implemented the policies which have already been initiated and
- To evaluate the personnel staff and employees.

Importance

In modern times HRA have been widely accepted as tools with which managers can control the programmes and practices of the HR department. The importance of HRA has increased in recent years because of the following reasons.

1. A change in managerial philosophy and theory, as a result of which a management now feels that the employee's participation

in the activities of an organisation, and their identification with it, has a tremendous influence on the working of that organisation.

2. The changing role of government, which intervenes more often and more extensively now, to control man power management by an organisation with a view to protecting the interests of the employees, providing them with better working conditions and ensuring their economic security.
3. The increasing role played by trade union and their strength, as a result of which they often question managerial competence in industrial relations.
4. The rising wages, changes in the skills of technical and professional workers, and the increasing expenditure incurred on the HR department.

Need for HRA[2]

According to Yoder, the need for HRA is largely influenced by several conditions. Some of these are:

- *The number of employees:* Very small units, because of the very small number of persons they employ, require comparatively little in the way of a formal audit.
- *Organisational structure:* Continuing feedback is facilitated if an organisation has a HR department.
- *Communication and feedback:* An effective two way communication system often reduces the need for a formal audit.
- *Location and dispersion:* The need for a formal audit is directly proportional to the number of isolated plants.
- *Status of an HR manager:* If he participates in top management plans, reports, discussions and decisions, the need for a formal audit may be less frequently felt.
- *Administrative style:* The greater the delegation of authority and decentralisation of power, the greater the value of a regular and formal audit.

Scope

The scope of HRA is very wide. It represents a 'whole man' approach, i.e., it assumes that the management of human resources involves much more than the practice of recruiting, hiring, retaining and firing employees. It examines the concept of people management by supervisors at all levels. The field of HRA includes:

- Job analysis

- Recruitment
- Testing
- Selection
- Training
- Management development
- Promotions and transfers
- Rating
- Labour relations
- Morale development
- Employee benefits and services
- Employee communication
- Employee counseling
- Wage and salary administration
- Collective bargaining
- Human Resource Research.

Frequency and Types

It is a common practice to have an annual evaluation or audit. At the end of each calendar year, a report is presented, covering statistical information on the activities performed, the results achieved, the costs and expenditure involved and comparisons of objectives and accomplishments. By a perusal of this report, a great deal of useful information can be had about personnel activities. In some organisations, however this personnel audit is conducted periodically, generally in accordance with the needs of each organisation. For example attitude or morale surveys on particular subjects or topic may be conducted, or special reports may be prepared on such issues as grievances, the working of seniority rules or the effects of overtime practices and collective bargaining agreements.

Two practices are generally followed while conducting a HRA. In some cases, the audit is conducted by those employed in the organisation itself generally by auditors or accountants. In other cases, the services of outside experts are engaged. The former is known as internal audit, while the letter is known as external audit. The advantages of having an outside audit are:

- He has a background of knowledge of what others are doing in similar situations.
- He has a professional attitude toward his work, and
- He is objective in that he personally will not become a party to recommend changes.

While appointing an outside auditor certain conditions should be kept in mind regarding his work.

1. He cannot work miracles. He can diagnose ills and recommend treatment.
2. He must receive top management's support.
3. He cannot and should not relieve management of its responsibility for making the decisions. He can recommend, but the acceptance of his recommendations rests with management.

Audit Report[3]

The report should invariably be submitted, within a reasonable time, after the audit work is over. It should avoid the journalistic style, be based solely on the findings, be presented in a factual manner that is reading available for future reference, make use of graphic techniques where appropriate and not be any longer than is necessary. The following items should be contained in the report:

- Table of contents.
- Summary and conclusion, in which the entire reports is summarized for the top executives.
- Preface giving a brief statement of the objectives.
- The report proper, in which a major division is covered as a special section. Each section should be complete and should certain as many supporting data as are practical without making it too voluminous. Other data should be included in appendix.
- Summary. This is more complete than summary and conclusions at the beginning of the report.
- Appendix: This includes supporting data that would be too voluminous to appear in the body of the report.
- It should be signed by all members making the audit.

Certain aspects of the audit report may be available to the employees. Other phases of audit may be appropriate to give only to top management.

References

1. K.B. Aswasthappa, *Personnel and Human Resource Management*, McGraw Hill, New Delhi, 2003.
2. D. Yoder, HG, Henneman, J.G. Turnbull and C. Stone, *Handbook of Personnel Management and Industrial Relations*, McGraw Hill Book, New York, 1858.
3. CB Mamoria, *Personnel Management*, HPH, 1996.

Chapter thirteen

HUMAN RESOURCE INFORMATION SYSTEM (HRIS)

There is hardly any sphere of activity which is not touched by computer. This human child has surpassed its patron in almost every aspect, so also in the human resource management. In HRM traditionally, most of the desired information was available from individual personnel files, the compiling of which time was consuming before computers became readily available. Use of computers for collecting, storing, maintaining, retrieving and validating human resource data is popularly called Human Resource Information System (HRIS).

HRIS is usually part of the organisation;s larger Managerial Information System (MIS). HRIS need not be complex or even computerized. But computerisation has its own advantage of providing more accurate and timely data for decision-making.

The areas of application of HRIS are many. Some of them include training management, risk managements, and turn over analysis, succession planning, financial planning and other related areas.

Steps[1]

Proper planning is absolutely necessary for successful implementation of an HRIS. The steps describe the specific procedures involved in successfully developing and implementing on HRIS are:

1. *Inception of an idea:* The idea for having an HRIS must originate some where. The originator of the idea should prepare preliminary report showing the need for an HRIS and what it can do for the organisations.
2. *Feasibility of study:* Feasibility study evaluates the present system and details the benefits of an HRIS. It evaluates the costs are benefits of an HRIS.

3. *Selecting a project team:* Once the feasibility study has been accepted and the resources allocated, a project tam should be selected. The project team should consists of an HR representative who is knowledgeable about the organisations HR functions and activities and about the organisation itself.
4. *Defining the requirements:* A statement of requirements specifies in detail exactly what the HRIS will do. A large part of the statement of requirements normally deals with the details of the reports that will be produced. Naturally the statement describes other specific requirements. This includes written descriptions of how users, collect and prepare data, obtain approvals, complete forms, retrieve data, and perform other non technical tasks associated with HRIS.
5. *Vendor Analysis:* This step determines what hard ware and software are available that will best meet the organisations needs for the lowest price. This is a difficult task. The best approach is usually not to ask vendors if a particular package can meet the organisations requirements. The results of this analysis will determine whether to purchase an off the shelf package or develop the system internally.
6. *Package contract negotiation:* After a vendor has been selected, the contract must be negotiated. The contract stipulates the vendor is responsibilities with regard to software, installation, service, maintenance, training and documentation.
7. *Training:* Training usually begins as soon as possible after the contract has been signed. The members of the project team are trained to use the HRIS. Towards the end of the implementation the HR representative will train managers from other departments in how to submit information to the HRIS and how to request information from it.
8. *Tailoring the system:* This step involves making changes to the system to best fit the needs of the organisation. An alternative approach is to develop programmes that augment the vendor's programme rather than altering it.
9. *Collecting the data:* Prior to start up the system, data must be collected and entered into the system.
10. *Testing the system:* Once the system has been tailored to the organisations needs and the data entered, a period of testing follows. The purpose of testing follows. The purpose of testing phase is to verify the output of the HRIS and to make sure it is doing what it is supposed to do. All reports should be critically analyzed for accuracy.

11. *Starting up:* It begins when all the current actions are put into the system and reports are produced. It is wise to attempt start up during a lull period so that maximum possible time can be devoted to the HRIS.
12. *Running in parallel:* Even after the new HRIS has been tested; it is desirable to run the new system in parallel with the old system for a period of time. This allows for the comparison of outputs of both the system and examination of any inaccuracies.
13. *Maintenance:* It normally takes several weeks or even months of the HR people to feel or even months for the HR people to feel comfortable with the new system. During this stabilisation period, any remaining errors and adjustments should be handled.
14. *Evaluation:* After the HRIS has been in place for a reasonable length of time, the system should be evaluated.

Subsystems

A computerized HRIS is an information system that makes use of computers to monitor, control and influence the movement of human beings from the time they indicate their intention to join an organisation, till the time they separate from it after joining. It consists of following such systems:

- Recruitment Information System.
- Personnel Information System.
- Man Power Planning Information System.
- Training Information System.
- Health Information System.
- Appraisal Information System.
- Payroll Information System.

Personnel Statistic System

Recruitment system	*Personnel Information system*	*Man Power Planning Information system*
1. General recruitment	1. Employee personnel details	1. HR recruitment forecast
2. Trainee recruitment	2. Transfer details	2. HR mobilization
3. Placement data bank	3. Promotion and increment	3. Succession planning

Contd.

Contd.

4. Advertisement system	4. Previous experience	4. Career planning
	5. Skills	
Training Information system	*Health Information system*	*Payroll*
1. HR development	1. Medical test reports	
2. Data for need based training	2. Employee health	
3. Training cost analysis	3. Monitor for maintenance	
4. Training monitor		
Annual Appraisal system		Personnel Statistics system
1. Merit rating		1. Employee profiles
2. Development requirements		2. Employee productivity
3. Promotion recommendation		3. Compensation pattern
		4. Turn over trends.

Needs and Advantages[2]

HRIS refers to the system of gathering, classifying, processing, recording and disseminating the information required for efficient and effective management of human resources in an organisation. Need for HRIS arises due to–

1. Large organisations employ a very large number of people. It becomes necessary to employ data based technology for tackling personnel problems.
2. In a geographically dispersed company every office requires timely and accurate information for manpower management.
3. Modern day compensation package is complex consisting of many allowances and deductions.
4. An employer has to comply with several labour laws. HRIS would store and retrieve data quickly and çorrectly enabling the employer to comply with statutory requirements.
5. With the help of a HRIS, employee records and files, can be integrated for fast retrieval, cross referencing and fire casting.
6. Necessary flexibility for adaptation to changes in environment can be built into mechanized information system.

Advantages[3]

The advantages of HRIS are also many which are:

- Clear definition of goals.
- Reduction in the amount and cost of stored human resources data.
- Availability of timely and accurate information about human assets.
- Development of performance standards for the human resource division.
- More meaningful career planning and counseling at all levels.
- Individual development through linkage between performance, rewards and job training.
- Higher capability to quickly and effectively staff project teams for problem solving.
- Implementation of training programmes based on knowledge of organisational needs.
- Ability to respond to every changing statutory and other environment.
- High status for the human resource functions due to its capability for strategic planning within the total organisation.

References

1. K.B. Aswasthapa, *Personnel and Human Resources Management*, Tata McGraw Hill, New Delhi, 2003.
2. CB. Mamonia, *Personnel Management*, HPH, 1996
3. *Ibid*.

Chapter fourteen

GENERAL ISSUES OF HRM

COUNSELLING

Human Resource Management aims to promote the common interests of employer and employed in the success of the business, but whatever steps you take to achieve this aim, you will find that there are some people whom you cannot fit into your scheme of things. In spite of all efforts to train a motivate them, they may be incapable of meeting acceptable standards. Sometimes you may be forced to accept that in special circumstances the needs of the organisation have to over ride the needs of some individuals in it. New technology or a history of over manning may mean that you can no longer retain some staff. There will also be some people who cannot or will not fit themselves to the organisation's recruitment's while others will have real or imaginary grievances. A problem solving technique is to be adopted to handle these matters, involving those individuals, who are ill disciplined, cannot cope with their work or who have grievances.

Counselling[1] is a very good remedial action for solving disciplinary problems, grievances and redundancy. He helps to get the true facts and to achieve the willing co-operation of the employee in implementing an agreed solution. So co-operation and better result are ensured if one adopts the following non directive counseling approach.

- Listen with intelligence and sympathy. Someone in difficulties cannot fail to benefit if he is allowed to discuss his problem with a sympathetic listener.
- Get the problem clearly stated and accepted as a problem by the interview as well as the interviewer. The interviewee should be

helped to define the problem for himself. If he does this he is much more likely to be interested in solving it.

- When defining the problem and discussing possible solutions a considerably amount of listening and questioning may be necessary before the point becomes clear, especially when strong emotions are involved their presence and clarity of expression seldom go together.
- When trying to get the employee's point of view. It is often helpful to reflect back to him his key statements in your own words. This checks your understanding ~nd fells him that he is getting through.
- Stay alert and flexible. You should have a broad plan about how you would like to a likely the interview, but be prepared to change direction in the light of new information.
- Go through the facts of case, however unpleasant they may be, but retrain from making derogatory comments during the counseling.
- Try not to get drawn into a futile ornament about matters of opinion. If there is a difference in views about the facts, simply record it and check later.
- Observe behaviours as well as words, which can be misleading. Take note of gestures, manner, tone and inflexion, pauses and other ways of responding.
- Summarize where you have got to from time to time with a crystallising statement or question, such as "Am I right in thinking that your problem bolts down to this?" But do not put words in his mouth.
- Try to get the interviewee to summarize the situation and, in circumstances such as when an improvement in performance is required, suggest a possible solution. Agree with that solution if you possible can and encourage the individual to plan its implementation.

In counseling, the aim should be to get the root of the matter and, if there is no justification for being aggrieved, let the individual work this out for himself, with prompting from you as necessary.

STRESS

Stress is a dynamic condition in which an individual is confronted with an opportunity, constraint or demand released to what he/she desires and for which the outcome is perceived to be both uncertain and important.

Stress is not necessarily bad is and of itself. It has both negative and positive value. It is an opportunity when it offers potential gain. More typically stress is associated with constraints and demands. The constraints prevent an employee from doing what he/she desires while demands refer to the loss of something desired. A good performance review may lead to a promotion, greater responsibilities and a higher salary. But a poor review may prevent you from getting the promotion. An extremely poor review might even result in being fired.

Two conditions are necessary for potential stress to become actual stress. There must be uncertainty over the outcome and the outcome must be important. Regardless of the conditions, it is only when there is doubt or uncertainty regarding whether the opportunity will be seized, the constraint removed, or the loss avoided that there is stress. Stress is highest for these individuals who perceive they are uncertain as to whether they will win or lose and lowest for those individuals who think that winning or losing is a certainty. But importance is also critical. If winning or losing is an unimportant outcome, there is no stress. If keeping your job or earning a promotion does not help any importance for you, you have no reason to feel stress over having to undergo a performance review.

Stress and Selye's Analysis.

Selye has presented definition, types and stages and impact of stress for a clear-cut perception. The views are placed below to supplement the analysis.

Job stress is a mental stress. It has positive and negative impacts. It is "Eustress" when positive and it signifies achievement and exhilaration. Further, it is 'distress' when it is negative in orientation and the effect of negative stress is de-motivation, in-effectivity and low production/ performance. There are three stages of stress-low stress, optional stress and high stress. Stress and its impact are presented graphically by Selye (1974). (See Figure 3.13.1)

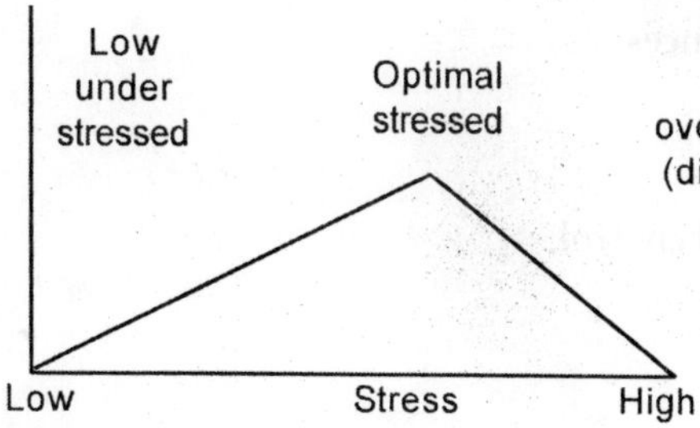

Consequences of Different Levels of Stress.

Basic	*Low stress*	*Optimum stress*	*High stress*
Reactions behaviours	Boredom/ Apathy Low: Motivation. Careless mistakes psychological withdrawal physical withdrawal activity	High Energy High motivation Heightened Perception High involvement	Exhaustion Anxiety and Nervousness in in Decisiveness and judgment
Performance Health effects	Low performance Dull health	High performance Good health	Poor performance Insomnia psychomatic illness

Fig 3.14.1: Selye's Stress and Job Performance Model.

Source: Selye, Hans, *Stress without Distress;* Signet Books, Philadelphia, 1974

Sources of Stress[2]

Potential stress

- Economic uncertainty
- Political uncertainty
- Technological uncertainty

Individual differences
- Perception
- Job experience
- Social support
- Belief in locus of control
- Hostility

Consequences
- Physiological

Organisational Factors
- Task depends
- Role demands
- Inter-personal demands
- Organisational structure
- Organisational leadership
- Organisational life stage

Individual Factors
- Family problems
- Economic problems
- Personality.

Source : Stephen Robbin's, *Organisational Behaviour.*

The above depicted model identifies there. Set of factors act as sources of potential stress:
- Environmental
- Organisational
- Individual.

Whether they lead to actual stress depends on individual differences such as job experience, personality. When stress is experienced by an individual, its symptoms can surface as physiological, psychological and behavioural outcomes.

Environmental: Just an environmental uncertainty influences the design of an organisation's structure, it also influences stress levels among employees in that organisation. Changes in the business cycle create economic uncertainties. When the economy is contracting, people become increasingly anxious about their security. Minor recessions, too, increase about their security. True, minor recessions, enhance stress levels. Down ward swings in the economy are often accompanied by permanent reductions in the workforce temporary lay offs, reduced pay, shorter work weeks, etc. Political threats and changes in some countries can be stress inducing. New innovations can make an employee's skill and experience obsolete in a very short period of time. Technological uncertainty therefore is a third type of environmental factor that can cause stress, computers, robotics, automation and other firms of technological innovation area threat to many people and cause them stress.

Organisational: Numerous factors within the organisation can cause stress. Pressures to avoid errors or complete tasks in a limited time period, work overload, a demanding and insensitive boss and unpleasant coworkers are a few examples.

Task demands are factors related to a person's job. They include the design of individual's job, working conditions and the physical work lay out. Assembly lines can put pressure on people when their. Speed is perceived as excessive. The more interdependence between a person's task and the tasks of others, the more potential stress there is. Autonomy however tends to lessen jobs stress where temperatures, noise or other working conditions are dangerous or undesirable can increase anxiety. So too, working in an over crowded room or in a visible location where interruptions are constant.

Role demands relate to pressures placed on a person as a function of the particular role he plays in the organisation. Role conflicts crate expectations that may be hard to reconcile or satisfy. Role overload is experienced when the employee is expected to do more than time permits. Role ambiguity is created when role expectations are not clearly understood and the employee is not sure what he is to do.

Interpersonal demands are pressures created by other employees. Lack of social support form colleagues and poor interpersonal relationships can cause considerable stress, especially among employees with a high social need.

Organisation structure defines the level of differentiation in the organisation, the degree of rules and regulations and the level of decision-making. Excessive rules and lack of participation in decisions that affect an employee are examples of structural variables that might be potential sources of stress.

Organisation leadership represents the managerial style of the organisation's senior executives. Some executives create a culture characterized by tension, fear and anxiety. They establish unrealistic pressures to perform in the short run, impose excessively tight controls and routinely fine employees who do not measure up.

Organisations go through a cycle. They are established; they grow, become mature and eventually decline. An organisations life stage creates different problems and pressures for employees. The established and decline stages are particularly stressful. Establishment is characterized by a great deal of excitement and uncertainty whereas decline stage requires cut backs, lay offs and a different set of uncertainties. Stress is least in maturity.

Individual: People hold family and personnel relationships dear. Martial difficulties, the breaking off of a relationship and discipline troubles with children are examples of relationship problems that create stress for employees.

Economic problems created by individuals over extending their financial resources are another set of personal troubles that can create stress for employees and distract their attention from their work.

Some people may have an inherent tendency to accentuate negative aspects of the world in general. If true, then a significant individual factor influencing stress is a person's basis dispositional nature. That is, stress symptoms express on the job may actually originate in the persons personality.

Individually stress is an additive phenomenon. Stress builds up. Each new and persistent stressor adds to an individuals stress level. A single stressor may seem relatively unimportant in and of itself, but if it is added to an already high level of stress, it can be dangerous. If we want to appraise the total amount of stress an individual is under, we have to sum up his opportunity stress constraint stress and demand stresses.

Individual Differences

Employees react in response to their perception of reality rather than to reality itself. Perception therefore will moderate the relationship between a potential stress condition and an employee's reaction to it. One person's fear that he shall lose his job because his company is lying off personnel may be perceived by another as an opportunity to get a large allowance and start his own business. Similarly what one employee perceives as an efficient and challenging work environment may be viewed as threatening and demanding by others. So the stress potential is environmental, organisational and individual factors do not lie in their objective condition. Rather it lies in an employee's interpretation of those factors.

Job experience is a great stress reducer. Uncertainty and newness of job situations create stress. But as we gain experience that stress disappeared or at least significantly decreases. This same phenomenon seems to apply to work situations. Experience on the job tends to be negatively related to work stress.

Increasing evidence shows that social support can buffer the impact of stress. It acts as a palliative, mitigating the negative effects of even high strain jobs.

Those people with an internal locus of control believe they control their own destiny. Those with an external locus believe their lives are controlled by outside forces. Internal perceive their jobs to be less stressful than do externals.

Hostility also contributes to individual stress. It creates aggressiveness, anger and cynical mistrust of others.

Consequences of stress

Stress shows, itself in a number of ways. An individuals who is experiencing a high level of stress may develop high blood pressures, irritability loss of appetite, accident prognoses, etc. These can be discussed under three categories.

1. *Physiological:* Most of the early concern with stress was directed at physiological symptoms. There was primarily because the topic was researched by specialists in the health and medical sciences. The research led to the conclusion that stress could create changes in metabolism, increase heart and breathing rates, increase blood pressure, headaches and induce heart attacks. The link between stress and particular physiological symptoms is not clear. This is the attributed to the complexity of the system and the difficulty of objectively measuring them.

2. *Psychological:* Stress can cause dissatisfaction stress shows itself in other psychological states for instance tension, anxiety, irritability, boredom procrastination.

3. *Behavioural:* Behaviorally related stress systems include changes in productivity, absence as turnover as well as changes in eating habits, smoking or consumption of alcohol, rapid speech and sleep disorders.

A significant amount of research has investigated the stress performance relationship. The most widely studied partner in the stress performance literature is the inverted 'U' relationship. The logic underlying the inverted 'U' is that low to moderate, levels of stress stimulate the body and increase its ability to react. Individuals then often perform their tasks better, more intensively or more rapidly. But too much stress places unattainable demands or constraints on a person which results lower performance. This inverted 'U' pattern may also describe the reaction to stress over time as well as to changes in stress intensity. That is, even moderate levels of stress can have a negative influence on performance over the long term as the continued intensity of the stress wears down the individuals and saps his energy resources. In spite of the popularity and initiative appeal of the inverted 'U' model, it does not get a lot of empirical support.

Management of Stress

From the organisation's stand point management may not be concerned when employees experience low to moderate levels of stress. But high levels of stress, or even low levels sustained over long periods of item, can lead to reduced employee performance and require action by management.

There are two approaches of managing stress. They are:

1. Individual approach
2. Organisational approach

Individual approach: An employee can take personal responsibility for reducing his stress level. Individual strategies that have proven effective include implementing time management techniques, increasing physical exercise, relaxation training and explaining social support network.

Many people manage their time properly. The well organised employee can often accomplish twice as much of the person who is poorly organised some time management principles are:

- Making daily lists of activities to be accomplished.
- Prioritising activities by importance and urgency.
- Scheduling activities according to priorities set and
- Knowing the daily cycle and handling the mot demanding parts of the job during the high part of the cycle.

Non competitive physical exercise such as aerobics, jogging, swimming and riding bicycle have been recommended by physicians as a way to deal with excessive stress levels. Individuals can teach themselves to reduce tension through relaxation techniques such as meditation, hypnosis and biofeedback. The objective is to reach a state of deep relaxation, where one feels physically relaxed. Expanding social support network can be a means for tension reduction.

Organisational approaches: Several factors that cause stress particularly task and role demands and organisation structure are controlled by management. The can be modified or changed, strategies might management want to consider include improved personnel selection, job placement, use of realistic goal setting, redesigning of jobs, increased employee involvement, improved organisational communication and establishment of corporate wellness programmes. Certain jobs are more stressful than others. Selection and placement decisions should take these facts into consideration. Individuals perform better when they have specific and challenging goals and receive feedback on how well they are progressing towards these goals. The use of goals can reduce stress as well as provide motivation. Goal feedback reduces uncertainties as to actual job performance. The result is less employee frustration, role ambiguity and stress. Redesigning jobs to give employees more responsibility, more meaningful work, more autonomy and increased feedback can reduce stress because these factors give the employee greater control over work activities and lessen dependence on others.

Role stress is detrimental to a large extent because employees feel uncertain about goals, expectations, how they will be evaluated, etc. By giving these employees a voice in those decisions that directly affect their job performances, management can increase employee control and reduce this role stress. Therefore, management must consider increasing employee involvement in decision-making.

Increasing formal organisational communication with employees reduces uncertainty by lessening role ambiguity and role conflict. Finally organisationally supported wellness programmes reduce stresses. These programmes focus on the employees' total physical and mental condition.

To reiterate job stress it can be said that Job overload is a glaring problem at work places. Certainly in the 21st century with Walter Kietchel (2001) one must agree that the new work, new workplace and new work culture will reign. New Logic of organisation is a paradigm shift from resource based organisation to knowledge based organisation. Certainly, with addition of new technology, globalize competitive advantage people of the organisations are over stressed. To have a check on 'burn out' organisations are preparing innovative schemes. Necessarily, there comes the role of HR manager in synthesising employees expectations with organisational requirements.

M. T. Malteson and J. M. Ivan Cevich in his book *Controlling Stress in the Workplace: An Organisational Guide* (1987) highlighted what stress is?. It extraordinary demand of the organisation. It is undue constraints by the organisation. And it is a check on the available opportunities. Stress can be constructive one and people under such stress are called Rust out. Contrary destructive stress has negative impact on the organisation, on the employees both and the people under this stress are called 'Burn out'. M. Friedman, R. H. Rosenman, V. A. Price and amongst other who analyzed the causes of job stress in organisation. To put those few in nut shell are- occupational demand, role conflicts, and ambiguity overload and under load, job change, strained interpersonal and group relations, faculty and ineffective communications, Conflict with the management and new life style. As such proper management of stress is the headache of the HR manager and for that HR practices develop coping individual and organisational strategies. HR managers are trying to counsel the employees as to career path, clarify organisation's mission and role of the employees. Along with this, they are striving to provide congenial working condition, employees counseling to as the stress free work.

To tell the truth HR manager as Counselor tries to establish a working relationship with counsel in formal as well as informal way- one is planned and other is casual. So performance counseling is on the job front and as performance by the boss to the subordinates. And the focus of counseling is on developmental and problem solving aspect of the employees, with a objective of removing tress on performance and building personal effectiveness.

Salary Management/ Compensation Management

The very purpose of compensation management is to provide a pay structure that will attract, retain and motivate knowledge worker. And the compensation plan should be in conformity with price rise and appropriate expectations of the employees. Compensation comprises of pay and benefits. Fairness or Equity is the key to salary administration. Further effective compensation management is to

a/ Attract Talent.
b. Retain Talent
c. Ensure Equity.

So, to provide a sound compensation is central to maintain Human Resources in an organisation. For this there is the need of timely pay hikes. As per study by Global HR consulting Firm Hewitt Associates-2007 (TOI: 17/3/07) India's tops the world list in pay hikes. During 2004, 2005, 2006 and 2007 the pay hike percentages are 13.7%, 14.1%, 14.4% and 14.5% respectively, which is ascending year by year. Contrary in Global Scenario Philippines is the 2nd country as to pay hike which is 8.4% in 2007. And the corresponding figure for China in 2007 is 8.2%. Further the pay bike is lowest in Japan which 2.6% in 2006 and 2.7% in 2007. Evidently, the conclusion is globalisation increased competition for talent search that brought this bonanza to Indian knowledge workers. And for salary administration there is the need of:

a. Pyroll	The sum of all financial record of salaries, wages, bonuses and deduction.
b. Payroll	A paper document issued by employer to employee for services rendered
c. Pay slip	A document employee receives as deposit transition

d. A payroll serving programme	A method of automatic deduction from pay check and deposit into employees savings account
e. Payroll card	A debit card to access employees pacy check

Source: Wikipedia: orgn/ payroll

Moreover as to this Dale S Beach provided certain principles of Compensation management which are noted below.

- The enterprise should have a clear cut plan to determine differential pay level in terms of divergent job requirements involving varied skill, effort, responsibility and working conditions.
- An attempt should be made to keep the general level of wages and salaries of the enterprise in line with that obtained in the labour market or industry.
- Adequate care should be taken to distinguish people from the jobs.
- Irrespective of individual considerations, care should be taken to ensure equal pay for equal work depending upon flexibility of jobs of course, variations may be permitted within a pay range.
- There should be a plan to adopt equitable measure for recognising individual differences in ability and contribution.
- Attempt should be made to provide some procedure for handling wage grievances
- Adequate care should be taken to inform the employees and the union, if any, about the procedure followed in determining wage rates. One thing should be noted that if "Principle of Equity" is applied in compensation management good human relations will exist.

Pension Pinch: Future Projections

The number of retirees is rising. Simultaneously, working population is shrinking day by day. People in sweet 65+ by 2050 will be a fifth of Indian population (TOI: May 15, 2006)

Further, a report relating to salary and benefit to pensioners is presented here as to the challenges of compensation and retirement benefits. As per CAG Report, Pension to retired employees under Central Government is likely to surpass the salaries and allowances of the present workforce in coming days. The Government pay Rs. 39, 074 crore to pension during 2006-07, which is slightly lower than the salary bill of the working staff which is Rs. 40, 047 cr. As such the Centre's pension liability is increased by almost 58% which is around Rs. 14000 crore during 2006-07. It is likely to exceed salary bill in 2007-08. The report reveals that between 1992 and 2007 pay and allowances to Central Government employees rose by average 5. 47%. Contrary to it pension surged 16. 20% on average during the same period. The pension burden is due to rise in life expectancy, increase in retirement age and increase in pension payment as per inflation ratio. According to 2001 census on March 2001 total Central Government employees was 38. 76 lakh which was 2. 6% lower than the workforce in March 1995 (39. 82 lakh).

Moreover, as per a statistical calculation by Sibani Swain and Pranob Sen submitted to Planning Commission, in 2004, the pension will rise to 45. 5 lakh in 2006-07 from 38. 3 lakh in 1999-2000. CAG report noted that during Eighth Plan ratio of salary : pension was Rs. 30. 606 cr: Rs. 15684. And the same for 10th Plan (2002-07) is Rs. 36, 765 cr : Rs. 25, 539. Further it is to be marked, the salary bill here is not inclusive of traveling allowances, productivity linked bonus, and other bonus, encashment of Earned leave and honorarium, etc. (Times of India : 11th December 2007).

Now-a-days a new method Performance Based Pay (PBP) is being introduced to inculcate new work culture amongst employees.

Employees Incentives and Benefits

Employee commitment programmes are linked with employees oriented incentive scheme and benefits. Incentives are offered to reward the efforts and performance of individual employees. At times Group incentives are also awarded. Moreover, fringe benefits are those monetary and non-monetary benefits given to the employees during and post-employment period which are connected with employment but not to the employees' contribution to the organisation (Rao: 2005). As such fringe benefits are linked to retirement benefits (Provident Fund, Gratuity, and Pension) bonus, workmen's compensation, housing, medical facilities, paid holiday, shift premium, etc. The benefit of fringe benefit programme is creating/ building loyalty of employees (Pigors and Myers). HR Managers prepares benefit plans to accommodate employees and associations demand and as a social security and welfare measures.

Health and Safety

Healthy workplace and safety at work are the prime requisites of good and congenial working conditions that motivate people to work more. And it is the responsibility of HR department and line managers to provide health and safety measures. Legal provisions regarding health are covered under the Factories Act 1948 (Section 11 to 20). Also use of tobacco and sexual harassment to work women employees are strictly prohibited as a corollary to Health and safety measures.

Grievance Handling

In modern day organisations with high expectations of employees Grievances are inevitable. As such grievance redressal is also the way to minimize dissatisfaction amongst the employees. A grievance, as Jucius explained, is a discontent or dissatisfaction which an employee feels to be unfair, unjust or inequitable. A grievance may be factual, imaginary and disguised (Carrrell, Avrin, 2001) and the cause of employees grievances may be due to :

- Economic consideration (Wages, salary, etc.)
- Work environment (Unfair rules)
- Supervision (supervisors biasness)
- Work group- Imbalanced interpersonal relationship.
- Miscellaneous- transfer, medical facilities promotion, etc.

As a matter of fact, grievances should be minimized. If HR practitioners fail to redress grievance it has pernicious effect on the productivity of the organisation. Also it helps in rising absenteeism and labour wherever and it creates a trouble some chaotic work situation. Necessarily an appropriate grievance handling procedure is the need of the organisation for smooth functioning. So, organisations are now falling open door policy to unearth grievances of the employees. And the CEOs are trying to identify, analyze and redress promptly the grievances for mutual benefit.

Discipline

Discipline is used to impose penalties for wrong doers. It may be positive and negative in orientation. When employees willingly practice self control and respect organisation's rules it is termed as positive discipline. On the contrary where the fear of punishment put the employees in right track it is negative discipline. Negative disciplinary action involves fines, transfers, demotion, lay-off, retirement, etc. And the few common causes that invite disciplinary actions are unauthorized absence form duty, theft, misappropriation, insubordination, smoking, sexual harassment, accepting bribes, etc.

HRA-Human Resource Accounting

HRA is a method by which human resource balance sheet is prepared. It is a process of identifying data as to human resources. In brief it can be said HRA is connected with measuring the cost of organisation as to recruit, select, hire, train and develop human assert. It also involves measuring the value of the employees of the organisation in terms of economic value (Flasshoitz: 1974). To this Renis Likert, in his book *The Human Organisation* laid down certain basic objectives.

1. HRA provides information as to cost of acquiring, developing and human resources.
2. HRA identifies value additions of the organisation in terms of appreciation or depreciation.
3. HRA is the medium through which monitoring of human capital is made.
4. HRA provides effective and innovative HR practices on analysing cost effectively.

Necessarily, a SWOT (Strength, Weakness, Opportunity and Threat) analysis in terms of financial implications by HRA helps the management in planning HR hiring and maintenance. In one word the HRA is of much help to the organisation in analysing the effectiveness of HR policies and practices in investing in HR and in decision-making as to HR in general. True, it is not an easy affair as it involves limitations. One of the important short comings of HRA is it suffers from utilising appropriate measurement technique to value human asserts in the organisation.

Work Motivation

In organisation people are to be motivated for better and efficient performance. As such HR people are consistently trying to motivate them with innovative measures. Simply motivation means fulfillment of needs of people for greater productivity of the organisation. The theory of motivation is enriched by Maslow

(Hierachy of Needs Theory), Herzberg, (Two Factor Theory), Alderfer (ERG Theory), McClleland, (Need Theory) Adam (Equity Theory) and many others and the message of motivation is goal directed and need fulfillment of the employees be it physical, social, official and psychological. And for better work it is the role of HR manager to identify needs of the employees and to fulfil the needs as per organisational capabilities. To this it is to be noted that two basic principles are followed to motivate the people in the organisation-carrot and stick, the reward and punishment. And pay fringe benefits, job enlargement promotions, and job enrichment are few important motivations at work places. Essentially, motivation is a problem; organisations are looking for a solution.

Empowerment

Today's work is knowledge based. People are much more empowered. Use of participative management, sound merit pay system and designed job enrichment are certain techniques of empowerment. And in empowering people the role of performed leadership is of much help. Here also the role of effective communication between the employee and the employer is called for.

Care for Family: HR Practices New Initiative

Concept of "We the Employee" is gaining momentum with more and more assertion of their Rights. Employees have a right to see their family better of; and family should not suffer at the cost of productivity of the organisation. As a matter of fact organisations recognize that if they are not family friendly, they will have a seemingly difficult time in retaining talent. As an important retention tool organisations are caring more for the families of the employees. For this workforce are given opinion of workplace that will help them in balancing the demand of familiar lives and work. Amongst the many scheme the following are worth noting.

1. Special schemes for children.
2. Scholarships.
3. Medical benefits.
4. Permission to take young kids to work place.

For example at NIIT this scheme for kids is practised under the name "Little NIITian." Another is 'Little Nittian Care Leave' (LNCL)-

Leave with half pay for half of the work for the day to take care of child. Another organisation 24/7 customer has initiated schemes for its employees namely :

1. Family Insurance Scheme,
2. Employee Welfare Fund,
3. Family Oriented Reward Programme
4. Reward and Recognition
5. Parent's Day
6. Day Care control.

Moreover another organisation *cellebrum,* instituted a scheme Home Away From Home" with the purpose of creating an atmosphere where basic needs of the employees are met.

A Reward System: Need of HRM

Really, an appropriate Reward System, an integral part of strategic Human Resource Practices, is necessary for developing a sound motivation process for the success of the organisation or organisational excellence. As such good reward system is essentially a war-on-talents, and concerned with soft (culture and process) and hard (Organisational structure) part of a system. In this context a reward system model of Brown Duncan. is presented here in figure 3.13.2 (Duncan, 2001).

FUTURE OF HRM

The 1990s have brought a revolutionary change in our administration. Post-liberalisation is marked by a shift from common economy to a market driven economy, from shattered market to competitive market, from monopoly to competition and from domestic trade to global trade. Such a shift calls for a different approach to human resource activities. During the pre-economic liberalisation, the human resource managers had adopted reactive strategies to people's problems. The need of the hour is proactive approach, a strategy which helps human resource managers for see events and takes appropriate actions before the events occur. Proactive strategies call for awareness about the likely challenges, the human resource managers, will face in the days to come. Essentially the future of HRM is based upon the new challenges.

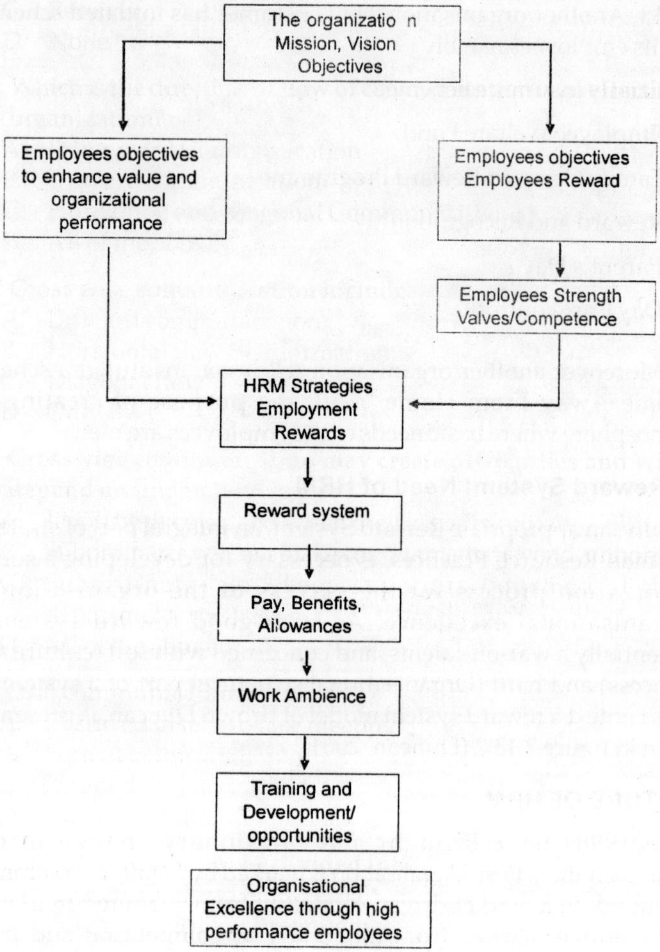

Fig. 3.14.2

Source: Adopted from K. Prasad (2001): Strategic HR

The significant changes that are likely to take place in the field of HRM on the basis of new challenges are as follows.[3]

1. Globalisation

The demise of capitalism, the breaking up of trade barriers and the rise of networked information have unleashed a revolution is business. Market capitalism guides every country on the earth good and services flow across borders more frequently than over, vast information networks instantly link nations, companies and the people. The result is globalisation the 21st century capitalism. Growing, internationalism of business has its impact on HRM. So in future, the HRM will cope with the problems of unfamiliar laws, languages, practices, competitions, attitudes, management styles work ethics and some. So the human resource managers will know that international operational have:

- More functions, such as taxation and coordination of departments.
- More heterogeneous functions such as coordination of multiple salary currencies.
- More involvement in the employees' personnel life, such as housing, health, education and recreation, etc.

2. Corporate Reorganisation

The past three to four years brought us news about corporate mergers, take over and massive reorganisation. It is difficult to imagine circumstances that pose a great challenge for HRM than reorganisation resulting from acquisition, merger, divestiture or a take over threat. The employees of both the taking over as well as taken over companies will have anxious moments because of

- Fear of loss of job.
- Job changes including new role and assignments.
- Transfers to new geographic location.
- Changes in remuneration and benefits.
- Changes in career possibilities.
- Changes in organisational power, status and prestige.
- Changes in corporate culture and loss of identity in the company.

All these above factors have natural impact on HRM. Competition from Multi National Companies (MNCs) and domestic industries have completed many companies to resort to downsising and flattening their organisational structures. Some years back, Peter

F Drucker in his new book *The New Realities,* argued that only flat structures would survive the 1990s. His prediction has come true. So due to reorganisation of flattened structures, HRM will experience in future:

- Increased growth opportunities for performance.
- Faster decision-making and market response
- Up gradation of skills within rank.
- Better internal communication and interaction
- Reduced man power cost.

3. New Organisational Forms

The practice of HRM is shaped by the organisational forms in which people are employed. Big organisations have grown bigger in the sense that the world economy is dominated by transnational organisations. But the employment potential of these giant companies is declining. Business process re-engineering with its philosophy of living of ancillary and expensive tasks to suppliers and automating the remaining functions is the latest contributor to this trend. The trend will affect the HRM in future in following ways:

- Smaller forms and establishments will mean a more personalized style.
- Smaller units will require less complex and sophisticated systems of HRM.
- Smaller units will less able to sustain a specialist HRM function.
- More contribution of HRM will be in facilitating the processes which support the development of the enterprise rather than, as traditional personnel management has done in administering systems for controlling people.

4. Changing Demographics of Workforce

The major challenge that has resulted from changing workforce demographics concerns duel workforce was resulted. Career couples, couples where both partners are actively pursuing professional careers. Men or women moving through organisational ranks to upper level positions need experience in a variety of roles in different organisational units. The increasing number of dual career processionals will limit individual flexibility in accepting such assignments and will hinder organisation flexibility in acquiring and developing talent in future. Again the future of HRM will experience, other demographic changes in the workforce. They are:

- Increasing number of working mothers.
- Increasing decline of blue collar employees who are giving way to white collar employees.
- Increasing awareness and education among workers.

5. Changes Employee Expectations

With the changes in workforce demographics, employee expectations and attitudes also have shifted. Traditional elements, such as job security, attractive remuneration, housing and the like do not attract and motivate to days workforce. In future practice of HRM, employee expectations are need to be discussed. Employee will demand empowerment and expect equality with the management. Empowerment resets in redefining jobs, both in the shop floors and board rooms. As workmen will be given more control over their jobs, whole classes of inspectors will become redundant, not be because they will do a bad job but because there shall be no need for them. By means of empowerment the worker will bring their around and even can gain knowledge about work methods. Expectation of equality will break up the traditional employee employer relationship, top and bottom in HRM. Lastly in future HRM, another expectation is that the electronics and telecommunication revolution will improve the quality of work life. Innovations in communication and computer technology will accelerate the pace of change, and as a result, lead to many innovations in HRM.

6. Renewed Focus on People

In traditional HRM, managers believed in structures, strategies and systems. I.e. '35'. For decades this philosophy served companies well. It supported successive waves of growth as companies integrated horizontally in 1950s diversified in 1960s and expanded into global markets in the 1970s and early 1980s. But in 1990s technological, competitive and market changes have eroded its effectiveness. So in future, HRM, there should be a renewed focus on people the human resource.

7. Managing the Managers

For future HRM, managing the managers is the biggest challenge. Managers are unique tribe in any society. In the post liberalisation era, freedom given to the managers is grossly missed to get rid off talented and hard working juniors. Managers feel slighted when their juniors turn out to be better performs. Inset of only managing their allotted functions, managers assume the role of employers and fire, those whom they feel are too smart. Consequently many talented and able young men are forced to leave. So far future HRM, the most difficult task is "how to manage this tribe"?

8. Interests of the Weaker Sections of the Society

Another important challenge for future HRM is to protect the interests of weaker sections of the society. The dramatic increase of women, minorities and other backward communities in the workforce has resulted in the need for organisations to re-examine their policies, practices and values. We believe that much has already been done for them but facts reveal a different story. In the name of global competitor, productivity and quality, the interests of weaker sections of the society should not be scarified in future HRM.

9. New Industrial Relations Approach

There is almost a metamorphosis at the industrial relations front. Strikes, lockouts and loss of man days are declining considerably. Trade union membership has fallen drastically all over the world and the future of labour movement itself is in danger. So no doubt it will aggravate the precise of HRM in future. In future the need is to adopt a proactive strategy towards industrial relations, an approach which enable HR specialists to look into the challenges unfolding in the future.

10. Development Planning

Personnel Management will not remain confined to administration of personnel services. It will be involved increasingly in organisational planning, organisational structure, compensation, personnel research, etc. Greater cost consciousness and profit orientation will be required on the part of the personnel departments.

11. Concept of AIMA

All India Management Association (AIMA) has its own concept regarding future of HRM. Regarding HR functions, the focus in the coming years would be on the following lines. :-

- HRM to become integral part of business.
- Empowerment of employees.
- Focus on productivity through team building
- Dynamic/Flattened/Matrix organisational structure.
- People sensitive management style and practices.
- Management of the changing workforce skill/sex/turnover.
- Managing the changing work diversification.
- Efficient use of information technology.
- Strengthening organisational communication.
- Greater focus on man-machine interface.
- Institutionalising employee involvement.

Thus in future HRM will be face new challenges and perform new responsibilities. To meet the future, five 'T' (5Ts) are recommended for HRM, i.e.

- Technology Up gradation
- Techniques of management
- Training
- Transparency
- Team work

It will have to recognize human resources as the vital instrument in realising corporate goals. Autocratic leadership will have to give way to participate leadership.

References

For Part 3 : Human Resource Management

1. E. B. Flippo, *Principles of Personnel Management*, MGraw Hill Book, New York, 1980.
2. K. B. Ashwathappa, *Personnel and HRM*, Tata MGraw Hill Publication.
3. *Ibid.*
4. *Ibid.*
5. S. George Odiorne, *Personel Administration by Objectives*, Richard, D Irwin, New York, 1971.
6. C.B. Gupta, *Human Resource Management.*
7. E.B. Flippo, *op. cit.*
8. C.D. Miller, H. W. Form, *Industrial Sociology*, Harper and Row, New York, 1964.

9. K.B. Ashwathappa, *op. cit.*
10. D. Yoder, H. G. Heneman, J. G. Turnbull and C. Stone, Handbook of Personnel Management and Industrial Relations, Mc Graw Hill Book Co., New York, 1958.
11. C.B. Mamoria, *op. cit.*
12. K.B. Aswathappa, *Personnel and Human Resource Management*, Tata McGraw Publishing. 2003.
13. C. B. Mamoria, *Personnel Management*, Himalaya Publishing.
14. ibid.
15. Armstrong, *A Text book of HRM*, 1995.
16. S. R. Robbins, *Organisation Behaviour* PMI Pvt. Ltd., New Delhi, 1996.
17. K. B. Aswatappa, *op. cit.*

SUGGESTED READINGS

Aswathappa, K.B. Personnel and Human Resource Management, Tata McGraw Publishing. 2003

Carroll, J., and H. L. Josi, Management by Objectives, Macmillan & Co., New York, 1973.

Chris Hendry, Human Resource Management- A Strategic approach to Employment, B. H. Contemporary Business Series, 1995.

Cole, G. A., Personnel Management- Theory and Practice, D. D. Publications, 1993.

Cynthia D. Fisher, et al., Human Resource Management, Hougton Mifflin Co., Boston, 1997.

Chris Hendry, Human Resource Management- A Strategic approach to Employment, B. H. Contemporary Business Series, 1995.

Cole, G. A., Personnel Management- Theory and Practice, D. D. Publications, 1993.

Cynfhia D. Fisher, et al., Human Resource Management, Hougton Mifflin Co., Boston, 1997.

Dale S. Beach, *Personnel- The Management of People at Work*, Fourth Edition Macmillan & Co., New York, 1980.

David A. Decenzo and Stephen P. Robbins, Personnel / Human Resource Management, Third Edition, Prentice-Hall of India, New Delhi, 1989.

David J. Cherrington, Organisational Behaviour, Allyn & Bacon, Boston, 1989.

David R. Hampton, Contemporary Management, McGraw-Hill, 1981.

Dave Ulrich (1996). Human Resource Champion, Harvard Business School Press.

David Allen, (2001) Getting things Done: The Art of Stress free Productivity, New York, Viking.

Dale S. Beach, Personnel- The Management of People at Work, Fourth Edition Macmillan & Co., New York, 1980.

David A. Decenzo and Stephen P. Robbins, Personnel Human Resource Management, Third Edition, Prentice-Hall of India, New Delhi, 1989.

David J. Cherrington, Organisational Behaviour, Allyn & Bacon, Boston, 1989. David R. Hampton, Contemporary Management, McGraw-Hill, 1981.

Edmond, R. Gray and Larry R. Smeltzer, Management- The Competitive Edge, Macmillan & Co., New York, 1990.

Edwin B. Flippo, Personnel Management, Sixth Edition, McGraw0Hill, New York, 1984.

Elmer H. Burack and Robert D. Smith, Personnel Management- A Human Resource Systems Approach, West Publishing Co., st. Paul, 2000.

Fred Luthans, Organisational Behaviour, McGraw-Hill, New York, 2000.

Garry Dessler, Personnel Management, Prentice-Hall International, New York, 1988.

John Storey, Human Resource Management, (Ed), Routledge, 1995.

John, H. Bernardian and Joyce, E. A. Russell, Human Resource Management- An Experimental Approach, McGraw-Hill, New York, 1999.

Jucuius, Michael J. Personnel Management, Homewood Richard D. Irwin, 1976.

Keith Davis and Newstrom, Human Behaviour at Work- Organisational Behaviour, McGraw-Hill, New York, 1993.

Mahesh V. S., Thresholds of Motivation- The Corporation as a Nursery for Human Growth, Tata McGraw- Hill Publishing Co., New Delhi, 1993.

Michael Armstrong, A Handbook of Personnel Management Practices, Kogan Page, 1988.

Milkovich and Boudreau, Personnel- Human Resource Management, Richard D. Irwin, 1990.

M. Armstrmg (2006). A Hand Book of Human Resource Management Practices.

Martin E J H (2006). HR Show one the money, Presenting an explanatory model. (http://ww. lulu. com/contatu).

Mark Forster (2006), Do it Tomorrow and Other Secrets of time Management, Hodder and Stoughtin Religions.

Stephen, P. Robbins, Dimensions of Organisational Behaviour, Prentice-Hall of India, New Delhi, 1993.

Steven L. McShane and Mary Ann Von Glinow, Organisational Behviour, Tata McGraw-Hill, 2000.

Terry, L. Leap, Michael D. Crino, Personnel/Human Resource Management, Macmillan & Co., 1990.

Thomas, H. Stone, Understanding Personnel Management, CBS College Publishing, 1989.

Toffer, Alvin, Power Shift, Bantom Books, New Yoek, 1992.

Wayne F. Cascio, Managing Human Resources, McGraw-Hill, New York, 1995.

Wayne, F. Cascio, and Elios M. Awad, Human Resource Management, Reston, New York, 1981.

Wayne, Mondey R. and Robert, M. Noe III, Personnel- The Management of Human Resources, Allyn & Bacon, Boston, 1981.

White and Bednar, Organisational Behaviour-Understanding and Managing People at Work, Boston, Allyn & Bacon, Boston, 1986.

Wiliam, P. Anthony, et al., Strategic Human Resource Management, Dryden Press, 1993.

William W., Werther, Jr and Keith Davis, Human Resources and Personnel Management, Fourth Edition, McGraw-Hill, New York, 1993.

Yoder, Dale, Personnel Management and Industrial Relations, Prentice-Hall of India, New Delhi, 1975.

Edmond, R. Gray and Larry R. Smeltzer, Management- The Competitive Edge, Macmillan & Co., New York, 1990.

Flippo, Edwin B. Personnel Management, Sixth Edition, McGraw Hill, New York, 1984.

Burack Elmer H and Robert D. Smith, Personnel Management- A Human Resource Systems Approach, West Publishing Co., St. Paul, 2000.

Garry Dessler, *Personnel Management*, Prentice-Hall International, New York, 1988.

John Storey, *Human Resource Management*, (Ed), Routledge, 1995.

John, H. Bernardin and Joyce, E. A. Russell, *Human Resource Management—An Experimental Approach*, McGraw-Hill, New York, 1999.

Jucuius, Michael J. *Personnel Management*, Homewood Richard D. Irwin, 1976.

Milkovich and Boudreau, *Personnel-Human Resource Management*, Richard D. Irwin, 1988.

L Terry, Michael Leap and D. Crino, *Personal/Human Resource Management*, Macmillan & Co., 1990.

H. Stone Thomas, *Understanding Personnel Management*, CBS College Publishing, 1989.

W. F. Cascio Waine, *Managing Human Resources*, McGraw-Hill, New York, 1995.

P. Anthony William, et. al., *Strategic Human Resource Management*, Dryden Press, 1993.

W. William, Werther, Jr. and Keith Davis, *Human Resources and Personnel Management*, Fourth Edition, McGraw Hill, New York, 1993.

Werther and Dale Yoder, *Personnel Management and Industrial Relations*, Prentice Hall of India New Delhi, 1975.

J. Fitz-enz, (2001) *How to Measure Human Resource Management* 3rd Ed, NY, McGraw Hill.

BRAINSTORMING QUESTIONS

1. **What is true of Management?**
   I. **As manager, people carryout the management functions of planning, organizing staffing, leading and controlling**
   II. **Management applies to any wind of organization.**
   III. **Managing implies effectiveness and efficiency.**
   IV. **The aim of all managers is same - to crate surplus.**
   A. Only I & II
   B. II & IV
   C. I & II & IV
   D. All of the above*

2. **The 'non-managers' generally mean:**
   A. The person who outside of organization
   B. The persons who are have no subordinate*
   C. Both
   D. None

3. **Management can not be applied to:**
   A. Small organization
   B. Non-profit organization
   C. Service organization
   D. None of these*

4. **'Enterprise' is not referred to:**
   A. Business
   B. Hospital
   C Universities
   D. None*

5. **Which statement is true?**
   I. **All managers perform managerial functions of planning, organizing, staffing, leading and controlling**
   II. **Top level managers spend more time on planning and organizing.**

III. Leading takes much time of lower level managers.

A. Only I
B. Only II & III
C. Only I & III
D. All*

6. Robert L. Katz identified how many skills of administrators.

A. Two
B. Three*
C. Four
D. None

7. Which of the following managerial skills are not given by Robert L. Katz.

A. Technical skill
B. Design skill*
C. Conceptual skill
D. Human skill

8. Technical skills are of greater importance at

A. Top level manager
B. Middle level manager
C. Lower level manager*
D. None of the alone

9. At top level management which skill is relatively more valuable?

A. Conceptual skills*
B. Technical skills
C. Human skills
D. None of these

10. In 'Search of Excellence' Thomas Peters and Robert Waterman identified characteristics of excellent enterprises. They

I. Were oriented towards actions.
II. Learned about their customers
III. Promoted managerial autonomy
IV. Focussed on business they know best Which of the above is wrong?

A. Only I
B. Only II
C. Only III & IV
D. None*

11. **The greatest opportunity for increasing productivity is surely to be found in knowledge work itself, and especially in management' who said this.**
    A. Taylor
    B. Thomas Peters
    C. Peter F Drucker*
    D. None

12. **Which statement is wrong ?**
    A. Productivity implies effectiveness and efficiency in individual and organizational performance
    B. Effectiveness is achievement of objectives
    C. Efficiency is the achievement of the ends with the least amount of resources
    D. None*

13. **Assertion**
    I. Like other practices managing is an Art.
    Assertion
    II. As organized knowledge management is science.
    A. Only I is correct
    B. Only II is correct
    C. Both I and II are correct*
    D. None of these

14. **'Theory is in its lowest form a classification, a set of pigeon holes, a filing cabinet in which fact can accumulate. Nothing is more lost that a loose fact" who said this?**
    A. Homans
    B. Fayol
    C. Gratt
    D. None

15. **Which of the following is not a management technique ?**
    A. Budgeting
    B. Programme Evaluation and Review Technique (PERT)
    C. Critical Path Method (CPM)
    D. None*

16. **Match Section I with Section II**

Section I	**Section II**
a. Managerial practice followed for a long period	**1. Producing**

b. Mental images of anything formed by generalization from particulars.	**2. Concepts**
c. Output input ratio within a time period with due consideration for quality.	**3. Management Fad**
	4. Management Technique
d. Cost accounting	**5. Quality Circle**

A. a b c d
   1 2 3 5

B. a b c d*
   3 2 1 4

C. a b c d
   2 3 1 4

D. a b c d
   1 2 3 4

17. Which of the following is not the function of managers?

A. Planning
B. Staffing
C. Leading
D. None*

18. 'Getting thing done through people' is the definition of

A. Work contract
B. Administration
C. Management*
D. All of the above

19. Which Book – author phrase is wrong ?

A In search of excellence – Thomas J Peter and Robert H. Waterman
B The one Minute Manager- Kenneth H Blanchard
C Theory Z - William Ouchi
D None*

20. Which Book-author phrase is wrong ?

A. The lot Art Japanese Management-Richard Tanner Pascale and Anthony G. Athos
B Management: Tasks, Responsibilities, Practices – Peter F. Drunker
C Both A & B
D None*

21. Which is not the major concern of Taylor

A. High productivity
B. Application of Scientific Method
C. Rule of Thumb*
D. Higher wages to worker

22. Match I and II

	I		II
a.	Max Weber	1.	Application of psychology to industry and management.
b.	Hugo Munsterberg	2.	Called for scientific selection of workers and harmonious cooperation between labour and management.
c.	Henry Fayol	3.	Father of modern management theory.
d.	Henry and Gantt	4.	Bureaucratic theory
		5.	Father of social system approach.

A. a b c d
4 2 3 5

B. a b c d
4 1 3 2

C. a b c d
4 5 2 1

D.* a b c d
4 1 3 2

23. Application of psychology to advertising, marketing and personnel was developed by

A. Water D. Scott*
B. Hugo Munsterberg
C. Wiliam Gilbreth
D. None

24. Who introduced quality control in Japan ?

A. W. Edward Deming*
B. Peter F. Drucker
C. William Ouchi
D. None

25. Cherter Barnard in his book 'The Functions of Executive' (1938) suggested

A. Comprehensive social system approach to managing*
B. Developed concept of 'Quality Circle'
C. Replaced the rule of thumb with science the organized knowledge
D. None

26. Who observed 'that eventually people get promoted to a level where they are incompetent'?

A. Laurence Peter*
B. William Ouchi
C. Both A & B
D. None

27. Which of the following is not the element of managerial function as given by Fayol ?

A. Commanding
B. Controlling
C. Coordinating
D. Staffing*

28. Whose thoughts are not linked to Industrial psychology

A. Hugo Munsterberg
B. William Gilbreth
C. Walter Dill Scott
D. None*

29. In developing Human Relations theory who worked with Etton Mayo ?

A. Hugo Munsterbeng
B. F.J. Roethlisberger*
C. Both A&B
D. None

30. 'Hawthorne Effect' was connected with

A. Scientific Management
B. Human Relatives Theory*
C. Social System Theory
D. Conflict Theory

31. Which is wrong ?

A. W. Edwards Deming- American
B. Etton Mayo – Harvard University
C. Henri Fayol-French Industrialists
D. None*

32. General activities of an industrial undertaking are

A. Planning, organizing, staffing, leading and controlling
B. Financial, security, academic technical, commercial, financial *
C. Both A&B
D. None

33. Which is not included in Mc Kinsey's 7-S approach ?

A. Style
B. Structure
C. Shard value
D. Simple Form*

34. Henry Mintzbeg had developed

A. Managerial Role Approach*
B. Theory Z
C. Motivational Theory
D. None

35. Henry Meintzberg advocated ten rules of managers that can be fitted into three heads. Which is the not correct head.

A. Interpersonal Role
B. Informational Role
C. Decision Role
D. None *

36. Who said the classical managerial functions-planning, organizing, coordinating controlling as 'Folklore' ?

A. Henry Mintzberg*
B. Koontz
B. McKinsey
D. None

37. Which of the following is not a decision Role as defined by Henry Mintzberg ?

A. The disturbance handler Role
B. The reference allocater role
C. The disseminator role *
D. The negotiator role

38. The focus of socio-technical systems approach is on

A. Blue collar and lower level office work *
B. Decision-making
C. Inter personal behaviour
D. None

39. 'Skill' in McKinsey's 7's approach means

A. Personal skills-technical, human or conceptual
B. Organizational capability *
C. Control techniques
D. Leadership qualities

40. Which is true of ?

A. Frank Girlbreth is known for time and motion studies
B. Lilian Gilbreth is known for her focs on human aspects of work
C. Both A&B correct *
D. Only B is wrong

41. Which has impact on management ?

A. Technical upgradation
B. Globalisation
C. Political and legal environment
D. All of the above *

42. The concept 'Social Responsibility' was developed by.

A. Howard R.Bowen (In book Social Responsibilities of the Businessman)*

B. WE Fulmer (Readings in Strategic Management)

C. RT Pascale and A.G. Athos (The Art of Japanese Management)

D. Cherter I Barnard (The Functions of the Executive)

43. Which is not correct ?

A. The mission of business is maximizing profits *

B. The mission of business is social responsibility and social action.

C. The mission of business is the production and distribution of goods and services.

D. None

44. The term 'Social Audit' was first proposed in 1950s by

A. Howard R Bowen*

B. Osborne and Gaebler

C. Keith Davis

D. None

45. A process that has a commitment to systematic assessment of and reporting on some meaningful, definable domain of the company's activities that have social impact is

A. Social Audit *

B. Social Responsiveness

C. Social Responsibility

D. Business Ethics.

46. Management of enterprise needs

A. Personal ethics

B. Accounting ethics

C. Business ethics

D. All of the above*

47. International business engages in transactions across national boundaries. The transactions include.

A. Transfer of goods and services.

B. Transfer of technology

C. Transfer of managerial know -how.

D. All of the above *

48. Which form is not confirmed to international business.

A. Licensing Agreement
B. Management contracts
C. Joint ventures
D. None*

49. 'Le plan' and Cadre is feature of which country's managerial practice ?

A. France* B. U.K.
C. India D. None

50. 'Authority' and 'Co-determination' are the managerial practices of which country ?

A. France B. Italy
C. Germany* D. None

51. The concept of 'Wa' and 'Inhaw' was present in which country respectively?

A. Korea and Japan B. Japan and Korea (South)*
C. Japan and France D. France and Japan

52. 'Life time Employment' is not the management practices of

A. Japan B. Korea*
C. Both A & B D. All of the above

53. Which is not a part of Japanese management?

A. Life time employment
B. Concern for seniority
C. Bottom up approach in decision-making
D. None*

54. Though 'Theory Z' is developed from Japanese management, decision-making in Japan and US are

A. Same
B. Different*
C. Sometimes same/some time different
D. None

55. Selected Japanese managerial practices are adopted in U.S. are called

A. Theory X B. Theory Y
C. Theory Z * D. All of the above

56. 'Comparative Management is defined as the study and analysis of management in different environments and the resources that enterprises show different results in various countries'. The statement is by

A. Richard N Farmer*
B. William Ouchi
C. Peter F. Drucker
D. None

57. Pioneers in Comparative Managements are

A. Richard N Farmer and Barry M Richman *
B. Richard N Farmer and William O uchi
C. Barry M Richman and Thomas Peter
D. None

58. The 'Geocentric orientation of International business' means

A. Total organization is view as an interdependent system operating in many countries.
B. Nationals have better understanding of local environment.
C. Staffing of foreign operations on a regional basis
D. None

59. 'Global Market' means

A. The whole world as one market*
B. Markets of different countries
C. Membership has privileges
D. None

60. Planning and Controlling are

A. Separable
B. Inseparable*
C. Both A & B
D. None

61. Planning does not involve

A. Selecting missions and objectives
B. Decision-making
C. Future course of action
D. None*

62. Which is the sequence of planning and ascending order

I. Setting objectives
II. Need of organization as to objectives

III. Kind of people
IV. Leadership
V. Furnishing of standard
A. V, I, II, III, IV
B. I, II, III, II
C. I, II, III, V, IV
D I, II, III, IV, V*

63. Controlling of planning are mediated by
I. Implementation of plans*
II. Planning proposals
III. Barriers of plan
IV. None

64. Efficacy of a plan refers to
A. Its contribution to the purpose and objectives *
B. Capability of planning
C. Strength of planning organizations
D. None

65. Which is wrong as to classification of planning ?
A. Purpose or Mission plans
B. Programme plans
C. Budget plans
D. None *

66. 'Synergy' in management means :
A. Two plus two equals to Four (whole is equal to parts)
B. Two plus two equals to three (whole is less than parts)
C. Two plus two equals to five (whole is greater than parts)*
D. None

67. Zero-base budget is
A. Variable budget
B. Programme budget
C. Combination of A & B
D. None

68. Out of steps in planning given below choose the correct ascending order
A. Numbering plans
B. Choosing an alternative
C. Aware of opportunities
D. Selecting objectives
E. Comparing alternatives
F. Identifying alternatives

A. A B C D E F B. A C E B D F
C. A F B E D C D. C D F E B A*

69. 'a' is looking ahead and 'b' is looking back.

A. a- planning; b-control*
B. a-control, b- planning
C. Both A & B D. None

70. ' Management by objectives is viewed in a larger context than that of a mere appraisal procedure. It regards appraisal as only one of several sub-systems operating within a larger system of goal-oriented management' is given by

A. George S. Odiorne* B. R.T. Pascale
C. Howard R. Bowen D None

71. 'Objective' includes

A. Important ends B. Organisational activities
C. Individual activities D. All of the above*

72. Which of the following is not the KRA (Key Result Areas) of a business, as per Peter F Drucker?

A. Innovation B. Worker Performance
C. Profitability D. None *

73. MBO can be as per different views

A. An appraisal tool
B. Motivational technique
C. Planning and control device
D. All of the alone*

74. Which is not the benefit of MBO ?

A. Improvement of managing
B. Encouragement and personal commitment
C. Development of effective control
D. Emphasis on short-term goals.*

75. Which is not the weakness of MBO ?

A. Inflexibility
B. Short-run goals
C. Difficulty of Goal setting
D. Classification of organization*

76. 'TOWS' Matrix, developed by Heinz Weihrich must start with

A. Strength
B. Opportunity
C. Threat *
D. Weakness

77. Boston Consulting Group developed

A. 'TWOS' matrix
B. Business porotfolio matrix*
C. Both
D. None

78. Which has a wider scope

A. 'TOWS' matrix over 'BP' matrix
B. 'BP' matrix over Tows.
C. Either
D. Neither

79. The core of planning is

A. Decision-making *
B. Leadership
C. Communication
D. Controlling

80. Effective decision-making must be

A. Economical
B. Rational*
C. Programmed
D. None of the above

81. The focus of Herbert Simon's satisfying model of decision-making is

A. Choosing a course of action that is good enough or satisfactory *
B. Selecting most economical alternative
C. Choosing a complete rational choice
D. None

82. In decision-making

A. Complete rationality is possible
B. Limited rationality is the rule*
C. Sometimes complete rationality and sometimes limited rationality prevails.
D. None

83. Cost effective Analysis is

A. Least costly way to reach an objective *
B. Costly way to reach an objective
C. Way to reach an objective
D. None of these

84. In selecting an alternative from among alternatives which is not a basic approach ?

A. Experimentation
B. Research and Analysis
C. Experience
D. None*

85. Which is true of decision-making?

A. It is made with some amount of uncertainty but degree will vary
B. Under normal conditions of decision-making under uncertainty three techniques-risk analysis, decision tree and preference theory is used
C. Higher level managers are accustomed to take longer risks than lower ones.
D. All of the above *

86. From management point of view creativity and innovations are

A. One factor – infer changeable term
B. Two factors-two different terms*
C. Both A&B
D. None

87. Creativity means

A. Use of new ideas
B. Ability and power to develop new ideas*
C. Borrowing of new ideas
D. None

88. Innovation means

A. Use of new ideas*
B. Ability and power to develop new ideas
C. Borrowing of new ideas
D. None

89. 'Brain storming' is

A. Technique to enhance creativity*
B. Management technique
C. A step in performance appraisal
D. None

90. The 'father of brainstorming ' is

A. Alex F Osborn *
B. William J Gordon
C. Ronald R Wood
D. Peter F Drucker

91. Which is not included in a part of creative process?

A. Unconscious scanning
B. Intuition
C. Insight
D. None *

92. The rules of 'brain storming are

A. No ideas are ever criticized.
B. The improvement of ideas by others is encouraged.
C. Both A & B*
D. None

93. 'Synectics' is originally known as

A. Obsorn Technique
B. Gardon Technique*
C. Drucker Technique
D. None

94. Good managers have to meet the criteria

A. Be honest
B. Be frugal
C. Be prepared
D. All of the above*

95. 'Managers tend to be promoted to the level of their incompetence" is named as the

A. The Peter Principle*
B. The Osborn Principle
C. Gardon principle
D. None

96. 'Need-want-Satisfaction' chain is linked to

A. Leadership
B. Controlling
C. Decision-making
D. None*

97. 'Motivators' means

A. Entire class of desires
B. Entire class of needs
C. Things that induce an individual to perform*
D. None

98. 'Metaphor 'Carrot and Stick' is related to which theory

A. Decision Theory
B. Motivation Theory*
C. Leadership Theory
D. None

99. 'Theory 'X' and Theory 'Y' is developed by

A. Douglas Mc Gregor*
B. Fredrick Herzberg
C. David C Mc Clelland
D. William Ouchi

100. Hierarchy of needs theory was provided by Abraham Maslow. He was a

A. Psychologist*
B. Industrialist
C. Doctor
D. None

101. Human needs given by Maslow are placed below. Put them in hierarchical order as per Maslow's theory

I. Social needs
II. Safety needs
III. Self Actualization needs
IV. Esteem needs
V. Physical needs

A. I, II, III, IV
B. I, II, V, IV, III
C. V, I, IV, III, II
D. V, II, I, IV, III *

102. Which is not the other name of 'Love needs' of Maslow?

A. Social needs
B. Affiliation needs
C. Acceptance needs
D. None*

103. Who found little evidence of a study to support Maslow's theory?

A. Edward Lawler and J Lloyd Suttle
B. Douglas T. Hall and Khalil Nougaim
C. Both A&B *
D. None

104. 'Two Factor theory' was developed by

A. Herzberg*
B. Maslaw
C. Alderfor
D. None

105. The two factors in Herzberg's theory of motivation are

A. Job context factor and job content factor *
B. 'X' content and 'Y' content
C. Need factors and Satisfaction factors.
D. None

106. The other name for one of the two factors of motivations of Hezberg are

A. Hygiene factor
B. Maintenance factor
C. Job context factor
D. All of the above*

107. Hygiene factor of Herzberg does not include

A. Working condition
B. Interpersonal relations
C. Supervision
D. None*

108. Which is true of motivation?

A. Expectancy Theory - Lyman W. Porter and Edward E. Lawler
B. Equity Theory – Victor Vroom
C. Reinforcement Theory-BF Skinner*
D. ERG Theory-David C McCelelland

109. Job enrichment is related to

A. Herzberg's theory of motivation *
B. B.F. Skinner's theory of motivation
C. J. Stacy Adam's theory of motivation
D. None

110. Different views and assumption about human nature are expressed by McGregor in theory

A. 'X' & 'Y' *
B. 'Y' & 'Z'
C. 'Z' & 'X'
D. None

111. Which is not true relating to motivation.

A. Hutzberg-Two sets of motivating factors dissatisfier and satisfier
B. Vroom-Expect high goals
C. Porter Lawler-Performance related to rewards and satisfaction
D. None *

112. Which statement is true?

A. Leadership is an important aspect of managing *
B. Leadership and managing are same
C. The essence of leadership is not follower ship.
D. None.

113. Which is not the ingredient of leadership?

A. Power
B. Understanding of people
C. Inspiring fellowmen
D. None *

114. 'Leaders are born and not made' is the theme of

A. Great man theory *
B. Trait theory
C. Likert theory
D. None

115. Ralph M. Stogdil's theory of leadership is

A. Trait theory*
B. Great man theory
C. Situational theory
D. None

116. 'Specific traits related to leadership ability' is theme of leadership theory advocated by

A. Ralph M. Stogdil*
B. Likert
C. Blake and Mouton
D. None

117. The types of leadership based on authority are -

A. Autocratic, democratic and free-rein*
B. Exploitative –authoritative, benevolent -authoritative, consultative and participative
C. Impoverished management, country club management, team manager, autocratic task manager
D. None

118. Out of Likert's four systems approach which system had the greatest success leaders

A. System I (Exploitative Authoritative)
B. System II (Benevolent Authoritative)
C. System III Consultative

D. System IV (Participative Group)*

119. Which system of likert has complete faith, trust and confidence in subordinates on all matters?

A. System 1(Exploitative)
B. System 2 (Benevolent Authoritative)
C. System 3 (Consultative)
D. System 4 (Participative) *

120. Likert's theory of 4 systems was developed on

A. Small group*
B. Big group
C. Not an empirical study
C. None

121. Managerial Grid approach was developed by

A. Robert Blake and Jane Mouton *
B. Rensis Likert and Ralph M Stogdill
C. Robert Tannenbaum and Warren H Schmidt
D. None

122. 'Concern for production and concern for people' is the theme of which theory

A. Managerial Grid Theory of Blake and Mouton *
B. Four Systems Theory of Rensis Likert
C. Leadership Continuum concept of Tannenbaum and Schmidst
D. None

123. The major defect of Managerial Grid approach is

A. It does not tells us why a manager falls into one part or another of the Grid *
B. It is not broad based.
C. It is not based on a empirical study of
D. None

124. Which style is odd man out in Management Grid theory of Blake and Mouton.

A. 1.1 Management
B. 9.9 Management
C. 5.5 Management
D. 9.5 Management *

125. 'Leadership as a continuum theory' was first develop in 1958 by Robert Tannenbaum and Warren H. Schmidt was revised in

A. 1972
B. 1973 *
C. 1974
D. None

126. 'Leadership continuum theory 'of Tannonbaum and Schmidst is not dependent on

A. Leader
B. Follower
C. Situation
D. Production*

127. Rise of Hilter in Germany in 1930, Musslim in Italy amount to which theory of leadership

A. Leadership as continuum.
B. Four system of management
C. Grid Management
D. Contingence theory *

128. Fred E Fielder's theory of Leadership suggests

A. People become leader not because of traits but because of various situations *
B. People became leader because of traits
C. People became leader by birth
D. None

129. In Fielder's contingency approach to Leadership what are critical dimensions of leadership situation that help to determine style of effective leadership

A. Position Power
B. Task structure
C. Leader-Member Relations
D. All of the above*

130. The leadership style according to Fred E Fielder are

A. Two-Task Oriented Leader and Inter Personal Relations achievement oriented leader *
B. Three-Country club, participatory and team manager
C. Three-Autocratic, democratic and free rein
D. None

131. In defining favorableness of situation of leadership Fred E Fielder developed

A. Least Preferred Coworker Scale (LPC)
B. Assumed Similarity between opposites (ASO) scale
C. Both A & B *
D. Neither A or B

132. In modern times which scale (testing technique-of FE Fielder) is commonly used in research

A. LPC Scale *
B. ASO Scale
C. Anchored Scale
D. None

133. The contribution of FE Fielder theory of Leadership is

A. Effective leadership style depends on situation*
B. Much concern for production
C. Least concern for people
D. None

134. Path-Goal-Theory of leadership is the work of:

A. Robert House *
B. F.E. Fielder
C. Tannenbaum
D. None

135. According to leadership theory of Robert House:

A. Functions of leaders are to set goals for subordinates, and find path to fulfil them and remove obstacles.*
B. Functions of the leaders are to care for production
C. Functions of the leaders are to teach morals to followers
D. None

136. Path Goal Theory of Leadership of Robert House suggests out of supportive leadership, participative leadership, instrumental leadership and achievement oriented leadership

A. There is one best way to lead
B. The appropriate styles depends on situation *
C. Both A & B
D. None

137. Noise is not found in:

A. Sender
B. Transmission
C. Receiver
D. None *

138. Which is the direction of flow of communication is an effective organization?

A. Downward Communication
B. Upward communication
C. Horizontal and diagonal Communication
D. All of the above *

139. Cross wise communication includes:

A. Upward communication
B. Horizontal flow of information
C. Diagonal flow
D Only B &C *

140. Crosswise communication may create difficulties and will depend on understanding:

A. It will be encouraged when they are appropriate
B. Subordinates will not make commitments beyond authority
C. Subordinates will keep superiors informed of the departmental activities
D. All of the above *

141. Oral communication is

A. Occurred in face to face meeting*
B. Formal or informal
C. Planned and accidental
D. All of the above

142. Communication can be divided into

A. Written, Oral and Non-verbal*
B. Programmed, Non Programmed
C. Structured, Non Structured
D. None

143. Which is not Barrier in communication?

A. Lack of planning
B. Semantic distortion
C. Poor listening and Premature evaluation
D. None*

144. Breakdown of communication occur in

A. Encoding of the messages by the sender
B. In the transmission of the message
C. In the decoding and understanding of the message
D. All of the above*

145. Which is not electronic media in communication?

A. Telecommunication
B. Teleconferencing
C. Internet
D. None*

146. Controlling means

A. Measurement and correction of performance *
B. Planning at first hand
C. An operating tool
D. None

147. Exponents of control in Management are

A. Giovanni Bgiglioni and Arthur G. Bedeian*
B. Fayol and Lilian Girlbraith
C. Tannenbaum and Schmdit
D. None

148. Basic control process involves three steps

I. Establishing standards
II. Measuring performance against these standards.
III. Correcting variations from standards
IV. Punishment to Actors.

A. Only I, III, IV
B. Only I & II
C. Only III & IV
D. Only I & II & III *

149. Which of the following is not a control point for strategic control?

A. Physical standards, cost standards, intangible standards
B. Capital standards and revenue standards, goals as standards
C. Programme standards and strategic plans
D. All of these *

150. Controlling is not linked to

A. Setting standards
B. Measuring performance
C. Taking corrective actions
D. All of the above*

151. 'Effective control requires attention to those factors to evaluating performance against plans' refers to

A. Principle of critical-point control *
B. Peter Principle
C. Principle of scientific management
D. None

152. Management control is usually perceived as a feedback system similar to that which

A. Operates in the common household thrermostat*
B. Operates in the engine of a car
C. Operates in the process of computer
D. None

153. In Management control 'real-time information' is information

A. About what is happening while it is happening *
B. About the techniques of control
C. About the feed back of control
D. None

154. A hunter will always aim ahead of a duck's flight to correct for the time lag between a shot and a hoped for it' This examplifies

A. Feedback system in management control *
B. Feed forward in management control
C. Both
D. None

155. Budgeting is

A. Formulation of plans
B. For future period
C. In numerical terms
D. All of the above *

156. In financial terms Budgets are
A. Revenue budgets-plans for revenues
B. Expense budgets-explanations for expenditure
C. Capital budgets-capital expenditure for plant, machinery, equipment
D. All of the above *

157. Over budgeting hiding ineffectiveness, causing inflexibility and overriding enterprise goals are:
A. Aids to budgeting
B. Dangers to budgeting
C. Features of budgeting
D. None

158. Production Management refers to
A. Activities necessary to produce and deliver a service as well as physical product *
B. Activities necessary to manufacture products
C. Activities in a system
D. None

159. In operation management system there is
A. Inputs-customer, labour, management and fixed assets
B. Transformation process-planning, operating and controlling system
C. Outputs-products and services
D. All of the above *

160. Which is true with preventive control
I. A highly qualified manager will make fewer mistakes
II. There by it reduces the need for direct control
III. There by it eliminates the need for direct control
IV. Only
A. I
B. Only II
C. Only I &
III D. I & II *

161. Return on Investment (ROI) approach is
A. A successfully used control technique *
B. A scale for individual performance management
C. A technique to measure leader behaviour
D. None

162. What is difference between direct control and preventive control

A. Former management is taking corrective steps on past practices. But in later case management will look into problems and thus eliminates undesirable element *

B. The two concepts are same

C. The former future directed and later is past directed

D. None

163. An organization is

I. A system or pattern of relationships in any kind of undertakings.

II. An enterprise itself

III. A Cooperation of two or more persons

IV. Behaviour of all participants in a group

A. I&II　　B. I&III&III

C II&III, & IV　　D. I, II, III & IV *

164. 'Satisfying' a term denotes the tendencies of manager, normally in instances of bounded rationality, in making decision is choosing course of action which is good enough under circumstances. This concept is developed by:

A. Beheling and Shrieshem　　B. Herbert Simon*

B. Peter F Drucker　　D. None

165. Match I & II in relation to definition of management

I	II
a. Functional concept: As a process, management is what manager performs	**1. Koontz, S. George, Mooney & Railey**
b. Human Relations concept: Management as a technique of getting things done by people	**2. John F Mee, F.W. Taylor**
c. Leadership and decision-making concept management as an act and science of decision-making	**3. Louis A Allen, William Spriegel George Terry, Henry Fayol**
D. Productive concept management as a technique of increasing productivity	**4. Ralph Davis, Ross Moore Donald Jclough**

E. Integration concept :manage ment as the coordinator of human and national resources

5. Lawrene Appleby, Barry M Richman, Keith & Gubellini

A. a b c d e
1 2 3 4 5 1 3 5

B. a b c d e
1 3 5 2 4

C. a b c d e
2 4 1 3 5

D. a b c d e
3 1 4 2 5

166. Management principles are important because

A. It increases the effectiveness of the organisation
B. It provides training programme for managers
C. It helps to understand nature of management
D. All of these *

167. Which is not the branch of management

A. Production management
B. Personnel management
C. Office management
D. None of the above*

168. Who coined the word 'POSDCORB'

A. Luther Gulick*
B. Lyndall Urwick
C. Both A & B
D. J.L. Massie

169. The management functions are divided into forecasting, planning, organizing, commanding, co-ordinatiing and control by

A. Luther Gulick
B. Lyndal Urwick*
C. J.C. Massie
D. None

170. Which is not part of 'POSDCORB' concept

A. Planning
B. Budgeting
C. Coordination
D. Reading *

171. Organizing, planning, reading, measuring and controlling are managerial functions advocated by

A. J.L. Massie
B. Koontz and O'Donnel
C. C.I. B arnard
D. None*
(Newman and Summer)

172. Management functions are classified into decision-making, staffing, organizing, planning, controlling, communicating and directing by

A. Newman and Summer
B. J.L. Massie*
C. C.I. Barnard
D. None

173. According to CI Barnard which is not a management function?

A. Providing communication
B. Securing efforts
C. Formulating and defending the purpose
D. Directing *

174. Who gave 'innovating as a distinct and separate function of management' ?

A. Eaverest Dale*
B. Cherter I Barnard
C. J.L. Massie
D. None

175. Who is not the follower of F.W. Taylor

A. Henry Gantt
B. Frank Gilbreth
C. Lilian Girlbreth
D. Roethlisberger *

176. 'The Human Side of Enterprise' was written by

A. Elton Mayo
B. C.I Barnard
C. Doglas M. McGregor *
D. None

177. Who does not belong to neo-classical thinkers beginning with Hawthrne studies

A. Roethlisberger
B. Dickson
C. Lippitt
D. None*

178. Who is odd man out?
- A. Mc Greger
- B. C.I Barnard
- C. Herbert Simon*
- D. None

179. Who is odd man at
- A. Mc Gregor
- B. Abraham Maslow
- C. Rensis Likert*
- D. None

180. Classical Theory of organisation relates to
- A. Closed system
- B. Static view
- C. Motivation through economic rewards
- D. All of the above

181. Which is not true of classical theory of organization?
- A. It neglects human factor
- B. It is identified with rigid bureaucratic structure
- C. It is based on empirical research *
- D. None

182. 'Feedback' in systems approach keeps organisation
- A. To adopt to environmental change *
- B. To predict future events
- C. To understand group behaviour
- D. None

183. Who said 'As long as we refer to Taylor as the father of scientific management, we would do justice to Fayol and his work to call him the father of principles of management
- A. Theo Haimann *
- B. Peter F Drucker
- C. Elton Mayo
- D. None

184. The critics attached neo-classical theory on the grounds
- A. Certain assumptions are not true
- B. Limited application
- C. More emphasis on Human aspect
- D. All of the above*

185. George Odiorne's name is connected with

A. MBO*
B. ROI
C. Both
D. None

186. According to Reddin MBO means

A. Establishment of objectives in such effectiveness areas
B. Each manager identifies his key effectiveness areas where he should show skills
C. Individual objectives should be related to and be par of the total organisation plan
D. All of the above

187. MBO is not connected with

A. George Odiorne
B. Reddin
C. John Humble
D. None

188. MBO process is related to

A. Control goal setting and freedom of implementation
B. Manager-sub-ordinate involvement and matching goals and resources
C. Review and appraisal of performance
D. All of the above *

189. Which is not the weakness of MBO?

A. Inflexibility and failure to teach philosophy
B. Difficulty in goal setting and problem for publication.
C. Emphasis on short term goals and costly and time consuming
D. None of the above *

190. Who observed MBO is self defeating in the long run because it fails to take into account the deeper emotional components of motivation.

A. Harry Levinso *
B. John Humble
C. George Odiorne
D. None

191. In relation to MBO 'Self-defeating and overemphasis' are

A. Limitations*
B. Elements
C. Benefits
D. None

192. Why MBO is needed?

A. For emphasis on change and maximum information granted.
B. For emphasis on effectiveness and interpersonal relationship
C. For group focus instead of individual focus
D. All of the above*

193. Why MBO Failed?

A. Due to lack of commitment and no follow-up action
B. Due to over emphasis on appraisal objectives handed over to subordinates
C. Due to making it mechanical and poor implementation method
D. All of the above *

194.

(a) **Organisation is the form of every human association for the attainment of common purpose 1. Gary Johns**
(b) **'Organisation are social invention for accomplishing goals, through group efforts' 2. Luthans**
(c) **Organizational behaviour is the result of interaction and interdependency between formal organizational and human factor available 3. Litterer**
(d) **Organisations are intervening elements between wants and their satisfaction and must be established before the wants are satisfied. 4. Money and Reiley 5. 'Peter F. Drucker**

A. a b c d
1352

B. abcd
3521

C. abcd
1243

D. abcd*
4123

195. Which is not the contributing field of orgnisational behaviour

A. Economics
B. Medicine
C. Semantics*
D. None of the above

196. Which is not correct.
A. OB does not exist in vacuum
B. OB is an inexact science
C. OB is both science and Arts
D. OB does not exist at multiple levels *

197. What is primary dependent variables in OB
A. Productivity
B. Absenteeism and Turnover
C. Job satisfaction
D. All of the above

198. Who observed 'Organizations are usually formed to satisfy objectives that can best be met collectively?
A. Argyris*
B. C.I Barnard
C. Elton Mayo
D. None

199. According to Hicks and Gullett why people organize
A. To enlarge abilities
B. To compress the time required to accomplish a objective
C. To take advantage of the accumulated knowledge of previous generations
D. None *

200. According to 'LA Allen' Sound organization
A. Facilitates administration
B. Facilitates growth and diversification
C. Utilitizes resources to optimum level and prompts creating
D. All of the above *

201. In his article 'Advanced Management' Alvin Brown identified a number of weakness of poor organization structure, which is not included in them ?
A. Failure to act and wrong actions
B. Lack of quantity of effort and lack of quality of effort
C. Write of effort
D. None*

202. I. Organisation structure of management authority must match with the demands of its environment.

II. Organisation structure of management must authority coincide with its technology
III. Individual sub-system must coincide with the technical requirements of subsystem
IV. Leadership behaviour must be appropriate to situational demands

According to Fred Luthans which are identified as contingencies to OB.

A I & II
B. II &III
C. III & IV
D. I, II, III & IV*

203. 'Field Theory is B=F (P,E)

Where B=Behaviour ; F=Function, P=Person and E=Environment is given by

A. Kurt Levin (Psychologist)*
B. FE Fielder
C. Rensis Likert
D. None

204. Who observed 'the peak of creative ability is among people between the ages 30 and 40?

A. Lehman*
B. Einstein
C. Fielder
D. None

205. Relatively permanent change in behaviour resulting from interactions with the environment is called

A. Learning*
B. Attitude
C. Creativity
D. None

206. Which is wrong?

I. Attitude is a perception with a frame of reference
II. Perception is the process by which information enters our mind and is interpreted in order to give some sensible meaning to the world around us.

III. Personality is a set of traits and characteristics, habits patterns and conditioned response to certain stimuli that formulate the impression an individual makes upon others.

IV. Valves are emotionally changed priorities and are passionately defended

A. Only I & IV
B. I & II
C. I & II & III
D. None*

207. What is not the key area that managers should pay attention while designing organizational structure?

A. Work specialization and departmentalization
B. Chain of command and span of control
C. Centralization and decentralization
D. None of the above*

208. Organization structure involves

A. Arrangement of Activities
B. Assignment of personnel to these activities
C. Fulfillment of organizational goals
D. All of the above*

209. 'Organization is the process of so combination of the work, which individuals or groups have to perform with the facilities necessary for its execution, that the duties so performed provide the best channel for the efficient, systematic, positive and coordinate application of the available effort was the view of

A. Sheldon*
B. Simon
C. Barnard
D. None

210. Work can be performed more efficiently if

A. Employees are allowed to specialize
B. Employees are motivated
C. Both A & B*
D. None

211. Determination, identification and enumeration of activities, grouping and assigning activities, and delegation of authority are the initial process of

A. Workers participation
B. Designing of basic structure*
C. Motivation process
D. Decision-making process

212. Which of the following is not the feature of good organizational structure

A. Flexibility
B. Simplicity
C. Unity of Direction
D. None of the above*

213. Good organizational structure has the benefits of

A. Encouraging creativity
B. Increasing cooperation among members
C. Facilitates good communication
D. All of the above.

214. 'Run around' in organization means.

A. Organizing structure in a horizontally,
B. Decentralization in the principle
C. Managers can not know who is responsible for what and people are sent to wrong people to get work done*
D. None

215. 'To whom do I go if I have a problem? And To whom I am responsible' The answer to this is

A. Chain of command*
B. Hierarchy
C. Span of control
D. None

216. Common organizational designs are

A. Simple, Bureaucracy and Matrix *
B. Complex, Bureaucracy and Matrix
C. Linear, complex and Bureaucracy
D. None

217. A boundary less organization seeks to

A. Eliminates the chain of command
B. Have limit less spans of control
C. Replace departments with empowered terms
D. All of the above*

218. 'Network' organization is

A. Boundary less organization
B. Small, core and centralized organization *
C. Both A & B
D. None

219. Which is true?

A. Flexible structures are labeled as organic structure
B. Bureaucratic structures are similar to mechanistic structure*
C. Both A & B
D. None

220. Which is not the basic characteristics of mechanistic structure?

A. Hierarchy and Functional specialization
B. Impersonal relations
C. Promotion on technical competence and excellence
D. None*

221. Which of the following variables are not responsible for determining the need for centralized and decentralized structure

A. Mission of the organization and size of organ
B. Competence of the top management and competence of subordinated
C. Creativity in the organization and adequacy of communication
D. None of the above *

222. Difference between formal and informal organization are linked to variables

A. Structure
B. Line of command
C. Pattern of command
D. All of the above*

223. 'Successful organizations vary with environment' is the opinion of

A. Thompson
B. FW Riggs
C. Lawrence and Lorsch *
D. None

224. Which factors are not responsible for structural differences?

A. Environment of structure
B. Size and strategy of structure
C. Technology
D. None*

225. Line structure is also known as

A. Scalar organization
B. Military organization
C. Vertical or departmental organization
D. All of the above*

226. Chief characteristics of line organizations are

A. It implies vertical relationships
B. The principle of units of command is followed
C. It defines authority and responsibility
D. All of the above*

227. The merits of line organizations are

A. Simplicity and flexibility
B. United control and prompt decisions
C. Orderly communication and fixed responsibilities
D. Autocratic approach and over loading *

228. A specialized staff in organization perform tasks in

A. Advisory capacity
B. Service capacity
C. Central capacity
D. All of the above *

229. 'Project organization' is

A. Temporary and one-time arrangement
B. To handle new problem arising out of the existing approaches
C. An addition to the existing organization
D. All of the above *

230. 'Project organizations should not be regarded as a panacea for overcoming all functional organization weakness. It should only complement or supplement and not supplant the functional development'. The view is expressed by

A. Middleton*
B. Sheldon
C. Lawrence and Lorsch
D. None

231. The concept of 'Functional Organization' originated with

A. Fayol
B. Taylor*
C. Mayo
D. None

232. A matrix organisation is a

A. Functional structure
B. Project structure
C. Combination and interaction of both functional and project structure *
D. None

233. An important aspect of Matrix organization is

A. Each person working on the project has three supervision –project manager, functional manager and finance manager
B. Each person working on the project has one supervisor- The functional Manager
C. Each person working on the project has two supervisors- Project Manager and Functional Manager *
D. None

234. Who has contributed to 'Motivation by defining it with satisfaction of unsatisfied needs'.

A. Viteless *
B. Fayol
C. Alderfer
D. McClleland

235. Who said, 'Motivation is the core of management'

A. Likert *
B. Maslow
C. Herzberg
D. None

236. 'Motivation refers to the way in which urges, drives desires aspirations, strivings or needs direct, control or explain the behaviour of human beings' is given by

A. Mc Farland*
B. Likert
C. Skinner
D. None

237. Which is wrong as to 'motivation'?

A. Motivation is an internal feeling
B. Motivation can be either positive or negative
C. Motivation produces goal-directed behaviour
D. None*

238. Which is not a fact as to Maslow's need model of motivation?

A. Sequential arrangement of needs

B. Descriptive ones

C. Satisfied needs causes performance

D. None*

239. Which is not a fact as to Harzeberg's model of motivation?

A. No hierarchical needs but two potent needs.

B. It is prescriptive one

C. It deals with work oriented motivational problem of professional workers

D. None*

240. 'Herzberg's two factor theory is a grossly over simplified portrayl of the mechanism by which job satisfaction or dissatisfaction comes about' is the view of

A. Alderfer, Shinner and Likert

B. J. Stacy Adam, Fielder and Alderfer

C. Dunnette, Campbell and Hackel *

D. None

241. The contributing factors of two factor Theory is

A. It increases manager's basic understanding of human behaviour

B. It is a worthy work of motivation at work.

C. Both A & B *

D. Neither A or B

242. 'Job Enrichment' is a direct growth of

A. Maslow's need theory

B. Likert's four system of management

C. Alderfer's ERG theory

D. Herzberg's two factor theory *

243. Mc Clelland's theory of need for achievement, need for affiliation and need for power resembles to the motivation theory of

A. Maslow *

B. Likert

C. Both A&B

D. None

244. Match I & II

I	II
McClleland's Need theory states	**Maslow's Need Theory**
a. Need for power	**1. Esteem need**
b. Need for Achievement	**2. Self-Actualization**
c. .Need for Affiliation	**3. Social need**

A. a b c *
1 2 3

B. a b c
3 2 1

C. a b c
2 3 1

D. a b c
3 2 1

245. 'Porter-Lawler Model' contributes to

A. Decision-making
B. Work motivation *
C Communication
D. Leadership

246. Which theory is related Human Resources model of Mc Gregor

I. Theory X
II. Theory Y
III. Theory Z

A I & II *
B I & III
C II & III
D None

247. The full name of McClleland who is a theorist on Motivation is

A. William C McClleland
B. Fred W. Mc Clleland
C. David Mc Clleland *
D. Mc Clleland

248. Which of the following is financial incentive?

A. Responsibility
B. Supervision
C. Bonus Plan *
D. None

249. Studies by theorists supported Equity. Theory of Stacy Adam. They are

A. Arrrowood, Andrew, Goodman and Friedman
B. Pritchard, Dunnette and Jorgenson
C. Both A & B *
D. None

250. Equity theory although easily understood, is complex and difficult to undersand opined by

A. Dunham*
B. Arrowood
C. Dunnette
D. None

251. William Ouchi developed

A. Theory 'W'
B. Theory 'V'
C. Theory 'Z' *
D. All of the above

252. Match I & II

a.	Salvatore Maddi	1.	Immaturity-Maturity model*
b.	Daniel Levinson	2.	Definition of personality
c.	Argyris	3.	Adult life stages
d.	Douglas T. Hall	4.	Career Stage model
A.	a b c d 1 2 3 4	C.	a b c d 4 3 2 1
B.	a b c d 1 4 2 3	D.	a b c d * 2 3 1 4

253. Which factors have no impact on personality?

A. Biological factor
B. Family and social factor
C. Cultural and situational factors
D. None *

254. 'Situation exerts an important press on the individual' pointed out by

A. Seligman
B. Argyris
C. Milgram *
D. None

255. Personality has key influence on

A. Work performance*
B. Physical strength of the person
C. Both A & B
D. None

256. Personality can be grouped into

A. A Type-Achievement oriented, punctual and have competitive drive
B. B Type-Early going, No time sense
C. Both A & B *
D. None of the above

257. 'Psychological notion is that man is motivated more by unseen forces than he is controlled by conscious and rational thought'. To this theory who is related

A. Sigmund Freud*
B. Seligman
C. Both
C. None

258. Carl Jung, Alfred Adler, Karen Korney and Eric Fromm propounded

A. Psycho analytical theory of personality *
B. Physiognomy Theory
C. Trait theory
D. None

259. Psychoanalytical theory of personality centers round

A. Id, ego
B. Ego, Super Ego.
C. Super Ego, Ego and Id*
D. None

260. Match I & II

I	II
a. William Sheldon	**1. Extrovert and Introvert theory**
b. Carl Jung	**2. Physiognomy Theory of Endomorph, Mesomorph and Ectomorph**
c. Cattell and All-port	**3. Self Theory**
d. Carl Roger	**4. Trait Theory**

A. a b c d
   1 2 3 4

B. a b c d
   4 2 1 3

C. a b c d*
   2 1 4 3

D. a b c d

261. Every person is unique but major similarities are there among individuals. They are

A. Inteiligence and set reflexiveness
B. Language and Tool making
C. Externally registered gains
D. All of the above

262. 'EPI' is a scale developed by HJ Eysenck to measure personality who was

A. A professor of Psychology at London University*
B. A professor of Psychology at Yale University
C. A professor of Psychology at Hull University
D. None

263. Rollo May deals with

A. Anxiety*
B. Personality scales
C. Self-concept
D. None

264. 'Two heads are better than one' It means

A. Leadership
B. Work Culture
C. Group decision*
D. None

265. 'Risk-Shift' phenomenon out in attached to

A. Individual decision-making
B. Group-decision-making*
C. Both A & B.
D. None

266. Which is not correct?

I. Groups are more 'Vigilant' than individuals
II. Groups can generate more ideas than individuals
III. Groups can evaluate ideas better than individuals

A I & II
B. II & III
C. I & II & III
D. None*

267. What is true of Delphi Technique?

A. It is a technique of participative decision-making
B. The key to recess of Delphi technique lies in its anonymity
C. Both A & B *
D. None

268. The A-I-S model (Activity, Interaction and Sentiment) of group behaviour was developed by

A. George Homans*
B. Harrison (E. Frank Hassison)
C. Janis (Irving Janis)
D. None

269. Who coined the world 'Group-Think"

A Irving Janis*
B. Harrison
C. Both
D. None

270. 'Group think' was examined by

A. Jains
B. Harrison
C. Both*
D. None

272. Management is generally considered to have three major dimension. Which of the following is not?

A. Technical
B. Conceptual
C. Human
D. Social *

273. Henry Ford, Alfred, P.Solan, Henri Fayol, F.W. Tayol were recognized as

A. Behavioural Thinkers
B. Early management Pioneers *
C. Thinkers on decision- making
D. None

274. The illumination studies (1929) which tried to examine the relationship between light intensity on the shop floor of manual work sites and employees productivity is the theory of

A. Herbert Simon
B. Frederick W. Taylor
C. Elton Mayo*
D. All of the above

275. Who provides criteria how to 'know good theory when we see one'

A. John Minor in 'Theories of Organizational Behaviour'
B. Douglas Mc Gregor in Human Side of Enterprise
C. Both A & B
D. None of the above

276. With social learning which psychologist more associated

A. Albert Bandura*
B. Ivan Pvlov
C. John B. Waston
D. None

277. Attribution refers to

A. How people explain the cause of another beaviour
B. How people explain the cause of their own behaviour
C. How people explain the cause of another's behaviour or their own behaviour*
D. None

278. Common problems in social perception is

A. Stereotyping
B. Halo effect
C. Both A&B*
D. None

279. The term 'personality' comes from latin word

A. Per Sona*
B. Perso na
C. Per rsona
D. Persona

280. Peoples' attempts to understand themselves are called

A. Self-concept*
B. Self efficacy
C. Self System
D. None

281. Who said, To some extent, a person's personality is like all other people's, like some other people's and like no other peoples'

A. Kluckhohn and Murray*
B. Levinson
C. Hall
D. Argyris

282. To understand organization behaviour the theories are provided by

A. Levinson
B. Hall
C. Argyris
D. All of the above*

283. The dimensions to job satisfaction is / are

A. Job satisfaction is an emotional response to a job situation
B. Job Satisfaction is often determined by how well outcomes meet or exceed expectations
C. Job satisfaction represents several related activities
D. All of the above*

284. Smith, Kendall and Hulin have identified five dimensions of job satisfaction which are/is not

A. The work itself and pay
B. Promotion opportunities and supervision
C. Coworkers
D. None*

285. Which of the following is not the dimension of job satisfaction?

A. Work itself and pay
B. Promotions and supervision
C. Work group and working conditions
D. None *

286. Which of the following is not the outcome of job satisfaction?

A. Satisfaction and productivity
B. Satisfaction and turnover
C. Satisfaction and absenteeism
D. None*

287. As per Meyer and Allen what is /are not dimensions of organizational commitment

A. Affective commitment (Employee's emotional attachment)
B. Continuance commitment (Association with learning organization)
C. Normative commitment (obligation to stay with organization)
D. Critical commitment (criticize the organization) *

288. Motivation can be traced to the latin word movere which means

A. To move*
B. To motivate
B To ask
D. To possess

289. Who proposed sophisticated wage incentive models to motivate workers ?

A. Taylor
B. Frank Gilbreth
C. Henry L. Gantt
D. All of the above*

290. Whose motivation theory is based on 'Cognitive concept of expectancy'?

A. Victor Vroom
B. P. Lyman porter
C. Ed Lawler
D. All *

291. In which theory first 'money was felt to be the only incentive

A. Scientific management *
B. Needs Theory
C. Expectancy Theory
D. None

292. Esteem and self actualization (Maslow). Responsibility recognition, achievement and advancement of Hazberg; and growth and personal development of Alderfer are

A. Higher-level needs *
B. Lower-lend needs
C. Money needs
D. None

293. Maslow outlines his needs theory in his classic paper

A. Labour letter
B. A theory of Human Motivation *
C. Fair pay for fair play
D. Motivation now directions for theory

294. Maslow provided love needs for motivation, by which he seems working to identity the love level need like

A. Freud*
B. Seligman
C. Levinson
D. None

295. Herzberg's theory is clearly related to

A. Maslow's theory*
B. Skinners theory
C. Fielder's theory
D. None

296. Match I & II

a.	**Hygine factor of Herzberg (Preventive and environmental in Nature)**	1.	**Lower order of needs of Maslow**
		2.	**Higher order of needs of Maslow**
A.	**Motivators**		

A. a b* 1 2
B. a b 2 1
C. a b 1&2
D. None 2&2

297. Hygine factors of Herzberg are linked to

A. Prevent dissatisfaction
B. Do not lead to satisfaction
C. They serve as a take off point for motivation; So by themselves they do not motivate
D. All of the above*

298. After providing high wages, salaries, excellent fringe-benefit packages, employees are not proper motivated. To answer this which motivation theory provides explanation?

A. Herzberg's two factor theory *
B. Likert's four systems of management
C. Blake and Moutons Grid theory
D. None

299. Herzberg's importance is that

A. Added much to the better understanding of job content factors and satisfaction
B. Contributes to job design technique of job enrichment
C. Both A & B *
D. None

300. Alderfer's Motivation Theory suggests

A. More of a continuum needs
B. Hierarchy of needs
C. There is no need to fulfill lower order of need before higher order of need is motivating
D. A & C both *

301. What motivates people to work under Vroom's expectancy theory of motivation?

A. Self actualization need
B. Responsibility need
C. Cognitive antecedents *
D. All of the above

302. VIE Theory of motivation is of

A. Maslow
B. Herzbeg
C. Vroom*
D. None

303. Herzberg theory of motivation is a theory of

A. Performance Appraisal
B. Job satisfaction*
C. Job evaluation
D. None

304. Porter-Lawler motivation model suggests

A. Performance leads to satisfaction
B. Satisfaction leads to performance *
C. Both A&B
D. Neither A or B

305. Job Design is an important

A. Area of work motivation
B. Area of study of organizational behaviour
C. Both A&B *
D. None

306. Which pioneering scientific managers examined jobs with techniques such as time and Motion Analysis?

A. F.W. Taylor
B. Franck Gilbreth
C. Neither
D. Both *

307. Job enrichment is concerned with designing job that

A. Includes a greater variety of work content.
B. Requires a high level of knowledge and skill
C. Give workers more autonomy and responsibility in terms of planning directing and controlling their own performance
D. All of the above *

308. A job characteristics model of work motivation was developed by

A. J. Richard Hackman
B. Greg Oldham
C. Both A & B *
D. None

309. Social Information Processing approach (SIPA) model of work motivation was developed by

A. General Salancik
B. Jeffrey Pfeffer
C. Both A & B*
D None

310. Which is not included in the core job characteristic approach (Hackman and Oldham)

A. Skill variety
B. Task identity
C. Task Significance
D. All of the above *

311. QWL-(Quality of Work Life) described as

A. Concern about the impact of work on people as well as on organizational effectiveness
B. The idea of participation in organizational problem solving and decision-making
C. Both A & B *
D. None

312. Who is regarded as 'father of employee motivation theory?'

A. Taylor *
B. Maslow
C. Herzberg
D. None

313. Edwin Locke says that goal setting is usually the underlying explanation of other theory/theories of

A. Vroom's VIE Theory *
B. Maslow's Hierarchy of Needs theory
C. Herzberg's two factor theory
D. All of the above

314. Who carried out research to test the Linkage between goal setting and performance?

A. Gary P. Latham and his colleagues *
B. General Salancik and his colleagues
C. Greg oldham and his colleages
D. None

315. Management by Objectives (MBO) is usually attributed to

A. Peter F Drucker *
B. Edwin Locke
C. Latham
D. None

316. The application of goal setting to organizational system performance is

A. MBO *
B. Job Enlargement
C. Job enrichment
D. None

317. A dysfunction of highly cohesive groups and committees that has selected a lot of attention recently has been called by Irving Janis.

A. Groupthink *
B. Team approach
C. Brainstorming
D. None

318. Individual conflict can be

A. Due to frustration
B. Due to competing goal
C. Due to different roles
D. All of the above *

319. Structural conflict can be of

A. Hierarchical conflict, functional conflict
B. Hierarchical conflict, functional conflict and line-staff conflict

C. Hierarchical conflict, functional conflict, line staff conflict and formal informal conflict *
D. None

320. Which is not true of conflict?
A. Conflict is inevitable
B. Conflict is integral to the nature of change
C. A minimum level of conflict is optimal
D. None *

321. Who defines stress simply as the interaction of the individual with the environment?
A. Ivancevich and Matteson*
B. Newman
C. Robert Eliot
D. None

322. 'Burnout' and 'Stress' are
A. Different
B. Same and used Interchangeably *
C. Almost same with slight difference
D. None

323. 'Managers rise to their level of incompetence in bureaucracies is
Peter Principle (Lawrence J. Peter) *
Partension's law (C. Northcote Pakinson)
Bennis Law (Warsin Bennis)
None of these

324. 'Bureaucratic staff increase in inverse portion to the amount of work done' is
A. Peter Principle
B. Parkinson's law*
C. Benins law
D. None

325. Match I and II

I	II
(a) Functional design	**1. Innovation is major objective**
(b) Project design	**2. Performance, cost, price, technology and Efficiency-**

(c) Product/Matrix design **3. Efficiency is the major objective**

A. a b c
1 2 3

B. a b c*
3 2 1

C. a b c
2 1 3

326. Which of the following are / is not the characteristics of organizational culture

A. Observed behavioural regularities
B. Norms and philosophy
C. Dominant values and rules
D. None *

327. Who is not a manager?

A. Coaches
B. Conductors
C. Sales executives
D. None *

328. Manager is a

A. People responsible for directing the efforts aimed at helping organizations to achieve their goals
B. People whose aim is to create surplus
C. Both A & B*
D. None

329. 'How well managers do their jobs ',is called

A. Organizational performance
B. Personal performance
C. Managerial performance *
D. None

330. 'Doing', things right' and 'doing the right thing' are chronologically

A. Efficiency and effectiveness
B. Effectiveness and efficiency
C. Either A or B
D. None

331. Match I and II

(a) A systematic method of handling activities

1. Leading **2. Controlling**

(b) The process of establishing goals and a suitable course of action for achieving those goals.

3. Planning **4. Organizing**

(c) The process of engaging two or more people in working together in a Structured way to achieve a specific goals or set of goals. **5. Process**

(d) The process of directing and influencing the task related activities of group members or an entire organization.

(e) The process of ensuring that actual activities conform to planned definition

A. a b c d e
1 2 3 4 5

B. a b c d e
5 4 3 2 1

C. a b c d e
1 2 5 3 4

D. a b c d e*
5 3 4 1 2

332. According to Mintzberg which is not the role of manager?

A. Liaison
B. Monitor
C. Negotiation
D. None *

333. The skills of managers technical, human and conceptual were identified by Henry Fayol and popularized by

A. Robert L Katz*
B. Henry Mintzberg
C. Elton Mayo
D. None

334. A management approach formulated by FW Taylor between

A. 1980-1930*
B. 1900-1930
C. 1919-1930
D. None

335. Scientific management theory came to forefront due to

A. The need to pay more to workers
B. The need to increase productivity*
C. The need to involve workers in management
D. None

336. Which of the following is not a theorist of scientific management?

A. Frederic W Taylor
B. Henry L Gantt
C. Franck and Lilian Gilbreth
D. None

337. The principles the development of a true science of management, the scientific selection of workers, the scientific education and development of workers and intimate, friendly cooperation between management and worker belong to

A. Workers participation theory
B. Scientific management theory *
C. Cooperative system theory
D. Bureaucratic theory

338. Critical Path Method (CPM) and Programme Evaluation and Review Technique (PERT) were chronologically developed by

A. Du Pont and Navy *
B. Navy and Du Pont
C. F.W. Taylor
D. None

339. The classical theorists are

A. Heri Fayol and Weber
B. Marry Parker Follett and Charter I Barnard
C. Both A & B *
D. None

340. Concept of 'Zone indifference' was given by

A. Marry Parker Follet
B. Charter I Barnard *
C. Fayol
D. None

341. 'Holistic' model of control was the idea of

A. Marry Parker Follet *
B. Charter I Barnard
C. Fayol
D. None

342. 'How managers interact with other employees' is

A. Human Relations *
B. Participation
C. Communication
D. Motivation

343. Which is the key to systems control

A. Feedback *
B. Flow
C. Synergy
D. None

344. 'Management for a small planet' which places ecological concerns was by

A. Edward and Jean Gerner Stead *
B. Simon and March
C. Fayol and Taylor
D. None

345. The study of rights and of who is or who should be benefited or harmed by an action is called

A. Responsibility
B. Ethics*
C. Rule of Law
D. None

346. Tools in ethics are

A. Values and Rights
B. Moral Rules and Duties
C. Relationships
D. All of the above*

347. A capacity or circumstance that inabilities a corporation to earn higher than average profits in a particular industry is called

A. Competitive Advantage* B. Side-agreements
C. Market Rivalry D. None

348. What are the ways of which companies go international

A. Exporting and Licensing
B. Franchise and Joint venture
C. Global strategic partnership
D. All of the above*

349. Globalization refers to

A. New perspective or attitude about relationship with other countries
B. Business relationships across international boundaries
C. Both A & B*
D. None

350. 'Presence of many different cultural backgrounds within an organization and coexistence of people from these different backgrounds are called respective

A. Diversity and Multiculturalism
B. Multiculturalism and diversity *
C. Corporate culture and social culture
D. Social culture and corporate culture

351. 'TQM' has been defined by

A. Marshall Sashkin and Kenneth Kiser *
B. Edwards Deming
C. William Shewhart
D. None

352. The process of identifying and selecting a course of action to solve a specific problem is called

A. Conflict management B. Strategic management
C. Decision-making * D. None

353. Plans designed to meet an organization's broad goals are

A. Strategic plans* B. Operational plan
C. Mission statement D. None

354. The management process that involves on organization's engaging in strategic planning and then action on these plans is called

A. Strategic management *
B. Performance management
C. Time management
C. Operation management

355. As per Hofer and Schendel's view strategic management process involve

A. Strategic planning
B. Strategy implementation
C. Both A & B *
D. None

356. Michale Porter's approach to corporate strategy is

A. Three Forces model
B. Four Forces model
C. Five Forces model*
D. Six Forces model

357. 'Wealth of Nation' deals with specialization of labour was by

A. Adam Smith *
B. Lawrence and Lorsch
C. F. Drucker
D. Robert Waterman

358. 'Integration term is used in place of 'Coordination' to designate the degree to which members of various departments work together in unified memory by

A. Lawrence and Lorsch
B. Adoom Smith
C. Ton Feter
D. Robert Waterman

359. A job in which an individual acts as a liaison between departments / organization that are in frequent contact is called

A. Coordination
B. Liasioning role
C. Bacodary spanning sole
D. None

360. Who attempted to distinguish between two organizational systems- mechanic and organic

A. Burns and Stalker
B. Lawrence and Lorsch
C. Peter and Waterman
D. None

361. John French and Bertram Raven identified 5 bases of power which one/are not included

A. Reward power and coercive power
B. Legitimate power and expert power
C. Referent power
D. None

362. Authority is

A. Form of Power
B. Form of Influence
C. Form of Coercion
D. None

363. Organization structure

A. Run themselves
B. Do not run themselves
C. Both A & B
D. None

364. Two or more people who interact with and influence each other towards a common purpose is

A. Team
B. Committee
C. Command Team
D Project Team

365. ' In Union there is strength' is one of the 14 principles of Fayol. The original term used by Fayol for this is

A. Esprit de corpse*
B Rule of thumb
C Bureaucracy
D Six Sigma

366. Planning process is not a

A. Rational approach*
B. Numberizing Game and Selected Goals.
C. Futurities commitment
D. None.

367. Human Resource Management is concerned with

A. Products
B. Service
C. People*
D. None.

368. Which is concerned with Human Resource Management?

A. Acquisition of employees
B. Development of employees
C. Maintenance of employees
D. All of the above*

369. Training as per HRM jargon is linked to

A. Maintenance
B. Development*
C. Acquisition
D. None of the above

370. Which of the following is not linked to HRM?

A. Organizational Development*
B. Training
C. Motivation and incentives
D. Compensation

371. Dimensions of personnel management is /are

A. Personnel aspect B. Welfare aspect
C. Industrial aspects D. All of the above*

372. HRM in 21st century is affected by

A. Globalization B. Economic compulsions
C. Technological Development D. All of the above*

373. Recruitment and selection are

A. Same B. Different from each other*
C. Interchangeably used D. None of the above

374. Leadership is

A. Influencing people * B. Forcing people
C. Bribing people D. All of these

375. Match I & II

	I	II
a.	Likert's Theory	1. Identifies two dimensions concern for production and concern for people.
b.	Management Grid Theory	2. Focuses autocratic democratic and free-rein styles.
c.	Leadership Styleson authority system	3. Identified 4 of Management
d.	F.E. Fidder	4. Leadership and situation one interlinked.
e.	Tannenbnbaum and Schmidt	5. Leadership as ....

A. a b c d e
1 3 5 2 4
B. a b c d e
1 2 4 5 3
C. a b c d e
5 3 1 4 2
D. a b c d e
3 1 2 4 5

376. Communication is commonly important function of

A. Decision-making B. Leading*
C. Organizing D. Staffing

377. Which of the following is part of communication process?

A. Sender, Message, Receiver, Noise*
B. Message, Receiver, Sender
C. Receiver, Noise, Message
D. All of the above

378. Importance of communication in organization as per Chester I Barnard , is

A. To set goals for organization
B. To lessen the burden of organization
C. To establish link between people for achievement of goals.
D. None of the above

378. I. Purpose of communication is to effect change
II. Communication is essential for internal functioning as it combines managerial function.
III. It is helpful in deciding goals of organization.
IV. It helps employees' motivation.
Which is true?

A I,   B I & II,
C I , II & III   D I, II, III & IV

379. Encoding in communication is corrected with

A. Sender*   B. Noise
C. Receiver   D. None

380. Delphi Technique was developed in 1950 at Rand Corporation Think Tank by

A. N.C. Dalkey and his associates*
B. Douglas Mc Gregror and his associates
C. Max Weber and his associates
D. None

381. The classical organization is most often associated with

A. Bureaucracy*   B. Centralization
C. Decentralization   D. None

382. Which one is not the characteristic of bureaucratic structure?

A. Specialization and division of labour
B. Hierarchy and Rule bound
C. Impersonal Relationship
D. None*

383. Recruitment process is affected by organization

A. Size
B. Working conditions
C. Salary structure
D. All of the above*

384. Which statement is true?

I. Recruitment is garlanding as many as eligible job candidates

II. Selection is garlanding as many as eligible job candidates.

III. Recruitment is a process of picking people from a pool of applicants

IV. Selection is a process of picking people from a pool of applicants.

A. I & IV*
B. I, II & III,
C. II, III & IV
D. I, III & IV.

385. Barriers to effective selection are

A. Fairness
B. Reliability of method
C. Outside pressure
D. All of the above*

386. To motivate employees to higher productivity' is the object of

A. Transfer
B. Performance Appraisal
C. Promotion*
D. Training

387. The needs of Training are to

A. Increase productivity
B. Improve quality
C. Improve organizational climate
D. All of the above*

388. Performance appraisal is not linked to

A. Training
B. Promotion
C. Transfer
D. None of the above*

389. Errors in performance appraisal are

A. Halo effect
B. Central Tendency
C. Spillover effect
D. All of the above*

390. Human resource audit is influenced by

A. The number of employees
B. Communication and feed back
C. Status of an HR manager
D. None of the above

391. The remedial action for solving disciplinary problems, grievances and redundancy is

A. Counseling*
B. Stress
C. Job analysis
D. None of the action

392. Stress has

A. Positive impact
B. Negative impacts
C. Both bad and good effects*
D. None of the above